## Praise for *Cambodia's Curse*

"Brinkley cuts a clear narrative path through the bewildering, cynical politics and violent social life of one of the world's most brutalized and hard-up countries."

—*Foreign Affairs*

"As a young reporter, Brinkley won a Pulitzer Prize in 1980 for his coverage of the Cambodian refugee crisis. Returning to the region 30 years later, Brinkley—now a professor of journalism at Stanford—chose his subject well . . . [he] admirably . . . demonstrates that Hun Sen's administration has been a disaster for many Cambodians."

—*San Francisco Chronicle*

"A riveting piece of literary reportage."

—*Publishers Weekly*

"An excellent . . . account of a country whose historic poverty, exacerbated by the Vietnam War, remains remarkably unchanged."

—*Kirkus*

"A heartbreaking but vital status report on a people who deserve far better."

—*Booklist*

"*Cambodia's Curse* will make you rage and make you grieve. With devastating data, no spin profiles, and poignant anecdotes, Joel Brinkley spares no one in his ruthless scrutiny. Cambodian officials range from venal to vicious to pathological. Outsiders and donors are nonchalant, naïve, or enablers—of both the feckless and knowing varieties. Corruption has succeeded the Khmer Rouge as torturer and killer. Trapped in an unending nightmare are the Cambodian people, passive and resigned. Just about everybody has forgotten them. With deep compassion and fury Brinkley makes us once again bear witness."

—Winston Lord, former U.S. ambassador to China and
former president of the Council on Foreign Relations

"Based on months of field work and hundreds of conversations, *Cambodia's Curse* is a saddening, sure-footed analysis of the way that power and corruption operate in Cambodia today. Joel Brinkley never loses sight of the victims. His book is withering, heart-felt, and persuasive."

—David Chandler, professor emeritus, Monash University; author of
*A History of Cambodia* and *The Tragedy of Cambodian History*

## Also by Joel Brinkley:

*The Circus Master's Mission* (a novel)

*Defining Vision: The Battle for the Future of Television*

*U.S. vs. Microsoft: The Inside Story of the Landmark Case*
   (with Steve Lohr)

# CAMBODIA'S
# CURSE

## THE MODERN HISTORY
## OF A TROUBLED LAND

## JOEL BRINKLEY

PUBLICAFFAIRS
New York

Hardcover first published in 2011 in the United States by PublicAffairs™,
a Member of the Perseus Books Group.

Paperback first published in 2012 by PublicAffairs

Book Design by Trish Wilkinson
Set in Minion Pro

The Library of Congress has cataloged the hardcover as follows:

Brinkley, Joel, 1952–
    Cambodia's curse : the modern history of a troubled land / Joel Brinkley.—
1st ed.
        p.   cm.
    Includes bibliographical references and index.
    ISBN 978-1-58648-787-4 (hardcover)
        1. Cambodia—History—1979– 2. Cambodia—Politics and government—
1979– 3. Democracy—Cambodia. 4. Social change—Cambodia.
5. Cambodia—Social conditions—21st century. 6. Pol Pot—Influence. I. Title.
DS554.8.B75 2011
959.604—dc22                                                  2010044806

ISBN 978-1-61039-183-2 (paperback)
ISBN 978-1-61039-001-9 (e-book)
LSC-C
10  9  8  7

*For Charlotte and Veronica*

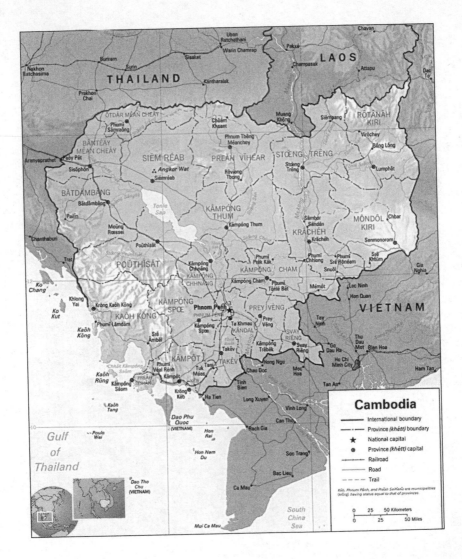

**THAILAND**

Nakhon
Ratchasima

Buriram

Surin

Prakhon
Chai

Sisaket

Kantharalak

Uban
Ratchathani

Warin Chamrap

Pakxé

Champasak

**LAOS**

Chavan

Attapu

Dac
To

ÔTDÂR MÉAN CHEÁY

Phumi
Sâmraông

Chôam
Khsant

Muang
Không

Siémpang

**RÔTÂNÂH
KIRI**

Virôchey

Bâng Lông

Phnum Tbêng
Méanchey

**BÂNTÉAY
MÉAN CHEÁY**

Aranyaprathet

Poy Pet

Sisôphôn

**SIÉM RÉAB**

Angkor Wat

Siémréab

**PREÂH VIHEAR**

Rôvieng
Tbong

**STŒNG TRÊNG**

Stœng
Trêng

Lumphât

**BÂTDÂMBÂNG**

Bâtdâmbâng

Pailin

Chanthaburi

Moung
Roessei

Tonle
Sap

**KÂMPÓNG
THUM**

Kâmpóng Thum

Sâmbôr

Sândân

**KRÂCHÉH**

Krâchéh

**MÔNDÔL
KIRI**

Chbar

Senmonorom

Trat

**POÛTHISÂT**

Poûthisât

Kâmpóng
Chhnâng

**KÂMPÓNG
CHHNÂNG**

Phumi
Prêk Kâk

**KÂMPÓNG** CHAM

Kâmpóng Cham

Phumi
Chhlong

Phumi
Srê Rônéam

Snuôl

Srê
Khtum

Gia
Nghia

Ko
Chang

Khlong
Yai

Krông Kaôh Kông

**KÂMPÓNG
SPŒ**

Phumi Lâmdâm

**KAÔH KÔNG**

Kaôh
Kông

Srê
Âmbôl

**Phnom Penh**

PHNUM PÉNH

Kâmpóng
Spœ

Ta Khmau

**KÂNDAL**

Phumi
Tônlé Bêt

**PREY VÊNG**

Prey
Vêng

Mémôt

Loc Ninh

Hon Quan

Tay
Ninh

**VIETNAM**

Ko
Kut

Kaôh
Rûng

**KÂMPÓT**

Phumi
Véal Rénh

Kâmpóng
Sâom

PREÂH
SÉHANU

Kâmpót

Tuk
Méas

Tani

**TAKÉV**

Takêv

Kâmpóng
Trâbêk

**SVAY
RIÊNG**

Svay
Riêng

Gò
Dau Ha

Thu
Dau
Mot

Ho Chi
Minh City

Biên Hoa

Ham Tan

Kaôh
Tang

Krông
Kéb

Ha Tien

Mong Ngu

Chau Doc

Tinh
Biên

Moc
Hoa

Tan An

Long Xuyen

Vinh Long

Can Tho

Bach Gia

Soc Trang

Bac Lieu

Ca Mau

Mui Ca Mau

*Gulf
of
Thailand*

Poulo
Wai

Dao Phu
Quoc
(VIETNAM)

Hon
Rai

Hon Nam
Du

Dao Tho
Chu
(VIETNAM)

*South
China
Sea*

### Cambodia

—————— International boundary

- - - - - - Province *(khétt)* boundary

★ National capital

⊙ Province *(khétt)* capital

+-+-+-+ Railroad

—————— Road

- - - - - Trail

*Kêb, Phnum Pênh, and Preâh Seihanu are municipalities (krông) having status equal to that of provinces.*

| 0 | 25 | 50 Kilometers |
| 0 | 25 | 50 Miles |

# CONTENTS

Photo insert on text between pages 154–155

# PREFACE

I was twenty-seven years old when I was first sent to Cambodia. At that time, barely four years out of college, I worked for the *Louisville Courier-Journal* in Kentucky. I was covering the Jefferson County School Board, writing about achievement-test scores and high school yearbook sales. Most recently, I'd helped compile the fall school bus–schedule supplement. The closest I'd ever come to international reporting was an overnight trip to Edmonton, Alberta, where I was assigned to write about a shopping mall.

Still, one afternoon my editor, Bill Cox, tapped me on the shoulder and said, "Oh, by the way, we'd like you to go cover the Vietnamese invasion of Cambodia and the refugee crisis." "Oh, by the way," he said—almost as if he meant: if you don't have anything better to do.

At first I wasn't sure I believed him. After all, Cox was a jokester. While the circus was in town, he had managed to convince the circus masters to truck a full-size buffalo over to the newspaper. Cox brought it up the freight elevator and rode it around the newsroom, waving an oversize cowboy hat. So I did some investigation. It turned out that Jay Mather, a staff photographer, had seen a television clip about a Louisville physician who was working on the Thai-Cambodian border, treating refugees. Mather convinced the photo editor to send a reporter and photographer there to write about this doctor and the larger story.

This was 1979. The Vietnam War had ended just four years earlier, but the convulsions it caused in neighboring states played out for years following. In Cambodia a few months after Saigon fell, Communist insurgents known as the Khmer Rouge overthrew Lon Nol, the military dictator who had been Washington's man in Phnom Penh.

Today the story of the Khmer Rouge crimes is well known. Two million Cambodians, one-quarter of the nation's population, were killed during Pol Pot's three and one-half years in power. He willfully destroyed every fixture and totem of twentieth-century life. Eighty percent of Cambodia's teachers were killed and 95 percent of the doctors, along with almost everyone else who had an education. Cambodia, as Pol Pot liked to say, was returned to year zero.

But in the autumn of 1979, little of this was known. Rumors of genocide had leaked out, but the regime roundly denied them, and a cottage industry of Khmer Rouge apologists had grown up in the West. Some government officials reported on what was happening, but hardly anyone in the United States wanted to listen. The Vietnam War's wounds were fresh; the last place Americans wanted to focus attention was Southeast Asia. They were preoccupied with energy crises, intelligence scandals, and, soon enough, the hostages in Iran.

In December 1978 Vietnam had invaded Cambodia and quickly deposed the Khmer Rouge regime. In the months that followed, tens of thousands of refugees stumbled toward Thailand, bringing with them deadly diseases, emaciated bodies, and stories so terrible they were hard to believe—the world's first clear image of the Khmer Rouge horrors. That's where I was going.

In those days, before the Internet, newspapers were flush with cash, and the *Courier-Journal* wanted to spend all of its travel money before the end of the budget year—or risk not getting as much the next year. I was delighted to help. So in October 1979 I prepared to leave for Southeast Asia. Mather, the photographer who had come up with the idea, was coming with me.

One afternoon we headed over to the Jefferson County Health Department to get inoculations. An elderly nurse with a gray bun of hair asked us where we were going, and I said, "Cambodia."

"Cambodia?" she asked. "Spell it."

So I spelled it, and she rummaged around in a file drawer until finally she pulled out a tattered sheet that looked yellow with age. Looking down at the paper through dirty reading glasses, she read off a litany of deadly infectious diseases, "Let's see, you're going to need malaria, cholera, tuberculosis, tetanus, typhoid, diphtheria" . . .

So I said, "Well, we'll take 'em all."

The nurse shook her head. "No," she insisted, "you can only get three diseases at a time. You've got to pick three diseases."

"Which three diseases do you think we should take?"

"I'm sorry," she said shaking her head. "I can't pick your diseases for you. Everybody's got to pick their own diseases."

I picked cholera, diphtheria, and tetanus. I came home with typhoid.

Reporting abroad years later, working for the *New York Times*, I was fortunate to have all the advantages big papers provided for foreign correspondents: drivers, guides, translators, assistants. Jay and I had none of that. We were on our own, and we were naifs.

Journalists then weren't easily able to reach Cambodia's capital, Phnom Penh. Khmer Rouge fighters were still exchanging fire with the Vietnamese. So Jay and I started in Bangkok, where I had a few interviews, and then we drove to the Cambodian border—a several-hour trip on bad roads traversed by almost as many water buffalo as cars. We stayed at a hotel in Aranyaprathet, on the Cambodian border. Our rooms' doors each had a padlock hasp, but it was up to us to buy the locks. Inside, the bed was a straw mat. The sink emptied onto the floor; the water washed around my feet as it wended its way to the drain in the middle of the room.

The first day, we drove to the border. A Thai officer looked at our passports and the permit we had picked up in Bangkok, then gesticulated that we needed something else—apparently a stamp. He motioned us back toward Bangkok. We didn't speak Thai and hadn't any idea what we were supposed to do. Disheartened, we drove back toward Bangkok, but along the way we saw an abandoned American air base. Several cars sat in front of the building closest to the road. Maybe someone there spoke English and could tell us what to do.

Inside, a Thai military officer sat behind a desk. He didn't speak English either, but I showed the permit and gesticulated a question. He took the permits from us, reached into a drawer, pulled out a stamp, and stamped our forms. Jay and I looked at each other and smiled. Serendipity.

We crossed the border and drove on, looking for refugee camps. After a while, we came upon a big truck stacked high with sacks of rice, so we followed it. The driver stopped in front of a crude shelter. Inside lay dozens of sick and dying Cambodians, all wearing the black pajamas that were the communal clothing for everyone in Democratic Kampuchea, the perverse name of the Khmer Rouge state. Just beyond it lay a vast refugee camp. It stretched to the horizon. We spent the day there and found several other camps in the following days. Here's what I wrote:

> Gaunt, glassy-eyed and possessionless, they crouch in the heat, hungry and diseased. They stoop over small, dry plots of rock-hard soil. And they wait.
>
> They wait in tight lines for hours to get today's ration of food from international relief agencies: a bowl of rice gruel, two bananas, a bucket of brown drinking water.
>
> They wait for doctors to heal them.
>
> Some wait for news of family, though many know their relatives are dead; they remember watching brothers and sisters, parents and children being murdered, or struggling for a last breath before starvation.
>
> They wait for another assault by Thai soldiers who come to rape their women. Or for Vietnamese troops to launch an all-out offensive that would drive them across the border into Thailand.

And some wait to learn where the next steps in their miserable lives will lead them. Meanwhile, they sweat, swat at mosquitoes and inhale the stench of hundreds of thousands of suffering and dying countrymen.

Death and destitution.

Seven million Cambodians have been caught between the two since 1975. About 3 million are already dead, and many who remain alive could die soon from disease or starvation.

The lucky ones are the million or so Cambodians who escaped the grip of the Communist Khmer Rouge, dodged gunfire from Vietnamese invaders and trekked hundreds of miles with little or no food to sanctuary in refugee camps on the Thai border.

But what kind of sanctuary is it?

For many it's a rectangle of hard, bare ground the size of a desk top.

It's a plastic sheet for cover, so low overhead that it rubs the noses of some who sleep.

It's the searing odor of sweat, defecation and death. It's the ceaseless buzzing of a million flies and the hack of 10,000 coughs.

It's row upon row of blank-faced sufferers whose futures hold no promise or respite.

Life in a refugee camp is hellish, unbearable. The relief worker who ends the first day wet-eyed can't always blame the choking dust. But compared with life in Cambodia since 1975, many refugees say their plight doesn't seem so bad.

Talk to them.

As they tell of years of horror and misery that Westerners can barely comprehend, their faces are expressionless and dull. Their voices go flat, as if they're talking about a dull day at work. Their tales end with a nodding acknowledgment of the death of their nation and culture.


I fell ill on the way home, flying through Hong Kong and Chicago a few days before Thanksgiving. Back in Louisville, my doctor had no experience with tropical diseases and at first misdiagnosed the illness, saying it was probably malaria. Later, after getting the result of a blood test, he realized what it was: typhoid. He prescribed antibiotics. But I stayed home in bed, sweaty, feverish, and hallucinatory. On Thanksgiving Day a friend brought me a big turkey drumstick. But I had no appetite. After about ten days, I began to recover, went back to the office, and wrote a five-day series on Cambodia.

Back then, before the Internet, even before Nexis and other newspaper data banks, when a regional paper wrote something, no one else saw it. For us, we heard only from readers in Kentucky and southern Indiana. After that, our words and pictures simply faded into memory. That was the nature of newspaper work back then.

———

Twenty-nine years later, in the summer of 2008, I was heading back to Cambodia for the first time. In the interim I had left the *Courier-Journal* and taken a job with the *New York Times*, where I worked as a reporter, editor, and foreign correspondent for nearly twenty-five years. I had reported from more than fifty countries, though I had never made it back to Cambodia. But I had a big question on my mind.

A decade after their invasion, the Vietnamese had pulled out of Cambodia, in 1989, and left a puppet Marxist government in place. The Khmer Rouge, still directed by Pol Pot, continued waging a guerrilla war against the occupiers and their government. The country seemed unable to pull itself out of the morass.

In 1992 and 1993 the United Nations occupied Cambodia. The state became a UN protectorate—the first and last time the United Nations tried anything so ambitious. The UN deployed 16,000 troops and 5,000 civil administrators. It ran the country for two years, and the whole enterprise cost $3 billion. The United Nations gave Cambodia a constitution that afforded the people—5 million Khmer Rouge survivors—all the human rights and privileges of a modern democratic state. Then the UN staged elections. To everyone's surprise, 90 percent of the electorate voted. The UN claimed that showed a hunger for democracy. Once the new government took office, the UN pulled out.

No other nation had ever been given a chance like that. The world had come together out of guilt and concern (and self-interest) to help pull this little nation out of the mire and give it an opportunity to start over, to enter the modern age. What happened? What had the new democratically elected government done with this extraordinary, unprecedented gift? To find out, in August 2008 I set off for Cambodia once again.*

On my third morning in Phnom Penh I was eating breakfast at the Intercontinental Hotel—a far cry from that place in Aranyaprathet in 1979. I picked up a copy of the *Phnom Penh Post*, an English-language daily. As I read a small story on page 3, I sat up straight and would have exclaimed out loud, had I not been in the dining room.

Hun Chea, a nephew of Prime Minster Hun Sen, had been driving his Cadillac Escalade SUV at high speed in downtown Phnom Penh when he ran over a man on a motorbike. The accident ripped off the motorbike driver's arm and leg.

Hun Chea tried to flee, the paper said, but running over the motorbike had shredded one of his tires. He had to pull over. But here's the part that captured my attention: As the motorbike driver, a crane operator, lay bleeding to death in the street, "numerous traffic police passed the scene without stopping. But the wreck drew the attention of about 20 military police, who removed the license plate from the SUV."

They removed Hun Chea's license plate? A few days later I asked Cambodia's minister of information, Khieu Kanharith, about the incident. The police removed the license plate? He had to think for a

---

*In pursuit of this and related questions, *Foreign Affairs* hired me to write an article. Portions of this book first appeared in *Foreign Affairs*.

moment but finally managed to say, "You try to cover the plates because it's harder to sell a car if it's been in an accident." As a reporter, sometimes it's hard to keep a straight face. But then, being the information minister in Cambodia is a tough job.

---

Two years researching and two long summers reporting in Cambodia answered my question: What had Cambodia done with that singular chance, that great gift the United Nations had bestowed? As it turned out, in the twenty-first century a corrupt, autocratic leader was running the country. The United Nations, in hindsight, had overestimated its ability to effect democratic change.

Cambodia was the first major state-building effort of the late twentieth century. The most dramatic examples before Cambodia were Germany and Japan. Both became thriving democracies; they showed it could be done. But these states had been on their knees, defeated and destroyed by war. When the occupying troops arrived, neither Germany nor Japan had any remaining homegrown leaders or oligarchs, no one who had anything much to protect. The people embraced the democratic changes Western occupiers brought along, and no one of note with wealth or power was left to stand in the way. That's why those occupations succeeded.

Cambodia's story was different, though the United Nations' leaders seemed unable to recognize that. They were starry-eyed about the broad international cooperation that had suddenly come about after the fall of the Soviet Union just a year or two earlier. Surely, the United States, Russia, China, Europe, Japan, and Vietnam, working together, could make this work. After all, this nation, like Germany and Japan, had been destroyed in a civil war of sorts. In Washington, the State Department plunged into the planning. The assistant secretary of state for the region, Richard Solomon, grabbed the issue as his own and pushed it hard—even as some more senior officials began expressing doubts.

In fact, the Cambodian "war" had ended in 1979, more than a decade before the UN occupation began. An old leader had regained his strength while new ones had emerged. Prince Norodom Sihanouk, the consummate self-interested monarch who was extremely popular with most of the Cambodian people, had ruled Cambodia since 1941, until a military coup deposed him in 1970. The Khmer Rouge brought him back as their titular head of state—though he was imprisoned in his palace during their reign. Then, as the UN troops began arriving in 1992, they made him honorary king again. But he wanted nothing less than his old job back—the all-powerful monarch, just like the kings who had ruled Cambodia since the beginning of time. Now, however, he had competitors.

During the Vietnamese occupation, from 1979 to 1989, a young Khmer Rouge officer named Hun Sen was named prime minister. He was barely educated, but clever and utterly ruthless—as one might expect of a young man trained by the Khmer Rouge and then the Vietnamese military. The prime minister's job was handed to him in 1985; he was not about to give it up.

A third competitor arose, Norodom Ranariddh, one of Sihanouk's sons. He had led a hapless guerrilla organization, funded by the United States. Its goal was to drive the Vietnamese and their appointed government, including Hun Sen, out of the country. After Vietnam pulled out, Ranariddh coveted power too. He seemed to know or care little about governance. But as prime minister, he knew he would be able to enrich himself. Ranariddh was not as clever as Hun Sen, but he was of royal lineage, which gave him a strong advantage.

So, past examples like Germany and Japan—even South Korea—simply were not useful models for this grand experiment. In fact, the Cambodian venture was unprecedented. Even before the UN troops left, the three aspiring leaders were grappling for power, as if the UN election had never taken place. Their contest lasted many years.

The troops may have left, but the United Nations was still there, running a phalanx of charitable organizations—UNICEF, UNESCO, the World Food Program (WFP), and the rest. The United States

Agency for International Development (USAID), the World Bank, and other major relief agencies from around the world worked alongside the UN. In fact, in time, 2,000 different donors and nongovernmental organizations (NGOs) set up shop in Cambodia. As the power struggles grew heated, even violent, the government grew ever more corrupt, and the donors began pushing the leaders to live up to their promises, to serve their people.

Hun Sen, Ranariddh, and the king offered little more than lip service to those demands, but that seemed to be enough. The donors kept giving money, hundreds of millions of dollars, year after year— even as the nation headed for a military showdown to settle the power struggle once and for all.

Successive American ambassadors played their own roles. The first one, Charles Twining, marveled at the wonder of Cambodia's new beginning and tended to be charitable even as the situation deteriorated. Then came Kenneth Quinn, who decided, logically enough, that he could do the most good by forming a close relationship with Prime Minister Hun Sen. But in Washington by then, Hun Sen was the villain of Cambodia, roundly despised for his corrupt and oppressive policies. So Quinn grew to be a polarizing figure because he alone stood up to defend the prime minister.

Quinn aside, the United States and other Western nations had lined up behind the lone remaining opposition leader of any consequence, Sam Rainsy. He talked the talk of a democrat but was far more popular in Washington than he was in Cambodia. He survived repeated legal attacks and an assassination attempt. But over time his allies began noticing the dictatorial way he ran his own political party. For all Rainsy's talk of democracy, it was hard to tell whether he was just a poseur.

Fighting finally broke out between Ranariddh and Hun Sen in 1997. Hun Sen became the uncontested leader. After that, successive American ambassadors arrived with a different point of view. The horrors of the Pol Pot era had receded from memory, replaced by more recent genocidal moments in Rwanda, Bosnia, Darfur. So these later ambassadors, particularly Kent Wiedemann, tended to view the government's corruption and venality with little if any sympathy. Wiedemann admitted that he effectively turned American policy toward Cambodia over to the human-rights advocates. Washington no longer cared.

The United Nations had invested years of effort and $3 billion but then dropped the matter—except to continue bragging about its success, even as Cambodia's leaders fell back into old patterns of selfinterested turpitude. As a result, even today, Cambodians remain among the most abused people in the world.

# CAMBODIA'S CURSE

# INTRODUCTION

When American visitors came to see Joseph Mussomeli, while he was the U.S. ambassador to Cambodia, he would adopt a melodramatic tone as he told them: "Be careful because Cambodia is the most dangerous place you will ever visit. You will fall in love with it, and eventually it will break your heart."

Yes, Cambodia is an alluring place, exotic and peaceful now after decades of genocide and war. Many in the West still feel sympathy, even responsibility, for the horrors of the Khmer Rouge years, when 2 million people died. As a result, visitors often smile as they watch ordinary Cambodians go about their lives in relative tranquility. "People in America," Ambassador Mussomeli observed, "all they know of Cambodia is the Khmer Rouge." So it's no wonder that tourists and visitors often "fall in love" with the state they see today.

On the streets of Phnom Penh hundreds of young people buzz past on motorbikes, carrying wives and children and every manner of cargo—mattresses, plate glass, even pigs and other livestock. Motorbikes outnumber cars by at least fifty to one. Espresso bars and stylish restaurants dot the cityscape—primarily for the thousands of international aid workers who still live and work here. One new twenty-seven-story skyscraper, a bank, is up, and several others are under construction, rising quickly in competition for the city's sky.

Everywhere you look in this most tropical of lands, flowers are abloom. Trees show off bright red, yellow, orange, or blue blossoms that rustle gently in the breeze. Now and then, you can spot a wild monkey jumping from branch to branch, even in the city center. Look up at the palm or mango trees, and you'll see ripe coconuts and fruits just waiting to be plucked. In fact, amid the litter in the streets—where in the United States you'd see half-crushed Bud Light cans and plastic water bottles—you'll find bristly, red lychee-nut shells and coconuts with drinking straws poking out of small holes.

Therein lies the central conundrum of Cambodian society. This is a nation so abundant that for all of time Cambodians have been able, as people here put it, "to live by nature"—to grow rice, pick fruit, catch fish, and live in homes built from nearby trees and vegetation. With all that plenitude there for the taking, who needs the modern world?

In Saharan Africa, the Brazilian Amazon, and other remote places, indigenous tribes live by this credo. But Cambodia is the only place where the bulk of the nation, more than three-quarters of its people, still lives more or less as they did 1,000 years ago. Until the 1940s, the nation had no schools outside the capital. The populace relied upon village monks who taught the principles of Buddhism and not much else. The state had not a single middle school, high school, or college. In large areas of the nation, the first schools were not built until the 1990s. Still, in some remote areas even now, most children still do not attend school at all. Fortunately, most villages do have a school now, and every region has its health clinic. But little else has changed.

A few miles south of Pailin, in the far-western corner of the state, near the Thai border, Ten Keng sits unsmiling under her primitive house shucking corn just harvested. "I have no education," she says with no apparent shame. Most everyone she knows is illiterate. In fact, the national teachers' union estimated that 60 percent of the nation's women could not read or write.

She's thirty-six, and her eight-year-old daughter, a first grader, sits on a bench behind her mother doing her homework—Khmer-language workbook exercises. If this little girl lives true to the averages, she will leave school after the second or third grade, as nearly half the nation's children do, and begin helping her mother in the cornfields or rice paddies.

Ten Keng's house is perhaps fifteen by twenty feet, one room with hardly any visible possessions, and sits on wooden poles about ten feet above the ground. There's no electricity, running water, natural or bottled gas for cooking, telephone service, radio or television, or other clear evidence of the modern world. Ten Keng cooks for her family over an open fire; she burns sticks and twigs and places her earthen pot over the flames, perched on three rocks.

Narrow palm fronds woven into a bamboo frame serve as her home's exterior walls. The roof is thatched. A crude log ladder climbs to the open front doorway. Hammocks hang underneath. That's where the family sleeps. A trench out back serves as the bathroom.

Around the house fruit hangs heavy from a papaya tree; clutches of nearly ripe coconuts cling to several palms. And a young mangosteen tree proffers dozens of purplish brown fruit that look ready to pick. A bucketful of tiny black seeds lie on a tarp, drying in the sun. Sesame seeds, Ten Keng says as she shoos away a gray-and-white duckling and a black rooster pecking at them. The seeds will bring a small fortune at market—maybe $60 or $70. Ten Keng's family needs it, even amid this natural abundance.

In a good year—that is, a year with a lot of rain—the family can earn 2 million riel, the Cambodian currency, or about $500. In a drought year, she says, the total may fall to $125—about 34 cents a day on average—for the entire year. And lately, those drought years come more and more often. Growing rice and corn, picking fruit, catching fish, "most years we have just enough to eat," she relates, betraying neither sadness nor self-pity. That's just the way it is, she seems to be thinking, but she also doesn't smile. Cambodians outside the cities and tourist areas are a dour people. Every day is a struggle. Life holds few opportunities for joy.

That impoverished people like Ten Keng and her family live here may not seem unusual. Every country, even the United States, has desperately poor communities. But in Cambodia, Ten Keng's reality is the norm. At least 80 percent of the nation's 13.4 million people live in rural areas, more or less as she does.

Paul Mason, a social worker, has worked in Cambodia for nearly two decades, and he recalls standing with a colleague beside a harvested rice field a few years ago when the colleague stood on top of his car, looked around in every direction, and remarked: "It probably looked like this here 350 years ago!" In the years since, Mason says he has seen some changes. A smattering of rural homes now have metal roofs—an anthropologist's measure of social advancement. What's more, in the past few years, motorbikes have shown up parked outside some of those Middle Ages huts.

However, this measure of progress can come only at a high cost. Bought used, motorbikes generally sell for $200 or $250. That's almost half the average annual wage for Cambodians. "To get motorbikes often they have sold part of their land," said Sara Colm, the Cambodia representative for Human Rights Watch. "I have seen that in remote villages." With no education, the buyers, eager for this new mobility, may not fully realize the implications until it's too late. "Then they don't have enough land to feed themselves," Colm said, shaking her head.

Across the country, some people now also have small black-and-white televisions, powered with car batteries, leading to an incongruous sight: TV antennae atop tall bamboo poles strapped to the side of tiny palm-frond houses.

"See?" Mou Neam said with a broad grin. He is the village chief of a small settlement in eastern Cambodia, near the Vietnam border. He had just turned on his little television. The battery sat on the floor amid a welter of wires and alligator clips. After a moment, a fuzzy black-and-white image of a Thai soap opera came on the screen, and Mou Neam boasted: "We can watch TV for a week on one charge!"

As it turns out, however, layering bits of the modern world into a society still living in the Middle Ages is causing disruption—not broader progress.

———————

Cambodia sits at the center of a poverty-stricken region. But by almost every measure, Cambodia is the poorest.

As a people Cambodians are generally short and thin. Obesity seems not to be a feature of society here. And it's no wonder. "The vast majority of rural poor consume only rice," said Jean-Pierre de Margerie, an earnest French Canadian who heads the World Food Program office here. A diet of only rice, only starch, leads to stunting, wasting. "Seventy percent have access to meat protein, on average, only once per week."

Ten Keng said she can afford to buy meat "maybe two to four times a month, but just a few grams." Millions cannot afford to buy enough food to provide even the minimum daily caloric count, roughly 2,000 calories, to avoid malnutrition. So children suffer stunting—a failure to develop physically or mentally for lack of protein in the diet. That means they will grow up short and, in many cases, not very smart. "If you don't provide a well-balanced diet to age two, you risk physical and mental damage that is irreversible," de Margerie warned. "Our goal is to get stunting down to 30 percent" of the children "in five years." In the meantime, almost one child in ten dies before reaching the age of five of either illness or malnutrition. Cambodia's child mortality rate is 60 percent higher than in Vietnam or Thailand, its neighbors.

But if you travel the corridors of government in Phnom Penh, you'll find Cambodia's only portly people: senior government ministers. Their diets are rich in fatty foods. Their obesity serves as an emblem of their wealth—just as it did for kings and noblemen in ancient times.

Thailand, Cambodia's western neighbor, has a gross domestic product per capita more than four times higher than Cambodia's. The average annual income for the Thai is about $3,000, compared to just under $600 for Cambodians—the second lowest in Asia. But then Thailand has largely been at peace for centuries. Its most significant military adventures were successive invasions of Cambodia in the sixteenth to nineteenth centuries.

Among the Southeast Asian nations, only Burma is poorer, on a per-capita basis. Yet Kent Wiedemann, who was chief of the U.S. mission in Burma just before he became ambassador to Cambodia in 1999, observed that the average Burmese "were actually more productive and much better off on a material basis than the rural people in Cambodia—even though the Burmese are under a much worse political regime." Even North Koreans are more prosperous. The average income there is almost triple Cambodia's.

Ask any Cambodian leader why the nation remains so stagnant while most of its neighbors prosper, and he will blame the Khmer Rouge years. "We are a war-torn country just now standing up from the ashes," Nam Tum, chairman of the provincial council in Kampong Thom Province, said in 2009, echoing similar remarks by dozens of officials, thirty years after the Khmer Rouge fell from power. In Phnom Penh at that time, the United Nations and Cambodia were putting several Khmer Rouge leaders on trial. But so much time had passed that the leaders were old and frail. Some of them were likely to pass away before they could stand trial. Pol Pot was already long dead.

At the same time, though, Vietnam's experience over the same period complicates Nam Tum's argument. Vietnam suffered a devastating war with the United States in the 1960s and '70s that killed 3 million Vietnamese and destroyed most of the nation's infrastructure, just as the Khmer Rouge (and the American bombing of eastern provinces) did in Cambodia.

The war in Vietnam ended just four years before the Khmer Rouge defeat in 1979. Yet today Vietnam's gross domestic product per capita is almost ten times higher than Cambodia's. Only 19 percent of the economy is based on agriculture, compared to more than one-third for Cambodia. Vietnam manufactures pharmaceuticals, semiconductors, and high-tensile steel. Cambodia manufactures T-shirts, rubber, and cement. Life expectancy in Vietnam stands at seventy-four years. In Cambodia it is sixty-one, one of the lowest in the world. (In the United States it is seventy-eight years.)

Most Vietnamese students stay in school until at least the tenth grade. By the tenth grade in Cambodia, all but 13 percent of the students have dropped out. Vietnam's national literacy rate is above 90 percent. UN agencies say that Cambodia's hovers around 70 percent, though available evidence suggests that may be far too generous. Most Cambodians over thirty-five or forty years of age have had little if any schooling at all. The explanations behind these and many other cultural and economic disparities lie in part in the nations' origins. Vietnamese are ancestors of the Chinese, while Cambodians emigrated from the Indian subcontinent. From China, the Vietnamese inherited a hunger for education, a drive to succeed—attitudes that Cambodian culture discourages.

Author David Ayres wrote in his book on Cambodian education, *Anatomy of a Crisis,* that in Vietnam, "traditional education provided an avenue for social mobility through the arduous series of mandarin examinations." In contrast, "Cambodia's traditional education system had always reinforced the concept of helplessness, the idea that a person was unable to determine their position in society." Village monks taught children that, after they left the pagoda school when they were seven or eight years old, their only course was to make their life in the rice paddies, as everyone in their family had done for generations.

The two nations have fought wars from their earliest days, when the Vietnamese were known as the Champa and lived only in the North of the country. The rich, fertile Mekong Delta in the South was part of Cambodia for centuries—until June 4, 1949, in fact, when France, which was occupying both nations, simply awarded the territory to Vietnam. And North Vietnam, where most Vietnamese lived, early in the nation's history, was not blessed with the same fertile abundance as Cambodia. As a result, the Vietnamese never acquired a dependence on "living by nature."

Even with Vietnam's fertile South, an accident of nature has always given Cambodia an advantage. The Tonle Sap lake sits at the center of the nation, and a river flowing from it merges with the Mekong River, in central Phnom Penh. Each spring, when the Mekong swells, its current is so strong that it forces the Tonle Sap River to reverse course, carrying tons of rich and fertile mud, as well as millions of young fish, back up to the lake. When the lake floods, it deposits new, rich soil on thousands upon thousands of acres around its perimeter. The fish provide meals for millions of people through the year.

Cambodian civilization was born on the shores of the Tonle Sap. The wonder and reliability of this natural phenomenon still encourage many Cambodians to "live by nature." Even now, many Cambodians say they have no need for society's modern inducements.

For all the devastation the United States wrought on Vietnam during the Vietnam War—the U.S. Air Force pummeled the nation with 15 million tons of bombs and other munitions—nearly all of that was used in the North, while American aid workers and diplomats spent millions of dollars aiding and modernizing the South.

Kenneth Quinn was a young American foreign-service officer stationed south of Saigon in the late 1960s and early 1970s and remembers building irrigation canals and introducing farmers to a new strain of high-yield rice that would enable them to grow three crops a year instead of one. Suddenly, he said, these farmers had a bit of disposable income.

Quinn said he also learned what he called "the incredible power of roads." In Vietnam,

as far as the road went, the new rice went. Trucks from Saigon would pick up the crops. And where the roads went, there were dramatic changes in a relatively short period of time. Pretty soon you'd see metal roofs instead of thatch. You'd hear radio coming from some of the homes, and pretty soon you'd see TV antennas. Then you'd see a taxi service starting up—to take kids who finish elementary school to the middle school in a nearby town. And, more important, the Vietcong had more trouble recruiting these young people. The VC propaganda didn't ring true anymore. But where the roads stop, improvements in the standard of living stopped. The people lived as they did one hundred years ago.

The Vietnamese took to these changes. The Cambodians never did. Twenty years later Paul Mason was working in Cambodia as an agronomist on the Vietnam border. "On our side, the ground was all brown and cracked," he recalled. "Over the border, just meters away, were these verdant green fields." Today, more than 90 percent of Cambodia's roads remain unpaved. Cambodian farmers grow a single rice crop per year—the only nation in Asia that does not grow more—and almost none of their farmland is irrigated.

Vietnamese embrace change. Cambodians tend to resist it. Even now, Cambodia's Ministry of Agriculture cannot convince most farmers to adopt modern rice-cultivation strategies that would increase Cambodia's yield—also the lowest of any major rice-growing nation. "It's not possible to spread these concepts very fast," said Kith Seng, a senior Agriculture Ministry official. "It depends on the people's ability to understand in terms of their own environment, education, and economics."

The Khmer Rouge fell from power in 1979. Remnants hung on through the following two decades, fighting a guerrilla war from the western jungle. But in 1999 the last Khmer Rouge guerrilla officer was captured, and Cambodia knew true peace nationwide for the first time in decades. Yes, the Khmer Rouge had returned the nation to "year zero." Nearly every educated person was killed, and much of the infrastructure was destroyed or fell into disrepair. Since 1979, however, that infrastructure has been rebuilt. In truth, though, the nation was quite primitive on April 17, 1975, when Pol Pot's army marched into Phnom Penh. There were few schools, factories, hospitals, or other features of twentieth- or even nineteenth-century life to raze. The nation's physical infrastructure is far more advanced today. Its people are another matter.

Chan Sophal is chairman of the Siem Reap Provincial Council, in one of the nation's largest provinces. (Provinces are equivalent to American states.) He's a serious man, intelligent and determined, and he holds an important senior position. But when he was eighteen years old the Khmer Rouge seized power and put him to work with hundreds of others digging an irrigation canal in Banteay Meanchey Province.

Asked about that experience thirty years later, as he relates the story his voice gradually rises while he fidgets and shifts in his seat. "The regime was trying to do something to empower themselves, but they did not want to empower us. We must work hard and achieve. Or die." He leans forward in his chair and punctuates his remarks with his hands, jabbing at the air.

> We had to finish our work. We worked day and night. There was no need for them to give us food. Everyone was skinny.
>
> I still remember my father being dragged away and killed. Now, sometimes, I am reading some document about the past, or meeting friends from that period, and it all comes back. I think about it. Things remind me, and not just in dreams. When I'm awake. Reading a magazine, and then I remember my personal story, how I survived. People being arrested and taken to the killing fields. Sometimes I hear people say they had a narrow escape. Then I think of my neighbor, arrested and taken away and killed. I see it in the daytime, and I dream it in the nighttime.

He looks up at the ceiling and sounds at once both desperate and sorrowful, shaking his hands over his head. "The hunger, the hunger, the sickness, the fright. Seeing the killing. Reading documents from that period, it all comes back. And the torture. People around me dying of starvation." Unprompted, he goes on and seems to slip into a detached state, more and more excited. Hand to his heart, he proclaims: "The way they arrest you in the open. They want to show us, intimidate us. Anyone who does the same thing will be treated the same." Then suddenly he is still as he draws out his words in a deep, mournful tone—eyes wide, unblinking, staring into the middle distance. "I would like to inform you that I am very, very hungry. Very, very hungry. I cannot sleep because I am so hungry."

Chairman Chan Sophal has vivid symptoms of post-traumatic stress disorder, a serious mental condition afflicting people who have experienced severe trauma. He is not alone. Several research studies have demonstrated that one-third to one-half of all Cambodians who lived through the Khmer Rouge era have PTSD, borne of their traumatic experiences then. Watching as young soldiers executed family members. Waking to find the person lying next to you dead from starvation. In one clinical study of Cambodian refugees who came to the United States in the early 1980s and now live in Long Beach, California, 62 percent were diagnosed with PTSD—twenty-five years after their trauma.

The illness brings with it major depression, insomnia, and dulled, passive behavior punctuated with violent outbursts that come when reminded of the trauma. It can impair social and occupational functioning and is particularly virulent among the poor and uneducated.

"I am Khmer; I know the Khmer," Judge In Bopha of the Pursat Provincial Court said with a piercing look. "Cambodians have been poisoned by the struggle to survive." Chhay Sareth agreed. "We are a broken society," the longtime governor of Pursat Province averred.

Won't the nation grow out of it? After all, nearly two-thirds of the population now is under thirty; they were born after the Khmer Rouge fell from power. But in fact, Cambodia is the only nation in the world where it has been demonstrated that symptoms of PTSD and related traumatic illnesses are being passed from one generation to the next. "Why not?" asked Ing Kantha Phavi, minister of women's affairs and a medical doctor. "It is well known that children who grow up in a home with domestic violence are likely to commit domestic violence themselves. The next generation will be the same."

The Khmer Rouge legacy weighs heavily on the minds of even the young, though most of them may not realize that. It has altered the entire nation's personality, changed the way people relate to one another. "When I was a boy," recalled Muny Sothara, a middle-aged psychiatrist, "the view here was to be courageous. In school they taught us that the Cambodian personality was heroic. We had great kings, a big land. We were an important country."

Seanglim Bit left the country in 1975 and watched with horror as the Khmer Rouge destroyed his nation. Fifteen years later he wrote a book, called *The Warrior Heritage*, about Cambodians' view of themselves, as he remembered it from his youth. "To be Cambodian is to be a warrior, the creator and builder of Angkor Wat," he wrote. "More accurately, to be a Cambodian is to be a descendant of a people that produced architectural masterpieces of the Angkor era which rival the achievements of any of the ancient nations." Now, though, said Muny Sothara, "people are passive. The one who survives is the one who is skillful at being deaf and blind."

Youk Chhang runs the Documentation Center of Cambodia. It gathers records of the Khmer Rouge regime. He has a slightly different theory for the change in his nation's people. "I remember our whole village was called out to watch the execution of a couple" by the Khmer Rouge. "Nobody reacted. Everybody was passive. That is how you survived. You pretend to be deaf." Then, after the war, "people were hiding their past behavior. To survive during the Khmer Rouge, you had to steal, cheat, lie, point fingers at others, even kill. And now you are ashamed."

Hem Heng, the Cambodian ambassador to Washington, offered an example. His family, he said, was respected in their village, but in 1978 the Khmer Rouge ordered the family killed. Villagers made a deal with the soldiers: Kill another family instead. And, sure enough, Hem Heng recalled, Khmer Rouge soldiers executed "a Chinese family in our place." He frowned and looked at the floor, silent.

After the war, Youk Chhang said, many people felt guilty, ashamed. "So we act passively, like we're deaf, to hide our past behavior. The problem is, now people don't see this as a problem. Today it has become the norm for us. That's what's scary."

This learned behavior is one reason most Cambodians do not react to their leaders' misbehavior. They are silent when officials enrich themselves on public proceeds and live in mansions the size of small hotels. They say little when the government tramples on their rights and constitutional guarantees. They seem not to notice as their police and military commit larceny and barbarity that would be unconscionable almost anywhere else in the world. They are quiet when the government sells their property to wealthy businessmen and then soldiers forcibly evict them in the night.

But then these afflictions were prominent features of Khmer society in the time of the great kings of Angkor 1,000 years ago. The lineage of larceny is clear. Far more than almost any other state, modern Cambodia is a product of customs and practices set in stone a millennium ago.

# CHAPTER ONE

Decades ago, when Prime Minister Hun Sen was only thirty-two years old, Cambodia's king anointed him with a richly symbolic title: *samdech*. It means "of great nobility." As he grew older, he picked up more and more ceremonial appellatives so that soon his full title stretched almost all the way across a printed page: Samdech Akka Moha Sena Padei Techo Prime Minister Hun Sen. It means "The Noble, Supreme, Great, and All-Powerful Commander in Chief, Prime Minister Hun Sen." Though he is the son of rural peasants and dropped out of school at a young age, he carries himself as if he is a direct descendant of Cambodia's great kings. All that's lacking are the elephants.

Unlike Hun Sen, the first kings of Angkor, the Khmer kingdom, knew how to use their elephants. Angkor was a full-fledged regional power dating back to the time of Jayavarman II, who first unified the Khmer kingdom in the ninth century AD. England then was not yet a nation, and the isles fell to Viking invaders. At the same time, Muslim armies occupied nearly all of the Iberian Peninsula that later would become Spain. France was just forming as a nation.

By the turn of the fourteenth century the seat of the throne (also called Angkor) was the largest city in the world. Its population approached 1 million, populating a tract of land more than twice the size of Los Angeles. From 1296 to 1308 King Indravarman III, one of Jayavarman's heirs, ruled a vast Asian empire stretching across most of Southeast Asia, including much of Thailand, Laos, Vietnam, and Malaysia. Each time he ventured out of his palace, he put on a spectacular display of majesty.

The best surviving account of life there comes from Zhou Daguan, a Chinese chronicler who visited in 1295 and 1296. "All of his soldiers were gathered in front of him, with people bearing banners, musicians and drummers following behind," he wrote. The next contingent "was made up of three to five hundred women of the palace" who carried huge candles, alight even though it was daylight. Following them came carts drawn by goats, deer, and horses, all of them decorated with gold.

Next in line, riding on elephants, were the ministers and officials and relatives of the king. "Their red parasols, too many to count, were visible from far away. Next came the king's wives and concubines and their servants, some in litters and carts, others on horses or elephants, with well over a hundred gold-filigree parasols. Last came the King, standing on an elephant, the gold sword in his hand and tusks of his elephant encased in gold. He had more than twenty white parasols, their handles all made of gold. Surrounding him on all sides were elephants in very large numbers."

These displays helped cement Indravarman's image as the God-king. And like the kings who ruled before and after, he conscripted immense slave workforces to build temples and monuments to his gods. These palaces and shrines are all that remain of Angkor today—a vast monument to slave labor. Most famous among them is Angkor Wat, built in the early twelfth century. Though it was at first dedicated to the Hindu god Vishnu, as Cambodians gradually switched their allegiance to Buddhism from roughly the eleventh to thirteenth centuries, at one point they renovated Angkor Wat to make it a Buddhist temple.

The Hindu influence on Cambodia is both ancient and lasting. The people of Angkor emigrated from the Indian subcontinent centuries earlier. Archaeologists have found ceramic shards in a cave that dated back to 4000 BC, the earliest known human population of the area. Carbon dating also places the earliest written artifact, a stone tablet in the Khmer language, at about AD 600. Other tablets from that era were in Sanskrit, the early Hindi language. Features of Hinduism—shrines and some religious practices, for example—are still part of Cambodian society today.

Each year nearly two million tourists visit the monumental architecture of Angkor Wat and the ancient city's other remaining shrines, but the homes, shops, and everyday buildings of Angkor have long since turned to dust. In AD 245 the Chinese emperor sent a fact-finding mission to Cambodia, then known as Funan. The mission report found that "the people live in houses raised from the ground." They were simple abodes, consisting of a single room mounted on poles, which kept the residents high above the annual floodwaters. Wealthier people had taller poles, giving rise to the expression, still current in parts of Cambodia today, "He lives in a high house." Bamboo matting covered the walls, palm thatch the roofs. The people cooked over open fires using earthenware pots, Zhou observed. "For a stove they used three stones set into the ground."

Several homes shared a ditch latrine. When the smell grew to be overpowering, they would cover up the ditch and dig a new one, Zhou wrote. These ditches lay amid or just above the city's water table. Needless to say, dysentery was a common illness and often fatal.

Cambodia is hot and steamy year-round; the tropical sun feels like a torch. To cope, the men of Angkor wore loincloths, the women skirts. That's all. Zhou, a prudish Chinaman, devoted significant attention to Cambodia's bare-breasted women and the freewheeling sexual mores. Life held an uninhibited, earthy quality. The AD 245 Chinese fact-finding mission reported that the people are of a covetous nature. "Boys and girls follow their penchants without restraint." For their part, Khmer kings kept vast harems, hundreds of women—until near the end of the twentieth century.

Angkor's lifeblood was rice. The kings of Angkor built large reservoirs and complex irrigation canals for the farmers. After all, rice was the source of the kings' wealth, and, as Zhou reported, the irrigation allowed the farmers to grow three or four crops a year. Farmers hauled their rice to market on crude wooden oxcarts with hand-hewn wheels. These carts can still be seen on friezes at Angkor. They are identical to the oxcarts Cambodians use today. Then, as now, the nation's economy was structured around an expansive patronage network.

Zhou saw hints of it, remarking, "There's a market every day, from around six in the morning until midday. There are no stalls, only a kind of tumbleweed mat laid on the ground, each mat in its usual place. I gather there is a small fee paid to officials."

Historians of Cambodia, drawing on texts like Zhou's and the friezes at Angkor, conclude that the king sold positions in his government. Once his mandarins paid their fee, they had the right to gather up each rice harvest, take some for themselves, and pass the rest up to the next most senior official, until finally the bulk of it was delivered to the royal palace.

No one ever questioned this practice. It was part of Angkor's natural order. Hierarchy was everything. And each of Angkor's people belonged to one of only three classes: peasantry, officialdom, or royalty. Each family's place in that hierarchy was unchangeable, from one generation to the next—from one millennium to the next. Through the centuries, Angkor's kings never acquired the view that they were accountable to their people. Still, the people clamored for favors; they begged the king for financial assistance or to weigh in on land disputes—an endemic problem.

The king also stepped in if someone committed a crime or failed to play his proper role in the hierarchy exactly as required. "If there is a dispute among the peasants," Zhou observed, "it must be referred to the king, even if it is a small matter." Penalties were brutal, even savage. For the guilty, "they just dig a ditch in the ground outside the west gate of the city, put the criminal inside it, fill it up solid with earth and stones, then leave it at that. Otherwise, people have their fingers or toes amputated, or their nose cut off."

The kings of Angkor appeared to view their citizens as little more than pawns in service of their own agendas. They conscripted thousands as slaves. Others faced even worse fates, giving their lives in service of the kings' foreign policy.

Kings of that time paid homage to one another. Indravarman knew just what it took to please the king of Champa (now central Vietnam). "At night men were sent out in many directions, to well-frequented places in towns and villages," Zhou wrote. "When they met people out at night, they snared their head with a rope and took out their gall bladder by sticking a small knife into their right-hand side. When there were enough of these, they were given to the Champa king," who most likely cooked and ate them.

Cambodians believed independent spirits lived within their bodies. Therefore, when you ate another person's internal organs, you absorbed his power. It would seem that the kings of Champa held the same view. That superstition persists today.

Following a coup in 1970, a mob killed Lon Nil, brother of Prime Minister Lon Nol, along with another member of parliament. They cut out both men's livers, took them to a Chinese restaurant, and ordered the owner to cook and slice them, then serve the attendant crowd.

For all of the vast wealth and slaves' lives Cambodian kings expended to build their temples and palaces, for their subjects they built only what was necessary to sustain the commerce that provided their wealth. Historian David Chandler wrote that, beginning with the earliest kings, the principal public works were roads, bridges, and reservoirs—all vital to growing and transporting rice.

The same remains true today. In Bon Skol, that village about a hundred miles east of Phnom Penh, the village chief, Mou Neam, does not hesitate when asked what the government does for him now. "The roads, the bridges, the wells," he said.

About 680 people live in Bon Skol. Their homes are small abodes perched on poles a few feet above the ground, with thatched roofs and walls of bamboo matting. They cook their meals over open fires and set their earthen pots atop three rocks. Bathrooms are open pits back behind the homes. These latrines sit atop the water table. Dysentery is as commonplace in the 2000s as it was in the 1200s.

Historians believe the Angkor empire began to decline in the fifteenth century. It had reigned longer than the Roman Empire. Though no one knows exactly why Angkor lost its way, theories abound. Most likely, the city outgrew its ability to sustain itself. Cambodians have always had large families; even today it's not unusual for the most desperately poor couples to have as many as eight or ten children. It seems probable that Angkor's population swelled beyond the natural environment's ability to sustain it. Add to that periods of drought and the evolution of the Asian economy into the era of trade and international commerce during the 1600s.

Responding to mounting threats to the Angkorian way of life, over time the people began to leave. That was easy. They could dismantle their simple homes, load them onto oxcarts, and move someplace else in the Khmer kingdom where they could grow rice, pick fruit, and catch fish.

Yet as the Angkor empire died, Cambodia lost its soul. Until just five hundred years ago, it had been a great nation-state—strong, confident, powerful, respected, and feared. But as the state declined, its kings became helpless, even pathetic, vassals of their neighbors.

Cambodia's neighbors were quick to seize upon this weakness. The Siamese to the west and Vietnamese to the east began taking bites out of the state, beginning in the 1500s and 1600s. Meantime, the Vietnamese migrated southward until they outnumbered Cambodians in the southern delta region. Over time, they became the de facto rulers. Siamese military forays made inroads from the west.

Over the years a series of kings and their family members allied themselves with either Thai or Vietnamese rulers, whichever they thought could serve as protectors against the other neighbor's aggression. Hoping to outmaneuver the king, dissident members of the royal family would sometimes make secret alliances with different neighboring states. Through all of this intrigue, Cambodia continuously suffered invasions and civil wars.

For the first time Cambodian leaders acquired a new character trait: an overwhelming sense of dependency. For solutions to their problems, they had to look beyond themselves. They searched for saviors outside their borders—a far cry from the great medieval kings who held a vast, glittering empire together with cunning and military might.

The Thai and Vietnamese had little respect for the Cambodian people after the fall of Angkor. Their views were scathing. Writing in 1834 Vietnamese emperor Minh Mang called Cambodia a barbarian state because "the people do not know how to grow food." They used picks and hoes in the rice paddies, wielding them by hand; they didn't know even how to use oxen, the emperor complained. The sophisticated irrigation schemes the Angkorian kings devised had long since fallen into decay, and in other parts of the country no one even thought to irrigate their fields. "They grow enough rice to eat two meals a day" and saw no value in growing anything more, Emperor Minh Mang wrote. Without irrigation, Cambodians were wholly dependent on the rains to water their crops. At best they could grow one rice crop a year, and then only when the rains fell as expected—a pitiable state compared to the farmers who lived when the kings of Angkor ruled.

A few years later the Vietnamese emperor assigned his best general, Troung Minh Giang, to civilize the Cambodians. But in short order, the general gave up. "After studying the situation," he reported, "we have decided that Cambodian officials only know how to bribe and be bribed. Offices are sold. Nobody carries out orders; everyone works for his own account."

Centuries before, the kings of Angkor had set up an economic model that relied on patronage. The king sold government positions to his mandarins. Once ensconced, these aides would be awarded the right to collect rice from the farmers who lived in their respective territories and keep part of it—generally one-tenth of the crop. Over time, this model naturally evolved into full-throated corruption.

———————

Through the Angkor empire and into the twentieth century, Cambodia had not a single school. Only monks in village pagodas who taught young boys scripture and perhaps how to read. Girls received no education whatsoever. As a result, the men who bought their positions in the royal court had no training or knowledge in government administration. Most were illiterate. The very idea of working on behalf of the people to improve their lot was a foreign concept. These officers looked out only for themselves; their sole occupation was accruing personal wealth. This state of affairs had continued uninterrupted for centuries, and there was no reason to question it.

Cambodia's peasantry viewed the government with suspicion, even fear. Men were liable for military conscription at any time. The only other interaction families had with the government came when an official showed up to collect "taxes"—10 percent of each harvest. It's no wonder that the Khmer verb *to govern* literally means "to eat the kingdom."

It's also not surprising that most Cambodians lack ambition or any hope for a better life. Their religion, Theravadist Buddhism, taught them to shun status and eschew material possessions because "contentment is wealth," as the monks still say. In the pagoda schools, monks preached that children should be pleased with the lives they had and not aspire for more.

Theravadist Buddhism swept the country and much of the region in the fourteenth century, possibly because its credo fit so neatly with the Cambodian reality. As nearly every Cambodian recognized, social advancement of any kind was impossible. Material wealth was unattainable. Theravadist monks advised the people to be content with the status quo, and having no other option, they complied.

Centuries later the Vietnamese viewed this Cambodian personality trait with contempt. Emperor Minh Mang complained that the people's shortcomings, as he saw them, "stem from the laziness of the Cambodian people"—an unfortunate epithet that grew to be commonplace among foreigners.

The Thai practiced Theravadist Buddhism as well, but they also characterized the Cambodians as indolent and dumb. Chaophyraya Bodin, a Thai military commander, complained in the nineteenth century that "all the Khmer leaders and nobles, all the district chiefs and all the common people are ignorant, stupid, foolish and gullible. They have no idea what is true and what is false."

Into the mid-nineteenth century the Thai and the Vietnamese battled each other for dominance over Cambodia, and had events played out without interference, in time the two states would have divided up the whole of Cambodia and annexed their shares. That is how weak and hapless the Cambodian state had become. But in the mid-1800s King Norodom, who had spent his youth as a hostage in the Thai royal court, changed the course of Cambodian history.

The king signed a treaty with France in 1863, offering timber and mining rights in exchange for protection from Cambodia's neighbors. The French could easily deal with the Vietnamese threat, as they had recently occupied Vietnam, too. The Thai were a more difficult problem.

For the first few years the French were benign guardians, asking only for taxes and fees in return for their protection. But by the mid-1870s they began demanding change in Cambodia's ossified government. At their urging King Norodom promised to abolish slavery and end the monarchy's insistence that all land belonged to the crown. He also pledged to reform "tax collection," which had grown into a system of runaway thievery. But then Norodom employed a passive-aggressive tactic that would remain commonplace, even into the modern era. He signed orders for all of these reforms—but then declined to enforce them.

This didn't escape French notice. Over the following decades the French grew ever more frustrated with the Cambodian people. Just as the Thai and Vietnamese before them, the French viewed the populace as ignorant and torpid. As for the government bureaucracy, one French administrator described it as "worm-eaten debris," historian John Tully wrote. As ever, the government's legal and administrative officials were dedicated only to enriching themselves. The French calculated that they pocketed about 40 percent of the nation's revenue.

King Norodom was another problem altogether. The French complained frequently about his vast harem, which included four to five hundred women plus another thousand relatives and children. Tully wrote that a French report in 1894 caustically noted that the king's concubine city cost the government 160,000 francs a year—a very considerable sum one hundred years ago. The French also chafed at his addiction to opium and deep affection for alcohol.

When Norodom died in 1904, his successor, King Sisowath, worked with the French to at last evict the Thai from western Cambodia. Otherwise, he was a compliant king. Soon after he took office he really did abolish slavery, as Norodom had promised forty years earlier. He realized he had to give up something if he wanted the French to free his state from his hated enemy.

Having secured Cambodia's territorial integrity, through the midtwentieth century the French imposed onerous taxes and fees, but they offered little in return. Only in 1935 did they build the nation's first high school, in Phnom Penh. Even so, they used it primarily to educate members of the royal family and train mandarin children to work in the French administration.

In midcentury the French began sending a few dozen talented students to Paris to study, hoping they could educate a few of them to do serious work in the colonial government. These were young people, generally in their early twenties, who had no experience with the world outside their villages or perhaps Phnom Penh. They had never seen a television and perhaps not even a radio. Cambodia had little in the way of newspapers, and so they knew almost nothing of the world outside.

These young students arrived in Paris and found a society they had no idea existed. Most shocking for them were the French people, quite wealthy by Cambodian standards, who were free to do pretty much what they wanted. For many Cambodians this was transformative. Suddenly they questioned every founding principle of the Khmer state. Who said they could not aspire to more—to a life like these Frenchmen lived? Why should they be satisfied with the stunted lives Cambodians were indoctrinated to accept without question?

One of these students made this view plain in an article published in a Khmer student magazine. The author wrote, "The King is absolute. He attempts to destroy the people's interest when the people are in a position of weakness." The "absolute king uses nice words, but his heart remains wicked." The author of these words was a twenty-seven-year-old student named Saloth Sar. The world would know him later by his nom de guerre, Pol Pot.

Communism was fashionable in Europe at the time. Saloth Sar and some of the other Cambodians embraced it and then brought the movement home. After returning to Cambodia they would find common cause with Vietnamese rebels who were fighting the French for their own freedom.

Yet at a young age Saloth Sar was by no means ideologically pure. His older sister, Saloth Roeung, was the favorite concubine of the next king, Sisowath Monivong. As a young boy Saloth Sar liked to visit her at the palace—probably because giggling concubines would gather around him and, with their hands, offer sexual favors.

When King Sisowath Monivong died in 1941, Saloth Roeung sat at his bedside. The French chose Sisowath's nephew Norodom Sihanouk as the new king. He was nineteen years old, and, once again, the French assumed he would be compliant. But in fact, as king, he would be responsible for winning freedom from the French in 1953, a year before the Vietnamese won their own freedom at Dien Bien Phu.

Sihanouk was a complex man, a clever, vain, and dedicated narcissist who ruled Cambodia for twenty-nine years and wielded great influence for decades longer. He was responsible for significant social change—and also great damage. He talked the talk of limited democracy but was brutal and merciless with his political opponents. Hundreds simply disappeared. In spite of his democratic overtures, he wanted to be the political leader of his country, not just a monarch perched upon a throne. So in 1955 he resigned as king and formed a political party. He ruled as Prince Sihanouk, chief of state, for the next fifteen years.

He built schools and universities—primarily for bragging rights at international meetings—even though he had no educated faculty to staff them. He held Cambodia's first-ever democratic elections for parliament in 1946. But when he disapproved of the outcome, he and his allies staged a coup.

Prince Sihanouk's changes aside, Cambodian culture continued as it had for a millennium. Under Sihanouk, as historian Michael Vickery put it, government officials "grew wealthy while the books showed red," and the economy "was a continuation of the traditional practice of officials extracting a percentage of what they collected for the state; and no one of the elite was ever severely called to account or forced to repay what he had collected from the public till." After a thousand years, nothing had changed.

For almost a century, the French had served as Cambodia's patrons. Soon after independence, the United States stepped in to fill that role and began supplying copious quantities of foreign aid—so much money, Sihanouk said, that Cambodia was succumbing to the "dollar god." His mandarins were ladling vast personal fortunes from the foreign-aid accounts.

Sihanouk liked to inveigh against corruption but then lived a lifestyle of almost unimaginable extravagance. His wealth's source remained obscure. Years later, in the early 1990s, Secretary of State James Baker visited Sihanouk in Paris at the Cambodian ambassador's residence. With Baker was John Bolton, then an assistant secretary of state. "It was 10 a.m., and he was serving champagne," Bolton remembered with obvious disgust. "He reached down and poured a glass for his dog. It was like Louis XIV."

In 1963 Sihanouk told the United States he wanted no more aid money. Until that point the United States had supplied millions upon millions. The money, he complained, was "a corrupting influence," but he was also straining to keep Cambodia out of the Vietnam War. Distancing himself from Washington, be believed, would help ensure that. Still, this act, more than anything else, proved to be his undoing. Where would all his mandarins purloin their incomes now?

In 1965 Sihanouk cut off diplomatic relations with the United States altogether and threw his lot in with China, whose leaders courted and flattered him. That set his aides to plotting. After all, the Chinese were not nearly as generous as the Americans had been.

All of this occurred as several of those Cambodian students who had studied in France began building an underground Communist Party based in Phnom Penh. Party members tried to remain covert, but they couldn't hide from Sihanouk. He regarded the growth of the communist movement with great alarm and warned in 1961, during a tour of the provinces, that a Communist regime in Cambodia would "deprive the individual of all that is dear to him—basic freedoms and the joys of family life—and turn him into a producing machine which over time has all the human values sucked out of it." Over the next decade he arrested anyone he caught who appeared to be associated with the movement and generally treated its members with ruthless repression.

In the mid-1960s, the movement's leaders fled Phnom Penh, set up headquarters in the countryside, and, in 1967, began a national military uprising. The four Communist Party standing committee members who made that decision were Saloth Sar, who later changed his name to Pol Pot; Ieng Sary, who became the Khmer Rouge foreign minister; Nuon Chea, known as "Brother Number Two"; and So Phim, who was commander of the Communist Party's Eastern Zone.

By the beginning of 1970 the Khmer Communists controlled not quite 20 percent of Cambodia's territory—principally the rural areas around their headquarters. Their future appeared uncertain at best.

In March 1970, however, everything changed. A military coup forced Sihanouk out of office while he was on vacation in Paris. The new head of government was Lon Nol, the nation's richly corrupt prime minister. Before leaving for Paris, Sihanouk often remarked that Lon Nol and his compatriots were "more patriots of the dollar than patriots of Cambodia."

Phnom Penh officialdom cheered the news. Lon Nol was close to the United States. Restored relations with Washington would allow the mandarins to dip back into the till. Car dealers and building contractors jubilated. But these people, the economic elite of Phnom Penh, represented but a minuscule portion of Cambodian society. At least 90 percent of the population lived in the provinces, and these people were stunned and ashamed. They adored Sihanouk. To them he was just short of a god. How could anyone overthrow the God-king?

All over the country people demonstrated against the coup. Hundreds of villagers marched on Phnom Penh. In 1970 Lon Nol ordered his troops to open fire on them. They scattered, ran back into the jungle. Later, several of them told reporters they were so angry about that episode that they rushed to join the Khmer Rouge.

Fury, of course, consumed Sihanouk. He flew to Beijing to seek advice. And when he heard that the new regime was vilifying him on Cambodian radio, he declared that he wanted "justice"—in other words, revenge. While this poisonous state of mind consumed him, his friend Pham Van Dong, the premier of North Vietnam, asked him if now he was willing to work with the Khmer Rouge to overthrow Lon Nol, journalist Philip Short wrote in his biography, *Pol Pot*. Sihanouk said yes, and the North Vietnamese passed word along to Zhou Enlai, the Chinese premier.

A few days later, just a few weeks after the coup, Sihanouk announced that he had formed the National United Front of Kampuchea. He was now allied with the Khmer Rouge. The prince, on the radio, urged his subjects to join the Khmer Rouge. Thousands upon thousands heard him and complied. Then and only then did the Khmer Rouge movement begin to take off.

Much of the scholarship on the Khmer Rouge was written in the first few years after their reign. And most of that was colored by the general disdain, endemic among journalists and authors, for Richard Nixon, Henry Kissinger, and America's misadventure in Vietnam. It's hard to overstate the contempt so many people felt, especially Europeans. The more recent broad, scornful view of George W. Bush seems mild in comparison.

In this climate William Shawcross, a British journalist, wrote his seminal book, *Sideshow: Kissinger, Nixon, and the Destruction of Cambodia*. It concluded that the American bombing of Cambodia, intended to destroy Vietcong sanctuaries there, drove the peasantry to the Khmer Rouge and ensured their victory. The liberal media (and I was a card-carrying member; I read and admired his book while flying to Cambodia in 1979) heaped adulation on Shawcross.

Now, thirty years later, with passions cooled, it is quite clear that his conclusion was wrong. The American bombing began a year before the Lon Nol coup. Sihanouk had quietly acquiesced, saying he wanted to be sure the Vietnam War did not spread into his own country. And in 1970 the Khmer Rouge was still a negligible force.

At the same time, since the late 1950s Sihanouk had spent a decade cultivating the Chinese leadership, Mao Tse-tung and Zhou En-lai. They grew to be Sihanouk admirers and friends—at a time when China had very few friends. Mao gave Sihanouk a magnificent mansion on Anti-Imperialist Street in Beijing and feted him every time he came to town—which was often. The Chinese also happened to be the Khmer Rouge's primary patrons and advisers. Would Mao and Zhou have authorized Pol Pot to overthrow their very good friend, Prince Norodom Sihanouk?

Lon Nol was, of course, a different animal with different motivations. He gave the Americans carte blanche to bomb wherever they pleased. In 1970, shortly after Sihanouk was thrown from office, he told an American television interviewer why he thought Lon Nol was so eager to give the United States whatever it wanted: "Some officers in our army and many deputies and many members of government want to be your allies because they want your dollars. They don't think about the destiny or the fate of our homeland." Even angry and embittered, his words rang true. As before, he called them "more patriots for dollars than for Cambodia."

When Lon Nol took power, the Khmer Rouge controlled little more than the areas around their jungle redoubts. More recent scholarship has suggested that the American bombing, for all its wanton, deadly results, so disrupted the nation that it delayed the Khmer Rouge's ultimate victory until after the B-52 campaign had ended, in August 1973.

If Lon Nol had not staged his mercenary coup, most likely the Khmer Rouge would never have come to power. That is, of course, Sihanouk's view, but other Cambodians hold it, too. Hem Heng, the Cambodian ambassador to Washington, said, "If not for the Lon Nol coup, there would be no Khmer Rouge." But in his view, that did not let the United States off the hook. "They supported the coup," he said. "They supported Lon Nol." The available evidence suggests but does not necessarily prove that theory.

Years later Sihanouk told James Garrand, an Australian television documentary maker: "We cannot remake history," but "I don't think I made serious mistakes. You should see Mr. Lon Nol because if we have to go back to the starting point, would he still like to destroy his country by a coup d'état against Sihanouk? Or would he like to restore Sihanouk as head of state? I think your question should be put to Mr. Lon Nol."

Sihanouk is partially correct: Lon Nol does share responsibility for what was to come. But it is beyond question that after the prince was thrown from office, by allying himself with the Khmer Rouge and urging his countrymen to join, Sihanouk condemned his people to damnation.

# CHAPTER TWO

Vietnamese called Nui Sam a mountain, but really it is not much larger than a hill, part of a range called the Seven Mountains, just outside Chau Doc City in southern Vietnam. Each year villagers hold a festival at a beautiful Buddhist temple at Nui Sam's base. Another Buddhist shrine sits amid the brush on the hill's peak. But for Kenneth Quinn and other Americans serving in Vietnam during the war, the incline offered something far more interesting: a magnificent view of southeastern Cambodia, from the Vietnam border all the way up the meandering Mekong River.

In the late 1960s and early 1970s, Quinn was a young State Department officer serving as vice consul in Chau Doc, a four- or five-hour drive south of Saigon—and a long way from Dubuque, Iowa, where he grew up. His job: to win the hearts and minds of the South Vietnamese and prevent Vietcong from making inroads among the population. Toward that end Quinn and his colleagues were building roads and irrigation canals while offering hybrid seeds and advice to rice farmers. At the same time, in the North, the U.S. military was gradually losing the war.

Quinn enjoyed the job, especially since it had allowed him to fend off a draft notice that would have brought him to the same country, as a soldier, not a State Department officer. Soon after he arrived, another foreign-service officer had taken him up the hill to show him the impressive view. Once, in the late 1960s, he brought Eugene Rostow, undersecretary of state—the department's third most powerful officer—up the hill to have a look at the panorama. Rostow was an older man and had trouble clambering over rocks on the climb up. But he made it to the top and appreciated the sight—even though, like every American official then, Rostow regarded Cambodia as an irrelevant little country. The United States had only one interest there: to prevent Vietcong troops from using eastern Cambodia as a sanctuary. After the United States began bombing eastern Cambodia in 1969, the next year American and South Vietnamese troops briefly invaded the area, on a hunt for Vietcong bases.

In 1972 Quinn asked Nguyen thi LeSon, a beautiful young Vietnamese woman from Saigon, to marry him, and she accepted. So it was only natural that when she came to visit from Saigon, he took her up the hill to see the view. But when they reached the peak and looked out across the verdant plains of eastern Cambodia, they stood stockstill and stared.

Below them in all directions, almost as far as they could see, scattered pillars of black smoke reached skyward. Quinn had no idea what he was looking at. "It was not comprehensible to me. Was it some sort of ceremony? No, it was too big. There were still American air strikes, but this didn't look like that. It looked like dozens and dozens of fires in villages all over the area." At that time, "Cambodia seemed a strange and mysterious place," and when he asked his colleagues back at the consulate about what he had seen, "no one seemed able to explain it very well," except to say that maybe it had something to do with the Khmer Communists—a poorly understood insurgent group that later came to be known as the Khmer Rouge.

They had not been considered a threat. As Quinn and the other American officers saw it, "they were like the minor leagues, not even triple A. Just double A." They were thought to be allies of the North Vietnamese who, it was assumed, funded and armed them. But why would Vietnam want to burn dozens of villages in eastern Cambodia? None of it made sense.

A few days later, hundreds of Cambodian refugees began pouring into Vietnam across an old, little-used border crossing. This was quite unusual. Cambodians hate the Vietnamese. For many Cambodians, the Vietnamese are infamous for a story, probably apocryphal, of Cambodian workers digging a canal in western Vietnam in the nineteenth century. Vietnamese soldiers grabbed three of them, buried them up to their necks so their heads formed a narrow triangle, then placed a pot on their heads, started a fire, and boiled water for tea. In the 1950s Prince Sihanouk used an image dramatizing this scene on a scarf he gave out to supporters.

For the Cambodians to flee into Vietnam, something really terrible had to be happening. Quinn was curious. Maybe these people could explain what he and his fiancée had seen from the hilltop. He decided to go talk to them.

Quinn interviewed several dozen of the Cambodians. They informed him that the Khmer Rouge—that's what Sihanouk was calling them—was forcing villagers out of their homes across the East, herding them to collective farms, and burning their houses to be sure they did not return. By mid-1973 the Khmer Rouge now controlled much of the Cambodian countryside.

At the same time, the Communists were attacking any Vietnamese troops they encountered, trying to push them out of the country. For Quinn this was even more surprising. It was a State Department verity that the Khmer Communists were a weak appendage of Vietnam. Henry Kissinger liked to say that when "we settle Vietnam, we will also settle Cambodia." At about that time President Richard Nixon wrote to Prime Minister Lon Nol in Phnom Penh, saying, "The United States remains determined to provide maximum possible assistance to your heroic self defense," adding that "the continuing warfare in Cambodia results solely, I believe, from the unreasoning intransigence of the North Vietnamese—and their Khmer communist supporters."

Quinn now believed that Nixon and Kissinger were wrong. This was important, and he had to tell Washington. So he decided to write an "airgram." These were longer than normal research reports that included new, revelatory information. He spent almost a year researching and writing it while also doing his other work. When he finally finished, in February 1974, he found a friendly secretary in Saigon to type it for him, and then the embassy sent it off to other American embassies across Southeast Asia and a dozen offices in the State Department. For Quinn, this was the end result of a year's hard work; his airgram offered important news. For a young officer, this was exciting!

Quinn's airgram was fifty pages, single-spaced. Its primary message: The Cambodian Communists (he called them the "Khmer Krahom," meaning Cambodia Reds) were trying to remake Cambodian society through force and terror:

The Khmer Krahom's programs have much in common with those of totalitarian regimes in Nazi Germany and the Soviet Union, particularly regarding efforts to psychologically reconstruct individual members of society. In short, this process entails stripping away, through terror and other means, the traditional bases, structures and forces which have shaped and guided an individual's life until he is left as an atomized, isolated individual unit; and then rebuilding him according to party doctrine by substituting a series of new values, organizations and ethical norms for the ones taken away. The first half of this process can be found in the KK attack on religion, the destruction of vestiges of the Sihanouk regime, attacks on parental and monastical authority, prohibitions on traditional songs and dances, and the use of terror. Psychological atomization, which can result from these practices and which causes individuals to feel effectively isolated from the rest of their community, can be seen to have actually occurred: refugees from Kampot and Kandal Provinces have said they were so afraid of arrest and execution that even in their own homes they dared not utter a critical word and obediently complied with every KK directive.

Quinn's airgram was a revelation. No one outside of Cambodia knew anything about these Khmer Communists. But based on what Quinn had heard, they appeared to be extremely determined, brutal revolutionaries who were trying to remake Cambodian society. His airgram was the first warning, the earliest indication for the West, of the Khmer Rouge's genocidal intentions.

For Washington, another of Quinn's conclusions was even more controversial: The Communists were not allied with Vietnam. In fact, as his airgram put it, "The KK are strongly anti-Vietnamese and desire to force all Viet Cong and North Vietnamese Army units out of Cambodia." Wasn't one of the justifications for bombing eastern Cambodia that the attacks would also cripple Hanoi's allies, the Khmer Communists? Quinn couldn't wait to get the phone calls from Washington, maybe even see a story in the *New York Times* or the *Washington Post*.

In Phnom Penh Donald Jameson was a political officer in the U.S. Embassy. When Quinn's airgram arrived, he and others simply turned up their noses. "It had no impact," he said, "mainly because it was from outside. It's ingrained in every embassy: Protect your turf." Quinn's document brought just one visceral reaction: Why on earth did this young fellow think he had the right to do reporting on Cambodia? The Phnom Penh embassy sent a telex back to Quinn's consulate. Its message, in sum, was *We'll do the reporting on Cambodia, thank you.* Then, for good measure, a few weeks later a Defense Intelligence Agency official came down to see him. *Where'd you get this?* he asked with a belligerent tone. He then set out to tell Quinn why he was wrong.

Quinn's airgram had landed with a thud. The State Department is little different from other large organizations. Thirty-one-year-old junior officers are in no position to challenge corporate orthodoxies. Furthermore, in Quinn's case, his evidence was considered unreliable. State Department officials didn't place much value on the testimony of refugees. Who knows what their political motivations might be? What's more, refugees generally know little more than what they are able to see happening in their own little villages. They can offer no context. That was especially true for most of the poor, illiterate refugees Quinn interviewed, though there were exceptions, a few refugees who had broader knowledge. In fact, Quinn's sources had indeed led him to one false conclusion—that the Khmer Krahom in southeastern Cambodia were a breakaway sect that was anti-Vietnamese while the larger body of Khmer Communists remained firmly allied with Vietnam. The truth was that the Khmer Communists nationwide were both united and staunchly anti-Vietnamese.

Nevertheless, Quinn's airgram offered an essential truth that was prescient for its time: The Khmer Rouge was a brutal, murderous revolutionary group intent on destroying Cambodian society. Before February 1974 no one outside Cambodia had known that. Even in Phnom Penh, knowledge was scant.

Within the American Embassy no one really knew or cared about the Khmer Rouge. In fact, paradoxical as it may have seemed, the embassy wasn't particularly interested in Cambodia—except as events there affected the war in Vietnam. "The mind-set," Jameson said, "was that there was no one of interest out there but the Vietcong." Even if they had wanted to go look for themselves, embassy officers decided it was too dangerous. By 1974 the Khmer Rouge frontier was just ten miles outside Phnom Penh. But what was the point? "Washington and the embassy could have cared less about the Khmer Rouge."

The embassy did care a great deal about Lon Nol, the military leader who had deposed Sihanouk in that coup in 1970. He was the State Department's man, and he did more or less what he was told. In return, between 1970 and 1975 the United States provided about $1.85 billion in military and economic aid. Accounting for inflation, that's about $9 billion in 2010 dollars. All of that American aid money brought out the worst features of Cambodian society.

The government and the military fell into an orgy of theft that knew no bounds. In the field, army officers sold uniforms and ammunition, even artillery pieces, to the enemy. They stole their units' food rations and medicine, then sold them at market. They created staff rosters with thousands of ghost positions and pocketed the salaries. They even failed to report men killed or captured in battle so they could continue collecting their pay. And when all of that was done for the day, they drove back to Phnom Penh for dinner at the most expensive and flamboyant Western restaurants they could find. For the evening they rejoined the Phnom Penh bacchanal.

The United States Congress ordered an end to the bombing of Cambodia in August 1973. By that time American aircraft had dropped about 2.75 million tons of ordnance, causing massive carnage that has never been fully documented or accounted for. Yet Congress's ban was enacted not out of concern for the Cambodian victims. As Representative Tip O'Neill said during the floor debate, "Cambodia is not worth the life of one American flier."

The areas bombed, in eastern and central Cambodia, were hard to get to—and at war. Reporters, diplomats, and aid workers did not travel there. No one was able to total the destruction; no one counted the dead. The only accounts of the horror came from peasants who fled the bombing and the Khmer Rouge. They ran to Phnom Penh, whose population more than tripled to 3 million people. Most of the survivors were illiterate, and even if they were inclined to talk, they had no one to tell.

The Lon Nol government supported a large expansion of the target area for American bombers more or less in exchange for cash. The U.S. Embassy in Phnom Penh wasn't interested in the victims. And among the other Westerners in town, undoubtedly some of them agreed with Gen. William Westmoreland, the commander of U.S. forces in Vietnam. "The Oriental doesn't put the same high price on life as does a Westerner," he said in 1974. "Life is plentiful, life is cheap in the Orient." Today those parts of eastern Cambodia are pockmarked with bomb craters, most of them now fetid ponds—hideous scars of a terrible crime.

Lon Nol suffered a stroke in early 1971 and never fully recovered, though he did retake nominal command a short time later, awarding himself the title of field marshal. He famously declared that Cambodians had no need for "the sterile game of outmoded liberal democracy"—joining a parade of Cambodian leaders, before and after, who offered that view. But he seldom left his villa and succumbed to his weakness for spiritual solutions to real-world problems. Once, he had military aircraft sprinkle "magical" sand around Phnom Penh's perimeter to ward off enemies.

None of it worked. As the Khmer Rouge noose tightened around Phnom Penh, the United States began airlifting food, medicine, and military equipment into the city. Cambodians looted the supplies to the end. Finally, in early April 1975, as Khmer Rouge troops advanced on the city, the airlifts stopped, the United States evacuated its embassy, and the leadership of Lon Nol's government fled.

No one knew exactly what to expect from the Khmer Rouge. Its leadership remained a mystery; the movement had never explained its intentions. Quinn's prescient airgram had no impact, and in the meantime Sihanouk sent several U.S. senators a letter in which he predicted that the Khmer Rouge, his allies, planned to set up "a Swedish type of kingdom."

On April 17, 1975, the Khmer Rouge army marched into Phnom Penh. Over the next few frantic days, journalists covered what they saw before they were forced to leave. They watched, astounded, as Khmer Rouge soldiers, young peasants from the provinces, mostly uneducated teenage boys who had never been in a city before, swept through town. For them, Phnom Penh offered many mysteries. The boys didn't know what to make of telephones, or toilets. But they set to their job right away, evacuating Phnom Penh, forcing all of its residents, at gunpoint, to leave behind everything they owned and march toward the countryside. Hospital patients still in their white gowns stumbled along carrying their IV bottles. Screaming children ran in desperate search for their parents.

Yet while the mass evacuation of 3 million people was stupefying, the foreign correspondents saw little bloodshed before they were deported. And that is about all the world knew of the new Khmer

Rouge government. Some writers and analysts saw this as the beginning of a horror show. Others believed they were witnessing the early days of a new, utopian society.

----

C harles Twining, a thirty-three-year-old State Department officer, couldn't have been more excited about his new assignment: political officer in the U.S. Embassy in Phnom Penh. In 1974 he had left a foreign-service posting in Africa to spend a year at the Foreign Service Institute in Washington, learning to speak Khmer. He was supposed to take up his new post in June 1975. But then, of course, in April the United States lost its embassy in Phnom Penh. After that no one in Washington professed to know what was going on inside Cambodia. So the State Department assigned Twining to be America's "Cambodia watcher," as they called the position, and sent him to Bangkok.

When he arrived at the end of June 1975, he was quite familiar with the debate. "With the fall of Cambodia, we all knew the accounts about the evacuation of Phnom Penh, and I believed them," he said. "But did anyone have a good grasp on the situation in the other cities at the time? Hardly."

So Twining set out to find the truth. He drove out to Aranyaprathet, the tiny, primitive Thai town that sat right on the Cambodian border. He was a careful young man, not given to quick flights of judgment. He knew his audience for what they were: hidebound bureaucrats in Washington. Nixon had resigned from office, and, in theory, the State Department no longer had to tailor its policy judgments so that they conformed to Washington's convoluted explanations for its policies in Vietnam and the rest of Southeast Asia. The Vietnam War was over; the American troops were gone. But even so, the men who had made those judgments about the war and staked their careers on them still sat in the big chairs at the department. President Gerald Ford had been Nixon's vice president, after all. Ford was not making wholesale changes in staffing at State or anywhere else. Kissinger was still secretary of state. Twining also knew that the general public in the United States wanted nothing to do with Southeast Asia. Whatever he found, whatever he wrote, he knew he would face a tough audience.

At the border he found a few like-minded investigators. "I and a few other diplomats and journalists who had left Phnom Penh had gathered in Bangkok. During the summer of 1975, we were all trying to figure out what was happening, with no one having very much hard information. There was a lot of comparing of notes, almost a case of the blind leading the blind."

In one of his first airgrams back to Washington that summer, he simply summarized the reigning points of view, since he was not ready to form his own. The journalists and others "can be divided roughly into hardliners and softliners. The hardliners believe Cambodia has been going through a considerable bloodbath whose end is not yet in sight. The softliners reject this theory, stating that, although there are undeniable reports of atrocities being committed in some parts of the country, these should not be permitted to form" a conclusion. Later, when Twining heard his first atrocity accounts, he too didn't know what to make of them. The killing and mayhem were "so tinged with chaos that the reality was hard to decipher."

In Washington, meanwhile, the State Department had another problem—eighty-one Cambodian military officers were studying in the United States under the Pentagon's Military Assistance Program. On April 17, 1975, the department's consular division canceled their student visas. The Lon Nol government had sent them to the United States for training. But that government no longer existed. Suddenly, all of these men were classified as refugees.

Almost to a man, they wanted to go home. "Everyone wanted to go back," said Bay Sarit, who was a lieutenant colonel in Lon Nol's army, stationed at Fort Benning, Georgia, for fourteen months of training. He and his colleagues had heard the rumors of mass killings. "But we kept saying, 'Cambodians are not going to kill other Cambodians.' We just couldn't believe that. The government had just fallen. Maybe they'd kill a couple of high-ranking people. But that's all. The others were saying. 'We need to go back and fight!' I asked them, 'Fight who?' We were confused. We didn't know what to do."

In Cambodia the Khmer Rouge quickly assigned Bay Sarit's wife, Bay Sophany, to a work detail, "breaking rocks for a road." She knew where her husband was, but she also realized that if the Khmer Rouge caught her carrying anything written, proving education and literacy—or, worse still, some connection to Lon Nol's army—she'd have been executed. So "I wrote it on my upper thigh: 'Fort Benning Georgia.' They wouldn't look there. When it wore off, I wrote it again," so she would not forget.

The State Department had no idea how to deal with those officers. So they contracted the problem out. They hired a refugee assistance group to take care of the Cambodians until Washington figured out what to do with them. Cindy Coleman, who had a long and distinguished record of work with refugees, was named project director. By the fall of 1975, "the group was getting restive," Coleman said. "They had wives and family back home. They were threatening to kill themselves if they were not sent back."

The department told them they had to wait a few months until they could find a solution. Washington had no diplomatic relations with the new Cambodian regime. In the meantime, in the fall of 1975 all of the military officers, plus three dozen other Cambodian refugees who had somehow managed to make it to the United States, 114 Cambodians in all, were herded to Philadelphia and given quarters in a downtown YMCA. They still clamored about going home, Coleman said, "but none of us knew what was really going on in Cambodia."

On the Thai-Cambodian border, Twining knew he had to be careful. The people he was interviewing were just refugees, after all, and given the mind-set back at State, their views did not count for much. Through the summer and fall of 1975, his reports were factual, even anodyne. "Life in Cambodia is undoubtedly very harsh, particularly for urban dwellers suddenly yanked out of their relatively comfortable surroundings," he wrote in an airgram dated August 25, 1975. Food is scarce, but after talking to people from Koh Kong Province, in southwestern Cambodia, "one concludes that, in that province at least, it is possible to survive."

By December, nine months after the fall of Phnom Penh, Twining was beginning to hear stories so terrible he wasn't sure he believed them. Two Cambodians who had worked for the Catholic Relief Service in Phnom Penh before the Khmer Rouge came to power made it to the border. Their observations, Twining wrote, "are the best we have heard in recent months." The two told him about a village work camp in Sisphon, in the Northwest. "New arrivals," the former CRS worker said, "were strictly separated by sex in both the fields and at night. Sexual relations or talk of marriage was punished by public execution, the two claimed. As justification, the Khmer Communists said everyone must devote himself to strengthening the economy instead of thinking of raising a family. The death rate among children was extremely high. On the worst day, 30 died, primarily of malaria, and they were buried in a common grave. With a general shortage of food, stealing food was punished with public execution, usually by rifle or pistol."

Over the following months his reports grew darker. Twining began to think, "This can't be possible in this day and age. This is not 1942. This is 1975." Across the country, he wrote, work hours were long, typically from 5:30 a.m. to 10:30 p.m. In Siem Reap, "one hears regularly that people are hooked up to plows" since most oxen and other farm animals had already starved to death. Executions were commonplace; freedom was nonexistent. "As 1975 advanced and continued into 1976," he wrote in March 1976, "an increasing number of Cambodian farmers" are "complaining that the amount of work they were forced to do, with little food to eat, was inhuman."

Twining's reports went straight to the State Department's Bureau of East Asian and Pacific Affairs—the same bureau that was trying to decide what to do with the 114 Cambodians in Philadelphia. Into

1976 the bureau was "telling us they didn't have any hard information on Cambodia," Coleman said.

Meanwhile, at the YMCA, the refugees quickly fell into a classic Cambodian hierarchical structure. The senior officers demanded their own desks in the project office. Junior officers would not tell Coleman even what they wanted for lunch without asking their supervisors. And so the civilians, most of them illiterate rice farmers, "spent a lot of time looking confused." But all of them still wanted to go home.

State Department officials were telling Coleman she should try to encourage them to stay in the United States, "but they weren't saying that out loud" to the refugees, Coleman said—nor were they saying what they knew about conditions there. "We would dangle out the possibility" of staying, "but that always brought resounding boos. One of the guys told me he would self-immolate if he couldn't go home." Coleman wanted them to stay—"I grew close to these guys," she said. But neither she nor her clients really knew what awaited them if they went back home.

With every passing month, Twining's reports were growing more dire. On March 31 he wrote that Cambodia offered "a Spartan, miserable existence for people constantly living in fear, under strict control. Disease and executions have become commonplace. . . . Usually people are taken quietly outside a village, often on some pretext, and killed. The rest of the family will often be led away separately to die."

In April the State Department helped the refugees find a way to fly home, through Paris. The group's commanding officer, Maj. Kim Phuoc Tung, stepped out the day before he left to buy himself a new suit. When he came back to the YMCA, resplendent in his new outfit, Coleman told him, "You're going to look great in the rice paddy." He just smiled and said, "I have a wife and four children at home."

The last of the refugees boarded a plane for Paris, and then on to Phnom Penh, on April 16, 1976. Coleman hugged each one and cried. Some called her from Paris, in between planes. On the phone she started to cry again and pleaded with them, "Don't go. Don't go!" That day she vowed to find out what happened to each one of them. That became her crusade.

———

In the fall of 1976 Representative Stephen Solarz, a first-term congressman from New York, was visiting Thailand with eight of his House colleagues. It was one of his first "codels," as congressional delegations abroad are known. Solarz and the others were members of the House Foreign Affairs Committee, and their role on the codel was to attend meetings with government officials and others. But Solarz had another aim: He wanted to go to the Cambodian border and talk to refugees. "Of course, we knew about Lon Nol and the triumph of Khmer Rouge," Solarz said. "We knew that they had evacuated Phnom Penh and other cities. But that's about all we knew."

That wasn't entirely true—Twining had been sending refugee reports to the State Department for almost eighteen months. As he learned more, the tenor of them grew ever more gruesome and alarming. People were being fed only thin rice gruel, mostly water, maybe with some banana leaves mixed in, he wrote. Thousands were dying of disease and starvation. "Refugees told stories of people simply collapsing and dying while working in a field." But Solarz had seen none of these reports. Neither had anyone else outside the administration.

One afternoon, an American Embassy officer led Solarz up to Twining's office. The congressman told Twining what he wanted to do, and the next day they drove to Aranyaprathet. None of the other congressmen wanted to go; the drive was long, hot, and uncomfortable. And who really cared? Of all of them, why was Solarz alone so interested in this?

Explaining his motivations years later, sitting in his study at home, Solarz simply smiled and waved his hand toward a bookshelf on a far wall. There, almost from floor to ceiling, was his vast library on Hitler, Stalin, and the Holocaust—perhaps every English-language book that had ever been published. Cambodia, he said, "looked to me like another Holocaust." It also happened that Solarz's congressional district, in New York, was home to more Holocaust survivors than any other in the nation.

Twining knew just where to take Solarz. Together, they walked through a teeming refugee camp. The congressman was appalled. "There were eight to ten thousand people there—wretched, desperate. I heard incredible stories. For example, they killed everyone who had eyeglasses. Monks, they killed them by putting plastic bags over their heads." And he heard the infamous Khmer Rouge slogan, the justification for each killing: "Keeping you is no profit; losing you is no loss." Right next to Solarz, as he was recalling this venture, on the side table beside his armchair, sat the book *Surviving Treblinka*. A bookmark suggested he had already read more than half of it. "This was my first direct encounter with anything like this, and it immediately evoked impressions of what happened to the Jews. It resonated with me as a great moral challenge."

Back in Washington, Solarz managed to convince a colleague to stage a congressional hearing on the situation in Cambodia. Unfortunately, with the '76 election fast approaching and other more important congressional priorities (and in truth, to most members of Congress almost anything was more important), the hearing was not held until July 1977.

Twining testified. In his most recent report from the field he had written about a malaria epidemic that was killing hundreds if not thousands of people, largely because the Khmer Rouge had no medicine. Medical aides were injecting patients with Pepsi or coconut milk. Speaking to the subcommittee, Twining said, "Most reports are that executions continue," but now "the number who are dying from disease or malnutrition is greater than from executions."

Richard Holbrooke, the assistant secretary of state and Twining's boss, was more direct—the first time a senior government official had spoken out. "Some journalists and scholars guess that between half a million and 1.2 million have died since 1975," Holbrooke said, but he was unable to confirm that or any other number. Nonetheless, Holbrooke did say, "Based on all the evidence available to us, we have concluded that Cambodian authorities have flagrantly and systemically violated the most basic human rights. They have ordered or permitted extensive killings, forcibly relocated the urban population, brutally treated supporters of the previous government, and suppressed personal and political freedoms. My guess," Holbrooke added, "is that for every person executed, several have died of disease or malnutrition or other factors, which were avoidable if the government itself had not followed this kind of policy, which seeks to completely transform a society by applying purely draconian measures."

This was mid-1977. The Khmer Rouge had been in power for more than two years. Twining had filed hundreds of pages of refugee accounts. Journalists had by now written dozens of stories offering the same refugee testimony along with other reporting. Two important books offering even more detailed accounts were in bookstores; one of them was even excerpted in *Reader's Digest*.

Jimmy Carter was now president, and for the first time in American history, his administration had made human rights a central tenet of his foreign policy. Even so, the United States was still unwilling to accept as a probable fact that the Khmer Rouge were guilty of crimes against humanity. One reason was the loud, public declarations of people like Gareth Porter, codirector of an independent organization called the Indochina Resource Center in Washington. Porter was also invited to testify at that congressional hearing. Given the willful uncertainty that prevailed at the time, the subcommittee believed that, to be fair, he should be heard, too.

At that time, Porter was one of the most prominent Khmer Rouge champions in the United States. In Europe, meantime, Khmer Rouge apologists easily outnumbered those who believed a tragedy was under way. These people had been vociferous opponents of the Vietnam War—particularly the bombing of Cambodia. One certainty united most of them. The bombing, more than anything else, had inevitably led to the state of affairs in Cambodia. And to them, whatever the U.S. government had to say now was per force a lie. If the regime in Phnom Penh was anti-American, it could only be worthy of admiration.

The climate of distrust surrounding the Vietnam War had spread to Cambodia. Porter later explained that as a student journalist, "I uncovered a series of instances when government officials were propagandizing" on the Vietnam War. "They were lying." If government officials had been so dishonest about Vietnam, why should anyone believe anything they had to say about Cambodia?

Elsewhere at the time, Porter claimed in public that Twining and others in the Bangkok embassy "had predicted that millions of people would starve to death once the United States pulled out of Cambodia. When the regime clearly averted mass starvation, these people would have lost face. So they created the genocide claim." At about this time, Ieng Sary, Cambodia's foreign minister, told an Italian interviewer that "the Khmer revolution has no precedents," and those who claimed that Cambodia had executed hundreds of thousands of people "are crazy. Only hardened criminals have been sentenced."

Before the subcommittee Porter said simply that it was "a myth that between 1 million and 2 million Cambodians have been the victims of a regime led by genocidal maniacs." This falsehood, he added, grew out of self-serving government statements and irresponsible reporting in recent newspaper articles and books.*

A few weeks earlier Noam Chomsky, an author and academic, offered an article in the *Nation* that conflated the American bombing and the Khmer Rouge horrors and made the same broad argument

---

* In 2010, Porter said he had been waiting many years for someone to ask him, for publication, about his early views of the Khmer Rouge. "I've been well aware for many years that I was guilty of intellectual arrogance," he said. "I was right about the bloodbath in Vietnam, so I assumed I would be right about Cambodia."

as the other apologists. He cited "highly qualified specialists" whom he did not name, but "who have studied the full range of evidence available, and who concluded that executions have numbered at most in the thousands." He also claimed that "these were localized in areas of limited Khmer Rouge influence and unusual peasant discontent, where brutal revenge killings were aggravated by the threat of starvation resulting from the American destruction and killing. These reports also emphasize both the extraordinary brutality on both sides during the civil war (provoked by the American attacks) and repeated discoveries that massacre reports were false. They also testify to the extreme unreliability of refugee reports, and the need to treat them with great caution."

Reflecting on the hearing, Twining said, "It was easy to tell them what I knew but impossible to tell them what to do about it. I felt helpless." Despite Porter's testimony, Solarz said the hearing had helped him convince the House to pass a resolution "calling on the Carter administration to coordinate with other nations to free the Cambodian people. But of course it had no effect."

———

In February 1978, almost three years into the reign of the Khmer Rouge, the *Washington Post*'s Lewis Simons wrote a news analysis summing up his experience as a Southeast Asia correspondent. He conceded, first of all, that neither he nor anyone else really knew what was happening in Cambodia. If that is so, he wrote, "Why do most Americans assume that the Cambodian Communists run the most brutal regime since the Nazis? Is the answer, as the Cambodians and their tiny handful of foreign friends allege, that Western governments and news media are guilty of 'distortions and wild fabrications?'" Not necessarily, he concluded. But in that case, "Why is it that the United States, with its vast intelligence network, should know so little about events in Cambodia? The answer seems to be that Cambodia no longer counts for anything in the U.S. scheme of things. At least that's what the officials say. 'All of Indochina, as an intelligence target, is of very, very low priority now. And Cambodia is so low as to be almost nonexistent,' said one official."

Nobody knew, nobody cared. Less than a year later, when Vietnam invaded Cambodia and deposed the Khmer Rouge regime, Washington demonstrated that same indifference in spades.

# CHAPTER THREE

The Khmer Rouge, like most Cambodians, hated the Vietnamese. And from the beginning of their reign the two states had skirmished along the border. Finally, by the end of 1978, Vietnam had had enough. Thousands of troops poured over the border, and in short order they deposed the Khmer Rouge.

Millions of Cambodians quietly cheered as their historical enemy swept through the nation. Three years, eight months, and twenty days after they seized power, the Khmer Rouge slipped furtively into the night. For decades to come, Cambodians, with little prompting, would affirm that the Vietnamese saved their lives.

Skeletal, sick, and traumatized, hundreds of thousands stumbled toward Thailand for sanctuary, eating leaves, roots, and bugs along the way. Many died of starvation en route, or stepped on land mines, for Khmer Rouge soldiers had laid mines almost everywhere along the western border, to prevent their victims from fleeing. Those who made it to Thailand brought malaria, typhoid, cholera, and a host of other illnesses into the camps. Human-rights groups estimated that about 650,000 more people died in the year following the fall of the Khmer Rouge.

Waiting for the refugees in Aranyaprathet was Cindy Coleman. "As soon as the country opened up, I went," she said. She arrived in February, just a few weeks after the Khmer Rouge fell from power, armed with photos of the former military officers she had cared for. She stayed in that hotel with an empty lock hasp on the door and a straw mattress for a bed. "It was my first encounter with a Thai toilet," she said, laughing. "A hole in the floor and a bucket of water."

For three weeks she and an embassy aide who helped her wandered around the camps, searching. "We followed Thai relief trucks around," she said. "The Cambodians were parked in open fields. They still wore their black uniforms and red scarves. All of them. They were undernourished, very thin. No expressions on their faces, just dead-eyed stares. Their clothes were soiled. I passed around pictures. I also put up pictures on bulletin boards set up in Aranya. The boards were already full of pictures and letters. Lots of people were doing what I was doing. I showed the pictures to aid workers in camps—to anybody." But "not a soul" had seen or heard of her men.

The fighting continued for several months and prevented farmers from harvesting their rice. The timing could not have been worse—a famine on top of three and one-half years of starvation. If Charles Twining's airgrams had gotten little circulation, now news reporting from the border exploded. Only people who willfully closed their eyes and ears could have pretended not to know of the Khmer Rouge horrors. President Jimmy Carter called the Khmer Rouge "the world's worst human rights violators," something of an understatement. Yet in response to the Vietnamese invasion, the White House merely slapped more sanctions on Vietnam. Nothing was done for the 5 million Khmer Rouge victims, most of whom still had no food. And then Carter's focus, and much of the world's, quickly turned away.

In July 1979 tens of thousands of Vietnamese "boat people" fled their nation. For Americans this was in some ways pleasing news. By the thousands citizens were running from America's enemy, the Vietnamese Communists. So the boat people monopolized news coverage from the region.

Then, on November 4, 1979, students seized the American Embassy in Tehran and took about fifty Americans captive, setting off the Iranian hostage crisis that captivated the world for more than a year. The next month the Soviet Union invaded Afghanistan. As the United States slouched into the 1980 presidential campaign, the American hostages in Iran were the primary foreign-policy subject of debate. Cambodia was effectively invisible.

In January 1979 the Vietnamese discovered Tuol Sleng, a former high school in central Phnom Penh that the Khmer Rouge had turned into a torture and death house. Vietnamese journalists and soldiers first walked in to find rotting corpses still in shackles. Gruesome torture implements lay about, and in an outbuilding the soldiers found thousands of pages of records, including photographs of the victims. At least 15,000 Cambodians had been taken there, tortured until they confessed to being an enemy agent, and then killed—whacked on the back of the head with an iron pole.

That and all of the other evidence of the Khmer Rouge horror received wide public attention.* But for most people in Washington the news from Cambodia wasn't the Khmer Rouge's crimes against humanity. No, American officials seemed capable of hearing only one thing: Vietnam, the United States' bitter enemy, had conquered Cambodia. Did the Communist soldiers make up or exaggerate the Tuol Sleng business to justify their invasion? Would Vietnam invade Thailand next? Was the domino theory actually in play?

At a White House press conference, President Carter issued a warning "to both the Vietnamese and the Soviets who supply them" not to

---

*Soon after, a Cambodian friend showed Cindy Coleman that many of her former clients were on the lists of people killed at Tuol Sleng—many but not all, she quickly noted. She kept looking.

carry the fight into Thailand. In the following months, however, Vietnamese troops did spill over into Thailand more than once, chasing Khmer Rouge fighters. America had lost the Vietnam War. Were the worst fears of the politicians who started it now coming true?

Soon, the United Nations had to decide who would occupy Cambodia's seat at the UN then held by the Khmer Rouge. As with all UN debates, the United States had an outsized voice. Would the deposed Khmer Rouge regime keep the seat, or would the UN give it to the puppet government Vietnam had installed in Phnom Penh? Here were a rock and a hard place: Recognize a genocidal former government— or a Communist nation, an ally of the Soviet Union, and the only state that had ever won a war against the United States. "Thug number one, or thug number two," as one senior State Department official put it then.

Surprisingly, the United Nations chose to reseat the Khmer Rouge instead of "those puppets," as Washington referred to the government in Phnom Penh. To the State Department, giving a seat to Vietnam's government was effectively giving Moscow another vote in the General Assembly. And although the Khmer Rouge were butchers, they were out of power now, living in the jungle—and allied with China, Washington's new friend.

Washington's policy was even more cynical than the UN's. Zbigniew Brzezinski, the National Security adviser, told journalist and author Elizabeth Becker, "I encouraged the Chinese to support Pol Pot." He "was an abomination. We could never support him, but China could"—and so they did, for the next thirteen years.

After the UN vote, Robert Rosenstock, the lawyer who represented the United States on the UN Credentials Committee, found himself shaking hands with Ieng Sary, the former Khmer Rouge foreign minister. The man was beaming with gratitude. Rosenstock wanted to go wash his hands. "I realized enough at the time to feel there was something disgusting about shaking Ieng Sary's hand," he told author Samantha Powers. Khieu Samphan, the Khmer Rouge premier, said: "We thank the U.S. warmly."

When Ronald Reagan came into office in 1981, he resolutely refused to recognize Cambodia's quisling government. UN aid agencies were forbidden to set foot in Cambodia. No one was to have anything to do with the stooges Hanoi had installed in Phnom Penh. As for the Cambodian people, victims of genocide and famine, well, no one spent much if any time thinking about them.*

Vietnam appointed Heng Samrin, a longtime member of the Cambodian Communist Party, as prime minister. He had served as a Khmer Rouge division commander. Like many Khmer Rouge officers, Heng had feared Pol Pot would turn on him, so he deserted to Vietnam. In 1978 the Vietnamese military had chosen him to command a small group of Khmer Rouge deserters who would "lead" the invasion of Cambodia, to give it an indigenous face.

Once in office, Heng Samrin and the government's other leaders took direction from Hanoi. Vietnamese administrators sat in every government ministry and provincial office, and they worked to remake Cambodia as a Marxist-Leninist state. Nowhere was this more apparent than in the schools. Vietnam renovated existing schools and built some new ones, hanging pictures of Heng Samrin, Joseph Stalin, and Ho Chi Minh in the classrooms. The curriculum included mandatory courses on socialist solidarity and economic theory as

---

*A few academics did maintain an interest in the Cambodian people, but they were interested only in the dead. In the few years after the fall of the Khmer Rouge, some people who styled themselves as Cambodia experts tried to estimate the Khmer Rouge death count. Of course, nobody had counted, and Cambodia had not taken a census since 1962. These people, academics mostly, included some early admirers of the Khmer Rouge. They got into heated arguments about whether some of the dead were victims of the Khmer Rouge—or the American bombing campaign. Several of them finally derived a variety of estimates, ranging from about 1.7 to almost 3 million. Journalists and writers then settled on the safest way to portray these estimates by writing "at least 1.7 million." That became the accepted number. In fact, research for the Khmer Rouge trial in more recent times put the number at about 2 million.

well as Marxism-Leninism. Students were told they were being taught to be useful "new socialist workers."

None of this should have been a great leap for the government in Phnom Penh. Its leaders were former Khmer Rouge officers, and the Khmer Rouge was, after all, the unofficial name for the Communist Party of Cambodia. So is it any wonder that the Reagan administration disparaged this government, a proxy of Vietnam, a nation that was itself a proxy of the Soviet Union, President Reagan's "evil empire"?

In 1985 Heng Samrin stepped aside, and in his place Vietnam installed Hun Sen, a wily thirty-three-year-old former Khmer Rouge division commander. He had joined the Khmer Rouge cause in 1970, after he heard Prince Sihanouk on the radio urging Cambodians to enlist so they could fight Lon Nol. In 1977, when the Khmer Rouge leadership appeared to be turning on him, he fled to Vietnam. There, he became an officer of the small indigenous military force the Vietnamese sent across the border in late 1978. Since the Vietnamese occupation he had been serving as foreign minister.

In Washington Solarz found himself one of the only members of the U.S. government who spent any time thinking about the true victims, the Cambodian people. His worst fear, a new Holocaust, had actually come true. He pushed the Reagan administration to admit thousands of Cambodians as refugees, then sponsored a bill to provide aid to what he and others called "the noncommunist resistance" in Cambodia—two small military forces in the countryside aligned with Sihanouk. Unless Hun Sen and his Communist cohorts were thrown from office, Solarz realized, the United States could not send aid to the long-suffering Cambodian people.

Hun Sen became the focal point of Washington's ire, the Communist stooge in Phnom Penh who did Vietnam's bidding. "I thought of him, basically, as a thug," Solarz said. But Richard Bush, a senior aid to Solarz, noted that his boss looked at the situation through a different prism. While the rest of Washington saw Hun Sen and the others as Communist puppets of Vietnam, "Steve was concerned that the Cambodian *people* were being ruled by former Khmer Rouge leaders."

Over time charges made the rounds that some of the American aid, $215 million so far, was finding its way to the Khmer Rouge. Congress demanded an investigation, and Tom Fingar, who was in charge of the relevant division in the State Department's Bureau of Intelligence and Research, dispatched investigators to have a look. Sure enough, they found some leakage—including sharing of ammunition, joint defense of a bridge, and using one truck to transport both "noncommunist" and Khmer Rouge fighters to a fight. But Fingar saw this whole enterprise as a typical Washington fury about nothing, an "epi-phenomenon in a flea circus." His investigators, he said, "were trying to sort out exactly what was happening," while he and others "were also asking: Isn't the larger objective here defeating the Vietnamese puppets in Phnom Penh? Why are we providing aid? Isn't it to defeat Hun Sen?"

Cambodia was stuck in a mire, occupied by its mortal enemy, represented before the United Nations and the world by its former genocidal government, governed by Communist dictators despised in the West, locked out of any significant assistance or aid. Cambodia had 7.7 million people in April 1975. Left when the Khmer Rouge fell from power were fewer than 5 million of them, and they were hungry, sick, and alone.

At the time nobody in Cambodia understood the import of what was happening, but the first hint of a break came in March 1985, when Mikhail Gorbachev came to power in Moscow. The Soviet Union was broke, and almost right away Gorbachev cut aid to many of the nation's allies, including Vietnam. Without that aid Vietnam was in trouble— so much so that the next year the Sixth Party Congress took a radical step. It launched a program called Doi Moi, or economic renovation, an attempt to introduce a free-market economy, to "free the entrepreneurial spirit in Vietnam," the Party Congress said. Over time that decision worked miracles for Vietnam's economy. But it would take years, and in the meantime Vietnam was forced to reassess its own foreign adventures. The government was overstretched. Loath as they were to do it, in 1988 and 1989 the Vietnamese army withdrew from Cambodia—leaving Hun Sen's puppet Communist government in charge.

This was at least partly expected. For years, anticipating Vietnam's eventual withdrawal, Australia, Indonesia, and Japan, among others, had been holding occasional informal meetings in Jakarta in search of a compromise that could break the stalemate between the four competing Cambodian factions—the Hun Sen government; the Khmer Rouge; the royalist guerrilla group led by Prince Norodom Ranariddh, Sihanouk's son; and another led by Son Sann, an aging politician who had once been foreign minister when Sihanouk was king.

None of that amounted to much. But the Vietnamese withdrawal changed everything. All of a sudden, people began to ask: With the Vietnamese army gone, what's to stop the Khmer Rouge from marching back into Phnom Penh?

Mey Meakk was Pol Pot's personal secretary. He took notes at Brother No. 1's staff meetings, typed his memos and directives, broadcast his messages on Khmer Rouge radio. As he tells it, the man who ordered the murders of 2 million of his countrymen was living quite comfortably in the jungles of northeastern Cambodia. "He had a lot of money," Mey Meakk said, and photos of that time showed Pol Pot growing fat.

Henry Kamm, a *New York Times* reporter and author, visited him and wrote of the accommodations Pol Pot offered. "The Khmer Rouge guest house was the very latest in jungle luxury. It was clearly modeled on the sumptuous hunting lodges to which French planters of the past invited guests for weekend shoots. . . . Plates of fruit brought from Bangkok were renewed each day. The best Thai beer, Johnny Walker Black Label scotch, American soft drinks and Thai bottled water was served."

The Khmer Rouge leadership was besotted with copious aid from China, plus their men were cutting down vast forests and selling the tropical wood to Thai generals at the border. But when it was clear that the Vietnamese had truly pulled out, Pol Pot roused himself. "He wanted to take advantage of the situation and retake Phnom Penh by the end of 1989," Mey Meakk said. "He wanted to prepare the troops, aggressively organize." But his commanders resisted. "The troops were very tired. Some of them had been fighting for 20 years. The commanders were tired, too. They offered no encouragement. They didn't want to do it." So Pol Pot dropped that idea. But no one in the West knew that.

The French government appeared to be particularly excited about the Khmer Rouge threat. As the months passed, Paris issued increasingly urgent warnings. "But my impression was that the French motivation was the belief that they could engineer a renaissance of their role in Southeast Asia," said Quinn, who was then the deputy assistant secretary of state for the region. That was the common view at Foggy Bottom. His boss, Richard Solomon, the assistant secretary of state, was one of several State Department officials who remarked that "the French were said to be rummaging around in government warehouses, looking for Sihanouk's throne." France invited all the players to a conference on Cambodia, in Paris, during August 1989. The French spared no expense and hosted the event at the Kleber International Conference Center, an elegant venue. American delegates marveled at the dramatic mirrored bathrooms.

President George H. W. Bush had taken office in January 1989, and his secretary of state, James Baker, attended the conference, as did foreign ministers from two dozen other countries. Leaders of the four Cambodian factions were also present. John Bolton, then an assistant secretary of state, was with Baker when they first met Prime Minister Hun Sen—whom, of course, they disdained. "He was sitting in a chair, rocking back and forth, when suddenly he pitched over backwards," Bolton said, smiling and slowly shaking his head. "He got up and looked dazed. We both thought he must be drunk, or hung over."

The meeting's purpose was to find a compromise that the four Cambodian factions and the world powers could accept. China insisted that Hun Sen's government be disbanded; Moscow, of course, refused even to consider that. Even then the Russians remained loyal to Vietnam and its appointed government in Cambodia. The four

Cambodian groups' positions were mirrors of their patrons' views. The conference failed.

Back in western Cambodia, Pol Pot decided that if he could not retake Phnom Penh, at least he would try to capture Pailin, the provincial capital a few miles from the Thai border—but also the headquarters of Cambodia's rich gem-mining region. His military commanders leaped at that idea. They captured the town quickly and decisively, allowing the commanders to further enrich themselves. The ensuing gem and timber sales are estimated to have earned tens of millions of dollars a year that slipped directly into the pockets of Pol Pot and his henchmen.

In Paris, London, and Washington the Khmer Rouge's 1989 offensive in Pailin reaffirmed the conviction that Hun Sen's army was no match for Pol Pot's forces. The French were particularly distressed: What was to stop Pol Pot from retaking Phnom Penh? Now, Washington was listening. "It sounded reasonable to me," Bolton said. "The Vietnamese had pulled out. Surely Hun Sen could not serve on. He didn't have the capacity to stand up to the Khmer Rouge."

Just then, once again, the ground shifted under the city of Washington. In the first months of 1989, just after Bush took office, China brutally repressed pro-democracy protests at Tiananmen Square. Ten years earlier, it had briefly invaded northern Vietnam, to punish the state for unseating Beijing's allies, the Khmer Rouge. American officials had to ask themselves: Could China still be Washington's new best friend? In November the Berlin Wall fell. The cold war was over. The Soviet Union and China established normal relations. Policy makers faced a brave new world. The State Department had long argued that Hun Sen was "an illegitimate puppet of an expansionist Soviet-backed, Vietnamese government." Now every element of that description was out-of-date.

As ever, Cambodia was not Washington's first priority, or even its fifth. Still, beginning in 1990 Congress grew ever more distressed about the Khmer Rouge. The threat remains, warned George Mitchell, the Senate majority leader, that the Khmer Rouge could again turn Cambodia into a "vast killing field." A dozen senators began drafting a letter to President Bush saying, "The Khmer Rouge represents an unacceptable threat to the people of Cambodia, and that American policy should be based, first and foremost, upon preventing the return of the Khmer Rouge."

Finally, on July 18, 1990, Secretary of State Baker announced a change in American policy—a complete reversal. The United States would end its political and tacit military support of the Khmer Rouge more than eleven years after they had fallen from power, a decade after it had become perfectly clear that Pol Pot and his minions had murdered "at least 1.7 million" people, 25 percent of Cambodia's population. At a news conference in Paris, Baker said Washington had "achieved one of its policy goals," the withdrawal of Vietnam from Cambodian territory. "Another policy goal was to prevent the return of the Khmer Rouge. We've not been able to achieve that goal and, in fact, it would appear that the risks are greater as we move forward that that might occur. So we want to do everything we can to prevent a return of the Khmer Rouge to power." Toward that end, he said the United States would resume "humanitarian assistance" to Cambodia, reverse its policy on the UN seat—and talk to Vietnam.

Baker spoke just after a meeting with Eduard Shevardnadze, the Soviet foreign minister, and Shevardnadze, standing next to him at the podium, said American and Soviet positions on Cambodia had now "come much closer." Until that day, the world's powers had been at odds, making a solution to the Cambodian mire impossible. China supported the Khmer Rouge, and over the previous decade had supplied at least $1 billion in military aid. The Soviet Union supported Vietnam. The United States backed 15,000 ineffective "noncommunist" rebel fighters in the northern jungle. But the Bush administration's new position scrambled everything.

In short order China announced that it would normalize relations with Vietnam. It began cutting its aid to the Khmer Rouge. China had already normalized relations with the Soviet Union. So now, all of a sudden, all three countries agreed that they had to deal with Hun

Sen's government in Phnom Penh, even though most of them had to hold their noses. "This was remarkable," said Quinn, the State Department official. "The Soviet Union, China, Europe, and the U.S. all agreed. That's a home run! It caused China to settle with Vietnam. It caused us to settle with Vietnam. My goodness, it was wonderful, and my country played a major role."

Baker, sizing up the moment, told a meeting of Southeast Asian foreign ministers in New York that it was time the United Nations Security Council "laid its hands" on the Cambodia issue. Now, of course, every one of the permanent members of the Security Council—the United States, Britain, France, Russia, and China, the "Perm Five," as they were known—agreed. When would that ever happen again?

Back at the State Department, Richard Solomon suddenly realized: This is my chance! He was assistant secretary of state for East Asian and Pacific affairs, the most senior official directing policy in Southeast Asia. At State every officer continually asked himself: What can I take on that is *mine*?

Solomon's career to this point had been distinguished but not extraordinary. He had earned a Ph.D. in political science from MIT and taught at the University of Michigan before joining the foreign service. He'd held several middle-level, important-sounding jobs, but now he was an assistant secretary of state—quite a senior post. Unfortunately, as usually happened, higher-ups in the department managed his high-profile countries: China, Korea, and Japan. Cambodia, well, nobody held much interest. So Solomon grabbed it.

When Solomon took office in the spring of 1989, his instruction had been clear: Don't take the lead on Indochina issues. Support the French, who were arranging that conference in Paris. But Solomon had other plans. He called Quinn back from a posting in the Philippines to be his deputy—Quinn, who had written that first airgram on the Khmer Rouge threat. He told Quinn they had a chance to make a difference. Solomon had no background in Vietnam or Cambodia. "That's why he needed me," Quinn said. "This was huge for him. But nobody in the U.S. government thought there was any chance an agreement would be reached. They let Solomon go off, doing his thing," he said with a dismissive wave.

Solomon also found an ally in Rafeeuddin Ahmed, who was the UN special representative for Southeast Asia. Ahmed had been shuttling around the region for more than ten years, trying to find an opening in the Cambodia impasse. "I realized that for us to play a credible role, I must go to Phnom Penh, even though the People's Republic of Kampuchea was not recognized as a legitimate government, it was not recognized at the UN," Ahmed said. This was in 1987. "I looked for a precedent and found that Dag Hammarskjöld went to China after some American planes were shot down during the Korean War. China was not a recognized country at that time." He spent several hours talking to Hun Sen; he was impressed. And when the Security Council began a series of special meetings in 1990 to agree on a course of action in Cambodia, no one at the United Nations knew more about this problem than Ahmed. He attended every meeting.

At the first summit, the council agreed that a peaceful settlement would require "an enhanced United Nations role," a news release said. Yet no further details were offered. When Ahmed briefed the council during its second meeting, in February, he told the members that agreement would be hard to reach as long as the Chinese, Soviet, and Cambodian government representatives all remained so far apart. What could the UN do without cooperation from everyone?

In New York a few weeks after Baker's news conference in Paris, the Perm Five met again, and this time they quickly came to agreement on a plan so audacious that it scared some council members. The United Nations would actually take control of Cambodia; the state would become a UN protectorate. The four competing armies would be disarmed, their troops held in special camps until national elections were held and a new democratic government chosen. "This was something we had never done before—actually controlling, supervising, monitoring the way the government was functioning," Ahmed said. "But we believed we could do it."

Others were not so sure. Kent Wiedemann was serving as the Asia specialist on the National Security Council, in the White House. He described the whole operation as "a major, major experiment in the use of the United Nations as a peacekeeping force, to pull Cambodia out of the mire." Very quickly, however, he and others began to realize that this experiment was turning out to be ruinously expensive. The British government threw out the first alarms, complaining about the likely high cost of this enterprise. In Washington, Bolton echoed that view. "We estimated this would cost $2 billion, which I thought was astronomical. This whole plan, it was completely unprecedented, and I didn't think it would work." And no wonder.

---

The United Nations is an imperfect reflection of its membership, the 195 nations of the world. Almost from the day of its founding, it had been paralyzed by the same conflict that froze the world: the cold war. Almost every nation belonged to one of three camps: the East, the West, or the nonaligned Third World. Each camp fell into conflict with the others over almost anything of importance. Most often the United Nations Security Council suffered the same paralysis.

But then the cold war ended, and the shackles fell away. The UN found a new confidence; it took on more missions—more in the five-year period than in the previous four decades. UN leaders spoke fondly of the "new congeniality" among members of the Security Council. The UN, they said, was undergoing a "renaissance." Where better to demonstrate this than Cambodia? Cold war divisions had prevented a solution through the 1980s. Now the United Nations had a chance to be a player, to make a difference. It would take over and administer an entire nation, something it had never done before, and give Cambodians a chance for redemption, a new life, membership in the modern age. With that, the United Nations would finally prove its worth. And could there be a better moment for this?

The Berlin Wall had fallen. Former Soviet satellite states were reveling in new freedoms, and impressive new leaders were taking the stage. Václav Havel. Lech Wałęsa. Elsewhere, stunning resolutions were coming to frozen conflicts. In South Africa Nelson Mandela was released from jail and became president of the African National Congress. In Northern Ireland the Irish Republican Army began secret talks with the British government and soon announced a cease-fire. Surely, with the United Nations' help, wouldn't this fresh wind blow through Phnom Penh, too?

In fact, however, in Phnom Penh no bright new faces came forward. Nothing had changed. Cambodians could look only to Hun Sen and King Sihanouk, two sclerotic leaders with not a thought in their heads but to achieve complete, undisputed control of the nation. These were the men who would lead Cambodians into the new democratic age.

On October 23, 1991, the four Cambodian factions and representatives of nineteen nations met in Paris to sign the Paris Peace Accords. The Cambodians agreed to an immediate cease-fire, followed by the demobilization of rival armies, repatriation of 370,000 refugees still in camps on the Thai border—and national elections by mid-1993. The United Nations would administer the nation until then; soon it would deploy tens of thousands of troops and civilian administrators and begin the most ambitious peacekeeping operation it had ever undertaken.

The French staged a grand ceremony at the Kleber International Conference Center once again, where Secretary of State Baker told the gathering: "What makes the case of Cambodia so extraordinary and its claim for international support so compelling, is the magnitude of the suffering its people have endured." François Mitterand, the French president, sensed the unease some of the Cambodians felt. The Khmer Rouge wanted no part of this. But the Chinese had abandoned them, and Pol Pot realized he had no choice. Their representatives, Khieu Samphan and Son Sen, sat impassively through the ceremony—knowing, as they did, that they still had by far the largest military force in the field. The British representative, Lord Caithness, diplomatically omitted their names from the list of Khmer Rouge villains he recited: Pol Pot, Ieng Sary, and the rest—though he then pointedly added, "and certain others." Khieu Samphan had been president of the Khmer Rouge government, and Son Sen was now "supreme commander" of the Khmer Rouge rebel forces.

The participants, maybe thirty people, sat at tables arranged in a large square, covered with yellow tablecloths. Hun Sen sat right next to Khieu Samphan. When the prime minister glanced at the Khmer Rouge chief of state—and at the leaders of the other rebel factions, Prince Ranariddh and Son Sann—he knew that all of these men, dressed in dark suits now, had spent the past decade trying to kill him. He had nothing to gain here; he was already the prime minister. First the Khmer Rouge and then the Vietnamese had schooled him every day since he was a teenager to serve as an absolute, unflinching autocrat. They'd taught him to do whatever was necessary—threaten, punish, kill—to hold on to power. What on earth did the UN occupation, particularly those "free and fair elections," offer him?

The world's powers had just signed an agreement to expend billions of dollars, years of effort by tens of thousands of people from dozens of nations, untold political capital, and probably even a few lives—all to give a small nation in a remote part of Asia of no strategic interest to anyone the chance to start anew after two decades of horror. Nothing like this had ever happened before—anywhere, anytime.

Cambodia's leaders, watching this incredible ceremony as leaders of the world's major nations bestowed this great gift in a glittering French reception hall, sat lost in their own thoughts, hatching new plots, devising fresh schemes. Observing them, Mitterand warned, "A dark page of history has been turned. Cambodians want peace, which means that any spirit of revenge would now be as dangerous as forgetting the lessons of history." As Mitterand and others would soon learn, history was not the Cambodians' strong suit.

# CHAPTER FOUR

The first UN forces arrived in Cambodia months late, of course. But undeterred, by the end of May 1992 Yashushi Akashi and John Sanderson, the UN's two top mission commanders, were bumping along a rocky dirt road in far-western Cambodia, on their way to create an enduring metaphor.

Yashushi Akashi was the civilian director of the United Nations Transitional Authority in Cambodia, which came to be known as UNTAC. Sitting next to him was Maj. Gen. John Sanderson of Australia, the mission's military commander. A truck full of reporters followed just behind. Eventually, they reached a Khmer Rouge "checkpoint." More precisely, they looked out their windows at one young Khmer Rouge soldier standing beside a single crooked bamboo pole propped up on sticks to simulate a roadblock.

Akashi and Sanderson asked to pass. They were on their way to meet up with a new Dutch military unit that was trying to cross the border from Thailand. The policeman, not even eighteen years old, told Akashi and Sanderson that he was not authorized to let them through. They tried to reason with the boy, but he was insistent. He didn't have permission to let them pass.

Finally, the United Nations officials just turned around and drove back to Phnom Penh. There, they blustered and bleated about this grave affront. "We take this act quite seriously," Akashi declared before issuing his ultimate threat: *I'm going to tell the Security Council!*

The world watched with sky-high expectations as the United Nations arrived in Cambodia. This was the *new* UN, after all, taking on a mission more ambitious and more expensive than anything it had ever tried before, in a brave new world of comity and cooperation—Russia, China, and the United States all working together. Still, no one outside the high halls of government realized that from the day all parties signed the Paris Peace Accords, the preeminent concern was actually "Who's going to pay for this?"

Britain complained the loudest, though American officials, too, made it plain that the price tag looked to be far too high. Bolton was the key official in this debate. As the assistant secretary of state for international organizations, he was the bridge between the UN and the State Department, which would have to come up with the money. "What happened was that we learned that the cost would be unbelievable," Bolton said. "Since the UN had never undertaken a mission of this magnitude, there were no precedents—and the estimates that came in were in the billions. And this happened as it became more and more clear that the Khmer Rouge was not really a military threat to anyone after all."

This news seemed to wake everyone up. Wasn't the Khmer Rouge just about to march back into Phnom Penh, from which they would once again turn Cambodia into a "vast killing field," as Senator George Mitchell had warned? Hadn't sixty-six senators signed a letter to the president expressing their deep concern? Weren't newspaper editorial writers having a field day with this? In October 1991 the *New York Times* had opined, "Even in real life, horror stories can have sequels. There's a worrisome possibility that one entitled The Return of the Khmer Rouge might now be about to unfold in Cambodia."

Now, months later, everyone realized they'd been duped. Yes, the Khmer Rouge were still a ruthless, murderous force. But now they were far more interested in gaining personal wealth—betraying the very principles their movement had stood for. "They were loggers and miners, not soldiers—selling timber and gems to generals on the Thai border," Bolton said. The assault on Pailin, in late 1989, had been about money rather than power. "The military column never materialized. It was like the Wizard of Oz. Where were they?"

Bolton, no fan of the United Nations in any case, felt the United States had been deceived. But America had committed itself to Cambodia, and down the hall from Bolton, Solomon was charging ahead—knowing, he said, that some in the building thought he was on a quixotic mission. Bolton "didn't think the UN was up to running the show," Solomon said. "No one did, including Jim Baker."

As soon as the Perm Five agreed on the details of a settlement, Solomon said he rushed to tell Lawrence Eagleburger, who was deputy secretary of state. "Now we are going to have to pay for it, aren't we?" Solomon said Eagleburger told him. "And it was primarily going to be us. The Brits, they were out of Southeast Asia. So were the Russians." In a booklet Solomon wrote about this period, he noted that, in the Security Council and other official settings, the British were primarily concerned with averting "a costly UN settlement."

Rafeeuddin Ahmed, who had been the UN's special representative for Southeast Asia, attended every Perm Five meeting at which the Cambodia operation was discussed. He said the United Nations "didn't have any preconceived notion about what this would cost. But everyone knew it would be costly because this was something we had never done before—control, supervision, monitoring of an entire government and its functioning."

As months went by, a realization dawned: We can't afford this! So the Security Council began to cut, pare, and trim wherever it could, realizing that, if they weren't careful, this initiative could end up costing as much as $10 billion. Where would the UN get money like that?

The treasuries of the wealthy nations, of course. American and British diplomats were confronted with the question: Would taxpayers sit still while their governments spent $2 or $3 billion of their money—on Cambodia? Not likely.

Soon this dilemma over cost entered the public debate. "The process is unfolding in disturbing neglect of the question of who is to pay the bills," a *Washington Post* editorial said. "But to put the requisite thousands of military peacekeepers and thousand or more civilian administrators on the ground could take $2 billion. Is there not a cheaper model?" In response, the Security Council cut even more. "It was a creeping process of reducing the UN role," Bolton said, "scaling back the scope of the UN's political responsibility and oversight."

Yet even as the resources shrank, the United Nations staff never exhibited anything but exuberant confidence in their ability to pull it off. This was their big chance to prove they could be relevant in the new world. "We never got from the UN that they couldn't do it," Solomon said.

As they pared back, no one—in the United States, Britain, Russia, or the halls of the UN—ever said anything in public about the cost cutting or reduced expectations. As far as anyone in the public knew, the United Nations was going to take over the country, disarm the Khmer Rouge and other military forces, run major areas of government, repatriate refugees, stage elections. But on the ground the forces were thin and grossly inadequate. "No one would acknowledge that we had scaled back," Bolton said. "By the time it happened, it was a big, expensive fig leaf."

Confronted by an eighteen-year-old guard at a bamboo-pole checkpoint, Akashi and Sanderson knew full well that they didn't have the resources to take on the Khmer Rouge. Even when fully deployed, the UN would have just 16,000 troops on the ground. Fewer than 10 percent of them had yet shown up. Among the troops still missing were those Dutch soldiers stuck at the border. By comparison, thirteen years later, the United States had ten times as many troops on the ground in Iraq, a nation two and one-half times the size of Cambodia, and for years the United States and its allies could not pacify the state. Now the Khmer Rouge was refusing to let the UN in.

Of even more importance in 1992 was the realization that the Khmer Rouge was just as strong if not stronger than the UN forces—intimately familiar with the terrain and unburdened by rules of engagement. For the UN's part, no one had even defined the rules of engagement. What could be done about all of that? Nothing. The Khmer Rouge refused to disarm.

The Khmer Rouge leaders' public explanation was this: Hun Sen has refused to give up control of the government or his army, so why should we? And in fact Hun Sen hadn't. The UN did not have nearly enough civilian administrators to take command of the Cambodian government, as they had promised, or to disarm his army. And unless forced, Hun Sen had no intention of giving up control. For him, this was just another Cambodian power struggle, nothing more. Given his background, he was confident of his ability to win it. Discussing this, he had even slipped into the regal practice of referring to himself in the third person. "For Ranariddh and Son Sann and Pol Pot, the Paris Accords were useful," he told author David Roberts. "How else can they join the politics and compete politically with Hun Sen?"

If anyone had doubted Hun Sen's true intentions, he made them clear during the first Paris Peace Conference, in 1989, when he declared, "You can talk about sharing power in Paris, but not in Cambodia." Vietnam had handed him the nation in 1985. He had ruled it uncontested for seven years. He would not step down or share his throne without a fight. And now, with wide reportage of the bamboo-pole incident, Hun Sen and everyone else realized that the UN was not to be feared. It was nothing more than a paper force. A correspondent for the *Far Eastern Economic Review*, reporting from Cambodia at the time, put it this way: "The Cambodian people believed that the UN blue berets were like Jupiter threatening to unleash lightning against the Khmer Rouge. What do people see? UNTAC pulls back."

The fact remained that the Khmer Rouge had not been defeated. The UN's deputy military commander, Michael Loridon, a French brigadier general, urged his commander to attack and "deal with the Khmer Rouge problem once and for all." That never happened, though the debate continued for years, until the last UN officer boarded a plane home. From the first days of the UN occupation, everyone knew that over ten years the Vietnamese army, with hundreds of thousands of troops, had never been able to defeat the Khmer Rouge. So what could the UN possibly do now?

By December 1992, more than a year after the Paris Peace Accords, the United Nations finally had its full force of soldiers and administrators in country. They were too late. Every Cambodian already knew that Jupiter had never climbed up the mountain. Pol Pot and Hun Sen were ignoring the UN and facing no penalty. But the truth was, the UN force offered a great deal more than the prospect of military reconciliation. Most Cambodians loved having them in town.

The visitors spent money, more money, and then more money still—$3 billion in all. Every staffer was given a daily living allowance of $145 on top of his salary—a year's income for most Cambodians. Contractors had quickly put up apartment buildings and now were taking in $2,000, $3,000 a month—ridiculously high rents for Phnom Penh. Hotels were full, and new ones were under construction. Anyone who'd ever had a fleeting thought of running a restaurant scrambled to open one. Everyone with a car hired himself out as a driver. Brothels worked overtime; UN doctors treated thousands of their men and women for sexually transmitted diseases. Liquor vendors couldn't keep up with demand; restaurant and bar owners had to replace fixtures and furniture broken in drunken brawls almost every evening. UN vehicles and equipment routinely disappeared in the night, but no one was sure whether the thieves were Cambodian or renegade UN employees.

Michael Hayes, a young American from Massachusetts, had come to Phnom Penh looking for work. He'd been on the staff of the Asia Foundation in Bangkok. But this was the new boomtown. It was 1991, and he was just twenty-four years old. "I was staying at the Royale Hotel," where everyone from the West stayed—journalists, UN officers, drug dealers, NGOs. "I went to the dining room for breakfast and asked for a newspaper. The waitress told me there are no newspapers here. So I began thinking: Maybe I should be a journalist. I had a lot of friends who were journalists. Maybe I should start a newspaper." So he did. With help from the UN and his friends, he founded the *Phnom Penh Post* in 1992, the nation's first English-language paper, still publishing today. His first readers were thousands of UN staff members.

The United Nations supervised the drafting of a new constitution, one that was to guarantee Cambodians everything promised under the United Nations Universal Declaration of Human Rights, a document first written in 1948. The authors of its preamble still had the Holocaust in mind when they wrote: "Whereas disregard and contempt for human rights have resulted in barbarous acts which have outraged the conscience of mankind, and the advent of a world in which human beings shall enjoy freedom of speech and belief and freedom from fear and want has been proclaimed as the highest aspiration of the common people."

In Cambodia forty-four years later, that played just as well. And under the UN, freedoms of all kinds flowered. A group of political prisoners let out of jail opened a legal-aid organization. Under UN auspices new human-rights advocacy groups began work; education, agriculture, health assistance, and a host of other civil-society organizations opened shop. Groups like these had never been permitted by the Vietnamese, the Khmer Rouge, or the monarchy. But would the new government, whoever won the upcoming election, allow all of this to continue? In 1992 and early 1993 it was hard to tell. The candidates were too busy fighting.

Prince Ranariddh and Son Sann had more or less disarmed and disbanded their troops, as they had agreed in Paris. Not so for Hun Sen and Pol Pot. And in early 1993 Hun Sen launched a military offensive against the Khmer Rouge stronghold in Pailin, violating every promise and tenet of the Paris Peace Accords, just as the Khmer Rouge had. But he knew he would pay no price, and he might just eliminate the only remaining military that threatened him. The fighting lasted for months, and the United Nations had only this to say: "It is a significant offensive that appears to exceed the right of self defense contained in the 1991 peace agreement." That was all. The fighting ended in stalemate, but the real theater was the elections. Hun Sen knew the UN had declared that the Khmer Rouge was not permitted to put up any candidates. Instead, Hun Sen faced Prince Ranariddh, Sihanouk's son.

Prince Ranariddh had led an unremarkable but privileged life. He spent his young adulthood in France, earning various advanced degrees and teaching. He did not return to Cambodia until 1974, when he was thirty years old, but then left for the duration of the Khmer Rouge years. He came back in the mid-1980s to head his father's guerrilla group, called Funcinpec, which stood for the National United Front for an Independent, Neutral, Peaceful, and Cooperative Cambodia; the acronym was drawn from the name written in French. From the jungle Ranariddh's small force tried to fight the Vietnamese— helped with significant U.S. aid.

After his group gave up its arms in the early 1990s Ranariddh turned Funcinpec into a political party. Hun Sen knew Ranariddh would be a fearsome political competitor simply because he was royalty. Most Cambodians still revered his father, and at every occasion Ranariddh reminded voters that Funcinpec was actually his father's party. By voting for him, he was saying, they were voting to bring Sihanouk back.

So, just as his Khmer Rouge and Vietnamese tutors had taught him, Hun Sen went after Ranariddh with everything he had. In 1993 the United Nations reported more than one hundred political assassinations. Nearly all of the dead were Funcinpec officials. A few worked for another smaller Buddhist party.

Hun Sen's political party, the Cambodian People's Party, or CPP, controlled every province, every town and village—every political jurisdiction in the country. How could it not? Under Vietnam Cambodia had been a one-party state, and Hun Sen had led it. He directed his loyalists in all of these regional offices to bribe, or threaten, everyone to vote for him. The regional officers jumped into the fight with abandon. They burned down Funcinpec headquarters, disrupted rallies, and killed prominent party officials. After all, a few years earlier, when Vietnam ruled the nation, that had been the way things were done.

Hun Sen also controlled most of the nation's radio and television stations, though the UN had its own radio station, which was quite popular. When Funcinpec tried to set up a TV station to compete, Hun Sen's police seized the transmitter as it was being unloaded at the airport. At a political rally in April, a month before election day, Hun Sen explained, "We have been accused of seizing equipment belonging to two political parties. So I would like to clarify that the equipment has been seized because the parties have acted illegally. They have imported 63 cars without paying taxes, and they illegally set up radio stations in Phnom Penh without applying for proper authorization. And now they are bringing in television equipment without, as before, any permission at all."

Hun Sen was just beginning to make an art of these facile explanations for his government's belligerent actions. Of course, he was the acting head of government (even though the UN was supposed to be in charge), and the people who grabbed more than five dozen cars and seized all that broadcast equipment were his own employees following rules and taxation "policy," published nowhere, changeable at will. Cambodia then was still a pure dictatorship, with a bit of superficial UN oversight. If Hun Sen wanted to blame faceless bureaucrats following his own unwritten regulations, often invented on the spot, who was to stop him?

————————

The Paris Peace Accords had named Norodom Sihanouk, the former king of Cambodia, to be the ceremonial head of state during the UN occupation. At the ceremony in Paris in 1991, he had beamed with delight; this was a wonderful tribute. He was seventy now. But the situation in his country was deteriorating, and he was unwilling to take the blame. To him it was the UN's fault for failing to give him authority. "I am a dummy, a dancing figure in a religious parade, while they are beating the drum," he insisted, speaking to a large crowd.

As the violence worsened he grew frustrated. After CPP vigilantes seized a Funcinpec officer and gouged out one eye, Sihanouk left in disgust and flew to Beijing. As soon as he arrived at the grand palace Mao had built for him, he put out a statement saying: "I cannot fail to react when confronted with the increasing acts of political terrorism and the continuation, with absolute impunity, of politically motivated crimes." The prince said he was no longer willing to work with the UN. There he sat through the rest of the campaign, waiting for someone to tell him how invaluable he was and plead with him to return.

Meantime, Khmer Rouge guerrillas began kidnapping and killing UN workers. The news coverage from Cambodia was simply terrible, filled with nothing but shootings, kidnappings, violence, and intimidation. And so in April 1993, six weeks before the election, UN Secretary-General Boutros Boutros-Ghali felt compelled to visit Cambodia and try to salvage this, the most important operation the United Nations had ever undertaken. Just a week earlier, Khmer Rouge guerrillas had shot and killed three Bulgarian soldiers working for the UN.

The secretary-general insisted that UN enforcement had "contributed to reducing the number of violent incidents" and promised that the UN "will deploy its military personnel and police to protect voters and electoral agents." There wasn't much else he could say. Almost nothing was working out as planned. The Security Council had given Akashi and Sanderson far too few people to fulfill their mandate. Hun Sen still controlled the entire Cambodian government; he simply worked around the few UN administrators sent into the ministries. The cease-fire had lasted only a few weeks, and now the Khmer Rouge was threatening to attack polling places. When asked about these and the many other problems, over and over again Akashi would shake his head and acknowledge that "we have failed to achieve a neutral political environment," paraphrasing a promise in the Paris Peace Accords.

A burst of attention from the United States in July 1990 had gotten this affair started. Secretary Baker had announced that Washington was changing its position, and the UN dove blithely into the process of reconciling Cambodia's political forces. But Washington had turned away from Cambodia almost as soon as Baker stepped down from the podium. The month after Baker made his Cambodian announcement, Saddam Hussein invaded Kuwait, and the Bush administration applied all of its attention and energy to the Gulf War. Soon after that came the 1992 presidential campaign. "People lost interest in Cambodia; they were just going through the motions," Bolton said.

Solomon was gone; now he was U.S. ambassador to the Philippines. Then in January, a few weeks after Sihanouk left for Beijing, a new Democratic president took office in Washington. With the change from Republican to Democratic control, most everyone with any knowledge of or investment in the UN operation left the government. The United States would have to formulate a new policy. But as Bill Clinton moved into the White House with the nation's economy in shambles, one thing was certain: It would be months, if not years, before anyone in Washington paid attention to Cambodia again.

Across Cambodia the polls opened the morning of May 23, 1993, and stayed open for six days. Khmer Rouge gunners shelled polling and police stations in Kampong Thom, Kampong Chhnang, Siem Reap, and elsewhere. Election workers fled; several were killed. But the major national offensive the Khmer Rouge had promised never came to pass, and over the six days more than 4 million Cambodians voted, even including some Khmer Rouge soldiers—90 percent of the eligible voters.

Their decision was clear. Hun Sen lost.

---

The vote was critically important to five different constituencies, and the outcome disappointed almost all of them. Prince Ranariddh was the victor, but his margin was too small. His party won 58 seats in parliament—not a majority, nor even enough to form a coalition with the two smaller parties that together had won 11 seats. Two-thirds of the parliament's 120 members had to join to form a government.

Hun Sen won 51 seats. He came in second. All of his tactics, murders, maimings, promises, threats, and bribes had failed to do the trick. Now he couldn't form a government, either. Nonetheless, he was resolute. Trained since he was a teenager to embrace and employ all the tools of ruthless dictatorship, in a country ruled by absolute monarchs since the beginning of time, Hun Sen couldn't simply give up all his power and slink away.

Khmer Rouge leaders were angry. They despised Hun Sen—a "contemptible puppet," Pol Pot called him—and while Prince Ranariddh had been close to an ally when they all were fighting Hun Sen and the Vietnamese, he didn't have the votes to become prime minister. Would that lead to a Ranariddh coalition with Hun Sen, Pol Pot's hated enemy?

Sihanouk was upset, too. More than anything else, he wanted to be the all-powerful king again; he had enjoyed his latest taste of power, serving as ceremonial head of state. And his son had more or less promised that he would take the throne again. In rallies toward the end of the campaign, Ranariddh had repeatedly said, "Funcinpec was established by Sihanouk, and I am his son. If Funcinpec wins, it means the whole nation wins, and Prince Sihanouk will come back to rule the country as before." Certainly, that was an election stratagem; his son was playing off his father's continued popularity. But Sihanouk intended to hold him to it.

Only one party came out of the election a clear winner: the United Nations. For all the UN's shortcomings, mistakes, and failures, it had pulled off a successful election, despite threats, boycotts, and violence. It had repatriated 370,000 refugees who had been living on the Thai border. In New York the secretary-general's office quickly put out a news release saying the election was "a credit to the men and women of UNTAC"—in other words, to itself. In Phnom Penh Akashi was more generous, and accurate, when he said the Cambodian people "were the true winners in this election." The Cambodian people, in fact, saved him.

From that day forward the UN proclaimed its Transitional Authority in Cambodia a glittering success. They seemed to be saying, "Forget everything that happened before: the failure to disarm the parties, the violence, murder, and mayhem." The election was all that mattered. Even so, the UN never again took on an operation as ambitious as this one.

The problem for all of them now was that Cambodia had no election law. The new government, once it formed, was supposed to write one. In the meantime, neither the Cambodians nor the UN had rules for settling this. Maybe they could stage a run-off election? But Cambodia had no law or precedent for that, either. In fact, it had few precedents for elections of any kind, aside from the heavily manipulated parliamentary elections Sihanouk had staged when he was king. The only possible solution was a coalition government of some sort between Hun Sen and Ranariddh. The UN pushed this, but neither man would agree. They hated each other.

Hun Sen immediately stepped in to fill this regulatory void by declaring the election invalid because, he asserted, there had been so many irregularities, including ballot switching, insufficient ballot-box security, and fraud by the UN, which, Hun Sen's party charged, had run the elections hopelessly biased against him. The UN, his party said, was "directing propaganda to the Cambodian people to malign the CPP"—an odd charge given the volumes of "propaganda" Hun Sen's party had disseminated using all of its state-run television and radio stations and party officers in every one of the country's villages, towns, and provinces.

Hun Sen wanted to restage elections in five provinces. These happened to be the provinces where Ranariddh won. If that happened, certainly this time the CPP could make sure that the vote turned out right. Hun Sen made it clear that he would simply refuse to hand over power until his grievances were addressed.

Into this quandary stepped Sihanouk. Hun Sen sought him out in secret, and the former king, ever magnanimous, offered to climb back onto the throne. Both Ranariddh and Hun Sen could serve as his vice ministers. Hun Sen agreed, and Sihanouk announced the deal—but without having told his son.

Ranariddh immediately objected. Wait a minute, he told his father in a faxed letter. I won this election! What's more, you would bring into the government certain CPP officials directly implicated in the killing of Funcinpec officers during the campaign. He was talking primarily about his own half brother Prince Norodom Chakrapong. (A man whose father had lived with two wives and uncounted concubines was bound to have a half brother or two.) Chakrapong was now Hun Sen's deputy prime minister and was reputed to be an utterly ruthless enforcer. During the campaign he had called his brother "a foreigner" who is "afraid to live in Cambodia." Ranariddh, forty-nine, was just twenty months older than Chakrapong, but they had been hateful rivals most of their lives. In fact, in the letter, Ranariddh asked his father, "How can I work with Prince Chakrapong who holds no other thought than to kill me?"

When the United Nations had arrived in Cambodia, the United States opened a mission—not quite a full embassy, but America's first diplomatic presence in Phnom Penh since 1975. Charles Twining, the State Department's Cambodia watcher, was appointed chief of mission, and with growing dismay he observed Sihanouk and the others trying to manipulate the results of a free election to their own advantage. Almost as soon as Sihanouk announced his deal, Twining's mission put out what came to be called a "nonpaper" because it was not official American policy, approved at the top. Still, it lambasted Sihanouk's deal, calling it "a violation of the Paris Peace Accords and the spirit of the successful elections," adding that it "would undermine the entire electoral process and the transition to democracy." Nonpaper or not, everyone took notice. Very quickly, Sihanouk withdrew his offer, then took to his bed and professed to be ill.

A few days later came a new stratagem, this one from Prince Chakrapong, Hun Sen's deputy prime minister, along with several generals from Hun Sen's army. They announced that they could not accept the election results. As a result, they were creating an autonomous region in the East, seven provinces that together comprised 40 percent of Cambodia's territory. These provinces were seceding. Hun Sen professed to have nothing to do with this, though the ringleaders were senior members of his own government, his army, and party stalwarts who governed all of the provinces in question.

UN officials were apoplectic. They'd pulled off successful elections despite everything that had happened before. They'd redeemed themselves, even received congratulations from the secretary-general and kind regard from leaders around the world. Now all of it was falling apart. Cambodia's leaders, all of them, were plotting, scheming, bribing, and backstabbing to come out on top, as if the election had never taken place. You could be sure that Hun Sen had paid off those provincial leaders who'd gone along with this secession ploy. Sihanouk was calling in all his markers. And Ranariddh prepared to play his trump card: his dad. That's how Cambodia's leaders had always behaved.

This time was supposed to be different. For the very first time, the people of Cambodia had spoken. Nearly all of them had voted. They had embraced democracy and stated their wishes. The world had just spent $3 billion to make this happen. And by God, the UN vowed, Hun Sen and all those royals could not simply pretend that the voting had never occurred and go on as they always had.

But the secessionists began attacking and burning UN offices in their new "autonomous zone." A UN spokesman declared: "This is not acceptable." Even with all that outrage, though, the UN had nothing to hold up as a threat but this: "The international community is sure to react to further provocation." In public, Akashi continued insisting that the elections had been fair and free; the UN had full confidence in the results. But he did write a private letter to Hun Sen, and there he made no attempt to hide his disbelief in Hun Sen's disavowal of responsibility for the secession threat. With his own staff under attack, and the UN's reputation on the line, Akashi demanded to know what Hun Sen planned to do about this.

Two days later, the newly elected National Assembly met. Sihanouk addressed the body and told the assemblymen: "We must not make this day the beginning of the end of Cambodia. We have to find a way to avoid the partition of Cambodia." He spoke as if this were some alien threat that had to be repressed, though the leader was his own son, a man who had served for many years as Sihanouk's "chief of protocol." Minutes later another of his sons, Ranariddh, offered a resolution to reinstate Sihanouk as king again, to give him "full and special powers inherent in his capabilities and duties as chief of state in order that he may save our nation." The assembly immediately approved the motion by acclamation. His son's secession ploy was proving to be quite useful for Sihanouk, too. He called the assembly's resolution "historic and invaluable."

Later that day, Hun Sen made his own grand play. He traveled to Kampong Cham Province, less than one hundred miles away but still part of the so-called autonomous zone, and reported back: Good news! This province is back under central government control! His ploy was transparent. All the secessionists were members of Hun Sen's government, and so were all of the breakaway provinces. Hun Sen seemed to be hoping no one would notice that and instead proclaim him the hero who had saved the nation. That's not exactly how it worked out.

In the end, Sihanouk prevailed on Ranariddh and Hun Sen to share power—while he would once again serve as king. Ranariddh agreed this time because he was to be designated "first prime minister," since he had actually won the election. Hun Sen would be second prime minister. Hun Sen agreed only because he knew who would really be in charge. As for Prince Chakrapong, he simply slunk away, over the border into Vietnam.

Hun Sen, Ranariddh, and Sihanouk had sat in that ornate conference room in Paris two years earlier, each conniving to achieve an outcome that would place himself on top. Now, it seemed, each of them had come quite close. Sihanouk was king, but without all the powers he had held before 1970. Both Hun Sen and Ranariddh were heads of the government, but they had to share power.

Nevertheless, through all of its history, only one absolute leader had ruled Cambodia. All three men had accepted the new arrangement— but only temporarily. Each of them wanted to be the nation's absolute ruler and remained determined to make that happen. As Hun Sen had said a few years earlier, "You can talk about sharing power in Paris, but not in Cambodia."

The UN blessed the agreement as the best that could be achieved for Cambodia—and for itself. Prince Sihanouk was not so generous. A foreign-press interviewer asked him what had been achieved with almost $3 billion and an election. "It was a waste!" Sihanouk declared with a dark grimace and a firm shake of his fist. "I apologize. I present my apologies to the United Nations. We did not deserve those three billion dollars because the way we handled it was so bad, so bad."

# CHAPTER FIVE

Triumphant, 22,000 UN personnel began packing to leave in the fall of 1993. The United States opened a full embassy and confirmed Twining, its chief of mission, as ambassador. Many other nations set up new embassies, too.

Cambodia was launched as a new democratic nation, a friend to the West. "There was a lot of optimism in the air," Twining observed. Most surprising of all, former archenemies Hun Sen and Prince Ranariddh seemed to be getting along. A famous photo, in the *Far Eastern Economic Review,* showed both men, in 1994, wearing matching formal white Asian shirts and offering slightly bowed, smiling homage to each other and to the world. "You know, I would listen to them talking to each other," Twining said, "and they would affectionately refer to one another as 'big brother' and 'little brother.'"

Behind closed doors, however, a power struggle was already under way. Ranariddh was supposed to be the first prime minister, the top leader, but the government as it stood the day he took office was simply a vast, unbroken patronage network for the Cambodian People's Party—from Hun Sen's office all the way down to the village chiefs. Ranariddh needed to wrest control from Hun Sen and the CPP. This wasn't driven simply because of the prince's natural expectation that he should control the government he was elected to lead. More important, he had to find "rewarding jobs" for members of his party. A rewarding job in Cambodia was one that placed the officeholder amid a lucrative patronage stream.

Ranariddh and Hun Sen decided to divide up the ministries. And once the prince had learned which ones were his, he laid down the résumé requirements for anyone who hoped to hold a senior position. Ranariddh wanted to see his applicants' bank statements. "The price list quoted by Funcinpec officials for jobs in the administration ranges from $200 to $3,000, depending on how good the position will be for extracting bribes," Veng Sereyvudh, a senior Funcinpec officer, told the *Nation* at the time. After all, he added, unlike Hun Sen, the new Funcinpec ministers "come with empty hands, and they need houses." Hadn't the kings of Angkor used the same system to choose their mandarins?

The real question the leadership had to address was, who was going to be Cambodia's new patron. After all, the national tradition of dependency had continued for centuries now. In recent history, after the French patrons had left, the United States was the first generous benefactor, in the early 1970s. Then came the Khmer Rouge years, when China kept Pol Pot and the other leaders rich and fat while they starved and killed millions of their countrymen. "The group of decision makers lived very well," said Mey Meakk, Pol Pot's secretary. "But the poor people who served them, the working class like me, we were still very, very poor." So, in that way at least, Pol Pot had carried on the traditions of Cambodian leaders through the centuries.

Then came the Vietnam occupation. While Hanoi served as occupier and patron, the newly appointed Cambodian ministers had little if any previous experience in government—or as managers of a sophisticated graft network. In any case, under the Vietnamese, resources were scarce. So when Twining first met Hun Sen, "he lived in a modest two-story stucco house downtown." On the first floor was a meeting room with a carpet on the floor and seating for six or eight people. Upstairs

were a small dining area, a kitchen, and a couple of bedrooms. The entire place probably did not exceed 2,000 square feet. Obviously, Hun
Sen had not yet tapped into a lucrative money stream. (Later, by comparison, even his deputy, Sok An, had a home the size of a small
hotel—five stories and about 60,000 square feet of living space.)

In 1992, the United Nations had arrived with billions of dollars to
spend. The nation was awash in cash, though little of it went into the
government treasury. Every project the UN undertook offered opportunities for graft—or theft. All that UN money bloated the Cambodian economy. A lot of people got rich. But then, at the end of 1993,
the UN and all of its money and expertise were gone. That left "a huge
vacuum," Twining observed. "In the government, there wasn't a lot of
experience." Among the new ministers, "there wasn't a lot of education." But hadn't that always been true of Cambodia's mandarins?
They were there primarily for the money. After the UN left, they worried: Who would step up? Who would be the new patron, the next
funder? How could those new Funcinpec officers build their mansions and buy their fancy new cars? A hint of a possible answer had
come in Tokyo a year earlier. There, in June 1992, thirty-two nations
had come for a conference to talk about how to rebuild Cambodia.
Everyone was confident that the country would soon have a new democratic government. But the nation's infrastructure—homes, schools,
hospitals, roads, railways, power networks, and water systems, practically everything—still lay in shambles.

William Draper III, administrator of the United Nations Development Programme, told the conference that Cambodia remained "a
critical test for the post–Cold War world," and its case was "especially
poignant, not only because of the immense human suffering that has
already taken place there, but because Cambodia was the unwitting
victim of superpower confrontation." Now, Draper suggested, it was
time to repay Cambodians for all of this, with "one of the largest and
most complex development challenges ever faced by the international
community." Draper said the secretary-general had asked him to
come up with an estimate of the reconstruction money needed right

away, and he had it now: $595 million. Then a parade of world leaders stood up to talk about how important the mission was and how eager they were to help. China's vice foreign minister, Xu Dunxin, promised to be generous and pumped up Beijing's good friend Sihanouk. "Under the leadership of Prince Sihanouk," he said, "the Cambodian people will overcome their difficulties."

When the day had ended and each nation had turned in its pledge sheet, the world promised to provide Cambodia with $880 million— 30 percent more than Draper had requested. The UN authorities were to manage that money since, in 1992, they still occupied the nation. In truth, though, as the violence increased in the following months, most of the countries held back their pledges. But for the Cambodians, perhaps the most encouraging development of that meeting in 1992 was that the donors were promising to put on another of these funding conferences the next year.

Sure enough, just a few weeks after Hun Sen, Ranariddh, and Sihanouk announced their tripartite governing agreement in the summer of 1993, the French staged another funding conference, in Paris. The mood this time was different. The donor nations weren't just trying to help another poor, beleaguered place. Now they had ownership. They had paid billions of dollars to give Cambodia this chance. They were heavily invested in the outcome. So the attendees pledged another $119 million while promising to begin delivering the rest of the $880 million offered a year earlier.

In Washington that fall Quinn, the deputy assistant secretary of state, warned Congress that after the United Nations closed shop and sent its people back home, the United States should not turn away. Cambodia still faced major challenges. Not least, "traditional political problems like corruption could come to the fore and weaken the new government," because "Cambodia lacks the institutions and adequate numbers of trained personnel needed for a mature democracy."

That same fall Japan reported that many nations were beginning to make good on their pledges, to the tune of $714 million so far—while the United Nations said Cambodians had spent only $330 million of that money on the projects for which the money was intended. Where did the other $384 million go? Just a bookkeeping error, the new Cambodian government explained; we don't have systems in place yet to keep accurate records of the aid we receive. Undeterred, donors pledged another $773 million in 1994. Ranariddh had read a note from his father to the group in which Sihanouk urged them to fund a "new unconditional Marshall Plan" for Cambodia.

A year passed, and Paris was planning still another donor conference. But by now the donors were growing concerned. What had happened to all of that money they had already given? Representatives from several of the donor countries, including the United States, met with government officials in February 1995 to discuss the matter. Twining said he and the other ambassadors, concerned about the growing indications of corruption, had "all been talking about it among ourselves." One civil servant complained to Twining "about his minister siphoning off so much money that there was very little left to run the ministry."

The state seemed to be falling headlong back into its old corrupt ways. Police had begun setting up unofficial checkpoints on the highways where they pulled over drivers and shook them down. Schoolteachers were demanding bribes from students every day as a condition for staying in class. And then, of course, there was the disappearing foreign aid. At the least, Twining said, "we were talking about raising the civil-service salaries so the teachers didn't have to take 50 riel from their students" every morning.

At the February meeting Twining told the group, "All of the donor countries want to continue to support democracy and development in Cambodia," but "some of them are concerned about corruption and concerned about transparency. We are not threatening to cut our support at this time, but it is true that there is a lot of competition for our aid dollars." He urged the government, Hun Sen and Ranariddh, to make clear that they stood firm against corruption.

The next month, Second Prime Minister Hun Sen made an announcement, broadcast nationwide over state radio. Since the elections, he said, "corruption has become more widespread in all circles, like mushrooms sprouting during the rainy season." As a result, the government was preparing a comprehensive anticorruption law. It would define corruption and the punishment for corrupt individuals. A strong office should be established to investigate and crack down on corrupt practices. The office should be independent; it should have sufficient rights and powers to conduct investigations, make arrests, and imprison offenders. "Prominent persons who are honest, courageous and resolute in their tasks," he said, "should be appointed as members, and they should have a clear mandate."

As a further check, Hun Sen said, "a strong and responsible press network should be created to publish accurate news, enabling the masses to become aware of the problem of corruption." He asked the Cambodian press "to show its courage and responsibility in using democracy jointly with the government to achieve successes for the people who are currently striving to eliminate corruption."

"He said all the right things," Twining observed. "We were very impressed." And it worked. In Paris, some speakers talked about corruption and human-rights abuses. But the Cambodians talked up their proposed new law and also pointed out: We're a young nation, just emerging from genocide and war. Give us a chance!

The Cambodians asked for $295 million. The donors gave them $430 million. "That amount," First Prime Minister Ranariddh told reporters waiting for him at the Phnom Penh airport, "is double our need and much more than we require." He was grinning.

---

After Hun Sen and Ranariddh divided up the ministries, Sam Rainsy of the Funcinpec Party was appointed minister of finance. He was an erudite French Cambodian, educated at the Sorbonne, who'd worked as an investment banker in Paris before returning to Cambodia in 1993. In addition to Khmer, he spoke French and near-perfect English. Most Cambodians viewed him as an elitist, and as if to prove it, he typically wore expensive suits and round tortoise-shell eyeglasses. Cambodians, by and large, did not wear glasses. They couldn't afford them.

Since returning to Cambodia, Rainsy had devised and trade-marked a political personality that made him a dissident within the government. He inveighed against corruption, both political and financial—though rumors about corruption in his own ministry, never confirmed, swirled through Phnom Penh. While Sihanouk, Hun Sen, and Ranariddh plotted and schemed during the first weeks after the elections, Rainsy had remarked, "Everyone is ready to do anything to survive. They are showing no moral values, no signs of concern for the national interest or the common good."

Rainsy liked to play to the audience in the bleachers—foreign governments, particularly France and the United States. In his first months on the job, he won plaudits from them by announcing that he had improved tax collection so that the government could soon begin paying civil servants a living wage, reducing the incentive to take bribes. At about the same time, though, the parliament voted to raise its members' own pay from about $30 a month to $1,800—ostensibly to reduce the need to take bribes. Needless to say, that got more attention than Rainsy's 20 percent pay increase for civil servants.

But Rainsy's biggest problem was his mouth. "Over the last 10 years, people, especially leaders, tended to confuse their personal assets with the state's assets," he told the *Toronto Star* in June 1994. "They saw their personal interests as the national interest. This was the worst combination we could have, a jungle economy and former Communist cadres who use their discretionary powers to serve their personal interests. They've been doing whatever they want. They just use their political power to get rich by disposing of national assets like they are their own assets." A bit later he told the Associated Press,

"You cannot start a business here without all the officials asking you for money." And now, with a divided government, "instead of bribing one party, you have to bribe two."

Every time he made a remark like that, diplomats and aid-group officers stood up and clapped. But Cambodian government officials and the businessmen who were bribing them grew to loath Rainsy. And, needless to say, the corrupt officials in government outnumbered Rainsy and his kind by at least 1,000 to 1.

Rainsy managed to inspire foreign confidence in the government's future. But this may have left Rainsy with the view that he was invulnerable. He was wrong. In October 1994 Ranariddh and Hun Sen fired him, saying he was "not a team player." Rainsy's wife, Tioulong Saumura, offered a curious explanation for his fall: "My husband was not good at explaining what he was doing because of his poor communication skills." Rainsy may have been booted out of government. But he was not going to fade gracefully away.

Even with Hun Sen's lofty pronouncements about corruption and a free and open press, it quickly became clear that Cambodia remained a dangerous place for the reform-minded. Two months after Rainsy left office, two men riding by on a motorbike shot and killed Chan Dara, a young reporter for the *Koh Santepheap* (Island of Peace) newspaper, in Kampong Cham, about seventy-five miles northeast of Phnom Penh. Chan Dara had been writing stories about corruption in government—as Hun Sen had publicly requested. A few weeks earlier in downtown Phnom Penh assassins on a motorbike had gunned down Nguon Chan, the editor of the *Voice of Cambodian Youth* newspaper. He, too, had been reporting on corruption.

Information Minister Ieng Mouly, when questioned about Nguon Chan's murder, offered a surprising bit of candor. He told a reporter for the *Christian Science Monitor* that he could not "exclude the possibility that members of the police or the military were responsible for this assassination, but it doesn't mean it's the policy of the government." Ieng Mouly soon lost his job. And never again did a Cambodian government official even suggest complicity in one of those killings. From that day forward, as the killings continued year after year, the government's position was steadfast denial.

In his speech for the donors in 1995, Second Prime Minister Hun Sen had urged the news media "to publish accurate news, enabling the masses to become aware of the problem of corruption." He had also promised to write and enact an anticorruption law. A few days after that speech, Keat Chhon, the new finance minister, told reporters, "The royal government is seriously implementing internal legislation to combat corruption" and is "determined to adopt measures to that end: the establishment of an anti-corruption office, the drawing up of an anti-corruption law, the exercise of administrative reform, and the strengthening of education to fight corruption."

Nevertheless, since the meeting in Paris, where the government got everything it wanted—and more—the anticorruption legislation had disappeared from public discussion. The government had decided it didn't want anyone even to talk about the subject anymore. This approach was very much like King Norodom's insincere promise to the new French administration a century earlier that he would abolish slavery, quieting his masters so he could head off for an afternoon at his harem. That strategy would become commonplace in the coming years. But this time, Hun Sen, Ranariddh, and King Sihanouk all had personal agendas in mind.

In June 1994 Sihanouk, heading to China for medical treatment, said he would be more than willing to become the ruling monarch again. "I have no plan to take power now," he told the *Far Eastern Economic Review*. "But in case the situation becomes anarchic and desperate, I would have to take power for one or two years." Rumors that Sihanouk was coming back rippled through Phnom Penh, to his delight. He continually encouraged the talk. "The people see that unless Sihanouk takes power, there is no leader capable of reuniting the country and giving everyone faith and confidence," he said. "I don't want to be the man of factions. I want to be the man of national unity, national reconciliation."

Listening to all of this, Hun Sen warned him: If you try to come back, I will fight you with everything I have. "I don't admire much this regime," Sihanouk said after receiving Hun Sen's threat. "But I accept it." The fact that his own son was first prime minister in the government didn't seem to change Sihanouk's opinion. He obviously had little respect for Ranariddh. Just before he was appointed figurehead king, Sihanouk spoke to a luncheon with Ranariddh in the audience. He glanced at his son as he quipped with a biting tone: "They want to make me king so I am completely neutralized. That's why Prince Ranariddh wants his father to be king." From his sickbed in Beijing, Sihanouk sent a steady stream of fax messages to Funcinpec Party officials, all of them highly critical of his son.

It turned out this drama had other players, too. A month after Sihanouk left Phnom Penh, a column of military troop transports and armored personnel carriers rumbled along the road toward the capital from the east, carrying about three hundred men armed with rifles and rocket-propelled grenade launchers. When the force reached the outskirts of Phnom Penh in the early-morning hours, government troops surrounded the vehicles, and all of the soldiers surrendered. Who did they find leading this small renegade force, apparently attempting a coup? Prince Chakrapong, King Sihanouk's black-sheep son, who had slunk off to Vietnam after his secession scheme failed. The next day fourteen armed Thai soldiers, some dressed in Cambodian military uniforms, were caught at the Phnom Penh airport, apparently there to add "firepower" to the coup attempt.

Chakrapong, being a royal, was hustled onto a plane and sent back into exile the very next day. He said nothing about his intentions, but the reigning theory was this: Chakrapong planned to depose, if not kill, his hated brother, Ranariddh, and return his revered father, Sihanouk, to full power. Then Dad would give him a powerful new job in his government. The bizarre incident remained an enduring mystery but had the result of persuading both Ranariddh and Hun Sen to build up their personal guard forces so that soon each of these armies numbered in the hundreds.

Ranariddh was growing more and more frustrated with his place in government. Yes, Hun Sen had given him several ministries—in theory. But all of the bureaucrats down in the bowels of these agencies were CPP loyalists. What's more, the true source of power, since the time of Jayavarman II in the ninth century, was in the provinces. There, the people who grew rice created most of the nation's wealth. Hun Sen and his political party maintained complete control nationwide, and Ranariddh could do little to change that.

At a Funcinpec Party conference, Ranariddh vowed to demand true power sharing in the provinces. By then no one held any doubt that a drive for greater personal wealth, which came from enhanced power, was Ranariddh's principal aim. He had already made it known that he had no use for democracy, the central aim of the $3 billion UN effort. "The Western brand of democracy and freedom of press is not applicable in Cambodia," he remarked in 1995. Ninety percent of Cambodians had voted in the recent election, but democracy and freedom of the press were not proving to be useful for Ranariddh. By this time his government had charged fourteen journalists with antigovernment slander.

All the while, members of his own party were losing faith. Ranariddh had never served in government before becoming first prime minister. He remained aloof and uninterested in much beyond enriching himself and advancing his own personal interests. And then those almost daily faxes from the king were working to undermine him among his own staff. Even so, he remained oblivious. "I don't think Ranariddh knew that people in his own party were turning against him," said Quinn, the State Department official. "They wanted to bring the king back."

Hun Sen was no more of a democrat. How could he be, given his history? During a meeting in Paris in 1996 Cambodians held a demonstration against him. Hun Sen warned them: "You can hold a demonstration in France, but do not do it in Cambodia!"

Now, the co-prime ministers were not even talking to each other. Hun Sen told author David Roberts that he and Ranariddh do not "hug and kiss each other, we do not love each other. In fact we barely speak. We do not have regularly scheduled meetings because we have little to discuss."

If anyone doubted that Sihanouk, Hun Sen, and Ranariddh all were driven to win dominance, they had only to witness the political violence still endemic in the capital city. Perhaps the most heinous of these crimes was the hand-grenade attack on the Buddhist Liberal Party headquarters in September 1995. Two men on a motorbike, wearing helmets with tinted faceplates, drove up to party headquarters, threw a hand grenade into the reception room where dozens of people had gathered for a rally, and then sped off. Their bike had no license plate, which was not uncommon in Cambodia. Then they drove over to a nearby pagoda, where another crowd of party members waited for the rally, tossed another grenade into that crowd, and sped off, leaving blood, mayhem, and death in their wake. More than thirty people were injured, and at least ten of these eventually died from their wounds.

The tactic had a long history. One infamous grenade attack killed Ieu Koeuss, leader of the Democratic Party, in 1950. His party was struggling for dominance in the fight for independence from France. King Sihanouk and Ieu Koeuss's party were bickering. French police were arresting party members, and Democrats were squabbling among themselves. When someone tossed a grenade into party headquarters, Cambodians endlessly debated who had the greatest motivation to kill him, and the police never made an arrest.

Grenade attacks allowed perpetrators to make a strong statement without leaving fingerprints. Each government faction loudly blamed one another, and in the end no one was ever caught or charged. That led many to believe that the government must be responsible; why else would the police never make any arrests? This impression was convenient for Hun Sen and Ranariddh; it was useful to be feared.

The 1995 attack on the Buddhist Liberal Party headquarters followed the new democratic government's refusal to give the Buddhist party a permit to hold a rally. Hun Sen had warned on national television that if Son Sann, the party leader, proceeded with the party congress anyway and violence occurred—perhaps even a grenade attack—he would hold organizers personally responsible. If you violate my rules, he was saying, I will attack you—and then blame you for the casualties.

At that time the Buddhist party was locked in a leadership struggle of its own. Another politician who was friendly to the government was trying to oust Son Sann. So who threw the grenades? At a moment like that, Cambodia could be a hall of mirrors. That's why grenades were such a popular weapon of misdirection.

---

With the leaders consumed by their personal holy wars, Cambodian society drifted toward anarchy. Phnom Penh was rife with drug traffickers; a deputy police chief estimated that six hundred kilograms of heroin passed through the city each week, and allegations flew that government ministers, even Hun Sen, were deeply involved in the trade. The Cambodian military, mimicking the Khmer Rouge, was plundering the nation's forests, selling immensely valuable teak, rosewood, and mahogany-like lumber to the Thai. Shortly after taking office Hun Sen and Ranariddh, in one of their few collegial acts, wrote a letter to the Thai prime minister saying that, effective immediately, only the Defense Ministry had authority to export timber. The two of them told no one else in the government about this, meaning that the stream of illicit money would flow directly through the ministry to them. Just three weeks earlier the government had issued a strong public directive, saying timber exports were now "prohibited under any circumstances." Rainsy, still in government then, got hold of the letter to the Thai prime minister and made it public. As finance minister, all he could say was, "All state revenues should be centralized in the budget." But he was powerless to enforce this declaration.

Phnom Penh, once one of the region's most beautiful colonial cities, was now crowded with shanty towns crammed into almost every open space. Beggars and cripples lay about the streets; thousands of Cambodians had lost one or both legs to land mines. With no toilets or trash collection, fetid sewage and garbage lay in wait of the rainy season to carry it away—somewhere. Young children played in the trash, often naked because their parents could not afford diapers or clothes.

The government was doing nothing for its people. The statistics that limned their lives remained bleak and were growing worse. The life span for an average Cambodian was barely fifty years, a statistic pulled down by the depressing fates of mothers and their newborn children. Almost 20 percent of all newborns died before they reached age five. One mother in ten did not survive childbirth—among the worst rates in the world. Outside Phnom Penh, maternal care was almost nonexistent.

Hun Sen traveled the nation dedicating new schools, usually named for him and paid for by friends in business as thanks for the access the second prime minister gave them to government largesse. But, just like Sihanouk's school-building program in the 1960s, most of these new schools had no educated teachers. A school was lucky to have a teacher who had completed third grade. Even then, their pay was so low that teachers continued demanding daily bribes from their students. Only about two-thirds of the children even started school, and most of those dropped out after the second or third grade. For Hun Sen, each new school building was a onetime cost paid by someone else—and a magnificent gift for the voters. But Hun

Sen, like Sihanouk before him, was nowhere to be seen when the uneducated teachers were taking cash from their students and trying to educate them in subjects they did not understand themselves.

Education was hardly the only problem. People who lived outside the major cities—in other words, almost everyone—had access to nothing but noxious, dysentery-inducing drinking water. Fewer than one Cambodian in ten had a toilet. Malaria, dengue fever, encephalitis, hepatitis, meningitis, pneumonia, tuberculosis, typhoid, and dysentery all were commonplace, and the HIV/AIDS rate was growing so fast that it set off alarms around the world. "I heard about it in Fiji!" said Dr. Michael O'Leary, a World Health Organization (WHO) official based there in the 1990s.

Government leaders, when they even heard about their society's growing list of afflictions, tried to foist blame. Henry Kamm, a *New York Times* reporter, asked Om Radsady, chairman of the parliament's Foreign Affairs Committee, about the state's burgeoning dysfunction, and he blamed the West. "The big powers should take responsibility," he said. "When you buy a car, you get a service guarantee. Maybe we drove the car badly, but you should share responsibility."

Even so, in the West the nations that put up all that money for the UN operation clung to the conviction that their funds had been well spent. All told, the United States contributed $1.2 billion, and both Washington and the United Nations continued talking up the Cambodia operation as a great success.

When Clinton's secretary of state, Warren Christopher, visited Phnom Penh in August 1995, as part of a larger regional tour, he told Cambodia's leaders, "I have come here to salute the progress the Cambodian people have made with such dignity and courage toward peace and freedom. No people in the world more deserve these blessings of peace and prosperity and freedom." On the fifth anniversary of the Paris Peace Accords in 1996, UN Secretary-General Boutros Boutros-Ghali congratulated Hun Sen for his "statesmanship." Winston Lord, the new assistant secretary of state for the region, called Cambodia "a model UN success story," and his deputy cheerily reported that the concept of human rights "has permeated" the government.

Twining, the ambassador, was also inclined to be generous. He believed that most of the people in government had a steep learning curve, and no one should expect Cambodia to become a Jeffersonian democracy overnight. Twining had little pressure from Washington to step into the nation's intramural battles. As usual, the State Department didn't really care. "It's fair to say they had other fish to fry," Twining said. "There was some relief that the country was finally at peace. I think the view was that Cambodia needed sustenance but not a lot of attention. There were other things going on. For example, the Somalia debacle. As for Cambodia, it was considered a little better off than it had been before." And for Washington, that seemed to be enough.

But over time Washington also began adding modest cautions. In the fall of 1995 Lord told Congress, "Cambodia's emerging democracy continues to show impressive endurance. The Royal Cambodian Government has begun the process of building political and economic institutions suitable to the country's current needs." But Lord also felt compelled to offer a gentle warning: "As a friend, the U.S. has been candidly telling Cambodia's leaders in recent months of our concerns over recent trends, especially in cases involving freedom of expression and of the press, and how those trends might jeopardize international support for the process of change in Cambodia." At the annual donors' conference a few months earlier, Cambodia had received pledges of $500 million. That money made up more than half of the nation's annual budget. But Lord had warned that if the nation's leaders did not change their ways, they might not get so much money the next year.

Rainsy, who was starting a new political party, loudly urged the donor nations to "impose conditions," including "the establishment of a true rule of law, the strengthening of democratic institutions and mechanisms, and guarantees that fundamental human rights will be respected." And, of course, he added his signature issue: an end to corruption. All of this played well abroad. The *New Republic* called him

"Cambodia's stubborn saint." But as always, others in government saw him as a dangerous scoundrel. A year earlier he'd been booted out of the Finance Ministry. Now Rainsy had so many friends and admirers abroad that Hun Sen and Ranariddh grew quite worried about his ability to dissuade donors from giving.

Hun Sen blasted him. "In the past, there was the Khmer Rouge blocking all kinds of aid to Cambodia, now we have a second Pol Pot against aid to the Cambodian people," he told reporters. Then that summer, Ranariddh offered a motion to expel Rainsy from the parliament. Rainsy's friends in the bleachers howled. Human Rights Watch, the British House of Lords, Amnesty International, the International Parliamentary Union, and several U.S. congressmen warned of dire consequences and questioned the expulsion's legality. No matter. The parliament voted him out, nearly unanimously. Rainsy was a private citizen again. Soon after that he came by the U.S. Embassy one afternoon and asked Twining if he could reside there for a while. He cited threats and dangers to his person. But living at the embassy would also give him the certain imprimatur of strong support from the U.S. government. "When he left government, he began looking elsewhere for support," Twining said, in part because "he often spoke out a bit more forcefully than the traffic would bear. Once he came by and asked whether he could stay a bit. I persuaded him to go home and said we would protect him."

In the months leading up to the 1996 donor meeting, Ranariddh repeatedly vowed to speed up work on an anticorruption law, the one Hun Sen had promised to enact, and move it to the parliament for a vote. Cambodia's new ambassador to Washington, Var Huoth, wrote a letter to the *New York Times* protesting a critical story about his government. "An anti-corruption law is being drafted to be submitted to the National Assembly for adoption," he wrote, adding, "I do not have to remind you that Cambodia still suffers from the aftermath of the mass murder, starvation and destruction by the Khmer

Rouge." At the same time Rainsy continued his public attacks, harping on corruption again and again. By the time of the meeting in July, no new law had even been introduced, but the donor nations gave Cambodia $518 million anyway, a 4 percent increase. Ranariddh was jubilant—particularly since the donors obviously had paid no attention to Rainsy. "He looks ridiculous now," Ranariddh said with obvious glee.

If Ranariddh and Second Prime Minister Hun Sen were thinking analytically, then no doubt a recent metaphor came to mind: the leaders of the UN occupation force turning away after that Khmer Rouge child soldier, standing at the bamboo-pole checkpoint, refused to let them pass. Now, these donors were every bit as toothless. Once again Jupiter was throwing no thunderbolts from the mountaintop. Whatever Ranariddh and Hun Sen said, whatever they did, the donors would come through anyway. Cambodia had found a new and reliable patron. Undoubtedly, each of them was also plotting how he might end the democratic charade, knock the other guy off, and place himself at the top of the government—as each of them had intended all along.

As Twining left office at the end of 1995, after four brutal years he had lost much of his optimism. "We all wanted to keep things moving forward," he said. "But I sent a cable to Washington saying I wasn't sure how long this government would last."

# CHAPTER SIX

In 1996, as Twining's term as ambassador was winding down, the Clinton administration choose Ken Quinn to replace him. Just like Twining, Quinn's background gave him a deeply sympathetic view of the state. In fact, at his confirmation hearing, he told the senators that the climb with his fiancée up that South Vietnam mountain in 1973 had changed his life. "My involvement with Cambodia began on a hot and humid Mekong Delta afternoon in June 1973, when I climbed to the top of Nui Sam Mountain along the Vietnamese-Cambodian border and witnessed a spectacle that would forever change Cambodia and reorient my professional career," he said, sitting at the witness table, looking up at the panel of senators on the Foreign Relations Committee. "From that vantage point at the top of Nui Sam, as far as the eye could see, every single one of the dozens of hamlets that dotted the lush green Cambodian plain was ablaze. Thick black smoke billowed from every cluster of thatched dwellings in which thousands and thousands of Cambodian rice farmers and their families lived. I was stunned." He easily won confirmation and took office in early 1996 filled with a warm sense of honor and purpose. "I was thinking that what we were doing was noble," he said.

"We didn't have any defense interests, any economic interests or intelligence interests. We were doing this because it was the moral thing to do."

Then, like every ambassador new on the job, Quinn made the rounds of lunches, dinners, and meetings, "making my calls," as he put it, getting to know the political, diplomatic, and military communities. "I came away with a sense that one side was going to turn on the other. I went to a dinner put on by a deputy of mine, and I was stunned by the descriptions of the CPP as corrupt and pure evil. This was a totally different picture than what I had been told."

Twining, Quinn's predecessor, had come to more or less the same conclusion and had cabled Washington laying out his concerns. But Twining was a far more careful and cautious man. Serving as Cambodia watcher in the spring of 1975, he spoke to scores of refugees who had experienced unspeakable horrors. In his cables to Washington he offered vivid descriptions of individual living conditions. Cambodians, he wrote, "are living a Spartan, miserable existence for people living constantly in fear." But his cables were light on larger political conclusions.

Quinn had always taken a different approach. Interviewing refugees who crossed the border into Vietnam in 1973, Quinn had offered a far broader, more provocative analysis: The Khmer Rouge, he wrote, were "stripping away, through terror and other means, the traditional bases, structures and forces which have shaped and guided an individual's life until he is left as an atomized, isolated individual unit; and then rebuilding him according to party doctrine by substituting a series of new values, organizations and ethical norms for the ones taken away." And this was even before the Khmer Rouge had taken power. Part of Quinn's analysis had proved to be wrong; he thought only one part of the Khmer Rouge movement was antagonistic to Vietnam when in fact the entire movement was. Still, his airgram had been the first bold, cogent warning of what lay ahead.

Now, in March 1996, once again Quinn showed his penchant for dramatic action. Just thirty days after taking office, he got on a plane, flew back to Washington, and asked for a meeting with Assistant Secretary Lord and his aides. "This is not the positive situation I had expected," he told them.

Co-prime ministers Hun Sen and Ranariddh weren't even speaking to one another. Each was building his own personal army, while their bodyguard forces had already begun exchanging occasional gunfire. A few months earlier, Hun Sen had dispatched tanks and troops to arrest Prince Norodom Sirivudh, Sihanouk's half brother and general secretary of the Funcinpec Party. The prince, widely respected among diplomats and aid workers, had been heard suggesting, probably in jest, that it would be easy to hire thugs to assassinate Hun Sen. He was thrown in jail, tried, and sentenced to ten years in prison—but then deported instead.

The signs were clear: The situation in Cambodia was deteriorating. "This country is heading toward violence," Quinn warned. As he saw it, Lord and the others "were shocked and surprised." But then, just as had happened with Quinn's airgram and Twining's field reports, Washington did little if anything. They didn't really care.

As all of this transpired, in 1995 Sam Rainsy started a new political organization, the Khmer National Party, practically throwing his contempt for Hun Sen in the second prime minister's face. The parliament had not yet passed any of the laws needed to form new political parties. That enabled Hun Sen to call the party illegal. Rainsy didn't care.

He was not going to make Ranariddh's mistake of leaving the CPP in control of the provinces. So he decided to open his first provincial office. He chose a location near Sihanoukville in the South—"Really, just some guy's house with a banner on the front," said Ron Abney, an American who was serving as a political adviser. But Hun Sen saw even this as intolerable.

The day the office opened, in May 1996, two gunmen on a motor-bike, wearing the trademark black helmets with tinted faceplates, shot and killed Thun Bun Ly while he was walking to work. He was a senior member of Rainsy's new party and editor of *Khmer Ideal*, an opposition newspaper affiliated with Rainsy. "They could not have chosen a better time to kill Bun Ly as the killing took place at the exact time we opened our first office outside the capital," Rainsy declared. "It's a very clear sign of intimidation. They want to intimidate us and show us we cannot open our offices." Rainsy's followers staged an angry demonstration. Large throngs marched through the city's main streets carrying Thun Bun Ly's coffin on their shoulders.

Even so, soon after, thugs burned down Rainsy's new district office, killing a couple of party functionaries. Rainsy was beside himself. He began working the bleachers in earnest, particularly the United States—struggling to stoke international opposition to Hun Sen, whom he routinely blamed for his nation's "lawlessness and violence." The occasional expressions of support for the government that came from Washington officials infuriated him. His message for them, distilled, was this: Hun Sen is a vicious, evil dictator. Why can't you see that? What more evidence do you need?

With a new ambassador, Rainsy again tried to draw the U.S. Embassy into his battle. "He was forever trying to get us to take him into protective custody in our embassy," Quinn said. "Phoning us, saying, 'They are trying to kill me. Take me into the embassy.'" Rainsy, American officials believed, thought that if the United States placed a protective umbrella over him, Hun Sen could not touch him or his party. He would be America's man.

Once, when Rainsy made a particularly vehement request, Quinn said he sent his deputy, Carol Rodley, to deal with him. In fact, she said, "I had that discussion with Sam Rainsy more than once. I remember once delivering him to the French Embassy, and the ambassador was quite unhappy. Absolutely, he wanted to draw the United States into the conflict. It suited him to be America's candidate."

Asked about that later, Rainsy vehemently denied it. "It's ridiculous. It's wrong. I never asked for asylum. I don't need protection. I have a French passport. I can leave the country anytime I want to."*

While Rainsy spent a lot of time abroad, trying to convince foreign leaders of Hun Sen's perfidy, he also held rallies and solicited support at home. Not surprisingly, his campaign platform centered on the venality of his hated enemy. On Sunday morning, March 30, 1997, he called for a rally in a large public park in central Phnom Penh. King Sihanouk's palace was up the street. The park was a city block wide and a quarter mile long, and Rainsy chose the northeast corner, just across the street from the National Assembly, a grand Asian monument topped with a glittering golden tower and sinuous gilt finials. In that building Ranariddh had offered the motion to have him expelled from the parliament two years earlier. Despite that, Rainsy's party had formed a tenuous alliance with Funcinpec a few weeks earlier.

From where Rainsy stood, with his back to the assembly building, a large Buddhist pagoda complex was to his right. In front of him, on the far side of the street a block away, splendid residential mansions ran all the way down to the park's far end. Among the mansions was Hun Sen's. That street, and the park, ended at Suramarit Boulevard, a few blocks east of the Independence Monument, a memorial to the day the French occupiers left Cambodia. This was a consequential part of town, sort of like the National Mall in Washington, D.C.

---

*That was just the first of several untruths he proffered, and Abney noted that "he's done it to me two or three times, too." In fact, foreigners with long experience in Cambodia find that lying is all too common. Cambodians, like most Asians, need first of all to save face, avoid shame and embarrassment. Cambodians also choose to shun conflict and confrontation. So if brash Westerners ask embarrassing or hostile questions, "they should not be surprised when they are told lies," wrote Philip Short, author of Pol Pot: Anatomy of a Nightmare. Abney noted, "I had people look me in the eye and say, 'No I never said that.' And then I would tell them: 'Well, I'm the one you said it to.'"

The message of the morning's event was that Hun Sen had taken control of the nation's court system and turned it into his own personal tool. It was early, eight thirty, before the heat of the day could grow brutal. A vendor pushing a blue cart was doing brisk business selling stalks of sugar cane.

Rainsy stood on a chair and began inveighing against Hun Sen. He told his enthusiastic followers that Prince Norodom Sirivudh's arrest, conviction, and then expulsion from the country were proof that Hun Sen was using the courts for his own venal ends. Several supporters carried signs saying "Norodom Sirivudh Has Committed No Crime."

A few Phnom Penh police loitered nearby, far fewer than usually showed up for Rainsy rallies. But several dozen well-armed shock troops from Hun Sen's personal bodyguard unit, a 1,500-man force feared among his enemies, stood in a tight line about fifty yards away, watching silently. Rainsy noted later that he had never seen any of these bodyguards at his other rallies in Phnom Penh. But then he had never held an event just across the street from Hun Sen's home.

As always, Rainsy's target audience was as much the foreigners in the bleachers as the Cambodian voters. To that end he had invited Ron Abney, an American serving as the Cambodian country director for the International Republican Institute (known universally as the IRI), a federally funded organization based in Washington charged with promoting democracy around the world. Abney was an enthusiastic, garrulous fellow who had glued himself to Rainsy. His job, as he saw it, was to be sure Cambodia maintained a healthy and robust political opposition as the government grew increasingly authoritarian. Rainsy was his man.

The IRI leadership in Washington was no fan of Hun Sen. Lorne Craner, the institute's president, remarked that he thought most Cambodians were afraid of him. "Well, last time he lost an election," in 1993, "he threatened a civil war. Maybe the people are afraid of retribution" from him if they even say they don't support him. After all, for many years the centerpiece of Washington policy toward Cambodia had been to throw Hun Sen, the Communist stooge, out of office.

For Abney and his supervisors in Washington, Rainsy was the great hope. Abney now considered him a good friend. "I loved him like a brother." But he also knew that Rainsy had a lot to learn. "He didn't realize you couldn't just be a guy who opposed Hun Sen and get elected. We were very much focused on a setting up a campaign operation." The next national election was just over a year away. "We were setting up people in each commune" nationwide. But Rainsy, Abney said, "was on a campaign to get Washington to support him."

Abney showed up late, after the speeches. After all, he didn't speak Khmer. "When I got there, they were finishing up," he said. "People were starting to leave. I walked over and got right in front of Rainsy." Just then, someone threw a hand grenade into the crowd. "It hit me in the hip, and I fell," Abney said. Another grenade went off. And then another and another. Dozens and dozens of people fell to the ground, wounded or dead. "The scene was unbelievable. People cut in half, kids with their faces blown off." Thin smoke from the explosions muted the scene and gave off an acrid odor. Victims moaned and cried. Protest placards lay beside them, splattered with blood. The injured looked stunned. For many of them, the assault also brought back painful memories of their horrific experiences during the Khmer Rouge regime. Abney said he looked up and saw several people running away. "They ran through Hun Sen's bodyguards," he said. These were not Rainsy party followers, he deduced. Why did he think that? "I assumed they weren't because they weren't carrying placards."

Rainsy survived, thanks, he said, to his bodyguard, who pushed him to the ground, sacrificing his own life. Immediately after the attack, a policeman lifted Rainsy and cradled him in his arms. Rainsy's blue suit and white shirt were bloodied. The left lens of his glasses was cracked. But Rainsy was uninjured.

The grenades killed 16 people and wounded as many as 150 others— most of the people at the rally. No one could immediately figure out where the grenades had come from. In the hours after the attack, several survivors said they saw a white car driving slowly past on

Sothearos Boulevard. A window opened, and someone tossed three or four grenades into the crowd. Other witnesses spoke of a "burly man" on a motorcycle. Still others described men in vests or flak jackets who stood at the perimeter, threw grenades, and then ran through the line of Hun Sen's bodyguards—perhaps the same people Abney said he had seen.

Ambulances did not arrive for a half hour but then took most of the wounded to Calmette Hospital, which immediately appealed for blood donations. But not enough blood came in time. A thirteen-year-old girl who died from blood loss became the sixteenth casualty. She was just one of several children killed.

Rainsy, bloodied but unharmed, regained his composure quickly and immediately went on the attack. "Hun Sen, the bloody guy," he growled. He "should be arrested and sentenced." Within days his ally, the cominister of interior, asked the U.S. Embassy to bring in the FBI since Abney, an American, had been injured. Under American law the FBI can open investigations in foreign countries if an American is a target of a terrorist attack and is injured or killed. The ministry official's actual request was for an FBI sketch artist to help identify the attacker. But what he did not know was that FBI rules required a sketch artist to be accompanied by at least two special agents. When that became known, the CPP vociferously opposed allowing the FBI in. But, as Rainsy certainly appreciated, that brought America in as a critical player in his latest drama.

Hun Sen denied responsibility. In a radio broadcast later that day, he promised to arrest the attackers but then fell into his normal pugnacious manner, demanding the arrest of the rally's leaders because "they shared responsibility" for the bloodshed. He didn't explain how that could be so.

Hun Sen also ordered the Interior Ministry to prevent Cambodians with dual nationality from leaving the country. His target was clear: Rainsy had a French passport. One of Hun Sen's close aides, Om Yientieng, claimed that it was obvious that Rainsy had ordered the attack on himself. After all, unlike most of the people, he had escaped unharmed.

Newspapers and television stations worldwide covered the grenade attack. FBI special agent Tom Nicoletti happened to see a story about it on CNN. After paddling his canoe off Waikiki Beach and winning his first race with his Hawaiian outrigger team, he was lying on the couch recovering. Even in his late forties he was an active man, not surprising for someone who had been the cornerback on his college football team. He was six foot two and 225 pounds and had spent five years in the United States Marines. Now, in his spare time, he was a kayak and lumberjack-chopping competitor. He was also a nineteen-year veteran of the FBI.

Agents are given one chance in their career to choose a duty station. When Nicoletti's turn came up, he chose Maui, Hawaii, which had a station manned by just one agent. It was perfect. He could paddle almost anytime he wanted. Nicoletti got the job, but after he arrived in Hawaii and the special agent in charge learned of his background—he'd been the SWAT team leader in Washington, supervisor of undercover surveillance, and a member of the International Joint Terror Task Force, among other choice assignments—he was given a different job. He wasn't going to be able to loll around on the beach in Maui. He was put in charge of all the terrorism investigations involving American citizens in Southeast Asia. So much for a relaxing job.

When Nicoletti saw the story about the grenade attack, he realized: Here's work. "I immediately called the Strategic Information-Operations Center at FBI Headquarters," he said. "'There's been a grenade attack on an American citizen in Cambodia.' They hadn't heard about it. It took three or four days to get approval, but then I flew to the region." He needed to speak to the American victim first.

When Abney arrived at Calmette Hospital in Phnom Penh with a grenade fragment in his thigh, he looked around, aghast. "That place, it looked like an old Civil War hospital from the movies." The emergency room had scant equipment, all of it primitive by Western standards. "People were lying everywhere, and some of them were really hurt." A few hours later the IRI flew Abney to a hospital in Singapore. Doctors removed a jagged piece of shrapnel about the size of a grape. He stayed there four days.

On the third day, when he woke up he saw a big man, an American, standing over him. "He looked like John Wayne, even talked like him." The man introduced himself as Tom Nicoletti, a special agent with the Federal Bureau of Investigation. True to type, he told Abney: "We're here to get the guys who did this." He then asked, "Do you think you were a target of opportunity in this attack?"

"Yes," Abney told him, "a target of opportunity, but not the target." They talked for about an hour, and Abney said Nicoletti stood there over his bed the entire time. He gave not even the slightest indication of what he was thinking about the investigation, any theories he might have held about who was behind the attack, Abney said. "Nothing. Nothing at all."

The piece of shrapnel lay in a dish beside Abney's bed, and just before he left, Nicoletti asked if he could take it, as evidence. Yes, Abney said, "but you have to give me a receipt. I want it back." So Nicoletti pulled out one of his business cards and wrote on the back: "4/4/97. Received one small grenade fragment to be analyzed by FBI lab—to be returned to Mr. Abney when investigation completed. T. E. Nicoletti." Abney still has the card. He is still waiting. (Much later, Nicoletti admitted that the FBI office in Honolulu had lost or misplaced it, but he was too embarrassed to tell Abney.)

Nicoletti flew to Bangkok and wanted to move along to Phnom Penh right away. But the bureau wouldn't let him go. Getting clearance from Phnom Penh seemed to take forever.

The CPP was fighting hard to block the request. He also learned later that Ralph Horton, the senior FBI agent responsible for the region (the legal attaché, or legat, in FBI parlance), "had personal issues with Rainsy." He "didn't like him." Two weeks later, the bureau finally let him go. Nicoletti departed for Phnom Penh wondering, "What was I supposed to do? This was a postbomb investigation, and I was sent there seventeen days after the blast." It took ten more days before another agent, Peter Hoffman, and a sketch artist, Myke Taister, joined him in Phnom Penh. The three of them were stepping into a classic Cambodian hall of mirrors.

Almost every foreigner and opposition figure in Cambodia naturally assumed Hun Sen and his political party were behind the attack. For most foreigners Hun Sen remained Cambodia's bogeyman. Western news stories still referred to him as the "former Communist leader." Many policy makers in Washington, in particular, held the view that there was no such thing as a *former* Communist. He was widely hated in Congress and among other policy makers. The IRI, Abney's federally funded employer, held a particular animus for Hun Sen. With the - grenade attack and Abney's injury, that animus blossomed into a positive loathing. For the International Republican Institute and most everyone in Washington who was paying attention, this wanton assault perfectly fit the profile of Hun Sen all of them held in their heads.

The Cambodian People's Party had a history of attacking political opponents, often with hand grenades, and Rainsy had been taunting Hun Sen for months. The government and the municipality had granted Rainsy permits for the rally, even though they had grown into the habit of denying rally permits for opposition parties—as they had for the Buddhist party months earlier. And a phalanx of Hun Sen's personal bodyguards had been standing nearby—to abet the attackers? Otherwise, the regular police presence was unusually light compared to previous Rainsy rallies.

But then, as was so often the case, some other facts did not fit as neatly. In the first days after the attack, most witnesses said the grenades were thrown from a white car, or a man on a motorbike, or the men on foot who ran away. Only over time did the story coalesce into a single version. By the time the FBI agents began asking questions, all of Rainsy's staff and followers were saying it was men on foot who threw the grenades and then ran through the cordon of Hun

Sen's bodyguards standing nearby. Now, the story went, several of the victims, apparently unharmed, managed to get up off the ground and chase the apparent attackers. When these people rushed toward the bodyguards, the unit closed ranks, pulled out their weapons, and would not let them pass.

But then, grenade throwers on foot were not the CPP's signature assailants: two men on a motorbike wearing black helmets with tinted faceplates. And although one Chinese journalist was injured, Abney was the only attendee whose injury could trigger an FBI investigation. He arrived just as the rally was ending when people were leaving. In that case, why had the attackers waited until just then to throw their grenades?

The narrative was becoming complex. As Seth Mydans of the *New York Times* put it in his story the next day, "Although Mr. Hun Sen appears to have been behind previous smaller attacks on opposition politicians and journalists, one Western political analyst cautioned that it was not clear who had ordered today's attack. 'I don't know whose interests are served by this,' said the analyst, who spoke on condition of anonymity. 'It's a murky situation. This would be exactly the kind of thing Hun Sen's advisers have been advising him not to do.'" Even Abney, who was utterly convinced that Hun Sen was responsible, admitted, "I thought he was too smart to do something like that, right in front of the National Assembly building, down the street from the palace."

So if it wasn't Hun Sen, then who could have done it? Ranariddh and Rainsy were now allies of sorts, so Ranariddh would have little motivation to do such a thing. Actually, the person who gained most from the attack was Rainsy himself. Even with the terrible carnage, the attack was a huge political gift, one he would draw on for years to come. He was a victim. And had there ever been more powerful proof of Hun Sen's evil? Demonstrating that fact to the West was Rainsy's single-minded goal. He was obsessed, and this attack made the point better than anything ever before. As Rainsy put it that day, "I think, since the UN election, this is the worst attack."

At the same time, it is hard to see how any politician, anywhere, could be so savage and cruel that he would allow a murderous attack on his own people, killing a score of them, just to make a point against his political opponent—and simultaneously so brave that he was willing to risk his own life to make that point. Both suppositions were hard to accept. As Nicoletti put it, "Rainsy is no General Schwarzkopf. I don't think he is going to stand there while people are throwing grenades near him." So who did it?

Shortly after the FBI team arrived, Rainsy's office gave them typed statements from some of the survivors, describing what they had seen. Nearly all of them spoke of the phalanx of Hun Sen's personal bodyguards in riot gear who, they said, stepped aside so the attackers could pass.

The government set up an inquiry called the Joint Investigation Commission. Nicoletti and the other agents were supposed to be a part of that. But they were learning a lot on their own. Midway through the investigation they realized, as Nicoletti put it later, that the Cambodian investigators were pursuing "deliberate, deceptive and delaying actions" to impede the inquiry. Each political party's police officers were leaking information to their political leaders and sometimes to the news media. The Cambodian authorities were turning up no new information and "seemed reluctant to initiate any investigative efforts that might anger" Hun Sen, Nicoletti said.

So the FBI agents pursued the case on their own, interviewing people in hotel rooms and other private locations. They spoke to dozens and dozens of people, and soon they got a big break. Their sources gave them copies of police photos of the attack. The material did in fact show that "Hun Sen's bodyguard unit had formed a perimeter around the people at the rally," Nicoletti said, and that "a major in the unit made an opening in the line for the people who threw the grenades to go through. The bodyguard unit let people through the lines. Not more than 4 or 5 people. It seemed pre-arranged." Just as many people at the rally had said, when Sam Rainsy's followers had tried to chase the attackers, the bodyguards closed ranks, pulled their weapons, and would not let them through. With this in hand the agents went to see the major they had seen commanding the bodyguard unit in those photos.

They met at police headquarters, and a group of police from the Joint Investigation Commission was there, too, including the major general in charge. Also present were an army major general from Hun Sen's bodyguard unit—and the major Nicoletti and his fellow agent Hoffman had identified in the photos.

Hoffman started the questioning, asking the major, "When the grenade throwers were running toward your position, how many people were chasing them?"

"I have no intention to count how many people were chasing the throwers, and I have no knowledge that those people are the grenade throwers," the major said. (Reporters for *Mother Jones* acquired FBI tapes of this interview.)

"Do you have good eyesight?" Hoffman asked.

"No, no problem with the eyes. The reason is that there are a lot of demonstrators."

"So three or four people throw grenades into a crowd," Hoffman asked, "and you didn't see anything?"

"I see nothing."

Hoffman pushed the major harder: "You were briefed very clearly on who was allowed to come through the line."

"My briefing was that no one was allowed to run through the line."

Hoffman was growing exasperated. "Are these grenade throwers supermen? Can they just click their fingers"—he snapped his own fingers—"and they disappear?"

"I don't know."

Now Hoffman was angry. He pounded the table and declared, "If this country is going to move to freedom and democracy and away from dictatorship and communism, then you have to have people be allowed to speak freely! You have to have that, otherwise a democracy is just pretend."

Then it was Nicoletti's turn. His first few questions, he said, "established the fact that the only person who could order the movement of the bodyguard unit was Hun Sen himself. Hun Sen would pass his order through the unit's commander." That meant Hun Sen had sent the bodyguard unit to Sam Rainsy's rally, armed and ready. Nicoletti towered over the major, and very quickly, "I confronted the major with his placement in the line," he said. "He denied he was there." And then, "I showed him the photograph. He went ballistic"—screaming at Nicoletti.

Immediately, a door to the hall swung open, and a line of Hun Sen's bodyguards stormed into the room—grenades, machine guns, assault rifles clanking at their sides. They lined up behind the major, and he looked up at Nicoletti with an expression of pure, unadulterated hatred and fury. "He was really pissed," as Nicoletti put it.

The interview was over. But as Nicoletti walked toward the door, he shouted at the policemen who were there, members of the government's own Investigation Commission: "So where are your questions?" The government's investigators had stood there, silent, as Hoffman and Nicoletti broke the case. None of them wanted to touch his evidence.

Outside Gen. Huy Piseth, head of Hun Sen's bodyguard unit, was chuckling as he told Nicoletti and Hoffman, "You were very hard on the young major." He was not accustomed to anyone questioning authority. "I wish I had you in my unit."

After that, the investigation moved forward quickly. The agents found that when they were able to speak to Cambodians alone, out of earshot of their colleagues and supervisors, they were much more forthcoming. Cambodians "were very eager to talk to us, and they didn't want to talk to the police or the commission," Nicoletti said. "They didn't trust the police." That gave the agents a huge advantage. As the FBI put it in a report later, the agents "conducted extensive debriefings of eyewitnesses who offered information to the FBI but refused to cooperate with the Cambodian Police or the Investigation Commission. Numerous leads were developed."

After a few weeks Hoffman and Taister returned home, disgusted by what Nicoletti called the "sham of a Cambodian Investigative Commission." But Nicoletti stayed behind, to advise the Cambodian police, in theory, but actually to follow up on some leads.

Rainsy, of course, remained acutely interested in what the agents were doing. On May 22 Nicoletti met with Rainsy and his wife. They asked him what he had found. More specifically, they wanted to know when they would be given a copy of the FBI report. Never, Nicoletti told them. "That's not the way the FBI operates." But it has to be, Rainsy sputtered. He was incredulous. "The people have to know what Hun Sen has done!"

Nicoletti explained that it wasn't so simple. There were still "real questions about the allegations and the motives of the grenade thrower." Actually, by now Nicoletti had a pretty good idea about what had happened. From the leaked photos he thought he was close to identifying the ringleader of the attack, a man well known to be a CPP enforcer. But Nicoletti certainly wasn't going to tell Rainsy that because "I didn't think he was very honest." Whatever Nicoletti told him would likely be all over the Rainsy party newspapers the very next morning. So the agent tried to throw him off the scent.

Sensing that Nicoletti was withholding something, Rainsy erupted and threatened Nicoletti. "You'd better be careful," he told the agent. "You might become a target of violence." The FBI report eventually recounted this conversation and added: "Rainsy also predicted that another violent incident might occur in the near future." Questioned about this years later, Rainsy denied that the conversation with Nicoletti ever took place. "It's ridiculous," he said as he took off his glasses for emphasis and offered a grave expression. "No. This did not happen."

A few days after that meeting, Rainsy and his wife flew to Bangkok, where they held a press conference and handed out their own report on the attack. As the FBI later described the news conference, "he linked the FBI's investigation to a 'Preliminary Report' which Rainsy claimed pointed to Second Prime Minister Hun Sen as the culprit of the March 30, 1997, attack." With this "report," Rainsy attached a raft of papers, said to be English-language transcripts of the agents' interviews with various witnesses. Nicoletti explained later that Rainsy had put "a plant inside the police department" who must have passed transcripts on to him. Some of the translators the FBI used were Rainsy followers.

Even so, somebody had obviously doctored the transcripts. One document purported to quote Nicoletti, without explaining where he had been speaking, when, or to whom. The name of the translator had been blacked out, which was appropriate, given the ludicrous nature of his statement. According to Rainsy's transcript, "Mr. Thomas Nicoletti said: 'Those men who threw the grenades are not ordinary people. They are not students who live in the pagoda with the monks. They are Hun Sen's soldiers. They are probably the worst people in the world. In doing my job here, I don't have any political bias.'" Nicoletti scoffed, "I never said that." But the Thai press picked up the statement anyway.

Ralph Horton, head of the FBI's office in Bangkok, was furious. Didn't this prove his point? He had told Nicoletti that the case "was politicizing the FBI." Could he have asked for better evidence? Horton quickly put out his own statement, saying the bureau had drawn no such conclusions.

A few days later, it appeared that Rainsy was making good on his threat of violence. "I was advised by the police generals from both parties that one or two Khmer hit teams were after me," Nicoletti said. "The day after that, the *Phnom Penh Post* published a photo of me," showing him working at the crime scene, interviewing a witness. "Quinn also advised me that he had independent information that I was targeted."

So Nicoletti flew to Bangkok to discuss the situation with Horton. He'd been in Horton's office just a short while when the phone rang. A marine guard at the front gate said someone was there to see Nicoletti. It turned out to be a messenger from Rainsy who said he needed to talk to the agent. Horton and Nicoletti were appalled. "They'd followed me here," Nicoletti said. For Horton, who had never wanted the FBI to get involved with this case in the first place, "that was the icing on the cake. I couldn't argue with him anymore." Nicoletti left.

With that the FBI investigation effectively ended. Other agents would later return to Phnom Penh to dabble in the case. But it never moved much beyond the state it was in when Nicoletti went home. Some reports since then have said Nicoletti had been close to filing for a possible indictment, but he insisted that while the evidence was strong, "the investigative results were not up to United States standards. If I had been able to spend another two or three weeks there, a lot more would have been accomplished." As it was, for years to come Rainsy would continue insisting that Hun Sen was guilty, while Hun Sen could plausibly dismiss the charge because no firm evidence had ever come out to prove it. Wasn't that the Cambodian way?

---

While politicians battled in Phnom Penh, the Khmer Rouge leaders luxuriated in the wealth they were still accruing from lumber and gems. A good portion of western Cambodia remained under their full control. Their troops still harassed and killed at will.

Hun Sen recognized that he could not defeat the Khmer Rouge. The Vietnamese army had tried for ten years and failed. Skirmishes with Khmer Rouge troops generally ended as inconclusive standoffs. The two sides were locked in a stalemate. What's more, though the Royal Cambodian Armed Forces were supposed to have 148,000 soldiers and staff, Hun Sen had discovered that almost 10 percent of them didn't exist. His Ministry of Defense realized that military commanders had put 13,000 "ghost" soldiers on the payroll so that they could collect and pocket their salaries, just as Lon Nol's soldiers had done in the early 1970s. But now, twenty-five years later, the commanders had invented a new trick: These ghost soldiers had given birth to 15,244 ghost children—all of whom entitled their "fathers" to add child allowances to their pay. "I know there are some high officials including officials at the Ministry of Defense who have made deals with their lower commanders to hide the ghost soldiers in order to put cash in their pockets," Hun Sen said. He offered them amnesty if they came forward.

When Hun Sen realized he couldn't defeat the Khmer Rouge, he offered them amnesty, too. In mid-1996, small squads of Khmer Rouge soldiers began leaving the forest and defecting. Hun Sen let them keep their land. Then in August 1996, Ieng Sary, who with Pol Pot had founded the movement and served as Democratic Kampuchea's foreign minister, announced that he and some of his allies were turning coat.

Hun Sen arranged an elaborate welcoming ceremony for them in Pailin, their "capital." He allowed Ieng Sary to continue living there as a private citizen—with full control of the gem mines and timber rights that continued to enrich him. From that moment the Khmer Rouge movement began a slow and steady march toward its demise—but not before playing an important part in one more act of Cambodia's ongoing political drama.

In the spring of 1996 Sam Rainsy, Norodom Ranariddh, and Khieu Samphan, who had been the Khmer Rouge president, met secretly in Paris—to plot strategy. No record of that meeting exists, but Quinn hypothesized, "Perhaps they were looking to do some things to shake things up." All of these characters mistrusted each other. Each had tried to stab the others in the back at one point or another in the recent past. But they held a common passion. All of them held a virulent hatred of Hun Sen. The fruits of this meeting became visible the next year.

The day after Rainsy's contentious meeting with Nicoletti in May 1997, when the agent refused to give him the report and Rainsy warned him that he was in danger, suddenly the Khmer Rouge got interested in the grenade-attack investigation. Khmer Rouge leaders devoted their daily radio broadcast to a vicious diatribe against Nicoletti and the FBI, saying the bureau was a tool of the Hun Sen government. The speaker threatened reprisals. Never before had the Khmer Rouge shown interest in the grenade-attack investigation. Why now? Was this a part of Rainsy's threat?

All the while Phnom Penh was growing increasingly tense. By the spring of 1997 gun battles on the streets were becoming commonplace. Senior government officials from both the CPP and Funcinpec built sandbag bunkers around their houses; guards stood behind them, their automatic-rifle muzzles pointed toward the street.

Both Hun Sen and Ranariddh had personal bodyguard forces that now numbered in the thousands. Not infrequently the two sides exchanged fire. Some soldiers and bodyguards were routinely killed. Just outside Phnom Penh both sides reinforced encampments for large numbers of their personal militia members. "The place was stirred up," Quinn said, and he made a practice of driving around the city in the evening to "look at the guards outside the houses. Were they slumped down, smoking a cigarette, or maybe asleep?" If so, Quinn knew he could relax for the night. "Or did they have their helmets on, standing behind the sandbag with weapons out?"

It was obvious: A war was about to begin. Diplomats from Europe, Asia, and elsewhere began arriving to talk to Hun Sen and Ranariddh. Don't do it, they would say. Call it off. But no one was listening.

The embassy looked at all the intelligence and made an estimate of when the fighting would start. They placed the date on or about July 1. But then, out of the blue, Washington told Quinn that Secretary of State Madeleine Albright wanted to stop by for a visit at the end of June, as part of a larger visit to the region. The country was tumbling toward violence, but "she wanted to talk about a success story, and see Angkor Wat," Quinn said.

Albright was an inveterate tourist. Whenever she could she would visit countries that also gave her an opportunity to see major attractions. Of course, she did plan to meet with Hun Sen and Ranariddh, as other visiting diplomats had, and warn them not to squander the advances Cambodia had made, thanks to the UN occupation and the

$3 billion the world had invested in the state. So she was planning a two-day visit, one day in Phnom Penh for business and the second day at Angkor Wat.

Quinn had been sending regular cables telling the department about the deteriorating situation. But he had no way to know who actually read them. A few days earlier three influential senators—John F. Kerry, Democrat of Massachusetts; William Roth, Republican of Delaware; and Bill Frist, Republican of Tennessee—had written Albright a letter, saying that despite receiving almost $3.5 billion in international aid in recent years, Cambodia "has become the single fastest-growing narcotics transshipment point in the world; scores of journalists, human-rights workers and political activists have been killed in political violence; the government has failed to establish critical constitutional bodies or pass some of the country's most basic laws; and corruption has infested and overrun almost every government institution." Was this really the nation that everyone had spent $3 billion to create?

But these concerns fell on deaf ears. Albright was coming to celebrate a new democracy—though, in Washington, she also said, "I will make very clear that it is important for them to proceed down the democratic path." But Quinn could see that major violence was now inevitable. He told the State Department she shouldn't come. "People will set out to embarrass her," he wrote. "There will be violence. That will make her look weak." He feared that a bombing, grenade attack, or some other violent act by someone trying to embarrass the government would force her to flee. He was looking out for his secretary, but the department "reacted badly," Quinn said. The tenor was, "What's wrong with the ambassador? He isn't on the team. She's already announced she is coming."

In mid-June 1997 real fighting broke out between the two bodyguard units in Phnom Penh. Both sides fired assault rifles at each other and tossed grenades. Explosions rattled the city. Thousands of residents locked their doors, closed their shutters, and huddled together, trembling. One rocket landed in the yard just beside Quinn's house. It happened to be Quinn's birthday. "My family had arrived" for the celebration, he said. "They stayed in the States while I was there because there was no high school for my kids in Phnom Penh. We were watching a video, *The Thin Man*, when we heard a click. I asked, 'Did you hear that?' Then a big boom. We threw the kids on the floor. My wife and I lay on top of them." No one was hurt, and damage was minimal. But he called the State Department Operations Center to advise them of what had just happened.

Quinn was vindicated. The next day the department announced a change in plans. Yes, Phnom Penh was a dangerous place. Perhaps Ranariddh and Hun Sen could come out to meet Secretary Albright at the airport and have their talk. Then she could fly on to Angkor.

Needless to say, Ranariddh and Hun Sen were not talking to each other. They spoke with their guns. But they did manage to agree on one thing: There was no way two heads of state were going to drive out to the airport to meet with a *foreign minister*—even the American secretary of state. What were they, her supplicants? Ranariddh was a prince, heir to the throne, and the head of state. Hun Sen had been the nation's undisputed ruler for a decade—and obviously planned to assume that status again, very soon. If she wanted to see them, she would have to drive into town, come to their offices. No, they told her. We won't do it. Ranariddh showed considerable tact when he explained the decision. "She wanted us to come to the airport," he told reporters, "but Hun Sen and I agreed that if we just met her at the airport, we would be breaking the principles of protocol." But then he couldn't seem to help himself and added, "It's insulting."

Using the missile assault on Quinn's house as the pretext, the department canceled Albright's stop in Cambodia. She'd have to visit Angkor some other time. Nevertheless, the debate over her visit threw off the American Embassy's carefully calculated time line. Rather than starting on July 1, as expected, the violence would begin five days late.

The denouement was still days away, but angry argument dominated the weeks leading up to it. During his meeting in Paris the year before, Ranariddh had probably talked to Khieu Samphan about contributing Khmer Rouge troops to the battle. Hun Sen's personal forces were indisputably larger and better armed than Ranariddh's, and he was afraid that Hun Sen's warm welcome to Ieng Sary when he had defected meant that Ieng Sary's 2,000 troops might fight on Hun Sen's side. Without help from the Khmer Rouge, Ranariddh would be outmatched.

In late May, Hun Sen caught Ranariddh trying to import three tons of weapons and ammunition through the port at Sihanoukville. The shipping manifest, addressed to Ranariddh, described the ship's contents as "spare parts." When Hun Sen called him on it, Ranariddh insisted he had every right to import weapons for his forces; Hun Sen was certainly importing weaponry of his own. Hun Sen then accused Ranariddh of making alliances with the Khmer Rouge. Ranariddh threw the same accusation back at Hun Sen.

The U.S. Embassy held its Fourth of July party as usual. This was a glittering event, and normally everyone who was anyone in Phnom Penh wanted to be on the guest list. This year, though, almost no one from the government showed up. That was quite unusual. But then, clues surfaced. In early July, a diplomat said, a foreign intelligence service working in Phnom Penh began picking up information from Funcinpec officials about something they were calling Operation Crossbow. And on the morning of July 5 the service picked up word that a Funcinpec soldier was asking Nhiek Bun Chhay, the Funcinpec secretary-general, whether Operation Crossbow was on. Yes, he said, it is.

The fighting started on the outskirts of town, where Funcinpec's military was encamped, but then moved into Phnom Penh. Ranariddh's forces drove tanks and armored personnel carriers (APCs) into the city; gun- and rocket fire echoed across town. Trying to sort out who had instigated the violence, diplomats noted that Sok An, Hun Sen's powerful deputy, was trapped in his house, unable to escape. Ranariddh, on the other hand, had already flown to Paris. Asked why he was there, he explained that his military commanders had told him it was not safe to stay. It would later be revealed that he had bought the ticket weeks earlier.

Not until late that evening did columns of armor—tanks and APCs—begin approaching the capital from the South, where Hun Sen maintained his country estate and military compound. A few of his tanks, scrambled in a rush, ran out of gas on the way. But by the second day, July 6, 1997, Hun Sen had brought all of his forces into a fierce battle.

At the U.S. Embassy, "our building was shaking," Quinn said. "We began burning all the files. There were tanks in the streets. We took out our own weapons. We were ready to destroy the communications equipment, the codes."

But by the end of the second day, the fighting was all but over. Hun Sen had prevailed. Funcinpec forces were on the run. Hun Sen's soldiers captured and summarily executed dozens of Funcinpec officers. Funcinpec secretary-general Nhiek Bun Chhay said Hun Sen's forces captured five of his bodyguards, gouged out their eyes, and then killed them. He also accused Hun Sen's forces of executing thirty of his soldiers after they had surrendered and then burning their bodies.

Hun Sen's soldiers looted shops and businesses downtown while Funcinpec soldiers and officers began calling the U.S. Embassy, asking for refuge. Quinn now said he told his staff: If anyone comes to the embassy, let them in. Human-rights officials and others have long insisted, however, that the embassy actually turned these people away. But whatever happened at the embassy, Quinn did rent the ballroom of the Cambodiana Hotel and began sending people who needed refuge over there.

By day three, the city was quiet. The war was over.

Prince Ranariddh, mortally offended by his treatment by Hun Sen, had thought he could topple this peasant, this Communist, from power. He wanted to take his rightful place as Cambodia's undisputed leader. It turned out, however, that the Khmer Rouge had not come to fight for either side. Hun Sen's forces, despite Ranariddh's surprise initial attack, came to the battle with more troops and superior intelligence. They turned the battle around and defeated Ranariddh's troops.

Even with Hun Sen's long record of violent, perfidious behavior, Ranariddh was unquestionably the aggressor. But in Washington that same afternoon, the State Department spokesman, Nicholas Burns, read a statement condemning Hun Sen, saying the United States strongly opposed "the use of force to change the results of the 1993 election and the use of force by the forces of Hun Sen to effectively rupture the Paris accords of 1991."

Soon after, Washington announced it would end all foreign aid to Cambodia. "They never asked me," Quinn said, shaking his head. "On day three, when the fighting was all over, Washington ordered the evacuation of all Americans and nonessential embassy personnel. They never asked me about that either. I had to send my family away. I felt terrible. It didn't feel like we were respected, like we were being paid attention to." But then, Quinn knew full well that most everyone in Washington hated Hun Sen. He'd seen hints that Ranariddh was planning something, "and I'd sent bits and pieces of that in cables. But some people in Washington didn't necessarily want to believe that."

In Washington the issues were black-and-white. Hun Sen was the villain. Ranariddh and Rainsy were the heroes. But since he arrived in Phnom Penh, Quinn had been building a close working relationship with Hun Sen. He was the man in power. Wasn't that how an ambassador could be most effective? They held frequent meetings and had dinner at each other's homes. Quinn had even stood next to him when Hun Sen received an honorary degree from Iowa Wesleyan University, at a ceremony in Phnom Penh—bringing catcalls from across the city. What Quinn didn't bargain on was the disrespect, even hatred, this strategy would bring him, from human-rights officials, members of Congress—even some in his own department. To them, Quinn was a quisling.

This may explain why State Department officials paid so little mind to his cables suggesting that Ranariddh had started the battle.

"He was *boastful* of his relations with Hun Sen," Abney said, his voice laced with scorn. At a congressional hearing a few days after the fighting ended, Representative Dana Rohrabacher, Republican of California, demanded that "Ken Quinn, our ambassador in Phnom Penh, be immediately recalled from Cambodia to appear before this committee and to answer questions before this committee and to the American people about why there has been a less than forceful opposition to these horrible events we're witnessing in Cambodia."

Eni F. H. Faleomavaega, who represented American Samoa, echoed Rohrabacher's suspicions and went so far as to imply that Quinn might even have helped Hun Sen set off the attack. Rohrabacher's statement "seems to collaborate some of the things that I have heard also through the rumor mill about the activities of our ambassador there. Has he been participating in the process, or is he staying on neutral grounds, or is he trying to do something that is not in conformance with our policies towards Cambodia?"

When Abney testified, he piled on as well. The American Embassy "has continually refused to criticize Hun Sen and, in fact, has a relationship with him which frightens the outspoken critics of his strong-arm government."

A State Department official testified that the government had full confidence in Quinn. Still, most every member of Congress, every diplomat, every journalist and commentator, had settled on Hun Sen as the villain. After years of vilifying him, from the days he ruled Cambodia as a puppet of Hanoi and a "Communist stooge," this stance felt natural, even comfortable, for its certainty. Hun Sen had engineered a "coup" to depose Ranariddh, the senior prime minister. As that conviction took hold, the dislike of the man among most everyone who followed Cambodia thickened to detestation.

Hun Sen was now responsible for the conclusion most everyone now drew: The grandest nation-building operation the world body had ever undertaken had collapsed. Democracy was dead. Hun Sen had squandered the $3 billion gift to the long-suffering Cambodian people. "The four-year-old experiment with democracy is in dire straits, and a tyrant has seized power through the force of arms, intimidation, terror, and summary executions," said Representative Doug Bereuter, chairman of the House Subcommittee on Asia and the Pacific. "This is altogether too familiar ground for the Cambodian people. Few people have experienced as much pain, suffering and terror as the people of Cambodia over the last 30 years."

Benny Widyono, who had just completed his term as the UN's special representative in Cambodia, was one of just a few public officials to lay blame on another offending party. The United Nations "left the four parties intact and armed to the teeth," he told the *Washington Post.* Funding for the UN operation had been so drastically cut that "we gambled on the election," as if "that was the main thing in the agreement. We should have stayed longer in the post-conflict rebuilding process."

Brad Adams, a senior UN official in Cambodia, told a congressional committee, "It seems fair to ask why the international community would negotiate a peace treaty with strong provisions regarding human rights and democracy and then mount the largest, most expensive peacekeeping operation ever—involving 20,000 soldiers and an army of election and human rights monitors, all at a cost of over $2 billion—and then lose interest."

But Kofi Annan, the secretary-general, seemed to be living in a dream world. He continued to boast of the UN's great achievement, even a few days after the fighting ended. "The UN operation was successful in helping establish national institutions which could lead to stability and economic development," he averred.

Quinn was the most disappointed of all. In 1974 he had delivered the world's first warning about the coming Khmer Rouge horror. He had written his dissertation on the Khmer Rouge. As a deputy assistant secretary of state, he been an important player in the work to set up the UN occupation and election—the world's effort to redeem the state and its people. And he had arrived as ambassador "with an idealized view, that if they could find a way for everybody to live together and share, there can be a better life for everyone."

Naive, perhaps, but now, he said, "The international community paid a ton of money to help them restore their country, but then they put in place another game. All of them were trying to reshuffle the deck and climb back on top, push the others out of the way." Quinn had come to understand that "Cambodians are capable of doing awful, destructive things to their own country for their own gain. You come away so dispirited by their efforts to manipulate you as part of their effort to destabilize the country for their own benefit. Now all the things we had worked for, all of this lay shattered, pieces on the floor. Like Humpty Dumpty. All the promise, it fell apart. It was over."

In Washington, some people were so angry that, through gritted teeth, they began calling for regime change.

# CHAPTER SEVEN

For a people still reeling from the trauma of war, the continuing violence in the 1990s nourished the debilitating mental illnesses that still plagued so many Cambodians. During the street battles for control of the government, tens of thousands of people huddled in their homes, quivering, hearts racing.

Even when there was no actual fighting, all too often visitors found residents of villages nationwide terrified to venture beyond their town's perimeter, afraid a Khmer Rouge soldier might be behind any tree. At the same time, across the nation Cambodians routinely unearthed mass graves by accident. Each held dozens, or hundreds, of skeletal remains from Khmer Rouge execution grounds. Most often villagers piled the remains in barns or outbuildings the Khmer Rouge had once used. Even now, decades later, villagers say the skulls speak to them.

Seth Mydans of the *New York Times* visited one of these villages in May 1996 and observed a haunted landscape:

> When the air grows still and heavy here in this pretty village far from
> any paved road, people say they sometimes hear the sun-bleached

skulls of Cambodia's holocaust, piled nearby in the ruins of a school-house, talking to one another. "Sometimes we hear them crying," said Sim Than, a farmer. "You can hear the voices of women and children and men, just as if they were alive."

People say they still hear the faint ring of a lunch bell, as they did more than 17 years ago when the schoolhouse served as a prison and sometimes as a torture chamber. The worst, they say, is when they hear again the moans that came to them from a thick stand of bamboo where prisoners were clubbed to death in the back of the neck. When the people here walk their cows past the schoolhouse to graze, or when their children wander through, picking small yellow berries, they sometimes stoop to replace the skulls that the cows have knocked from among the many hundreds that are piled here.

Across Cambodia, at hundreds of former killing fields like this one, scattered bones and bits of clothing lie unburied and largely ignored. And in thousands of villages like this one, men and women who worked for the Khmer Rouge have returned to their formerly quiet lives, farming their fields and raising their children side by side with the families of people they abused and killed. Those anonymous bones and unpunished victimizers are part of the fabric of Cambodia today.

Most of the nation's Khmer Rouge survivors suffered from post-traumatic stress disorder, but through the 1990s no one in Cambodia recognized this or offered any treatment. No one paid any attention at all, allowing the illness to fester and, in some cases, worsen. For someone suffering from PTSD, most anything out of the ordinary could set off a heart-wrenching panic. For older people with heart trouble, these panics could trigger a heart attack.

One day in the late 1990s technicians set off a planned explosion at the edge of Phnom Penh. "Some old mines were being detonated by the Cambodian Mine Action Center to get rid of them," Quinn remembered. "This set off a major panic downtown because people heard the noise and thought it was 1975 again and that the city was about to be retaken by the Khmer Rouge. Markets closed, schools emptied, and people raced to find their families and get home to safety."

Devon Hinton, M.D., a psychiatrist and anthropologist at Harvard Medical School, studied this phenomenon for many years, primarily among Cambodian refugees in Lowell, Massachusetts. More than half of the Khmer Rouge survivors there had PTSD. As he saw it, this illness was just the tip of an iceberg sitting atop a distressingly diverse array of pernicious physical and mental illnesses—one complication that led to another and triggered another and then set off another still. Most of them suffered from one of several physical ailments that resulted from protracted trauma, including blurry vision, headaches, heart palpitations, constant buzzing in the ears, shortness of breath, and a painful neck and shoulders—mimicking the pain of carrying heavy buckets of dirt on a pole resting on the shoulder while working for the Khmer Rouge.

More than half of these survivors frequently experienced intense, sometimes violent, angry outbursts against members of their own families. Normal household disputes triggered these incidents, including something as simple as children who they perceived had acted disrespectfully. The victim might scream at his child, throw things, or strike him, while at the same time he experienced heart palpitations, shortness of breath, dizziness, and chest pain characteristic of a panic attack. At the very same time, he might also experience flashbacks of the events that precipitated the mental illness. Typically, the victim would recall working as a slave for the Khmer Rouge while starving, being tortured, or "forced to stand with biting ants crawling over the body," Hinton wrote in a study published in 2009.

These symptoms played directly into Cambodian spirituality. Across Southeast Asia people believe that spirits inhabit most objects and people. The little templelike shrines you see on stands in the yards near businesses or homes have nothing directly to do with Buddhism. In these shrines people leave food and other offerings for the spirits. Cambodians believe the spirits within them are particularly powerful. Anger sets them off, and they begin to cause mayhem within the body—boiling blood that rises in the body, eventually reaching the brain. That superstitious fear, by itself, is terrifying. Coupled with debilitating PTSD, it is even worse.

For these people there was no relief even when they went to sleep. Many Cambodians also suffered from sleep paralysis and an associated disorder known as "ghost sitting." Sixty percent of the men and women Hinton studied who had PTSD suffered from these two afflictions. "Clinical experience suggests that sleep paralysis occurs at a very high rate in the Cambodian population," he wrote in another published study. During sleep paralysis, "Cambodians frequently hallucinate certain supernatural beings," including "a ghost sent by a sorcerer to kill the victim by putting objects into the body, a demon that wants to scare the soul from the body—or the ghost of someone who was killed during the Pol Pot period." Others might hallucinate "near drowning experiences" or "having a plastic bag placed over the head," both common Khmer Rouge torture or execution techniques. These events seem to occur during a state halfway between sleep and wakefulness. They could last for roughly five to thirty minutes, and through all of it the victim feels paralyzed; he cannot move or speak. Cambodians call this "the ghost pushing you down."

One victim profiled in Hinton's study, a forty-one-year-old woman, said she repeatedly saw "the black shape of a man clutching a knife and walking toward her. With one hand he pointed the raised knife at her; with the other he grabbed her shirt front." Another victim, a forty-eight-year-old woman, "initially became conscious of her inability to move. Next she saw three ghastly demons, creatures with fur and long fangs, approach her. One of the ogres came close to her head." Another "held down her legs; yet another held her arms." Then, "ogres tried to scare her to death." Usually someone would hear her frightened murmuring and shake her fully awake. The woman, identified only as Chea, said she could not sleep the rest of the night. Instead, horrid images from the Khmer Rouge era came flooding back into her mind, including one when she saw soldiers leading three of her friends from her village, blindfolded, behind a stand of trees twenty yards away. "A minute later, Chea heard the sickening sound of a skull being cracked with a club."

Victims of sleep paralysis, ghost sitting, and related trauma wake up terrified, exhausted, and subject to panic attacks throughout the day. Some grow so anxious that they become dizzy, afraid they might fall down. Not surprisingly, they suffer chronic insomnia. They are afraid to go to sleep, which only exacerbates the problems.

Daryn Reicherter, M.D., a psychiatrist at Stanford University, discovered identical sleep paralysis and ghost-sitting symptoms among a different Cambodian refugee population, in San Jose, California. He also encountered the phenomenon of hysterical blindness. "The Khmer Rouge generally spared blind people," he noted. "So people used that as a coping strategy. They pretended to be blind." Now, "many of the Khmer Rouge victims' coping strategies today are maladaptive," or inappropriate. Some of his patients seem to go blind "when they are stressed." He imitated a patient in his office bumping around with his arms stretched out. "You can't really tell if it is fake or real. For him it might be real. It comes and goes, and it lingers to this day. I have seen some of this in Cambodia, too," Reicherter added. "It's at least the same there and probably worse."

These deeply troubled refugees in Massachusetts and California are largely dysfunctional. Numerous studies have shown that they can't hold jobs. In one study, in Massachusetts, 90 percent of the PTSD patients were unemployed. Decades after moving to the United States these people still spoke no English. They lived tormented lives on government assistance.

A study published in the *Journal of the American Medical Association* in 1995 looked at Cambodian refugees in Long Beach, California, who came to the United States in the early 1980s, just after the Khmer Rouge years. More than half suffered serious, debilitating depression. Two-thirds had PTSD. More than three-quarters of the adults had no education. Most were unemployed, desperately poor, and prone to irrational violence. More than one-quarter were disabled. They lived in slums and were emotionally incapable of interacting with others. In

San Jose, too, "they are still monolingual, illiterate, unacculturated, drunk," Reicherter said. "Most of these people cannot work. They are on disability still. They all have major depressive disorders."

Millions of Cambodians suffered from these and similar symptoms and disabilities resulting from the trauma they experienced decades earlier. The few studies conducted in the country confirmed that fact. Muny Sothara, a psychiatrist in Phnom Penh, described "a household provincial survey in Kampong Cham in 2004 that showed PTSD or symptoms of other psychotic disorders in 47 percent of the population."

Left untreated, these people passed their illness on to their children. Nigel Field, a professor at the Pacific Graduate School of Psychology in Northern California, is an expert on what he calls second-generation effects. He studied two hundred children in a Phnom Penh high school and found that the more they knew about their parents' traumatic experiences, the worse off they were. "Children, seeking approval, parrot their parents' aberrant behavior," Fields said. "There's also a tendency for children to become 'parents' for their parents, to try to help quell their parents' anxieties. These children tend to see danger when there is no danger," just like their parents. When asked to list the events they knew their parents were exposed to—starvation, torture, near death— "some of them get angry when they talk about it, showing the role reversal. They have higher anxiety, depression. These stresses take a toll on their lives."

Muny Sothara, the Cambodian psychiatrist, suggested that parents unwittingly teach PTSD to their children. They do this by "educating the child, warning about dangers. Saying 'don't participate; don't get involved. Be quiet.'" As Reicherter put it, "What we have learned is that if you have a traumatic childhood, you are more likely to get PTSD. So we have children who are growing up with violent parents who are drunk and beat them. That's the generation that's coming."

That new generation has already arrived. In about 2004 Cambodian officials estimated that one-quarter of the nation's men frequently beat their wives and children  one of the highest rates in the world. By the end of the decade, as more of the Khmer Rouge victims' children married and had children of their own, the rate had actually increased, to about one-third of the nation's families.

Hinton and Reicherter both reported that therapy helped some Cambodian refugees. But in the 1990s Cambodian psychiatry was not yet even in its infancy. The state had perhaps four or five psychiatrists nationwide. All of them worked for hospitals, dispensing outdated medications. Reicherter said he visited one village where "we saw one man, a schizophrenic apparently, with a dog collar, tied to a tree—how psychiatry was practiced a millennium ago. We gave him a shot. One shot. And they were able to let him go."

Members of the government didn't seem to care, even though many senior officials had the same symptoms. "Mental health is the last priority here," said Michael O'Leary, head of the World Health Organization office in Phnom Penh. "The ability to provide support is really quite limited."

Khieu Kanharith, the information minister, said he suffered a recurring nightmare, a hallmark of PTSD: "I go back to my home and most of my family is on the ground, on their knees," as they would be just before execution by the Khmer Rouge. Since 1979, "I actually have been back home only once, and it's in a village just up the road. I wrote on the wall of my house: I am alive! But it's too stressful to be there. I haven't been back. PTSD, everyone has it." The continuing war with the Khmer Rouge only amplified the people's pain.

At the same time, even months after the "coup" in 1997, the CPP and Funcinpec fought sporadic battles across the country—utterly heedless of anything but advancing their own positions. The people they were supposed to serve suffered the tortures of the damned. Terrified, tens of thousands of them fled to Thailand once again, just as they had in 1979.

Nothing could have seemed more discordant to the mood of the state, but Cambodia was supposed to hold national elections in July 1998, just a year after the battles between Ranariddh and Hun Sen.

Ranariddh was in exile, and Hun Sen promised to put him on trial for something close to treason if he ever dared to return. Ung Huot, an ineffectual Funcinpec placeholder, had been installed in Ranariddh's office to carry the party forward until the elections. But how could you have an election with only one major party running for office? Funcinpec had won the last election. But it was the "royalist" party, and without Prince Ranariddh, it stood not a chance.

Sure, in Iraq, Egypt, Yemen, and countless other authoritarian states the leaders staged one-party elections. But Cambodia was different. It was just four years out from the UN occupation and the national elections. The aid groups had settled into a routine of giving the government about $500 million a year, more than half of the government's budget. Hun Sen couldn't risk losing all of that largesse and what little was left of the world's goodwill.

In Washington, already, denunciations were flying fast and thick. Brad Adams, the UN official, told a receptive congressional committee, "Funcinpec, a royalist party, now has no members of the royal family in its leadership, rendering the party politically meaningless. Hun Sen has staked out a clear strategy: create the appearance of a constitutional, multi-party government and political system, such as by placing a malleable figure such as Ung Huot in the position of first prime minister, hold elections next year without any semblance of a real opposition, exercise control over all levers of government, dominate the electronic media and wait for the international community to hold its nose and declare the elections minimally free and fair."

In the end, the Japanese brokered a deal. Japan was eager for influence in Southeast Asia to counter China's growing clout and stepped in to help break this impasse. Ranariddh had asked his father, King Sihanouk, to pardon him. But Sihanouk refused—unless Ranariddh apologized. Sihanouk, at least, knew who had started the violence. And now father and son were not getting along too well.

Ranariddh refused to apologize, saying he was not willing to admit guilt—even though he knew he was, in fact, guilty. (In truth, though, both sides had been brewing for a fight. If Ranariddh hadn't started it, sooner or later Hun Sen probably would have.) That led to even more complex maneuvering.

Under the Japanese plan Hun Sen's courts put on a show trial and convicted Ranariddh of smuggling arms and conspiring with Khmer Rouge guerrillas to launch a coup. The court sentenced Ranariddh in absentia to thirty-five years in prison and fined him $54 million for damages to businesses that resulted from the fighting—and from the looting afterward, even though it was actually done by Hun Sen's troops. Once the verdict was in, Sihanouk pardoned his son, and Ranariddh came back in 1998. He commenced running for office again, as if nothing had ever occurred.

Tidy as this plan was, Ranariddh's image among Cambodians was now something less than pure and clean. This time around he also had a serious competitor in Sam Rainsy. The parliament had finally enacted a political-party law, and in a bold display of his own view of himself, Rainsy was now head of the Sam Rainsy Party.

All of these factors, by several accounts, made Hun Sen quite nervous. He'd lost the last election, and now he had two formidable opponents. He was not sure he could win. What to do? He fell back on his traditional strategies of intimidation. Soon, assailants began threatening, torturing, and killing Funcinpec officers, just as had happened before the last election. More than a dozen people died in the violence.

Perhaps the worst example was Thong Sophal, a Funcinpec official found in Kandal Province a month before the vote. His head and face were smashed beyond recognition; his eyes were gouged out, his ears cut away, his fingers chopped off. His legs, from his upper thigh to his feet, were stripped of all flesh and muscle so that only skeletal limbs remained. A grisly photo of this man appeared in the *Phnom Penh Post*, and a local police official called the death a suicide. Was that not an effective warning to all who dared defy the ruling party?

No one has ever proved that Hun Sen either ordered or sanctioned this attack, or any like it. But then Hun Sen liked to point out that he was all-powerful. He controlled everything. If he disapproved of these tactics, he could have stopped the murders and assaults. But he never even spoke out against them—except, oftentimes, to blame the victim for the crime. With all of that, Hun Sen left no doubt in anyone's mind that he was in fact responsible, and those who know him say he reveled in that.

The murders carried a clear message: *Stand up to me, and look what will happen to you. I'll gouge out your eyes, cut off your fingers, and then skin your legs before I kill you.* Hun Sen had learned this from years of serving the Khmer Rouge and a decade of serving Vietnam. As Paul Grove, a Cambodia specialist at the IRI, put it in his testimony to Congress, "The Chinese have a saying which may best describe the rationale behind these killings: Kill a chicken to teach the monkeys."

Although electoral observers complained of voter intimidation—the CPP controlled the village chief in every town across the nation—and vote buying, the overall violence was not as frequent or severe as in 1993. And while human-rights advocates screamed, Hun Sen actually found the beginnings of a valid political strategy that seemed to work for him. *I brought you stability,* he would say. *I have been fighting the Khmer Rouge for you. They are on their last legs now.* That tactic played well with the nation's emotionally wounded population. Stability was more important than anything else. Cambodians most of all wanted peace and quiet, qualities of life they had not seen since the late 1960s. They wanted to be left alone.

Diplomats complained that the deck was already stacked. More than 80 percent of the people lived in the countryside. In 1998 most of them did not have television or radio. Newspapers did not circulate outside the cities, and most of the rural residents could not read. What news of the campaign they were able to hear usually came from their village chiefs, every one of them a CPP stalwart.

What's more, Hun Sen controlled all of the government institutions set up to ensure free elections, the National Election Committee, the Constitution Council, and others. When Grove, the IRI Cambodia specialist, visited the election commission close to election day to see what it was doing to achieve free and fair elections, all that the commission's functionaries were interested in talking about was the challenge of installing "electric service in the commission's office," he told Congress. The Constitution Council, whose mission was to resolve election disputes, had never even been established.

Still, once again Cambodians embraced the election. More than 90 percent of the people voted, and foreign election observers judged election day to be both fair and free—showing that Hun Sen had learned how to put on the appearance of a clean election. It didn't matter how much bribery and murder occurred before election day. If the vote itself was judged to be clean, election observers would certify the vote—with at most a note suggesting problems during the campaign period.

After the 1998 election, international observers dubbed the vote "a miracle on the Mekong." Yet in later years the International Republican Institute, for one, refused even to participate. "Cambodia is not really worth observing," said Lorne Craner, the IRI's president. "The outcome is a foregone conclusion."

Ambassadors and other diplomats noted a little less violence, not quite so much vote buying, and usually remarked, "This is the best election so far." Hun Sen would feast on that, while opposition leaders despaired. Speaking of the United States, Mu Sochua, an opposition parliamentarian, was despondent. "You keep saying 'progress has been made.' Yes, but I have only one lifetime. I don't have 30 lives." In Phnom Penh, "praise from Washington goes a long way."

The results in 1998 were a virtual mirror of the voting in 1993, though the parties opposing Hun Sen split their vote this time. Hun Sen won the most votes, 41.4 percent. His party crowed about that. Funcinpec won 32.2 percent and Sam Rainsy 14.4 percent, most of that from the more educated, urban population. Hun Sen was declared the winner, as Ranariddh had been last time. But by adding Ranariddh's and Rainsy's votes, together they held the plurality, almost 46 percent to 41 percent. The opposition could control the government—if only they could form a coalition. The trouble was, Rainsy and Ranariddh despised each other. Rainsy considered Ranariddh a scoundrel in a royal cloak. Ranariddh saw Rainsy as a self-righteous hypocrite. So rather than talk about join-ing forces, they both used what was becoming the standard strategy for losing candidates: Declare the election rigged and fraudulent.

As it was, the National Election Committee, after finally figuring out how to turn on the lights, concocted a vote-allocation formula that awarded 53 percent of the seats in parliament to the CPP, even though the party had won only 41 percent of the vote. Still, two-thirds of the voting members were needed to form a coalition government.

Hun Sen planned to amend the constitution so that only a simple majority was required, now that he nearly had one. When King Si-hanouk warned him not to do it, however, he backed off—for the moment.

Meantime, a parade of foreign political leaders arrived in Phnom Penh, all of them determined to convince Rainsy and Ranariddh to join forces to push Hun Sen out of office. Steve Solarz, now a former member of Congress, "spent an hour in Ranariddh's house," Quinn said. "He begged him to join forces with Rainsy." Solarz said, "I tried my best, but they both refused."

In Washington the Senate Foreign Relations Committee called Stanley Roth, the new assistant secretary of state, to testify about the political deadlock. Consistent with the prevailing attitude in the capi-tal, he said, "Some six out of ten voters chose a party other than the ruling Cambodian People's Party." To get 60 percent Roth had counted all the smaller parties, some of which did not win even enough votes to earn a seat in parliament. In his view this "clearly demonstrates that efforts aimed at intimidating the Cambodian electorate failed." Then he told of the State Department's hope that the parties "negotiate a coalition government which reflects the will of the people as ex-pressed in their vote." And in their total vote, he noted again, 60 per-cent of the people voted against Hun Sen.

The truth was that Ranariddh didn't seem much interested in forming an opposition coalition. He was far more keen on working something out with Hun Sen that would place him astride the flow of graft money that streamed through senior government offices.

Negotiations dragged on for six months. All the while Hun Sen's party managed to peel away one Funcinpec supporter after another by offering lucrative government appointments and cash. Sun Thun, a teacher and prominent Sam Rainsy Party member in Kampong Thom Province, recounted his own experience: "They tried to buy me. They promised they would pay me and give me a position in government. I didn't accept. But a friend of mine did. They pay him 1 million riel salary. Now he's a deputy director in the education ministry. And now everybody calls him 'your excellency.'" In the end, Hun Sen and Ranariddh agreed that Hun Sen would return as prime minister while Ranariddh became speaker of the National Assembly—quite a lucrative post.

The problem was that this position did not give his many supporters and acolytes the positions they needed in government to buy big houses and put their children through school. Funcinpec was given ministries that offered few financial opportunities—Education, Health, Rural Development, and the like—while Hun Sen clung to Justice, Defense, Interior, Commerce, Construction, Industry, and Planning. But part of the deal Japan brokered offered another avenue to bring party members into the lucre. The state would create a senate. It would have little power—but enough status and influence to curry favor with moneyed interests. Seats would be apportioned according to votes in the last election.

Throughout the process Rainsy continued to rail about the inequity of it all, so he got nothing in the coalition deal, just his party's seats in parliament. And to demonstrate that Cambodia held no room for an opposition politician, when he returned from abroad for the opening of the National Assembly, police used clubs and electric batons to beat up several dozen of his supporters who had shown up to greet him. To say he was bitter would be a world-class understatement.

In September 1998 King Sihanouk called everyone to his palace in Siem Reap for a ceremonial opening of the new parliament. This entailed a flight, followed by a drive to Sihanouk's palace. Along the road from the airport, a small group of men hid behind bushes with an RPG-2 grenade launcher. The RPG-2, sometimes called the B-40, was an old, crude instrument—the first rocket-propelled grenade launcher designed in the former Soviet Union and supplied to its allies, starting in 1949. The North Vietnamese fired them at American troops during the Vietnam War. The Khmer Rouge used them. Though deadly, they weren't very accurate; they featured only a bolted-on iron site for aiming the weapon.

Soon enough, Hun Sen's motorcade approached, sirens blaring, and the launcher fired. The grenade missed; it whizzed past just in front of Hun Sen's windshield and exploded across the road, killing a young boy and wounding several other people. At first Hun Sen and his party did not know what had happened. But by the time they got to the palace for the ceremony, they realized, as Hun Sen put it, "this was a clear attempt on my life," adding, "They want to kill me, of course." But he named no names. A diplomat who attended the reception said Rainsy and Sihanouk "both looked ashen" after hearing the news.

After the party at Sihanouk's house, the new parliamentarians were sworn in at Angkor Wat. Hun Sen then flew directly back to Phnom Penh. Rainsy and Ranariddh fled the country. "Sure we are worried," a spokesman for Rainsy told reporters. "It seems like they are claiming this was an assassination attempt on Hun Sen, a free-standing accusation that could be used against anyone." Ranariddh pointed out that he had been in that convoy. Why would he order an attack when "my own car was very close?" he asked. Hok Lundy, Hun Sen's police chief and a brutal thug, stepped into the debate and quickly declared: "We have concluded that this was a clear attempt by the political parties that lost the election."

It is a testament to the peculiar character of Cambodia that neither Ranariddh nor anyone else said anything about that little boy who was killed. How would the United States, or France, or Finland, or Japan treat a little boy, an innocent bystander, killed in an attempt to assassinate the head of state? Everyone would know all about him.

Not so in Cambodia. The nation's leaders were so focused on themselves that he was irrelevant—collateral damage worthy not even of acknowledgment.

Like all the rest of these episodes, no one ended up being arrested. Rainsy and Ranariddh eventually slipped back into town, and everything went on as before—although now, for the first time, Hun Sen was the uncontested leader of his nation.

Hun Sen's hold on power drew on many strengths and strategies. Among them were nepotism and intermarriage. His brother Hun Neng was governor of Kampong Cham Province, and the governor's daughter was married to the deputy commissioner of police. Hun Neng's son Hun Seang Heng was married to Sok Sopheak, the daughter of another deputy commissioner of police. Hun Sen's son Hun Manith was married to Hok Chendavy, the daughter of Hok Lundy, the National Police commissioner until he died in a helicopter crash in 2008. After that, Hun Sen appointed his nephew-in-law to the job. He appointed his daughter, Hun Mana, as a senior assistant in his office. Another of Hun Sen's sons, Hun Many, was married to Yim Chay Lin, daughter of the secretary of state for rural development, while one of the prime minister's daughters was married to Sok Puthyvuth, the son of Sok An, the deputy prime minister.

That is just a taste; the government was riven with marital and professional nepotism. In a nation where no one trusted anyone else and everyone looked out only for himself, the family stood as the only social grouping in which people confidently relied on one another.

Hun Sen's friends called him clever, wily, and smart. His enemies, a far larger group, called him cunning, ruthless, and diabolical. But on one fact everyone agreed. He would accept nothing short of complete, unfettered control of his nation, just like the kings of yore. Now he had it and liked to brag about that. "I wish to state it very clearly this way," he said in a major speech. "No one can defeat Hun Sen. Only Hun Sen alone can defeat Hun Sen." But he once also protested: "Don't accuse me of loving power. The people gave it to me." Actually, it was Truong Chinh, the Vietnamese leader, who placed him in office during the Vietnamese occupation of Cambodia in the 1980s.

Hun Sen was born in 1952 in a tiny village in Kampong Cham Province, north of Phnom Penh. His parents were uneducated peasant farmers, and by his own account he studied at one of those village pagodas where the monks taught scripture and perhaps how to read and write. He says he then moved to Phnom Penh to continue his studies in a French school, the Lycée Indra Devi, though it was never explained how a peasant child managed to accomplish that. But the nation was at war, and when Hun Sen heard Prince Sihanouk urge young people to join the Khmer Rouge, that's exactly what he did, in 1970.

Most Cambodians have come up with accounts to explain their lives during the Khmer Rouge era. Millions of victims, of course, have terrible stories to tell. But many of the former Khmer Rouge soldiers and officers have crafted tales of their own. In their telling, they lived in the forest or worked as a Khmer Rouge slave in a remote area—stories that cannot be proved or disproved.

Unlike these Khmer Rouge veterans, Hun Sen has never talked publicly about his time as a Khmer Rouge soldier. He was promoted quickly, which suggests that he must have followed Pol Pot's doctrine quite faithfully. He fought in the battle to take Phnom Penh in 1975—and lost one eye. By 1978 he was a commander stationed in eastern Cambodia. When Khmer Rouge and Vietnamese troops began exchanging fire across the border—Vietnam briefly invaded eastern Cambodia in 1977—Pol Pot began seeing collaborators everywhere. All soldiers working on the border were presumed to be traitors. In this climate of suspicion it was just a matter of time before his Khmer Rouge superiors began to suspect him.

One day the regional office called Hun Sen in for a talk. People working in border areas knew they could be killed at any time. Whenever the central office called them back for interviews, they never returned. Hun Sen went to the meeting, he said, but put a pistol in his bag. A senior officer questioned him about his loyalty, and as the interview came to an end, Hun Sen put his hand on the pistol in his bag. But they let him go. Outside, he cut the office's communications lines, then took off for the border and defected to Vietnam. The Vietnamese put him in jail at first but then let him out and brought him into the planning for the invasion. Once Vietnam had seized Phnom Penh, they made him foreign minister.

Hun Sen seems to live up to every one of the descriptions his allies and enemies offer. He is undeniably smart. How else could he have outwitted so many of his political rivals, every one of whom was just as diabolical as he is, for so many years? He is ruthless, having allowed his government, or his party, to murder hundreds of political opponents over several decades. He is also cunning, as Christopher Hill discovered firsthand. In 2006 Hill was assistant secretary of state for East Asia and Pacific affairs, the same job Solomon and Lord had held before. He was in Phnom Penh for meetings. A few days earlier the government had arrested two prominent human-rights activists on trumped-up charges. When Hill met Hun Sen, "I told him: 'I don't really know Cambodia, but I do know Washington. And if you do things like this, pretty soon people are going to begin seeing you as another Burma.' Hun Sen huddled with his aides for a minute, then said: 'How about if we let them out at 2 p.m.?'

"'Well, that would be good,' I said.

"'But you didn't pressure me, right?' Hun Sen insisted. 'You're not going to say there was any pressure?'"

No, Hill told him. "I won't say there was any pressure."

"'Well, then,' Hun Sen said, 'I am releasing them as a gift to you.'"

Hill thanked him and left. Later, Joseph Mussomeli, who was the U.S. ambassador at the time, pointed out, "Yes, he made that promise to Chris Hill. But before Hill got there, Hun Sen had already promised to release them."

But Hun Sen is not all cunning and bluster. He is also a troubled man. By several accounts from people who know him well, Hun Sen suffers panic attacks. "He could be shaken, rattled, panicked," Quinn said. "When that happens, he can seem to lose touch with his sur-roundings and says things like 'What's going on, what's happening?'"

When confronted with options he does not like, Hun Sen often speaks of his fears of instability and war. He is zealous about protect-ing himself and his family. After the murder of Thun Bun Ly, the op-position newspaper editor, in 1996, angry Rainsy supporters paraded his coffin through the streets. Hun Sen called Quinn and pleaded with him to send protection for his two children who were in school in the United States. The State Department was not eager to cooper-ate with his request, but local police did send squad cars to check on the two. For that, Hun Sen was quite grateful.

For Hun Sen and people like him, "their background leaves them constantly afraid," Quinn said. "That fear of losing control constantly permeates them."

Assessing all this, Reicherter, the psychiatrist, said: "He definitely sounds like someone with anxiety. This is not the normal behavior of a leader, thinking that power could be taken from him at any time, which is a symptom of PTSD."

———

In 1999 Quinn had been in Phnom Penh for more than three years. The State Department appreciated his work, but his relationship with Hun Sen had made him a polarizing figure. Some senior Repub-lican members of the Senate held a strong interest in Cambodia and "realized this was something they had to keep an eye on," Ron Abney said. "They did it through us"—Abney and his colleagues at the IRI. The picture these senators received focused sharply on the dysfunc-tional political situation because the institute was a focal point for the animus toward Hun Sen—and deep suspicion of Ambassador Quinn.

After Abney was injured in the grenade attack, the institute's fixa-tion on Hun Sen blossomed. Grove had served in Cambodia during the mid-1990s and then had become the IRI's Cambodia specialist. Like others at IRI, he was a Rainsy fan. "Every time he came to town,"

Grove said, "we made sure he got up on the Hill to talk to people." Abney often went with him, and, as he watched, "Rainsy could really get congressmen excited," he said. "He was like the Aung San Suu Kyi of Cambodia, talking to them about all this inside stuff in Cambodian politics. They loved it!"*

At the end of the decade Grove took a new job as a senior aid for Republican senator Mitch McConnell, who happened to be chairman of the Senate Foreign Operations Appropriations Subcommittee—a body that held significant influence over how American money was spent abroad. McConnell was from Kentucky, where he had previously served as a county administrator. He had been in the Senate since 1985. The senator hadn't held especially strong opinions about Cambodia—until he hired Grove. Prior to 1998 he spoke about the state rarely. After Grove joined his staff McConnell visited the country, wrote op-eds denouncing Hun Sen, and was quoted widely. "Staff was able to bring issues to his attention," Grove modestly observed.

When the Clinton administration nominated Quinn's successor as ambassador to Cambodia in January 1999, McConnell put a hold on it, as senators can do. His nomination could not go forward unless and until McConnell lifted the hold. The senator had no particular problem with the nominee, Kent Wiedemann, a career diplomat who had most recently been chargé d'affaires in Burma. No, the goal of McConnell and his Republican allies was simple and straightforward: regime change. Hun Sen had to go. What better way to make that point than to refuse to send an ambassador? Whose idea was this? Sam Rainsy's.

Wiedemann's foreign-service career had been long and distinguished. He had served in Israel, Singapore, Poland, Taiwan, and China. The debate was not about him, and he knew it. "Not sending an ambassador was a very effective way of showing our distaste," he said. "And, yes indeed, Sam Rainsy was their client. He traveled to the U.S. and very

---

*Aung San Suu Kyi was the Burmese opposition leader who had spent much of her life under house arrest.

successfully gained the support of some of these Foreign Relations Committee staffers. And most importantly, the people at IRI very early on saw Sam Rainsy as a better champion of democracy."

Rainsy, of course, denied he had done any of this. "I don't understand things in Washington," he averred. "It would be too demanding for me to try to influence things on the Hill." (Given a chance later to explain this and other lies, Rainsy declined.) Another McConnell staffer told the senator that Wiedemann was not tough enough on the regime when he was chargé d'affaires in Burma. That also played into Wiedemann's problems.

Quinn said the State Department asked him to remain in office as the nomination debate dragged on, month after month. He agreed, and with obvious glee he called Rainsy to tell him, "I would be happy to stay indefinitely." That, of course, was just about the last thing Rainsy wanted to hear. As Quinn saw it from Phnom Penh, eventually "Rainsy called it off, and soon enough Wiedemann was confirmed."

In fact, cooler heads prevailed in the Senate. "John McCain and Chuck Robb weighed in," Wiedemann said. Friends and supporters told Rainsy that "things were moving in the direction of acceptance of having an ambassador, so he dropped his opposition." McConnell lifted his hold.

Wiedemann stepped into his new position on August 1, 1999. His attitude and the environment around him were wholly different from what they had been for either of his predecessors. Twining and Quinn had both had direct encounters with the horrors of the Khmer Rouge years. Both of them played important roles in the UN occupation. They had come to the job with a deep sympathy for the Cambodian people and cautious optimism about the nation's future after the United Nations had given it a major lift. The American mission during their tenures was hopeful: to help Cambodia create a democratic government that would heal the wounds of the Khmer Rouge era, lift its people out of poverty, and join the modern world.

Wiedemann, in contrast, had served in Burma, China, Israel, and Washington, among other places. He was dealing with Asian and Latin American affairs during the Khmer Rouge years and beyond. He, of course, had followed the news and felt sympathy for the Cambodian people—as did most everyone around the world. But he had no particular attachment to the country or its people, no personal stake in the United Nations' mission. And by the time he got there, most of the world had already concluded that the UN mission had failed. No one was left in government who had a strong interest in the state, like Solomon or Quinn—someone who could be an advocate for Cambodia while the rest of the government focused on higher priorities.

Now, the atmosphere for the American ambassador in Phnom Penh was also quite different. "It was still a very difficult time because the U.S. had seen the '97 events so negatively," he said. "We cut off aid, downsized the embassy." As a result, Wiedemann had an adversarial relationship with Hun Sen beginning the day he set foot in the country. Unlike Quinn, Wiedemann was able to establish only "a decent working relationship with Hun Sen, though a very prickly one. Especially when I would go in to protest something, like impunity or the murders. I would go into his office, and I could sense the anger he felt. His answers were short and abrupt. You could see him kind of twitch."

With all of that the United States was adopting a new mission in Cambodia. Actually, it abandoned any real sense of mission. "The reality is, at the State Department we are awfully busy doing China, doing North Korea nukes, doing Sudan," Wiedemann explained. "We don't really have much time to deal with Cambodia, Burma, the little countries. We don't have any major national interests there. So we let the human-rights folks handle it. We say, 'Let's make human rights the principal or perhaps the only foreign-policy objective.' So we bring all the human-rights groups into the tent. Human Rights Watch, Amnesty International, the IRI." These groups began to play "huge roles. And they all had an extreme and focused antipathy toward Hun Sen. In IRI's case, while I was there, their principal aim was promoting

Sam Rainsy. Hun Sen, he was absolutely illegitimate. He has to go. He needs to come down."

That meant the U.S. government was taking the de facto position as Hun Sen's avowed and determined enemy. Hun Sen's government didn't really know how to handle that. On advice, they hired a lobbyist in Washington. But that didn't work out. "We paid him $1 million, but he cheated us," said Khieu Kanharith, the information minister. "He was Cambodian. We decided we didn't want to have a lobbyist anymore." With or without a lobbyist, Hun Sen's government continued providing his antagonists new ammunition to use against him, month after month after month.

Hun Sen, left, and Ranariddh, when they were pretending to get along.

Sam Rainsy

Prince Norodom Sihanouk

Farmers planting rice more or less as their forebears did 1,000 years ago.

Tuy Khorn tries to dig furrows by tying a heavy rock to her primitive plow.

This twelfth-century Bayon temple carving shows an oxcart nearly identical to those used today.

Residents, including a land mine victim in the hammock, watch their village's only car-battery-powered television.

When a charity gave out free rice, Chan Yat, 76, was almost the only one who got any.

Farmers ferry live pigs to market.

School teacher Kdep Sokhin, 26, fears he will soon have 143 students, all by himself.

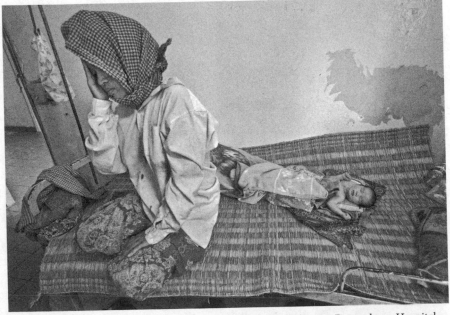

A mother, a bit of blood on her blouse, recovers from a C-section at Battambang Hospital.

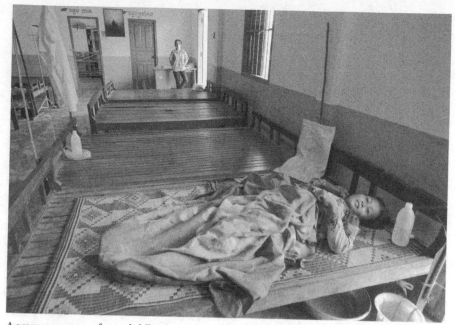

A woman recovers from childbirth at Pailin Referral Hospital. At the room's other end is the nurse with the slightly crossed eyes and the "Duty Room," where the nurses sleep.

Mith Ran tells the sorrowful story of his wife's death at Pailin Referral Hospital.

Let Ting, 22, was widowed after a military officer burned her husband to death.

Sam Nhea sits with his two barely-conscious children, one of whom is out of frame, in the Andong evictee camp.

Police man a checkpoint in Pursat Province where they stop drivers and demand bribes.

Pol Pot's younger brother, Saloth Nhep, 84, reflects on his life a few months before he died.

Youk Chhang, director of the Documentation Center of Cambodia, sits before a shrine holding skulls of Khmer Rouge victims.

Chhay Sareth, Pursat Province council chief, complained about the province's corrupt prosecutor.

Prime Minister Hun Sen's new mansion, theoretically built with money from his salary, has a heliport on the roof.

Deputy Prime Minister Sok An's house is the size of a small hotel.

Millions of Cambodians live in houses much like Mith Ran's simple abode.

# CHAPTER EIGHT

I t's hard to overstate how important trees are to Cambodians. Since the beginning of human habitation of this bucolic state, people have built their homes from tree trunks, limbs, and branches—even making use of the leaves. They've taken food from the fruit trees, burned tree limbs to cook their food, lived in the shade of trees as protection from the brutal heat, tapped tree resin to seal the hulls of their fishing boats, and much more. That is why so many people looked on with genuine distress as the Khmer Rouge, after their defeat, denuded northwestern Cambodia of vast forests and sold the lumber to Thai generals.

These weren't just any old trees. Cambodia is fortunate to be home to tropical trees that produce some of the world's most beautiful woods. Some provide exquisite-looking lumber that in appearance offers a rich, unique coloration. It's roughly a cross between walnut and mahogany with an attractive meandering grain. Some feature a blond-wood stripe, maybe three-quarters of an inch wide, that twists and turns through the tree. Cambodians call the lumber from these trees "luxury wood." It is prized and quite valuable. As a mark of status, senior government ministers place massive luxury-wood chairs in their offices. Intricate designs are carved into the six-foot-high seat backs, and the chairs are finished with a high-gloss varnish so they sparkle.

Shortly after taking office in 1993, Ranariddh and Hun Sen sent that letter to the Thai government saying they alone were authorized to sell this lumber, through the Ministry of Defense. In the following years they sold what the government called "concessions" to friends and cronies—dozens of them, involving thousands of acres of forest. The buyers would cut down all the trees, haul the lumber away, and then leave behind vast empty fields dotted with ugly stumps. (You can only guess into whose pockets the concession payments went.) And once Hun Sen and Ranariddh designated the Defense Ministry as the state's only legitimate tree broker, its own officers began freelancing in the forests, making their own fortunes by cutting down thousands of trees.

Through the 1990s all manner of Cambodians plunged into this orgy of deforestation. Patrons to roadside beer bars in Pailin, near the western border, sat in luxury-wood chairs pulled up to table tops made from one solid slab of this wood, four feet wide, six feet long—and seven inches deep. A fifteen-dollar-a-night guesthouse in Battambang featured massive luxury-wood beds with heavily carved headboards, eight feet tall. One of those blond stripes coursed through the footboard, and each of these beds weighed well over 1,000 pounds.

Cambodia's trees were fast disappearing. But early in the 2000s the World Bank office in Phnom Penh made saving the remaining forests a major priority. The bank was among the nation's largest foreign-aid donors and was also quite influential within the donor community. So when bank officers urged Hun Sen to hire a company to monitor the forests, he agreed—and even accepted the bank's choice for the job, a British advocacy organization named Global Witness. The group described its mission as follows: "Global Witness exposes the corrupt exploitation of natural resources and international trade systems, to drive campaigns that end impunity, resource-linked conflict, and human rights and environmental abuses."

Global Witness investigators had already worked in Cambodia, in 1995, and had written a report about Khmer Rouge timber sales. Boasting about this later, the group wrote, "In 1995, within five months of commencement, our very first campaign closed the Thai-Cambodia border to the $20 million per month timber trade between the Khmer Rouge and Thai logging companies." Now, Global Witness's take-no-prisoners investigators were doing what they best liked to do—under government contract! At the same time, in Phnom Penh, World Bank officers were working to close down the government's utterly corrupt land-concession schemes. The two were promising to shut the lumber business down.

In time Ian Porter, the World Bank's country director, said he had seen progress. "Forest concessions have been suspended," he said, "public disclosure has improved, and environment and social-impact assessments have been used for sustainable forestry management plans." But as it turned out, that was far from the end of the story.

———

Now that Hun Sen and his Cambodian People's Party controlled all of the government agencies that mattered, the ones that could make money, ministers and their allies showed just how imaginative and innovative they could be. They certainly weren't thinking up clever new ways to help their constituents—by most measures the health and welfare of Cambodians were at best stagnant. Instead, a local human-rights group uncovered a scandal in 2001 that showed how little regard government leaders actually accorded their own people, especially their children.

At this very time, in Mai Sai, Thailand, mothers were selling their twelve-year-old daughters to slave traffickers who subjected them to a hellish life as prisoners in brothels, karaoke bars, and strip joints. Sometimes those Thai traffickers had to pay off local police, but there was no indication that government officials in Bangkok were involved;

sometimes they even arrested traffickers. In Cambodia, however, very senior officials in the Interior Ministry and the Ministry of Foreign Affairs were directly profiting from the baby trade.

A Cambodian human-rights group first discovered the problem. The United Nations had helped form the Cambodian League for the Promotion and Defense of Human Rights in 1992 as part of the UN effort to create strong, private civil-society advocates for the people. Since the group's name was a mouthful, it quickly became known by its French-language acronym: Licadho. In 2001 two mothers visited the Licadho offices in Phnom Penh asking for help. They were divorced and impoverished, and both said a kind man had come to them, promising to help. He offered to take their babies—one was six months old, the other just four days—to a children's center that would care for them until the women got back on their feet. The mothers could visit their babies as often as they wanted. He gave each of them a bit of cash and took the babies away. But once they had given up their babies, the mothers were not permitted to see them. Licadho investigated and found that the children had been taken to "an orphanage run by an adoption facilitator who caters to the U.S. market," the group reported. And this was no isolated incident.

Across Cambodia hundreds of women were being tricked or coerced into giving up their babies. The children effectively were being sold to Americans. They were eager to adopt Cambodian children and did not know the babies had been stolen. Fees for such a service generally ran up to about $10,000. But the scam didn't simply end with unscrupulous baby brokers. For these babies to leave the country, each had to have a passport issued by the Ministries of Interior and Foreign Affairs. Officers in both ministries were demanding rich bribes from the brokers, and as usual they were passing part of the proceeds up to their superiors. Since nearly all of the children were being taken to the United States, the embassy got involved. When American officials began to get a whiff of the scam, they contracted with Licadho and a similar group, the Cambodian Human Rights and Development Association, to investigate the problem. The results were startling. "Some women turned away in the marketplace for a second to buy some fish, and when she turned around her baby was gone," Ambassador Wiedemann said. "Sometimes a woman would have a difficult birth, and someone would agree to treat her in the hospital—and take care of the baby. When she woke up, they'd say, 'Baby? What baby?' The babies were taken to warehouses of sorts. They might have fifty babies at a time. I visited a number of them."

With American backing, the investigators were able to question deputy ministers and other senior officials in both the Interior and the Foreign Affairs ministries. It could not be proved, but the investigators came away convinced that even the senior ministers were involved. In spite of the ministers' denials, Wiedemann does say, "This was run with official complicity up to very high levels. But I don't think Hun Sen knew about it. I told Hun Sen there was obvious government complicity. They knew it was going on, and they were being paid off."

Hun Sen responded well, Wiedemann said, and ordered the racket shut down. The United States refused to grant any more visas for Cambodian babies—infuriating Americans desperate to have children. "When we declared an end to adoptions," Wiedemann said, "I was hammered, terribly"—this time, for once, by Americans, not Cambodian officials.

In Washington, this news only heightened the hatred of Hun Sen. Senators and others were furious: He had ordered the grenade attack on Rainsy, their golden boy. He had engineered a coup to seize full, unfettered power. Now his people were stealing babies. Hun Sen was spitting in the face of the United States and all those other countries that had spent billions of dollars to give the Cambodian people a new life.

The political landscape in Cambodia was, nonetheless, changing. In 1998 Pol Pot died. The next year Cambodian police arrested Ta Mok, the very last Khmer Rouge commander. He had refused to accept amnesty. With that the Khmer Rouge movement was dead. The war was over. For the first time in more than thirty years, Cambodia was at peace. Hun Sen could no longer use the war as an excuse, though he could—and did—boast, with some justification, that he had defeated the Khmer Rouge.

In the meantime, as an indirect result of their decision to ignore Cambodia, the State Department had essentially turned relations over to human-rights groups. This meant that more and more negative information poured from these groups into the offices of the senators who remained obsessed with Hun Sen. The American press joined the hate feast. An editorial in the *Washington Post* labeled the prime minister "Saddam Hun Sen." The *New Republic* called him "Hun the Attila."

Senator Mitch McConnell was openly calling for regime change, and he began writing op-ed pieces in which his animus was on full display. The first one, in the *Boston Globe* in 2001, began with a swipe at Hun Sen. "Thirty years later, Cambodia has yet to recover from the genocide and social upheaval caused by the Pol Pot regime," he wrote. "Today, former Khmer Rouge cadre occupy senior levels of government, including Prime Minister Hun Sen, who defected to Vietnam in 1978 and marched into Phnom Penh with invading Vietnamese forces. In 1985 Hun Sen was tapped by Vietnam to be prime minister, a position he has managed to retain for 16 years through aggressive political intimidation, a bloody coup d'état, election chicanery, and fraud."

Soon McConnell introduced a bill that would increase aid to Cambodia by 50 percent—but only if Hun Sen was voted out of office. In the meantime, his subcommittee was considering a bill that would reduce aid to Cambodia's central government (nearly all had already been cut off after the "coup" in 1997) and provide $7 million to what it called the "democratic opposition," that is, Sam Rainsy. That prompted Khieu Kanharith, the information minister, to quip, "They say, 'Choose your leaders in a democratic way,' and then they go and say this?" But those bills went nowhere.

In Phnom Penh Wiedemann stood up for Rainsy, but he was a bit wary of the man. After all, Rainsy had helped convince Senator McConnell to put a hold on his own nomination. But Wiedemann was well aware that if the United States wanted to support a democratic opposition in Cambodia, Rainsy was the face of that opposition. "He was chosen by the human-rights groups, Amnesty International, IRI, and the others," Wiedemann said. "They picked him. He worked them very hard." So Wiedemann occasionally attended his rallies and sat next to him on the podium, if only to show that the United States was not going to let anything happen to him.

The ambassador was more dubious when it came to Rainsy's political abilities. He and Ranariddh, Wiedemann said, "lacked the personal dedication, perseverance, and understanding of postwar Cambodia to compete effectively" against Hun Sen. "I was surprised when Ranariddh and Sam Rainsy for months on end would simply abandon the field of competition in Cambodia and return to France—or, in Rainsy's case, to campaign mainly in the U.S., France, Australia, and a few other places." And besides, Rainsy "is not a country guy. He's not very comfortable out there in the provinces."

Still, just as Rainsy had with his predecessors, he called Wiedemann occasionally, complained that his life was in danger, and in his best wheedling tone asked to take up residence in the embassy. Wiedemann would dutifully meet with him and try to calm him down. But over time, he said, "I often had the impression, when Sam Rainsy called me saying, 'I am just about to be attacked by a squad of goons,' that he was crying wolf, that he did it to convey to us that he is sort of the hero in the current political scene in regard to democracy, and he is facing this horrible, venal enemy, and we should keep him under our wing."

Flawed as Rainsy was, there was no one to take his place. "One of the great tragedies of Cambodia was that from 1993 on, no new leadership has emerged," Wiedemann said. "It's the same players since back in the early 1990s. Most are venal, and most are engaged in a battle among themselves rather than for the good of the country." As

Carol Rodley, deputy chief of mission when Ken Quinn was ambassador, observed, "Cambodia needs a hero."

But as the Hun Sen haters in Washington continued to throw barbs at the illegitimate prime minister, the Communist stooge, the murderer, the coup leader, the baby stealer, Wiedemann did take it upon himself to make inquiries about the supposed "coup," that seminal event in the nation's recent history. "I looked into it very closely, talked with lots of Funcinpec people, including Nhiek Bun Chhay," the Funcinpec secretary-general. "And from everything I learned, yes indeed, Funcinpec launched it. They admitted it to me. And they would have won but for the simple fact that Hun Sen was better organized and had better intelligence." Even with that, the conventional wisdom held fast in Washington and around the world. There was no debate. Hun Sen alone was guilty.

Elections were coming up in 2002 for new communal governments. Whereas Cambodian provinces were equivalent to American states, communes were similar to counties. Since the fall of the Khmer Rouge every single leader of Cambodia's 1,621 communes had been appointed by Hun Sen's government. In fact, Cambodia had never before held open local elections of this sort. The UN election agreement had called for them in 1993, but political and military turmoil had so consumed the nation that more elections had not seemed possible until now. Of course, the same players were putting up candidates: Hun Sen, Norodom Ranariddh, and that darling of the Americans, Sam Rainsy. And all of them played true to form.

A collection of civil-society elections groups, including the Committee for Free and Fair Elections in Cambodia, sat down with the three parties eighteen months before election day and proposed several changes that, they all believed, would produce a more equitable vote. First, they suggested, voters should be allowed to pick among individual candidates instead of political parties. Behind that, of course, was the fact that Hun Sen's party had an unmatchable monopoly of local officials nationwide. Rainsy and Ranariddh immediately embraced the idea. Hun Sen said he kind of liked it but was not sure "as to how it could be implemented in technical terms." So it was not done.

The private groups said they wanted to find a way to ensure that more women stood as candidates. Once again, while Rainsy and Ranariddh endorsed the proposal, Hun Sen said this sounded like a good idea but worried that it clashed with the constitutional provisions for equality between men and women. Nothing was done.

Rainsy and Ranariddh both leaped at the suggestion to restructure the National Election Committee, which was an organ of the CPP. (This was the agency that had come up with the vote-allocation formula that awarded 53 percent of the seats in parliament to the CPP, even though the party had won only 41 percent of the vote.) Hun Sen said fine, but not until 2003, after the elections, because that's when the present commissioners' terms expired. Naturally, nothing was done in 2003—or in the years following.

In the meantime, when the National Democratic Institute sponsored candidate debates around the country, the elections commission ruled that television networks, all of them state controlled, would not air them. The stations did, however, offer copious coverage of vote buying—CPP officials handing out sarongs and household goods en masse to voters in rural villages.

The commune elections were the third since the UN occupation, and by now the parties had settled into a routine. Rainsy and Ranariddh spent much of their time abroad. Rainsy, particularly, behaved as if he were running for office in the United States. "Rainsy shrewdly exploited Western sympathy by not only noting but often exaggerating CPP human-rights abuses," Wiedemann said. But, the ambassador added, "Rainsy was undoubtedly more deft in generating sympathy and support in Washington than he was in Phnom Penh or in the Cambodian hinterland."

Meantime, Hun Sen deployed his vast network of party officials and local officers in every village, commune, and province to do what they could to ensure a CPP victory. After two elections, they had refined their strategies. Now, their third time up, they knew just what worked.

The United Nations sent a special representative to report on the election, which was to take place in February 2002. Almost as soon as he arrived, he learned that fifteen campaign officials had already been killed, and the elections were still two months away. "Twelve of the murders were from shootings," he said in a report to the UN. Of the remaining cases, at least two involved victims being beaten to death. "In only one case is there uncertainty about the cause: The body of Funcinpec candidate Ros Don was found in a ditch beside the road." And every one of the victims was an active worker for either Funcinpec or the Sam Rainsy Party. Not one CPP worker was killed. "Police investigations of such incidents and subsequent judicial processes show serious shortcomings," the UN found. "Investigating authorities remain reluctant to probe political motives, afraid they would be killed if they assigned blame to governing-party operatives." Cases brought to the National Election Committee sat in the in-box, never to be pursued.

But the CPP also used strategies that stopped short of murder. Village chiefs in many areas told tens of thousands of villagers that they had to hand over their voter-registration cards. The chiefs generally kept the cards for a few days and then gave them back, leaving the villagers with the impression that the chiefs would be able to check and see how they voted. Other village chiefs called all their villagers to the town square and urged them, en masse, "to swear oaths of allegiance to the ruling party," the UN said.

Several human-rights groups and newspapers reported on the murders and intimidation on a daily basis. The government routinely denied any responsibility. In fact, at the end of the campaign, the Ministry of the Interior, which managed the nation's police, issued a news release that proudly proclaimed that the ministry "has the honor to announce that since the beginning of the electoral campaign until the present, there has been no politically motivated crime."

For Wiedemann, that was just too much. Both of his predecessors, Twining and Quinn, had witnessed political violence at least this bad. They had issued the expected State Department mealymouthed statements intended to ensure that no one was offended. Typically, they went something like this: "We condemn this act of violence and call on all parties to refrain from provocative acts so that the Cambodian people can exercise their democratic rights without fear or intimidation."

But Wiedemann would have none of it. Before he spoke out he waited until the polls had closed—Hun Sen, not surprisingly, won control of 1,600 of the 1,621 communes. By then at least twenty opposition-party activists had been killed. Then Wiedemann pronounced the government's denial of any responsibility "appallingly irresponsible, insulting almost, and dismissive of the international community's concerns, expressed to the government time after time after time, when it is unwilling to accept the fact that there are some political killings." Cambodian newspapers eagerly devoured his remarks. Later, he explained: "I was absolutely convinced that the government was involved, and I was angered at the denials. It was just so obviously politically motivated. So I made a decision to go public with it."

Behind this was the fact that a new political order had taken hold. For Wiedemann and other diplomats, the hope, the idealism, that motivated them before had been crushed. So why hold back? "There was a lot of that kind of feeling among the diplomatic community, a huge frustration among everyone that the hopes of UNTAC and the international community had not worked out. We would wring our hands. And then, sitting in Phnom Penh, it was very easy to get pissed off by the antics of Hun Sen."

For his part, the prime minister bristled when asked about complaints that the elections fell short of international standards. He offered one of his typical nonsensical dismissals. "What are international standards?" Hun Sen asked rhetorically. "I don't understand. International standards exist only in sports. If your understanding of it is poor, go back and study it."

Now that the United States had turned away from Cambodia, except for those senators and staff whose mission was to topple Hun Sen, the embassy's mission gradually evolved from supporting democratic change to attacking corruption. The Agency for International Development was the lead office in this effort, and soon this consumed nearly all of the USAID officers' time.

The U.S. Embassy was alone in its efforts. "Broadly speaking, the American embassy was almost the only country out there speaking frankly about misbehavior of the regime—corruption, impunity," the ambassador said. "Maybe the Aussies sometimes, occasionally the Brits. In part I think it's a matter of our national style. Other countries tend to regard the process of change as something that takes a very, very long time. We are not so patient. We want results more quickly—and for good reason. People are suffering and dying."

Early on, USAID officers decided to charter a comprehensive study of corruption, to find out how extensive and costly the problem actually was. Everyone "knew" that corruption was widespread. But ask any government official about the problem, and most likely he would shake his head and lament the problem—while sitting on a fat wallet.

USAID hired Casals & Associates, an international consulting firm, to investigate the following questions: "the degree to which corruption exists in Cambodia; the types of corruption most harmful to democratic governance; the capacity of government, civil society and the media to combat and expose corruption." The research would take many months.

Meanwhile, year after year, international aid groups were still holding pledge conferences in Phnom Penh. Every one of the 2,000 or more aid agencies, from the World Bank to the Despondency Saving Wanderer Organization, prepared to tell Cambodian officials what they planned to spend in the coming year. Along with the pledges, however, the donors were also making certain demands. Leading up to these meetings each year, some of the donors were still berating their peers to make the donations conditional. The primary condition: Don't give any money until the government stops the political murders and passes that anticorruption law. Every year the list of demands grew longer and longer. And, beginning with Wiedemann, every year the U.S. ambassador, addressing the group, would berate the government for failing to make much if any progress.

As his term reached its end, Wiedemann began to see the pattern, and it made him angry. "Every single year, the donors get together," he said. "They decide among themselves in advance what they want to talk to the government about. They spend two days lambasting the government, the ministers, and you get all these promises of change. Then the donors turn in their pledges. And nothing changes. Year after year after year. All the things the donors do, that's money Hun Sen doesn't have to spend. You know he does get some legitimate money, from taxes on the garment industry and a few other things." And then more from illegal logging and selling off land rights to his cronies Wiedemann's frustration had reached the breaking point.

In 2001 he decided to tell Hun Sen and the rest of his government exactly what he thought. Every government minister came to these meetings, and Wiedemann was not timid. For a few days, at least, every minister played the role of toady to the agencies and nations that funneled millions into their budgets, serving hospitals and schools—as well as paying for their children's private schools and those shopping trips to Singapore. Each of the ambassadors from major nations spoke—Britain, France, the United States, and others. When Wiedemann's time came, "I was looking right at Hun Sen." Years of pent-up anger and frustration boiled inside him. He was thinking, he said, of "one time, there were these young women imported from Eastern Europe—Romania and Bulgaria. They were kept locked up in hotels so they could be used by senior officials in the Cambodian government. Licadho or some other aid group told me about it. We are the ones who got the girls out and took care of them until we sent them home."

Speaking to Hun Sen and the other ministers at the aid conference, he said, "It is very clear there is very heavy corruption in this country. Lots of places are corrupt, even the United States. But it's out of control in Cambodia. The thing is, you are slow to admit that it's happening. If it was just simple corruption at the lower levels, that would be one thing. But it's not. Every year we have brought it to your attention at every donor meeting." As he spoke Hun Sen and his aides "were squirming, angry," Wiedemann said. "Every year we get all these promises of change. Then the donors turn in their pledges. And nothing changes. Year after year after year. We are tired of this. Something has to be done." First, and foremost, he told them, you need to pass that anticorruption law.

In the months before the conference the government had announced that it had completed a draft of the anticorruption law and had sent it on for consideration by the Council of Ministers—essentially equivalent to the cabinet in the U.S. government. From the council the law would be sent on to the parliament.

Of course, over the past seven years the government had said exactly that many times. In 1995, for example, Son Soubert, second deputy president of the National Assembly, told the news media that the parliamentary committee on defense, interior, and investigations had nearly finished consideration of a tough anticorruption law. In 1996 Ranariddh vowed to speed up passage of the law. In 1999 the story changed. Now, the government was saying, several government ministries were drafting an anticorruption law. In July 2000 the *Cambodia Daily* reported that the Council of Ministers had approved the draft law.

During the pledge conference the year before Wiedemann spoke, the Asian Development Bank's country representative, Urooj Malik, had insisted once again that donors wanted to see real progress in the coming year. "The government's report card since the last meeting does not look good," Malik said at the time. The British ambassador, Stephen Bridges, added that there had been "little or no progress in judicial reform or anti-corruption efforts. These are key reform issues and are essential for the future development of the country." Hun Sen and his aides, as always, vowed that would be the year donors saw real progress. So the donors pledged $548 million.

A year later, when Wiedemann took the podium, nothing had changed. Nonetheless, when donors announced their pledges, they totaled $615 million, exceeding the government's request by $115 million. So it went—and so it would continue to go.

# CHAPTER NINE

The men arrived in the middle of the night with bulldozers and chain saws. They began by cutting a road through neighborhoods, rice paddies, even the grounds of the local temple. They reached the edge of the forest just after daybreak. The bulldozers, with engines revving, vertical exhaust pipes belching thick black clouds of smoke, plowed small trees to the ground, while men with chain saws got to work on the larger trees. All of this made quite a racket, of course. Angry villagers rose from their hammocks, then rushed to the forest half-a-mile away, a place intimately familiar to all of them. "No one told us" that the forest demolition was going to begin that day, said Um Huot, a village leader.

In this 75,000-acre forest, Um Huot and hundreds of others made their livelihood. They hunted for small animals, tapped trees for resin, harvested fruit and bamboo, cut rattan-palm vines to make baskets and furniture, plucked mushrooms and herbs from the forest floor, and chopped down an occasional tree for lumber. Using the forest's bounty, they "lived by nature," as Cambodians always had. They had no choice—no other livelihood was available to them. But when they reached the forest that morning, villagers found a heavily armed military unit guarding the men with bulldozers and chain saws. The soldiers drew their weapons and ordered the villagers to turn away.

The villagers knew full well that the company conducting this frontal assault on their forest intended to clear-cut it, knock down every tree, and haul the timber away for sale to builders in China or Taiwan, leaving behind only vast fields of stumps and sawdust. The villagers were certain of this because, a few years earlier, Hun Sen had staged an elaborate signing ceremony in Phnom Penh as he awarded rights to this forest to the company Pheapimex. The new owner, Lao Meng Khin, was a prominent tycoon and an *oknya*—roughly defined as one of Hun Sen's wealthy cronies.

To become an *oknya* was quite an honor in the Cambodian business community, and the title carried with it a rich tradition. In the 1800s, according to historian David Chandler, *oknya* were expected to give generous gifts to the king. In exchange they received titles and seals and insignia of rank—along with positions or business opportunities that made them even richer.

In 1993 Hun Sen decreed that anyone who donated at least $100,000—a princely sum in postwar Cambodia—for public works projects would win the *oknya* title, bestowed by the king. Holders of this title did favors for the prime minister, usually taking on building projects that helped Hun Sen enhance his own reputation. They got favors in return—like the right to buy forest concessions. *Oknya* has no direct translation in English. But the word originated in early Khmer, referring to someone who was a special devotee of Siva, the Hindu deity. In the modern context it was a wealthy person, a mandarin, a special devotee of Hun Sen.

Every time the prime minister visited a humble village in some remote area, he brought along several of his *oknya* who stood around him like acolytes as he asked the dirt-poor villagers what they most needed. Throughout the 1990s most often the villagers would say they needed a school. Hun Sen would spread his arms as a show of his beneficence, then point to an *oknya* and say: "Presented as requested." All of this was usually televised on one of the government-controlled channels. Then it was the *oknya*'s job to build that new school.

Mong Reththy probably built more schools than anyone else, many hundreds of them. He was an agricultural tycoon who ran the nation's largest palm-oil plantation and became one of Hun Sen's first *oknya*. He explained, "Before Samdech Hun Sen asks anyone to build a school or a temple, he asks if we accept this or not. When we go someplace really poor, I know in advance I am responsible for that. When Samdech turns to me and says, 'Mong Reththy will help,' I already know. Samdech does not force anyone."

Mong Reththy spoke of this while sitting at a formidable luxury-wood table on a raised, covered deck in the front yard of his house, a gated Greco-Asian mansion with Corinthian columns and gold-trimmed cornices. His fifty-fifth birthday party had been staged in this yard the day before—it was also, he pointed out, the twenty-first anniversary of his business. Overhead, hanging from two dozen wires stretching the width of the large front yard, dozens of flag-size white sheets fluttered and snapped in the breeze, creating a dramatic backdrop of light, shadow, and sound. To his left two dozen black standing fans were lined up in a row, power cables carefully coiled, waiting for servants to haul them back to storage. A young girl served tea, then sat in a chair twenty yards away, her eyes locked on Mong Reththy in case he decided to beckon her. Behind her in his garage sat a BMW 750i and a Lexus LX570—together about $180,000 worth of automobile.

Mong Reththy is also a senator, as are most *oknya*, which some Cambodians view as a serious conflict of interest. Mong Reththy "is the tycoon in the sector," said Kang Chandararot, a senior economist with a local NGO. "As a senator he makes it hard for newcomers to come into that sector." Mong Reththy disagreed: "Not surprisingly, in the Senate I am in charge of agriculture. I am also chief of the agro-industry associ- ation." He put his hand on his heart. "I do not use my role for family or personal benefit. Some individuals use such an opportunity to do that. But I am committed to doing something for the people. My business is another thing." Then he confided, "I have no education. I went to a temple school for only four years." But his business card lists a doctorate in business administration—a common dishonest conceit for prominent Cambodians. His voice carried a pleading tone as he said, "I hope you can see that I am a normal person."

Inside gated mansions like his all over Phnom Penh and other cities, *oknya* wait for the prime minister to call. When the call comes, they know they will have to travel to some godforsaken spot and spend a little money to make Hun Sen look good. But then when they need or want something, the prime minister is ready to return the favor—for a price. So it was in 2000 when *oknya* Lao Meng Khin asked to buy the rights to take out the last major forest in Pursat Province, in south-central Cambodia. They agreed on a price, to be paid directly to Hun Sen.

Another *oknya*, Ly Yong Phat, also a wealthy senator, actually bought the right to sell off tons of Cambodian land. Singapore was a veracious purchaser of sand; the city used it as landfill to create more real estate. For years it had bought sand from Indonesia, but sucking it from the bottom of the seabed had caused "very severe environmental damage in many Indonesian islands," the Indonesian Foreign Ministry had said. Indonesia banned sand dredging.

Almost right away, *oknya* Ly Yong Phat bought the right to begin sucking sand from the bottom of Cambodian rivers and seashores, for sale to Singapore. The *Phnom Penh Post* reported that sand dredgers were at work inside the Peam Krasp Wildlife Sanctuary, among other places. By the summer of 2010 riverbanks were beginning to collapse, dragging boat piers and outbuildings down into the water.

Eventually, Hun Sen issued what he called a "partial ban" on sand dredging. This still left him a loophole, allowing the continued sale of contracts as he pleased. Similarly, in 2002 Hun Sen issued a ban on logging. No one could cut down any more trees. Existing land concessions were canceled pending review—including Lao Meng Khin's. This was a sop to the World Bank and the other donors who were decrying the ongoing rape of Cambodia's forests. But, just like so many of these edicts, in the tradition of King Norodom's serial promises in the 1880s to abolish slavery, the moratorium existed only on paper. In the field it had little effect. Lao Meng Khin had already paid handsomely for his concession. No one was suggesting that Hun Sen had given the money back. For him and other *oknya* in the lumber business, the moratorium was nothing more than a brief pause.

After an appropriate period of time had passed, the government took up a new tactic. Now, the government was no longer selling lumber concessions. Instead, *oknya* and other tycoons could buy large plots of land to establish so-called plantations. It just so happened that they planned their plantations on the nation's dwindling forested acreage. All those trees would have to be cut down (and sold) to make room for new durian or kumquat farms.

Lao Meng Khin quickly came up with his own scheme: Once the "plantation" land was cleared, Pheapimex would use the property to create a vast eucalyptus farm with the intention of using the trees to feed a paper mill. That was the plan when the bulldozers showed up in early 2004—under armed guard provided by the Royal Cambodian Armed Forces. "I heard that the people are complaining about the cutting of the resin trees," *oknya* Lao Meng Khin offered. "But we are planting eucalyptus in a place that does not violate anyone's property rights."

No, the villagers did not own the forestland. Neither, actually, did Hun Sen. But shortly after Hun Sen announced the deal, more than seven hundred villagers showed up in Phnom Penh to protest the concession. "If they destroy the old forest, they might as well come to kill us," declared Luek Thuon, a sixty-six-year-old villager. "That forest is our rice pot."

After the bulldozers had wreaked havoc for a day, the villagers decided they would stage a sit-in at the forest's entrance. Um Huot, who had grown to be the voice of the protesters, organized it. He was a middle-aged man with an expression of serious purpose locked on his face. He sat on a small wooden porch in front of his modest home, under a corrugated metal roof, and explained the crime in stark terms. The Vietnamese occupiers, the Khmer Rouge, and others had deforested millions of acres in Pursat Province over the previous thirty years. Vast areas of land were clear-cut and now offered only stumps and weeds. Why, then, Um Huot asked, does Lao Meng Khin need this particular plot of land—the only forested land left—for his eucalyptus plantation? "There's plenty of empty land. Why don't they use some of that?"

The answer, Um Huot knew, was that the eucalyptus-plantation proposal was simply a cynical trick, a rationale for the rape of the area's last forest that made no sense to anyone who looked at it with any care. But then, who could challenge Hun Sen? Who could point out these fallacies? Did anyone have leverage over him? Or did Hun Sen and the rest of the Cambodian government, as so many diplomats and human-rights workers complained, live behind an unassailable shield of impunity?

Um Huot managed to recruit eight hundred villagers for the sit-in. They brought sleeping mats and stayed at the forest entrance around the clock, trying to block the bulldozers. And as so often happened in Cambodia, at 12:45 a.m. someone crept out of the woods and threw a hand grenade into the field of sleeping villagers. Eight people were wounded, fortunately none fatally. Um Huot decried the attack. The police, following the script, said the protesters had themselves ordered the grenade attack so they could blame it on the government. Why else was no one killed? It happened that Peter Leuprecht, the UN human-rights envoy, was in Phnom Penh at the time, and he exclaimed, "I deplore this grenade attack that was launched against peaceful protestors, and I hope that a serious investigation will be carried out."

As usual, no one was ever arrested or charged. The only positive result occurred a few days later when the Ministry of the Interior, responding to outrage from diplomats and human-rights officers, temporarily suspended the clear-cutting operation. Um Huot and the others viewed it as a stay of execution. They returned to the forest to pursue their livelihood—fully aware that they were living on borrowed time.

The fracas at the forest served as a coda to the World Bank's efforts to reform forestry management. Over the months leading up to the grenade attack, all of the bank's initiatives crumbled under the weight of official corruption and, within the bank itself, institutional torpor and incompetence.

In December 2002, 150 people gathered at the Forestry and Wildlife Ministry to protest ongoing deforestation at numerous sites around the country. Thousands of villagers were losing their livelihoods, just like those people in Pursat. The government loosed the police on the protesters. Officers kicked them and attacked using electric batons. Seven people were hospitalized; one was killed. Global Witness, the government's forest monitor, issued an acrid, accusatory report. Hun Sen, furious, fired Global Witness and kicked its investigators out of the country—something he had probably wanted to do for a long time.

Hun Sen had hired Global Witness only because the donors had left him little choice at that time. In the following years, he had bristled and bridled as he watched the group work against his interests. "We have the right to terminate visas for anyone who dares to abuse our national sovereignty, our political rights and inflict damage to our reputation," he said. "I will sue Global Witness because it has accused Cambodian police of killing people and injuring several others." After he dismissed the group the investigators left. But soon others arrived. Like a hound that sniffed a covey of quail, Global Witness could not let this investigation go. It didn't need a government contract or Hun Sen's permission. The group would finish its investigation and publish a report on its own.

The World Bank soon ran into troubles of its own—from its own internal office of investigations. For years, the bank had worked to reform the government's forest-concession program—the one that sold vast swaths of forest to *oknya* and other wealthy businessmen. The fruit of the bank's effort was the bogus logging moratorium and other theatrical administrative orders. Meantime, the trees, millions and millions of trees, continued falling all over the country. Trucks loaded with lumber clotted the state's roads. Hun Sen and his cronies grew ever richer from the concession payments that went directly to them, not the government.

In 2006 World Bank investigators from Washington found that their officers in Phnom Penh had so single-mindedly pursued concession reform and phony regulations that they'd ignored what was really going on. If they had bothered to lift their eyes from their desks and look out the window, they would have seen that the government had authorized "an estimated 3–4 million cubic meters of illegal logging," the investigators' report said. Yet all the while Ian Porter, the bank's Cambodia office director, lauded the enactment of new regulations. He seemed to have forgotten that the state had issued similar regulations years earlier. Shortly after taking office in 1993, Hun Sen and Ranariddh had announced a new rule that said timber exports were now "prohibited under any circumstances." Why did the bank think the new promises were any more believable?

Over the years, dozens of Cambodians told the bank's executive officers about the continuing deforestation. As the bank investigators finally put it, falling into World Bank internal jargon, "Bank was frequently made aware of numerous complaints of harms to local communities due to cutting of resin trees. Bank's failure to consider and investigate these problems does not comply with OP 4.01 and OP 4.36." In other words, the international communities' initiative to save Cambodia's forests was in shambles.

Against this backdrop the government faced national elections once again in the summer of 2003, the third since the UN occupation. The players remained the same, as did the issues. Violence diminished a bit. Still, opposition officers were killed, the CPP intimidated voters by multiple means, and all the parties tried to buy votes. Turnout dropped by about 10 percent over the previous elections in 1998. Analysts hypothesized that many voters realized that the election would not, could not, bring any real change. Whatever happened, they seemed to believe, Hun Sen would cling to power, while Ranariddh and Rainsy would scheme to maneuver the results to their own advantage.

Yet when the votes were tallied, Hun Sen found himself in a fix once again. This time the CPP won 47 percent of the vote, the Sam Rainsy Party 22 percent, and Funcinpec 21 percent. A variety of smaller parties won the rest of the vote, but none of them wound up with enough to claim a seat in parliament.

The CPP had "won," but Hun Sen still did not have the two-thirds supermajority needed to form a government. He would have to reach out to at least one of the opposition parties. Either one could push him over the top. But Rainsy and Ranariddh were not going to shake his hand so easily this time. Or so they said.

The two men formed a coalition called the Alliance of Democrats—a name intended to show the differences between their outlook and Hun Sen's. They created a platform, listing the demands that had to be met before they would join a governing coalition. Any Cambodian reading these conditions could immediately see their true intent: to effectively remove Hun Sen from power. This time Rainsy and Ranariddh had come up with a particularly clever scheme to overturn the election results, one that their fans in the international bleachers happily embraced. Both Rainsy and Ranariddh said they would not join any government unless Hun Sen signed a pact confirming these points:

- The government would establish a new nonpartisan National Election Committee. King Sihanouk would appoint the chairman and vice chairman.
- In each village nationwide a village committee representing all three parties would replace the CPP-appointed village chief.
- The parliament would enact a new election law to make elections freer and fairer by, for example, opening broadcast media to all candidates.

- The three parties would agree on judicial reform to remove the government's control of the court system.
- The parliament would pass an anticorruption law, and the government would establish an independent anticorruption commission (nine years after Hun Sen first proposed that idea).

Further proposals were intended to break Hun Sen's control of the government bureaucracy, the military, and the police. Finally, if any party chose to withdraw from the coalition, the parliament would have to take a vote of confidence in the government. If the government could not win that vote, new elections would be held—under the new, presumably fairer election law.

Having lived under Hun Sen's many-handed control of Cambodian governing institutions for a decade, the Alliance of Democrats knew precisely how to block him at every turn. Well aware of Rainsy and Ranariddh's intentions, Hun Sen refused to sign. His spokesman, Khieu Kanharith, said simply, "It is absurd for the losing parties to issue demands to the winning party."

The deadlock dragged on, month after month, and true to form Ranariddh spent most of his time at his home in Paris, saying he would come back when Hun Sen conceded. Rainsy hopscotched between Paris, Sydney, and Washington, still trying to convince foreign leaders of Hun Sen's perfidy.

Hun Sen, meantime, continued in power as if nothing had changed. Brazen murders of opposition leaders continued at a brisk pace, and in January 2004, four months into the election stalemate, two men on a black motorcycle with license plates removed, wearing helmets with dark-tinted faceplates, pulled up to a street stall where a man named Chea Vichea was reading a newspaper. They shot him dead and then sped off.

Chea Vichea was the nation's most prominent labor leader, president of the Free Trade Union of Workers of Cambodia. He had organized numerous workers' rights marches and demonstrations. He was a member of the Sam Rainsy Party. His death haunted the CPP for years—especially after the courts trumped up charges against two obviously innocent men and sentenced both to long prison terms.* The CPP was following what was now standard and established practice: Peel away some opposition-party members with blandishments and bribes. Kill the rest.

This behavior wasn't restricted to the Sam Rainsy Party, either. In January 2004 assailants broke into Meach Youen's home while he was sleeping and shot him in the face with an AK-47 assault rifle. He was an important Funcinpec official and the fifth opposition figure to be murdered in just that month.

The tactic was remarkably effective. Typically, a CPP enforcer would call or visit an opposition-party officer and offer him a senior position in government, one that came with the sobriquet "his excellency," along with a rich down payment and a coveted spot amid the cash flow. The officer could visit the Toyota dealer and drive home in his new Land Cruiser that very afternoon. It was an offer he could not refuse. Say no, the officer well knew, and he could end up like Chea Vichea or Meach Youen by the end of the week.

The defections and killings steadily reduced the opposition parties' strength. A few weeks later, as Rainsy's bargaining position slowly dissolved, he proclaimed that his party and Ranariddh's would merge. Ranariddh didn't have much to say about that; he was still in France. But Ranariddh had betrayed Rainsy before. Perhaps, Rainsy certainly thought, this would lock him in. At the same news conference he once again warned that Hun Sen was about to kill him and, true to form, appealed to his foreign friends to protect him.

---

*When an American journalist produced a film named *Who Killed Chea Vichea?* in the spring of 2010, he showed it at the Cannes Film Festival, but the Cambodian government banned the showing of the film. When union members tried to show it in Phnom Penh, police stormed in and tore down the screen. The film concluded that highly placed members of the Cambodian government had to know about the killing.

A few weeks later the two parties formally announced a "merger," as planned, but that lasted only a short while. In June Ranariddh finally struck a lucrative deal with Hun Sen that allowed his party to enter a coalition with the CPP—and leave Rainsy out in the cold.

Ranariddh had needed the previous months to negotiate the arrangement he wanted. The merger with Rainsy's party had been simply a bargaining tool. Under the resulting deal Hun Sen and Ranariddh would split "commissions," the payments *oknya* and others made to Hun Sen or Ranariddh to buy land for deforestation, commercial development, mineral mining, or other exploitative purposes. Sixty percent of these payments would go to Hun Sen, 40 percent to Ranariddh, Steven Heder reported in *Southeast Asian Affairs*.

When word of this leaked out, Funcinpec and Rainsy party members began tripping over each other in the scramble to pay Ranariddh large sums for the government positions they hoped to hold. Most of the money was wasted. In June, eleven months after the election, Ranariddh agreed on a platform for the new government that included not a word of the Alliance of Democrats' reform platform—or any place for Sam Rainsy Party members. Hun Sen would remain as prime minister, Ranariddh as president of the National Assembly.

Once again, Rainsy got nothing. Soon he was almost all by himself. Over the summer more than a hundred members of his political party defected to Funcinpec, Ranariddh's party. Ranariddh held a welcoming ceremony at his party headquarters and told the Rainsy Party deserters, "I will send the list of defectors to Prime Minister Hun Sen and let the government offer appropriate positions to them." Twisting the knife in Rainsy's heart one more time, he also urged more of his party members to defect.

But Rainsy was not the only one he betrayed. Ranariddh had worked out his own lucrative deal, and in the process he had abandoned his own party, too. Funcinpec would now control the Ministries of Health, Rural Development, Tourism, Public Works and

Transport, and Education as well as Culture and Fine Arts. With the possible exception of Public Works and Transport, none of the ministries offered any opportunity for significant graft. Once again, Hun Sen and Ranariddh had worked everything nicely for themselves, while doing nothing for their allies—or for the Cambodian people.

A few weeks after the new government took office, the U.S. Embassy greeted the duo with a comprehensive and devastating research report on what it called "grand corruption." It showed that government officials stole up to $500 million each and every year—about half of the state's annual budget—almost every dollar the government collected on its own. The other half of the budget consisted of donations from NGOs.

In effect, the government chieftains left the care of the people to foreign donors while using the state's own money to care for themselves. "The Royal Government of Cambodia collects very limited legal revenues, as large sums are lost to smuggling, bribes and other illegal practices," the report concluded. "Further losses are experienced once revenues enter the state financial system. Informants estimated annual diversions from government coffers ranging between $300 and $500 million."

A team of American consultants, working for USAID, had worked for much of a year and laid out a stunning description of a pervasive patronage system that affected every facet of Cambodian society. "Grand corruption involving illegal grants of logging concessions coexist with the nearly universal practice of small facilitation payments to speed or simply secure service delivery. Police and other officials demand small bribes in numerous guises. Students across the public school system pay unofficial daily fees to supplement salaries of teachers and administrators, and perhaps fill the pockets of high-level ministry officials. The same is true in public health, where access to services is often contingent on supplemental payments to doctors, nurses or other health-care personnel."

Among their findings was a pernicious tax system. As in most nations, taxes were collected ostensibly to pay for health, education, social development, and other state services for the people. Instead, each time a tax collector visited a business, he told the owner that he would forgive the tax debt if the businessman paid him a somewhat smaller bribe instead. Most businessmen complied—to save money and possible trouble if they refused. "Some observers have argued that such payments are taxes in another form. While there is some truth in this observation, this form of corruption places businesses in a legally and morally ambiguous position, tainted by their own actions, and readily subject to additional, irregular exactions from officials. The costs to citizens-at-large are even greater. Low formal tax payments lead to poor health and education services and second-rate infrastructure. And because potential foreign and indigenous investors refuse to do business in Cambodia, few jobs are created, and additional legal revenues are foregone." For these and many other instances of depravity and turpitude, the consultants found, no one was ever punished:

> Corruption is structured more or less as a pyramid, with petty exactions meeting the survival needs of policemen, teachers and health workers, but also shared with officials higher in the system. Patronage and mutual obligations are the center of an all-embracing system. Appointment to public office hinges on political connections or payment of surprisingly large sums, and these payments are recouped through a widely accepted right to collect bribes. And impunity is the norm.
>
> No one involved with the patronage of the state is punished, whether for massive pillaging or petty theft. In fact, those most at risk are individuals and organizations that dare to resist corruption. Most Cambodians regard resistance as a futile act.

The report was devastating. As Hun Sen considered his response, still another scandal spilled out, first reported by the *Phnom Penh*

*Post.* World Food Program officials discovered in August 2004 that about 4,000 tons of rice worth more than $2 million had been stolen en route to some of the nation's poorest areas, where it was supposed to feed Cambodia's most malnourished children. The thieves then sold the stolen rice for cash.

The WFP fed millions of children in desperately poor countries worldwide. Typically, it provided school lunches, as an inducement for parents to send their children to school. The lunches, rice and fish, were often the only meals the children would get each day. WFP and UNICEF surveys found that at least one-third of Cambodian children were malnourished. The WFP classified the situation as "alarming." UNICEF data showed that about 40 percent of Cambodia's children were "stunted" for lack of nutrition, and 10 percent suffered from wasting, meaning essentially that they were starving to death. Given those numbers, it was no surprise that one child in ten died before reaching age five. That is why the theft of WFP rice was so devastating for the children who were to have eaten it. Most likely, some of them died as a result, as the thieves should certainly have known.

The WFP fired several Cambodian employees, and newspapers reported that some senior government officials were implicated— though, of course, none were ever penalized. But Hun Sen was contrite. He promised to pay the WFP back, either in rice or in cash.

As for his formal response to the corruption report, he apparently realized that the annual donors meeting was just a few weeks away. This would be an inopportune time to lash out at the United States, the nation that had paid for the report. So Hun Sen pulled out that old chestnut, always available for troubled moments like this. He promised once again to pass the anticorruption law.

The amazing thing was that anyone believed him. Hun Sen had first proposed this law in 1995, another moment when donors were restive over corruption. The offer had quieted them for a while, and the government had then thrown up an imaginative array of excuses and roadblocks to explain away the failure to pass the bill. For example, answering questions during the previous donor meeting, Hun Sen had promised to pass the law by the end of June 2003. And in fact, that June a law was brought up before the parliament for a vote. But it failed because the assembly could not muster a quorum. Someone had stipulated that, for this particular vote on that particular day, seven-eighths of the assembly membership had to be present. Every opposition member was there. Somehow, though, just enough members of Hun Sen's own political party failed to show up. So the proposed law was shelved for another year.

When the 2004 donor meeting dawned, the donors were in a nasty mood. American ambassador Charles Ray dropped his diplomatic veneer and lambasted the Cambodian leadership. "Ordinary Cambodians," he told Hun Sen and the state's other leaders assembled before him, "are subject to a daunting array of small and medium exactions, some paid virtually on a daily basis." He noted that the corruption report had highlighted the significant loss in revenue due to smuggling, bribes, and other illegal practices. The total, up to $500 million, was roughly equal to the amount the donors gave each year. As an example, payments students made to teachers each morning, starting in the first grade, "suggest that children as young as six are already being schooled in the art of corruption and bribery."

When his turn came to speak, Hun Sen put away his usual scornful bombast and did not respond directly to the angry accusations. Cambodia, he said, was "at a crossroads in its difficult journey towards sustainable development and poverty reduction." He promised again that his administration would pass the long-awaited anticorruption law, aggressively fight corruption, strengthen government institutions, and improve governance.

All of the donors had heard that before. Some shook their heads and rolled their eyes. When they finally made their pledges the total came to only $504 million for the coming year—almost $100 million less than they had provided at the last meeting. Cambodia had asked the donors to pledge $1.8 billion to be paid over the next three years, "but the donors would have none of it," Verghese Mathews, the former Singapore ambassador to Cambodia, wrote in the *Straits Times*. "The donor community has been demanding good governance for years and is not amused at the unacceptably slow pace of reforms." Now, the former ambassador added, "the signal was clear—future aid would be conditional" on progress. But Hun Sen had heard that before, too, and experience had shown him that he needn't worry about it.

# CHAPTER TEN

When the government delivered some emergency food assistance, three hundred residents of Dang Rung village rioted. Some of them saw the sacks of free rice, scores of them, delivered to the village chief. But none of them got any. So they naturally assumed he had given the rice to his family, friends, and CPP cronies, leaving none for the rest of the villagers. "We didn't see even a grain of rice," fifty-six-year-old Saing Moeva said with a sneer. He was rolling a cigarette from a plastic bag holding a small bit of tobacco, leaning against a pillar holding up his one-room home. Asked if he had ever received any aid from the government, he chortled as he said, "Yes, every five years," at election time. "They come around and give us a sarong, 2.5 grams of seasoning, and a scarf." His sense of humor was rare among Cambodians. In fact, it was quite rare to see Cambodians laugh at all. Given their desperate situation, they seldom even smiled.

His wife, Mou Chouerm, rose from the hammock under the house and pointed at a small cultivated patch. "I grow mint and sell it at market," she said, her voice slurred. "I can earn 7,000 riel, maybe 10,000." That's roughly $1.75 to $2.50. The slur was the product of an ugly deformity. She'd had a stroke years earlier and lost control of the right side of her face. Her mouth drooped, baring her teeth, almost as if a lead weight pulled at it. She had looked like this since 1985, when she collapsed and her husband decided "to take her where they could treat her with traditional medicine. She had bad spirits, so we went to a secret spirit house about thirty kilometers from here. A traditional drama group played music to chase away the spirits. It didn't really help."

In 1985, during the Vietnamese occupation, professional health care was largely unavailable in the provinces. But the spirit treatment left more lasting damage. Not only did Mou Chouerm and Saing Moeva have to pay about $500 for the ceremony, "we also had to buy alcohol, beef, and other food for those people." To come up with the necessary funds, the family had to sell half of its land. Now Mou Chouerm still presented an ugly sneer, and they owned so little land that they could not produce enough rice to feed themselves. That is why they were so excited to hear that the Asian Development Bank was donating free rice to the poor.

A villager working for the local government had come by to take their names and location. But to get to their house, he had to pass a Funcinpec Party sign planted at the head of the dirt track leading to their home. And when he spoke to Saing Moeva, the odds that day were fifty-fifty that he was wearing a Human Rights Party T-shirt. During the recent campaign party workers had come by handing these out for free. "No, no, I am CPP," he objected, waving his arms, as if to say otherwise would suggest treason. "Any political party can put up a sign." In fact, those signs dotted the countryside, everywhere. "They asked me, and I said okay, but I didn't know they would put it on my property." As for the shirt, "I have only two, and I wear this one sometimes." He pointed to the other, a blue work shirt hanging from a nail under the house. Animated, he gesticulated urgently toward his pants, his only pair, torn over the left knee. "We are poor; we are very poor."

To prove the point, Mou Chouerm climbed the log ladder into their small house. The floor was almost bare. Practically their only possession was a twelve-inch National-brand black-and-white television sitting on a rusted folding TV table, wired to a car battery on the floor. To watch it they sat on the floor. She pointed to the tin ceiling, speckled with bright spots, the tropical sunlight shining through scores of tiny holes—so many that, when it rained, they could take a shower. She shook her head and, unable to shake her anger, she again said: "We didn't get any rice."

Down the dirt road, around a bend, Chan Yat sat quietly on a neighbor's stoop. At seventy-six, she was ancient. On average Cambodians could hope to live to about sixty. She had few teeth, so her lips curled into her mouth. She shaved her head. The furrows on her face seemed to testify to a difficult life. She was the poorest of the poor, and her reality had changed little if at all since she was born here in this village in 1933. Some of her neighbors now had battery-powered radios and television sets. A few had motor scooters. But nearly all of them lived on what they could forage or grow and slept in hammocks under their bamboo-walled homes. Some of those same huts were standing there, she said, when she was a little girl.

Chan Yat walked slowly to her own house, leaning on a cane, a bamboo sapling that happened to have a crook at the top. She lived in a miniature Cambodian house on stilts just two feet high. They held up an enclosure maybe five feet by five feet and no more than four feet tall. The walls were woven palm fronds halfway up toward the roof. The upper half was covered with empty Blue Diamond Cement bags tacked to the frame.

She spoke in a whisper. "Yes, I got some rice. A bag, fifty kilograms. The village chief brought it." Her son, a laborer, normally brought her a bit of food now and then. As she spoke a crowd gathered outside, fifteen or twenty people. Visitors were in town, asking about the rice! The villagers tried to outshout each other. "I didn't get any," said a middle-aged woman. "Not a grain. Nothing!" Another woman angrily insisted, "They gave the rice to the people who don't need it. Those people probably sold it. They didn't give any to the people who would actually eat it." She rubbed her stomach as if to say, I am hungry. A scrawny gray cat with a white belly sidled past her, scanning the ground for food. It pounced on a spider.

As the villagers grew angrier and angrier, Chan Yat, the only one there who had actually been given some of the rice, sat quietly, leaning on her bamboo cane, looking down at the dirt. "People here are very poor," a man shouted. "We didn't get any food. We never get any food! It all goes to them," he snarled, pointing in the direction of the village chief's house.

Kok Chuum had heard it all before. He had been village chief for seven years. He was a warm, voluble, soft-spoken fellow with cheekbones so high they seemed to be reaching for his forehead. As he sat at a table in the yard of his small compound, four buildings and sheds holding stores and equipment, he explained, "The food we get is not for everyone." Chickens, ducks, and pigs wandered about. "There's not enough. Some years only enough for four families. Some years twenty. We rotate. This year we got four tons, enough for forty families," more than half the village.

Even so, some people say they have never been given any rice—not even a grain, they like to say. "I know some people say that, hoping to get more," he explained in a quiet tone, showing no surprise. "But that's a lie. I think the problem here is the state of mind. Some people go to the water and come back with empty hands." He shook his head. His manner was sorrowful, not disparaging. "The way of thinking here is very low. They don't have any ambition. They go to school and come out without any idea of doing anything."

Kok Chuum was in his forties, and like most people his age, he had attended a temple school through the third grade where he did learn to read and write; that's all. But he was a man in motion, and that had obviously paid off. He was quite prosperous, by his village's standards.

Asked what he earns, he offered a counterintuitive answer, for Cambodians, and talked instead about how much he was able to save. "If I don't have a wedding to pay for or some other big expense, I can save 2 million riel a year." That's almost $500, roughly the average per-capita income for Cambodians. A few years earlier he had bought a rice mill—a primitive, almost cartoonish-looking device that sat in a shed. A gas-powered motor turned a ten-foot cloth belt that in turn spun gears, each almost three feet in perimeter. Kok Chuum used it to make rice-based animal feed for sale. The machine cost him $1,400 a few years earlier, "and I have not made my investment back yet."

He asked visitors to remove their shoes before climbing the log ladder to his house. Inside, his young daughter watched cartoons on a small battery-powered *color* television. The house was painted a dark red—the only one in his village with paint. Moralistic public-service posters decorated the walls. One showed a man sleeping under a tree, a straw hat pulled low over his eyes, next to a broken-down cart. His oxen were wandering away. Others offered picture stories preaching against alcoholism, drugs, domestic violence.

From his villagers came the constant refrain, punctuating every conversation: "I am poor" or "I am hungry." Kok Chuum had his own personal declaration, offered repeatedly: "I work very hard." He had learned to rely on no one else. After all, as the CPP village chief, Kok Chuum sat on the lowest rung of the government ladder. The position paid only $10 a month.

Asked what his government did for his constituents, he answered, "The dikes and canals. And they maintain the road and the bridges." Just what King Indravarman III had done for his people nearly a millennium earlier.

Kok Chuum's remarks, and those of the villagers, did not sit well with His Excellency Chhay Sareth, Pursat Province's longtime governor and now its provincial council chief. He sat in the provincial government's council room at one end of a twenty-five-foot conference table that seated at least forty people. Along the wall at the other end loomed a massive video conferencing system with a fifty-inch Sony LCD monitor, a camera on a tripod, and a rack of assorted equipment.

A few months earlier, Hun Sen had asked every province to install one. He'd been in western Cambodia for the dedication of a new $450 million golf course and sports complex. The prime minister was an enthusiastic golfer. He had built an eighteen-hole course at his country estate, and his official government Web site lists his scores ahead of everything else ("Number of pars: 51 percent"). But while visiting he had ordered each of the twenty-four provinces, the army, and border-control stations to install video conferencing systems because, he said, "This will allow me to give direct orders following my reading of local media." Ministries and departments should also convert to this "new gadget," the prime minister added.

Pursat was one of the nation's poorest provinces, and the equipment cost between $50,000 and $75,000. Chhay Sareth pointed to it, saying, "We need to use more machinery. Cambodia is behind other countries. We need to get to modern times." For now, though, he wanted to talk about a more primitive issue, the food aid. He leaned forward, pushing down hard on the table as he said in a sharp tone, "The government cannot satisfy everyone. The food aid is very limited. The people like to say the authorities don't take care of them. But sometimes the people don't receive the food aid because they are not home. They are away—job migration—and when they get back it is too late. But the poverty is not from this food-aid confusion. It's from laziness. Or, the people have lost the land they had for farming." Then the governor sat up straight, hands on his hips. "I don't agree that most people don't trust the government. I am here, president of the provincial council, and we lead from zero. Pol Pot killed everything. We are still rebuilding."

Chhay Sareth relaxed a bit and sat back in his chair. He wore a tan safari suit and gold wire-rim eyeglasses, an outfit identical to the one Hun Sen often wore.* Unlike some other governors, he did not present an ostentatious show of wealth. A plastic pen stuck out of his

---

*Eyeglasses were another indication of wealth. In the provinces, no one wore them, no matter how poor their eyesight might be. No one could afford them. In fact, optometry was not a profession commonly pursued.

pocket; on his wrist he wore a simple gold watch and on his left hand a small diamond ring.

His people, Chhay Sareth acknowledged, live a life that "is a kick-back to centuries ago. This is Cambodia's tradition." He was hardly the only official to refer to abject poverty, malnutrition, illiteracy, disease, and premature death as "Cambodia's tradition." He concluded, "I cannot say what my council will do, but we have a work plan, and we need to improve agriculture."

So say his colleagues, nationwide. In 2009 the parliament changed the law to give the provinces more money and greater control of their fates. To manage this it set up new provincial counsels. Flush with this new authority and the promise of new cash, a half-dozen governors and council chairmen described their vision for the twenty-first century. But, to a man, they echoed Chhay Sareth's tenth-century ideas.

Chan Sophal, chairman of the provincial council in Siem Reap Province, dressed in that same tan safari suit, the same gold-frame glasses, told of his ambition: "Better roads and irrigation for remote, rural people." His gold watch bore small images of the CPP's three iconic leaders, Prime Minister Hun Sen, Deputy Prime Minister Sok An, and Chea Sim, president of the senate. Viewed from across the chairman's desk, the three tiny faces brought to mind old publicity photos of The Three Stooges, Moe, Larry, and Curly. "Give them a better capability to farm," chairman Chan Sophal continued. "Help them improve their land so they can grow more rice."

In Kampong Thom Province, north of Phnom Penh, council chairman Nam Tum wore exactly the same uniform and offered a similar plan. "For a long time, people have relied on the tradition, living on forest products. We need to change the Cambodian tradition so that people don't live by nature anymore. Then we could have a real free market." He sat in the lobby of the governor's mansion in one of those high-back luxury-wood chairs with serpentine carvings. Two rows of these chairs faced each other, twelve of them in all. Behind him, hanging high on the wall, were portraits of the king and queen mother.

Two brown lizards crawled over the queen's face. "We must solve the problems of the agriculture sector so it can grow. The well-educated people were killed by the Khmer Rouge. So today's younger generation, the people who are trained and educated, if we want to grow as a nation we need to send these people back to help the farmers improve their rice."

In Battambang Province, Governor Prach Chann's safari suit was linen, not cotton. A gold pen stuck out of his breast pocket. He sat on one side of a conference table for twelve people, a microphone at each place. His massive, richly carved luxury-wood desk loomed at the end of the room. His views were consistent with those of his counterparts in other provinces: "The way people make a living is traditional. We want to pursue conservation and development to maintain our regional culture related to the development of agriculture." But like several of his colleagues, he also blamed his people, saying "their poverty is from laziness."

In Pailin Province, the governor, a former messenger for Pol Pot now wearing one of those signature tan safari suits, said he was too busy to talk as he climbed into his limousine in front of the provincial office building. In the lobby a bulletin board showed him cutting ribbons and kissing babies, in many cases wearing a military uniform so heavily encrusted with medals that it was a surprise he didn't walk with a stoop. Down the hall, the deputy governor, Mey Meakk, said simply: "Our main job is to build roads for accessibility and help them improve farming."

No one in government offered a view that differed from this one. No one mentioned manufacturing, service industries, technology. Nobody spoke of higher education. Not one official strayed from a vision of his country that differed at all from the goals of the Angkorian kings. But then most of these men, generally in their fifties and sixties, had little if any education themselves.

When these men were children there were no schools, save those temple classes for young children. Those people who managed to go to school in Phnom Penh generally left the country before 1975 or were killed by the Khmer Rouge. The same held true throughout the Cambodian government. Prime Minister Hun Sen said he left school when he was sixteen to join the Khmer Rouge, which would be quite unusual for a man his age who lived in the provinces. (Some biographies say he was eighteen, but they also list an assortment of bachelor and master's degrees as well as a Ph.D. that he never earned.) On the twenty-fifth anniversary of his appointment as prime minister, in January 2010, the *Cambodia Daily* published a long profile in which one of the prime minister's closest colleagues seemed to let the cat out of the bag. Cheam Yeap, a senior CPP legislator, said Hun Sen "only finished grade three or four before joining the resistance. Even though he studied a little bit, he learned very fast."

Aid workers, meantime, worried that the people's continuing ability to live by nature, as all of these government officials were advocating, was simply not sustainable. "They have eaten all the cobras, most of the lizards, the pythons," said Javier Merelo de Barbera Llobet, who worked for Catholic Relief Services in Battambang for more than two years. "The trees are gone. And the monkeys are almost all gone. They are a great delicacy now."

But starting in the mid-1990s Cambodia acquired a new industry, a new source of wealth. Several Asian nations, principally China, Malaysia, Singapore, and Taiwan, on their own initiative, began building garment factories in Cambodia. They saw the low-wage labor market as particularly attractive. Over the following years the number of these factories rose to more than three hundred. They employed as many as 380,000 Cambodians, primarily women. The workers made jeans, T-shirts, baseball caps, and sweaters, primarily, and sold almost three-quarters of their products to the United States. The factories grew to produce 70 percent of Cambodia's exports. The only real competition was rice.

The government encouraged expansion of the industry; it actually produced legitimate income—taxes and fees. But it also made the government quite vulnerable. As Ambassador Joseph Mussomeli put it, "The economy has three legs: garments, tourism, and agriculture. Levi Strauss or the Gap could destroy this country on a whim." When the world economic crisis hit in 2008, Mussomeli's dark vision came true. Orders from American retailers plummeted. Tens of thousands of Cambodians lost their jobs. But Hun Sen had a ready solution. "Unemployment hasn't caused a very big crisis for our country," he insisted, because "those people can go back to the fields and grow more rice."

Sorasak Pan, deputy minister of commerce, was one of the few who had a different idea, though his ambition was limited—he advocated a different sort of farming. "We can export Cambodian silk to America tax free," he said with smiling enthusiasm. "It's a handicraft for women who can raise silkworms at home. You know, if silkworms eat a different kind of leaf, they produce a different kind of silk. Here they can eat mulberry leaves. This hits two things, poverty and gender. It's true that Cambodian silk is rougher than Thai silk. But it lasts longer!"

Sorn Kimseng was deputy executive director of the Cambodian Chamber of Commerce. He represented Cambodian businesses, so that colored his opinion. Still he said, "Actually it is good we invest in agriculture. But if it is only agriculture, Cambodia cannot recover. We need to focus on industry more. If we focus only on agriculture, so much of the country will remain undeveloped. And when agriculture has a problem, we cannot control it."

In Channy, president and CEO of Acleda Bank, one of Cambodia's largest, with 220 branches across the nation, said, "I have a different view." He wore a blue suit and white shirt with a gold-and-blue-striped tie. His corner office was pleasant but not grand. Among dozens of Cambodian officials and businessmen, he alone said clearly, "We continue to get lost. We need to expand business, but to establish a company here is so complicated. It discourages entrepreneurship. You lose so much money, so much time. Here it takes at least forty-five days to start a company. In Singapore it takes thirty minutes, and you can do it online. The government needs to shorten registration time, remove barriers for imports." What's more, "the transport costs are three times what they are in Vietnam. There are time delays on imports, and you have to pay a lot on the way. Customs, capital control, agriculture . . . several parties are involved," meaning several agencies taking bribes. "If they do not remove these barriers, we cannot move forward."

Kang Chandararot, head of the Economics Unit at the Cambodia Institute for Development Study, worried about a related problem. "The prevailing risk," he said, "will continue to be conflict of interest in general. Businesspeople are at the same time members of government, making policy." He mentioned Mong Reththy, the *oknya* and senator who dominated the palm-oil business, as an example. "They can crowd competitors out. That makes it difficult to grow. That's why we need an anticorruption law." Mong Reththy himself suggested that not even an effective law would help. "Most companies have two sets of books," he said. Living without corruption, "that's impossible for Cambodians. It's just not possible. You are not Cambodian, so you cannot understand."

Cambodia's constitution forbade conflicts like Mong Reththy's. Article 101 said: "The functions of members of the Royal Government shall be incompatible with professional activities in trade or industry and with the holding of any position in the public service." But then no one in government paid any particular attention to the constitution, written during the UN occupation. As Sihanouk perceptively explained in 1996, "The public is not concerned about liberal democracy. Everything is very special in Cambodia. The reality is, their government is judged not so much on how democratic it is but how many bridges and roads and hospitals they build. The constitution is a paper monument. We consider it a monument."

Even without all of these obstacles, the nation was still hard-pressed to move forward when 88 percent of the nation's people had no electrical service. This group included almost everyone outside of the capital. "Eighty percent of our supply goes to Phnom Penh," said Keo Rattanak, director general of the Cambodian Electric Company. He was a tidy-looking businessman with two computer monitors on his desk and neat, color-coded file folders. Expanding electrical service to the rest of the nation, he seemed to say, was economically impossible because the government sucked his company dry. It ordered him to give subsidies to the poor, the vast majority of his customers, "but then they don't pay us back to make up the difference." The Asian Development Bank provided grants to expand service, but the money went through the government, and officials took a cut. "If we lose money here, it is impossible to subsidize" people in the provinces. "The poorest of the poor are in the countryside. We can't subsidize them. If the elephant falls, you can't expect the ants to support the elephant. So we have no strong incentive to reach out. Every time we reach out, we lose more money. I have been very vocal about this. We are part of the government. What do they say? We 'should be acting like a commercial enterprise and should be more efficient.' I would love to be able to do a lot more to lessen the impact of electricity on everyone in the economy, but I can't."

The government said it planned to build several hydroelectric dams that would, in theory, provide electricity to the provinces. China was promising to help pay for them. Few put much faith in that promise. For these and so many other problems, In Channy, the bank president, said, "We need a clear vision from the top. In our society, normally small people follow their leader."

In the meantime, Kamlesh Vyas, the Cambodia director of a South Asian NGO who tried to work with farmers in Battambang Province, shook his head as he offered his own analysis. "They are just following the past because that's all they can do. You can't impart new skills to people with no education."

Tuy Khorn was barefoot, trying her best to tie a heavy rock to a plow blade bound to a tree limb, pulled by an ox. She was trying to dig rice furrows. She was alone; the Khmer Rouge killed her husband in 1997.

Her seventeen-year-old daughter wanted to get married to bring a man (or boy) into the household to help out. Tuy Khorn said she was trying to discourage her. She wore a dirty red shirt, a pink sarong, and a white floppy hat in an unsuccessful effort to keep the brutal sunlight off her face. She was forty-two but looked much older. Each time she tied a knot on the big rock and ticked the ox with a stick so it began lumbering forward, the rock tumbled off her makeshift plow blade. Again and again. "Some years," she said, "I can grow enough rice to last through the year. But if there's no rain, I can't grow enough. I don't know what I will do if there's no rain, maybe just go by nature." What she meant was eating fruits and insects and whatever she could find in the wild.

Eighty percent of Cambodian farmers lived as she did, wholly dependent on the weather to survive. That year, 2009, Cambodia suffered a drought, and climate change already seemed to be bringing on drought conditions more and more often. While Cambodia's leaders promoted a vision of the future that seemed to mimic Jayavarman II's governorship in the ninth century AD, they failed to provide the people even as much as the ancient kings had offered. Mey Meakk, deputy governor of Pailin Province, put it this way: "I have no ability to compare life to the period of Jayavarman. But development of the country then was very, very high compared to this day."

Angkor thrived because of a sophisticated irrigation network. Zhou, the thirteenth-century Chinese chronicler, noted that the networks allowed farmers to harvest three, maybe four, rice crops a year. Almost no one in modern-day Cambodia grew more than one crop. Early in the twenty-first century somewhere between 4 and 10 percent of Cambodia's farmers had access to irrigation. Even those few people found it of limited value.

Just over two hundred families lived in the village of Sangkum, in Kampong Thom Province, and a lovely addition had come to the settlement a year earlier. An irrigation canal sloshed through the center of town, water sparkling and gurgling in the sun. In truth, the canal had been there for more than thirty years, since the Khmer Rouge forced villagers to dig it. Loch Pheach, the deputy village chief, had been one of those slave laborers. "The dirt was compacted, tough as wood. It was very hard work, and they didn't give us anything to eat," he recalled. "People died."

After the war the canal fell quickly into disrepair. Loch Pheach moved away and returned only in 2000. He found the canal still there, "a scar, a hideous reminder of that terrible time," now passing only a trickle of water—just enough to make mud. But in 2008 the Asian Development Bank provided money to renovate it. Now, one of the sluice gates flooded Loch Pheach's rice paddy. Still, "the canal has water only during the rainy season. We'll have water until November." So he and the other villagers with access to the canal water still can produce only one crop each year—and that only if it rains. They are little better off than Tuy Khorn, the woman trying to tie the rock to the plow.

Up and down the waterway, dozens of other families watched the water flow by but could not use it at all. No sluice gates were built to serve their land. With no electricity, they couldn't use a pump and wouldn't have been able to afford one even if it had been useful. So, as the water splashed past, they could look at, stick their hands in it—but then they had to turn their eyes to the sky and hope for rain. "If I had water all the time, I would keep plowing," Loch Pheach said. He was barefoot; his blue work shirt was ragged, his pants full of stains and holes. In a good year, he said, he produced 1 ton of rice on his 1 hectare plot of land (a hectare is about 2.5 acres). As it is, he said, he will have to send his teenage children to Thailand to work if the rains do not come. Asked what he eats, Loch Pheach looked puzzled. "Rice," he answered, as if there were no other possible answer. In truth, the Khmer verb *to eat* actually means "to eat rice." "Just rice. Maybe some fish, if we have money to buy it." So goes life beside an irrigation canal.

For all the emphasis Cambodians placed on rice cultivation, the nation provides the lowest yield per acre in Asia. Loch Pheach was able to grow 1 ton of rice on his hectare in a good year, still lower than the national average: 2.4 tons. In contrast, using modern agricultural techniques, Vietnam produced 4.9 tons per hectare, Laos 3.5, North Korea 3.8, Burma 4.0, Bangladesh 3.9—and Japan 6.5. Sorasak Pan, the deputy minister of commerce, lamented the sad state of agriculture. "We have only one rice harvest each year. Vietnam has three, Thailand has two. And we have no irrigation. So we have only one harvest, during the rainy season."

Even the piddling quantities of rice the nation did produce were of such poor quality that it could not be sold to developed countries. Exports were shipped to Thailand and Vietnam for processing because Cambodia did not own a modern rice mill—or a lab to certify that the rice was free of disease or harmful chemicals. The few small rice mills Cambodia did have were primitive, and "when rice is processed, the grains break into small fragments, which are not suitable for overseas markets," Chan Tong Yves, a deputy agriculture minister, told the *Phnom Penh Post*. Cambodian rice did not meet European or American standards. Outside of its neighbors, Cambodia was able to sell only to parts of Africa.

Kith Seng, the undersecretary of state in the Agriculture Ministry, spoke carefully, so as not offend his supervisors. But his message was clear: The government needed to do more. Kith Seng was a rare creature in the Cambodian government, a bureaucrat with education and expertise in his field. His office shelves held hundreds of agriculture journals, research studies, and books. He spoke halting English and said he earned a bachelor degree in agriculture from a French-run university in 1974.

Cambodia has never offered welfare or relief for the poor. The government has never made agricultural subsidies or even low-interest loans available to the public. "This is a totally free market," Kith Seng said with a rueful smile. "The government relies on the private sector. And whether they build a rice mill will depend on the market. The policy of the government is entirely free market. We leave all of that to the private sector." What that meant, really, was that the government did nothing. An "entirely free market" does not work even in wealthy nations. The United States, the wealthiest nation, still provides Medicare, Medicaid, Social Security, farm subsidies, unemployment benefits, food stamps, and a host of other aid for the poor and not so poor. Cambodia, one of the poorest nations, offered its citizens roads, bridges, and wells. More recently, it tried to offer rudimentary education and health care. But farmers, the hope and soul of the nation, were left entirely on their own.

When the world economic crisis hit in 2008, Rainsy offered one of his more moderate proposals. In a letter he asked Hun Sen to issue a $500 million stimulus package, for the many thousands of Cambodians who had lost their jobs. The government scoffed, saying, "Sam Rainsy should be able to address this. He is a parliamentarian." In other words, Rainsy should introduce a bill that the CPP majority would then reject. While the Asian Development Bank said the economic crisis was pulling 2 million people into even deeper poverty, Hun Sen called Rainsy's idea "not logical. It is opposition logic."

"My own idea, just me, is that first we need to have a strong farmer organization" to lobby the government, Kith Seng said. Burma, Thailand, and Vietnam all had rice growers' associations. "Now, the farmer has land but not credit. The farmer offers labor and technical skill. So the state needs to support them with low-interest credit. Now they leave that to the private sector, and the private lenders charge them 45 percent to 60 percent a year. Another of my ideas, and I raise it at meetings," to no apparent effect, "is to support a focus on new enterprise. Give a loan to the association of rice milling to buy new mills." That idea, too, went nowhere. What happened instead, he said, was that every year "there's a difference between the community level and the national level. At the community level, they talk about how they do not have enough to eat. At the national level, they still talk about having a rice surplus. And they sell that surplus to Vietnam and Thailand."

In 2009 the government declared a surplus of 2.5 million tons and committed to sell it to Vietnam, Thailand, and whoever else would buy it—leaving many thousands of Cambodians, like Cha Veun, wondering where they would find the rice they needed to survive. She was forty-six and had no teeth. She lived on a raised wooden platform, perhaps eight feet by eight feet, with no walls. She said she earned roughly 2,500 riel a day—about 50 cents. The people of her village, Bon Skol, near the border with Vietnam, made earthenware cooking pots for sale at market. And Cha Veun's pots served as a metaphor for her situation. Hers were miniature versions of the same cookery— toys, she explained. She had lived there all her life but owned no land and could only help other villagers with their crops. "But I don't earn enough to buy food." Has the government ever helped her? "Not yet. I want them to help me be not so poor. But it doesn't happen. And I don't have enough to eat."

Jean-Pierre de Margerie, head of the World Food Program office in Cambodia, observed that "lots of people here think food security is inventory. They refer to total production. But food access is the biggest problem. In fact, it's huge. Between 1.4 million and 1.5 million people are chronically food insecure," meaning they cannot get enough food to supply 2,000 calories a day. Aware of this, while government leaders sold off much of Cambodia's rice, and pocketed the proceeds, they also asked the Asian Development Bank to donate rice for Cambodia's poor. "The food-security concern in Cambodia is not whether the country is capable of producing sufficient food to feed its own population," said Arjun Goswami, the bank's country director. "It has been capable for several years now. The concern is whether" any of this abundance is made available to the nation's own people.

While rice sacks were stacked on trucks and ships for export, the Asian Development Bank declared an "unprecedented food-security emergency" and budgeted $38 million in "emergency food assistance"— $38 million worth of rice. That was the rice the people of Dang Rung village said they never got.

# CHAPTER ELEVEN

If education is the answer for Cambodian society, as so many experts
assert, then the nation is lost. In a nationwide survey only 2.6 percent of Cambodia's schoolteachers said they were providing students
"a high-quality education." That should be little surprise. Education is
by its very nature a reflection of the society it tries to teach. So every
foible and folly that crippled the nation can be found in the schools.

Every day, just before Chhith Sam Ath's two young sons headed
out the door for elementary school, their mother gave each of them
a small wad of cash. As soon as they entered the classroom, they
handed the teacher their money. So did all the other students, one by
one. Children who didn't make the daily payments were likely to get
bad grades. In some schools they were sent home or forced to stand
in the corner until it was time to leave.

Tens of thousands of poor families do not send their children to
school because they simply cannot afford to pay the bribes. In Cambodia, school has never been mandatory, so these children may end
up working in the rice paddies, or else their parents take them to Thailand to beg. The International Labor Organization estimated that 38
percent of Cambodia's children between ages seven and fifteen worked

at least part-time. "We can see them in restaurants, children selling things on the street. Pulling carts. Working in brick factories. Picking trash at dumps," said Rong Chhum, president of the national teachers' union. Others worked in neighboring countries as beggars or prostitutes. "A lot of children do not have any education at all." And so another generation is lost.

The problem isn't just children who don't go to school. For those who do choose education, "you go to school and learn how to bribe people," said Chhith Sam Ath, a nonprofit association leader, shaking his head. Teachers, in turn, had to give some of their bribe money to their principals. "We are required to pay 2,500 riel, 5,000 riel," between 50 cents and $1.20, "to the principal at the end of the month," Rong Chhum said. Principals, in turn, had to pass some of that money up to the local Education Ministry office. An NGO study called that "a facilitation fee," required before the ministry would release salaries and other state funds for the schools.

These fees and payments are all but untraceable. All government salaries and payments were made in cash, and they were not documented. "Everyone in government is paid in cash," said In Channy, president of Acleda Bank. In fact, "77 percent of the economy works on cash." What's more, that USAID corruption investigation said, "the national budget was described to the assessment team as non-existent or in even more derisive terms." Without a budget, there could be no accountability.

Bribing teachers was an evergreen story in the nation's newspapers. In late 2009 the *Phnom Penh Post* reported that the economic crisis had pushed teachers to double the amount of their bribes. "Oung Bunoun, 12, a third-grader at Tuol Svay Prey, said students have to pay money to their teachers, and that if they don't, they will receive lower grades," the paper wrote. "A teacher from Phnom Penh's Anuvath primary school, who declined to be named, said Monday that she has to collect money from her students because she cannot feed her family with the salary provided. 'It's not only me that takes money from them but also the other teachers,' she said. 'So why can't I?' Chea Cheat, president of the Municipal Department of Education, acknowledged that the department allows teachers to take money from students but said it would take action against any school that forces students to pay more than 500 riels." Even the education minister, Im Sethy, considered the bribes an unavoidable fact of life. "Our policy is to cut down on these irregularities, but if you look at the living conditions of these people, it's understandable," he said with a matter-of-fact tone.

Because of the bribes, poverty, and other factors, 15 to 20 percent of the nation's five and six year olds never entered school. The percentage was probably higher; the statistics conflicted. For those who did go to school, "the average class sizes are 75–80 students," the education minister said. "It's very hard for the teacher."

"After the first year, already 10 percent of them drop out," said Teruo Jinnai, head of the UNESCO office in Phnom Penh. "And then 10 percent after that. And by the time they finish the 6th grade, half of them are gone." Just under 13 percent go on to high school, and fewer still graduate. About 3 percent go on to college.

The percentages can be far lower in rural areas. "I would say only half go to school," said Mou Neam, village chief in Bon Skol, just west of the Vietnam border. "The village school goes up to the sixth grade. The few who go on to the higher grades go up the road to another school, two kilometers away."

In Dang Rung village in Pursat Province, village chief Kok Chuum said, "Fifty children entered first grade this year. Only two are in high school, and they will probably drop out after grade 9," when public education is no longer free.

The few students who reached high school had been so well schooled in the art of bribery that they had learned how to buy their way to a diploma. High school teachers would sell them answers to tests; they would also take money to change a grade or cover up absences. All of it came to a head at final exam time each summer. "It's like a battlefield," Education Minister Im Sethy said.

In the classroom students collaborated. They collected a pool of cash, two or three dollars each, and offered it to the teacher when he walked in with the final-exam papers. If he accepted the bribe, a student would then photocopy the answer key and pass it out to all the others who had contributed. If the teacher wouldn't play along, then street vendors sitting at folding tables outside the school sold answer sheets of uncertain provenance. Photocopy shops set up satellite businesses outside large urban schools, and each year newspapers published photos of students mobbing the vendors. In 2009 the *Cambodia Daily* quoted sixteen-year-old Kanhchana saying, "It will be a tough time for us during the exam if the teachers will not accept money." Another student, Nhan Theary, added, "We can do everything by ourselves, but the result will not be so good."

Every year Rong Chhum, the teachers' union president, issued a warning: Don't allow the students to cheat! That seemed counterintuitive since it was his members, the teachers, who facilitated the cheating. But the union took the position that their members had no choice but to take money because their pay was so low—as little as forty-five dollars a month.

Each year Im Sethy asked the Interior Ministry and the army to send squads of police and soldiers to the schools, and sometimes the officers shooed away the answer-key vendors sitting at tables. Other times they looked away. "Year by year we try to make it better," Im Sethy said. "For example, this year I ordered that the photocopy centers in schools be closed. We spread out the desks" so students could not share answer keys. Nevertheless, Rong Chhum disagreed. "The students pay off the police. It was the same as last year. There was still a lot of cheating." The result of all this, he said, "is 75 percent of public school students move through the system without getting even a basic knowledge of the subjects they study." He said this with a tone of dark certainty and a determined stare. "The majority of students seem to know nothing."

Students applying for medical school proved the point. In 2008 1,800 students took the entrance exam. To pass students had to get at least half of the answers right. Only 369 of them managed even that. The students rallied and protested and screamed and yelled until finally the medical school relented and said a score of 25 percent was enough to enter medical school, which entitled another 507 students to pass. Still, more than half the test takers, after cheating and bribing their way through school, had been unable to answer even one question out of four correctly.

At the National University of Management, "We used to require a thesis for graduation," said Seng Bunthoeun, the vice rector. "But students would just copy old cases. They cheated. So we dropped it." Just like their forebears, the students had managed to graduate but had learned little if anything at all.

---

When King Norodom first handed sovereignty over his state to France in 1863, the occupiers found a nation almost uniformly illiterate. Cambodia had not a single school, just those temple classes, where monks taught the children about Buddhism, the Cambodian oral tradition, and perhaps how to read sacred texts. Historians have concluded that the education system changed little, if at all, between the Angkorian period and the early twentieth century.

A primary goal of educators remained to reinforce the social hierarchy. Historian David Ayres showed that the Buddhist notion of individual helplessness is the central factor in that process. As he wrote, "Students were equipped to become citizens in a system in which they were taught to refer to themselves as slaves and to willingly accept the necessity of their subservience to individuals of higher social status."

From their earliest years Cambodian children learned that ambition and personal aspiration should not, could not, be a part of their character. Be satisfied with the life you have, the monks told them, no matter how poor or menial. Education "simply took children from the rice fields and then gave them back to the rice fields."

Girls were instructed to expect even less. They were not permitted to attend even the temple classes. Instead, their mothers taught them subservience and docility. Nothing embodied that idea more than the *Chbab Srey*, a piece of traditional literature that described a woman's place in the home, written in the form of a mother talking to her daughter. One passage said: "Dear, no matter what your husband did wrong, I tell you to be patient, don't say anything . . . don't curse, don't be the enemy. No matter how poor or stupid, you don't look down on him. . . . No matter what the husband says, angry and cursing, using strong words without end, complaining and cursing because he is not pleased, you should be patient with him and calm down your anger." The *Chbab Srey* was required reading in the schools until 2007, when Ing Kantha Phavi, the minister of women's affairs, managed to convince the Education Ministry to pull it from the curriculum. Nonetheless, she acknowledged, "it is still taught in rural areas." This in a nation where more than 80 percent of the people lived in rural areas.

Into the early twentieth century, the nation had not a single middle school, high school, or college. The French built the first high schools and middle schools in the 1930s, all of them in Phnom Penh. But the French occupiers weren't interested in educating children for the betterment of Cambodian society. No, these children were trained specifically to become administrators in the French colonial government. As government employees, they received better than decent pay, by Cambodian standards. Better still, the young bureaucrats immediately found themselves sitting astride the flow of graft money. Could there be a better job?

In the 1960s King Sihanouk began building more and more schools, even though almost no one in the nation was educated or equipped to teach. The building of schools did have the ancillary effect of involving the government in village life for the first time in Cambodian history. However, the paucity of educated teachers was a problem that would linger for decades.

In 2008 Suomi Sakai, head of the UNICEF office, explained why, on average, it took ten years for a child to finish elementary school.

"One reason is teacher training; some of the teachers in rural areas have no better than a third grade education." In the mid-1950s fewer than 1 child in 60 managed to complete elementary school. Just 1 child in 3,000 made it to high school.

Even with his new schools in chaos, Sihanouk decided to build a university system. A technical college opened in 1964 whose primary mission was to teach agronomy and other skills related to agriculture. But the students showed no interest. More than 90 percent of the technical university's 1,300 students majored in the liberal arts, the course work they needed to get a lucrative government job. They wanted to be modern-day mandarins. Just 117 studied agronomy. Sihanouk was appalled. "Students must adapt themselves to various professions," he declared. "Unfortunately everyone wants to be a red tape artist." He repeatedly warned that his government simply did not have enough jobs for everyone. The students ignored him, and most graduates remained unemployed.

But then the French had structured the primary and secondary education system to train Cambodians for government service. Sihanouk advocated reform, but it never came. Almost fifty years later, in 2009, Women's Affairs Minister Ing Kantha Phavi noted, "It's still the dream of every Cambodian to work in government. They can make a lot of money," she added with a smile, while offering the slippery-finger gesticulation for corruption. "Very few get hired now, but it is still the dream. These other areas," engineering, agriculture, technology, "they are not attractive subjects." What's more, "a lot of parents don't like to see their children working in these other areas."

Students remained so focused on becoming mandarins that the state had little choice but to build the National University of Management. It opened in its current form in 2004 and immediately became the most popular college in Cambodia's university system. "We have 15,000 students, and ours is by far the most popular major," said Vice Rector Seng Bunthoeun. "We teach them law, economics, history, English, general culture. But students don't like courses not related to management"—usually, he added, "because their parents push them to do that. They want to join the government, but each year the ministries take only about 30 students." So only about 10 percent of his graduates actually found jobs. "I try to help them," but he faced the same problem university rectors confronted during Sihanouk's time.

———————

Sun Thun taught social studies to middle school students in Kampong Thom Province, north of Phnom Penh. He offered lessons in democracy, human rights . . . and corruption. That's what got him into trouble. "My teaching on corruption is short," he said, thrusting forward a tattered paperback textbook. "It's all in here." He tapped the book urgently with his index finger. "But I explain it with real examples of corruption from the community. For example, during exams students have to pay money to teachers to pass. They have to pay money so they can cheat on the exams."

The principal somehow heard about this bit of course work and reported Sun Thun to the district office. An official charged him with "unprofessional behavior" and ordered him transferred to a school in the province's hinterlands. Sun Thun refused, and the teachers' association organized large demonstrations in Kampong Thom and Phnom Penh, outside the Education Ministry. Sun Thun was also the Cambodia Independent Teachers' Association local representative. He appealed, and the transfer was stayed while the appeal was considered.

Sitting in the yard outside the Kampong Thom office of the teachers' union, Sun Thun was dressed as a professional in a striped white shirt with a button-down collar, shirt tail out, and black pants. Agitated, angry, arms waving, his expression squint-eyed wary, he leaned far forward, almost as if he believed he needed to be in physical contact for his words to hold meaning. How did the school learn what he was teaching in his classroom? "The principal sneaked over to listen to me," he said, shaking his forefinger. "He knows I am president of the CITA," the teachers' union. "I started a debate on the budget and the payroll of the school," highlighting the inevitable kickbacks and corruption. "So the principal is not happy with me. A teacher, to be principal of the school, must make payoffs to his superiors. The teachers have to pay him or buy food or beer. I didn't pay him. That's why he turned me in, that plus my questions about the school budget."

Principal Te Kim Sien denied it all. "Sun Thun did wrong and abused his professional position," he said in his dark office that doubled as the school storeroom (like most, this school had no electricity). He wore a pink T-shirt and a grave expression. "I will not allow him to stir up trouble here anymore." He went on: "We don't sell exam results here. In Baray District, I have never heard of paying for exams." Keng Vantaa, a young teacher sitting beside him, chimed in without being asked and offered a confirmatory rebuttal. "We don't have to pay to get jobs. Teachers here are not interested in promotion. We like teaching. So there's no need to pay anyone." While insisting that not a hint of corruption tainted the school, the principal and his friend showed little hesitation describing the school system's underbelly. As illustration, they pointed to a new one-story classroom building.

Cambodia had held elections again in the summer of 2008, and this time Hun Sen, using all the aboveboard and underhanded tactics employed in previous elections, won a decisive majority. He needed no coalition partners. (He'd recently managed to change the law so the winner needed only 50 percent of the vote, not two-thirds.) Ranariddh had retired from government and taken a position in the royal palace.* And Sam Rainsy became a strident opposition leader with no role except to complain.

---

*Funcinpec actually expelled Ranariddh in 2006 after he was found to have left the country, whereupon he sold the party headquarters to a developer and pocketed the proceeds. Later, the courts charged the prince with fraud, convicted him in absentia, and sentenced him to eighteen months in prison. But Cambodian court sentences are malleable. Hun Sen forgave him, so he returned to Cambodia and left politics.

During the campaign Hun Sen promised Te Kim Sien's school a new building with twelve classrooms and a reception hall. On election day the building was partly built, and the lumber for the rest lay stacked beside it. It happened, though, that the majority of voters in the Baray District where Sun Thun taught had voted for the Sam Rainsy Party. The day after the election, workers showed up and hauled all the lumber away. "All construction materials were removed during the night and later sold at auction," Sun Thun said at the time. "I think the CPP spent a lot of money here, and when they didn't get the votes, they became spiteful." The episode received negative attention in the news media, and the workers eventually returned—with new marching orders. "After hauling away all of the lumber for the school after the election," said Keng Vantaa, "they built a new building, but the metal was so cheap they could not build two stories, as needed. So we got this." He pointed to the small one-story building with two or three classrooms. That did little to address the school's shortage of class space.

The school also had too few teachers, and like the majority of schools nationwide, most of them worked only part-time. They left early, cutting their classes short, or skipping them altogether, so they could work second jobs. The workday for middle and upper schools was supposed to be from 7:00 to 11:00 a.m. and then from 2:00 to 4:40 p.m., but "five teachers leave early every day because they have a job with an NGO," Sun Thun said. They didn't show up for their afternoon classes. The principal downplayed the problem. "Most of the teachers, their wives work," he averred. "But some have a grocery store, say, and leave early to work there."

This problem sprang up as a result of a directive from Phnom Penh intended to discourage teachers from demanding bribes from their students. "We are going to allow them to work after school—tutoring, for example," Im Sethy said in 2008, when he was deputy education minister. "We are encouraging teachers to solve their own problems." So teachers began taking after-school jobs that soon evolved into during-school jobs, including paid tutoring—while still taking bribes from their students.

Te Kim Sien may have been innocent of everything Sun Thun alleged, but across the country school principals were often considered part of the problem—as corrupt and self-interested as anyone in government. Many had paid their supervisors for their appointment, and so they felt entitled to recompense.

In another part of Kampong Thom Province, teachers at Phat Sanday secondary school charged their principal with billing the school district for ghost teachers, a hallowed Cambodian tradition. When the principal heard of the complaint, he held back (and probably kept for himself) two months of overtime pay belonging to the seven teachers who complained.

In Prey Veng Province, in the Southeast, the teachers' association pointed out that the principal of Neak Leung secondary school had built a fence around his house next to the school, extending it onto school property, grabbing more than 125 square yards. The principal professed to be trying to protect the land from "land-grabbing villagers," and Hoem Sophal, the provincial school director, offered a flippant explanation. He claimed that the teachers "were involved" in the principal's land grab, too. He didn't explain how. But then Hoem Sophal had little regard for teachers anyway. A few months earlier they had accused him of skimming from their salaries. His explanation then: He was volunteering as a monk and could not respond to the allegations "until I leave the monkhood." With all of that, for most teachers education remained a joyless profession.

Kdep Sokhin, a handsome young man, was one of those rare students who stayed in school through the twelfth grade. Then he attended a teachers college for two years. After that he started work at a small elementary school in western Kampong Thom Province, earning forty-eight dollars a month. One summer afternoon nineteen children, seven girls and twelve boys, all of them eleven or twelve years old, sat in his classroom at desks that had been drawn on, carved, and otherwise defaced by generations of children. They wore simple uniforms, black pants and plain white shirts. The girls' shirtsleeves offered a small white decorative bow, a rare feint toward formality.

Only the windows lit the room; this school, too, had no electricity. Two canisters holding clean water sat on a table by the door. Ten-inch-high lettering on the side told everyone that UNICEF had provided this. In 2003 UNICEF also built the bathrooms out back, a large sign said. Now the toilets were cracked, broken, and home to spiders and their webs. A ditch latrine beside it was the new bathroom. Elsewhere on the small school yard, a bare concrete pavilion served as the lunchroom. Two fire pits, each with three rocks, held up rusty grates.

Inside, Kdep Sokhin lectured about long division while writing examples on the chalkboard, smiling at the children as he spoke. He, too, wore a white shirt and jet-black pants, though stripes of yellow dust filled the creases behind his knees. He was twenty-six and had been teaching there for four years. "Teaching's not really fun," he said when class was over, that smile still affixed to his face. "The children are easy, but it's hard to survive on this salary and have money to buy petrol for my motorbike. There are only two teachers here and 143 students in grades 1 to 5."

On that day, however, his classroom was less than half full. "So many are absent. Some of the children went off with their fathers to work in paddies in Thailand." A teachers' union survey that year found that 54 percent of the nation's teachers said they do not teach regularly and "took no notice of students." The teachers blamed the government for this attitude, saying they weren't paid enough. But for Kdep Sokhin, the bigger problem was the other teacher at his school. "He wants to transfer to another school, near his family. I would be alone if he left. I have no idea where another teacher would come from." Most likely Kdep Sokhin would have 143 students all to himself.

In 2009 the World Bank published a special multivolume report on education and competitiveness. It echoed concerns that had been reverberating among donors and the nation's leaders for decades. Cambodia cannot grow until it "reforms its education system," the report said. As long as the workforce remained unskilled and barely educated, Cambodia will remain "the biggest laggard" in Asia. The year before, the International Republican Institute had surveyed the Cambodian public. Seventeen percent of the respondents said they had no education, while another 49 percent said they had attended only one or two years of primary school. So, in 2008, two-thirds of the public was barely literate. Pollsters spoke to 2,000 people face-to-face nationwide and said the survey had a margin of error of plus or minus 2.8 percent. The World Bank said that had to change if the Cambodians expected to become prosperous enough even to catch up with their neighbors. Other figures in the survey seemed to verify that. Almost 80 percent of the respondents said they earned less than one hundred dollars a month. Half of Cambodia's people earned less than fifty dollars a month. That's six hundred dollars a year.

Then in early 2010 the government gave an answer of sorts. Its new National Strategic Development Plan set back the nation's education targets, such as achieving universal enrollment and literacy. The previous plan, published in 2006, had offered the fanciful idea, for example, that 75 percent of all students would attend both primary and middle schools by 2010. When January 1, 2010, arrived, however, only about 30 percent of the nation's students were enrolled in middle school. The number had barely budged since 2006. So the government changed the goal—to 51 percent by 2013. Similarly, the earlier plan had promised that at least half of all children who lived in what it called "remote" rural areas would attend elementary school by 2010. Well, 2010 had dawned, and the government was far, far from its target. The new goal: By 2013, 22 percent of the little boys and girls who lived in remote areas would attend school.

Carol Rodley was deputy chief of mission in the U.S. Embassy during the late 1990s. Back then, just a few years after the UN occupation, "I heard a lot of distress about the state of the education system," she said. "They talked about the corruption in schools. It was shocking and really, really distressing to the middle class." She returned to Cambodia as U.S. ambassador in 2008 and quickly discerned a change. The anger had faded. In fact, it had disappeared. Instead of being upset, people were now simply dispirited. "They don't talk about it anymore. Now it's the status quo."

# CHAPTER TWELVE

Twenty-seven-year-old Leang Saroeun didn't much like his job. He worked for Lt. Col. Ou Bunthan of the Cambodian military, stationed in Pursat Province. The colonel hired him and his wife, twenty-two-year-old Let Ting, to chop lumber and do other chores. Shortly after they took the new position and moved into a small cottage on the officer's property, however, Ou Bunthan told them the job had another, sinister, element.

After warning him not to tell anyone, Ou Bunthan ordered Leang Saroeun to help him smuggle endangered species for sale to China and other places. In July 2009 the colonel sent him to pick up a pangolin that a poacher had captured in a protected national forest. Pangolins, also called scaly anteaters, were in danger of extinction. Capturing them was illegal in Cambodia and most of the world. Native to Southeast Asia, they are large beasts that some people refer to as walking pine cones. Their scales and claws are razor sharp, allowing them to climb trees, and they can grow to be six feet long, including the tail.

Leang Saroeun picked up the young animal, stuffed it into a bag, tied it to the back of his motorbike, and drove back toward the colonel's home. During the drive, though, the pangolin managed to claw his way out of the bag, jump down, and scamper into the woods. Leang Saroeun screeched to a halt and ran after the beast, but it was nighttime. Chasing after the beast in the dark was hopeless. Still, he searched for hours but finally gave up and drove home. When he called his boss to relate the bad news, Ou Bunthan was furious. "He accused my husband of selling it to someone," Let Ting related. A live pangolin was worth hundreds of dollars. "He told the colonel he didn't sell it. It ran into the forest." The colonel was not mollified. The next morning Ou Bunthan called, his voice icy, and summoned Leang Saroeun to his house twenty yards away. Let Ting stayed back at their cottage, but a few minutes later she heard her husband screaming and ran out to see what was wrong. "He was on fire, all over his body. He ran off and jumped into a cistern full of water. He climbed out and walked to the road, then slipped and fell down. He could not get up. He never walked again." Sobbing, Let Ting ran to him. A local police officer passing by stopped and "took pity on us. He drove us to the hospital." There, Leang Saroeun told his wife what had happened. "My husband told me he poured five liters of gasoline over him and then lit him with a cigarette lighter. My husband couldn't run away. The man had his pistol pointed at him and would have shot him to death."

Leang Saroeun was shuttled from hospital to hospital over the next several days but finally died. He'd been burned over 80 percent of his body, said Ek Sonsatthya, a nurse at one of the hospitals. "He was burned like a grilled fish," said his older brother, Map Narin.

Ngeth Theary, a local human-rights worker, had photographed him. The picture showed parts of his clothes still fused to his charred skin. Most of his face was black, locked in a terrible expression of pain and horror.

Cambodians are a conflicted people, generally passive, quiet, non-threatening—but also capable of extraordinary violence and brutality. Their history and religion have taught them "not to exhibit extremes of behavior," observed Youk Chhang, who runs the Documentation

Center of Cambodia. It collects records of the Khmer Rouge era. "So when they hold it in for so long, when they do resort to violence they get very emotional, which leads to extremes of violence."

Ing Kantha Phavi, the minister of women's affairs, is also a medical doctor, and she offered a clinical explanation, saying, "I think a lot of people are hiding a lot in their subconscious. You can see a person, perfectly normal, and then an hour later see him transformed into another person who will kill you." Part of it, she and others said, is the post-traumatic stress disorder so prevalent in society. Extreme anger and violent outbursts are common symptoms. But there's more.

Experts have found that compromise is next to impossible in Cambodian culture. A team of Swedish anthropologists in the mid-1990s studied Cambodian society and came to this conclusion. For Cambodians, like most Asians, they noted, few things are more important than saving face, protecting personal dignity. Yet "there is no cultural tradition for reconciling contrary opinions—or even for the acceptance of the existence of contrary opinions," the Swedes wrote in their book, *Every Home an Island*. As a result, in any debate one side or the other is certain to lose face. "So when Khmer men resort to violence— when young men form gangs, or when a husband beats his wife, almost to death," they are "impotent human beings who act out of frustration because their 'cultural heritage' offers no other way out of a humiliating situation. In most cases an act of violence is preferable to the loss of face."

Raoul-Marc Jennar, a Belgian who worked for the United Nations in Cambodia for many years, concluded that "killing was an everyday act, the automatic almost direct consequence of the negation of differences." Actually, following Jennar's logic, killing was an automatic tactic for eliminating differences of opinion. Quinn, the former ambassador, also found this personality characteristic remarkable. "We Americans are inculcated in the art of compromise," he said. "Not there. That's just not part of the Cambodian character."

Clinicians have found striking uniformity in Cambodian behavior and psychological state. "Cambodia is fascinating," said Daryn Reicherter, a psychiatrist who treated Cambodians in San Jose, California, and in Cambodia. "Unlike a lot of other countries, there is no diversity to the client population. There's a single story. Ask any of them, and you get the very same story. I wouldn't do it, but I could write the note before I even see the client. They all have major depressive disorders. They drink. I'd ask women if they had been raped. Every one of them said no. I told a case worker: 'It's amazing, none of them were raped.' She told me all of them had been raped, but they wouldn't talk about it to a man."

In most societies conflicts can be resolved in court. Not so in Cambodia. Leang Saroeun's death proved the point. It produced a couple of newspaper stories. Nothing long or prominent, just another episode in the running catalog of injustice, misery, and death. But when one reporter asked Top Chan Sereyvudth, Pursat Province's chief prosecutor, what he intended to do, the prosecutor said he was waiting for the police report before considering the case, then added, "But it is slanderous to say that Ou Bunthan burned Leang Saroeun." How could he know that before he'd even seen the police report? The answer: Top Chan Sereyvudth was the face of injustice in Cambodia.

Top Chan Sereyvudth was a little man, maybe five foot four, with a bit of fuzz on his chin that some might mistake for a beard. A few months earlier, through a bureaucratic sleight of hand, he had managed to have a case transferred from Banteay Meanchey Province, on the other side of the nation, into his own courtroom. The case in question involved a dispute with four villagers over ownership of some land. These villagers were locked in argument with none other than Top Chan Sereyvudth himself, who stood to gain five acres if he won the case. Bringing it into his own courtroom, where he was the prosecutor, therefore proved convenient. He managed to dispatch the quarrelsome villagers to jail. Given the graft and general inequity that plagued the courts, that would normally have been the end of it—if not for Chhay Sareth, council chief for Pursat Province.

Chhay Sareth had been out of town during the prosecutor's escapade, but he heard about it when scores of the victims' friends from Banteay Meanchey began raucous demonstrations in the center of town. "I was just informed that there were angry people in the street," the council chief said. "I was one hundred kilometers away. The case was getting bigger and bigger. I thought, 'If we don't stop it, Hun Sen will hear about it!' I told the police, 'Please don't do anything.'" After hurrying home, he called in the protesters, heard their story, and ordered the police to ensure their security—afraid, he said, that someone would order a grenade attack on these people, "and then they would blame the government for mistreating its own people." A few days later the case moved to trial.

By now the governor's concern was well known, and the trial judge, In Bopha, let the four men go. When asked why, he chose his words carefully. "It was determined that the crime was committed in Banteay Meanchey province and was out of our jurisdiction. So I ordered it forwarded back to Banteay Meanchey under article 290 of our code."

Not to be outdone, Top Chan Sereyvudth took the case to the court of appeals and asked that court to hold the men in jail during the appeal, he told a *Cambodia Daily* reporter. (It was too late; the men were already gone.) But when the reporter asked about the five acres he stood to gain in this dispute, the prosecutor abruptly hung up the phone.

It was because of people like Top Chan Sereyvudth that In Bopha, a judge in the same Pursat courthouse, paused for a moment when asked about Leang Saroeun's death and finally said, "In this case, from my point of view, the victim should not seek help from any institution under government control." Let Ting's only option, he said, was "go to an NGO for help."

When I approached Top Chan Sereyvudth outside his office and said I wanted to talk to him about both the land case and Leang

Saroeun's death, he said he had an urgent appointment, bolted to his car, and slammed the door. His driver whisked him away.

Meanwhile, Ang Vong Vattana, the minister of justice, was growing angry. After all, he had approved the prosecutor's request to transfer the case. Now, the minister thought, what was a governor doing messing around in his courts? "The minister of justice asked me why I got involved in this," council chief Chhay Sareth recalled with a slight shake of the head. "I told him: 'This problem came here from Banteay Meanchey, and when someone vomits on your leg, you have to react. So I got involved.' I respect these people, even though they came from Banteay Meanchey. I did not know about this case until they came here. The prosecutor brought this case here."

So then, why, after all of that, was Top Chan Sereyvudth still chief prosecutor in Pursat Province? The governor said he was asking the same question, "why the prosecutor, who was really involved in this case, why there is no punishment, no measure taken against him. I still wonder why. If you want to know more, I suggest you talk to the minister of justice."

A few days later, Justice Minister Ang Vong Vattana swept into an anteroom to his office in Phnom Penh and sat in one of the room's elegant chairs painted with gold leaf and upholstered with brown velvet. He was tall, balding, with gold wire-rim glasses. He wore a gray suit and a bothered expression. "What do you want?"

I asked him about transferring the land case into Top Chan Sereyvudth's courtroom. The minister answered with an imperial tone: "I have the right to transfer the case, and I did it."

But didn't the prosecutor have a personal interest in the case?

"People say he was involved, but nobody has shown me the proof."

Okay, then, was it proper for this same prosecutor to pronounce guilt in the Ou Bunthan case before he had even seen the police report? For a moment the minister simply glared with a pinched-lip, narrow-eyed stare. Then he stood up and stormed out of the room, muttering, "You waste my time."

Let Ting was six months pregnant when her husband died of his burn wounds. When I spoke to her, he had been cremated just the day before. Let Ting was sorrowful, but she did not cry.

The colonel kicked her off his property, so she had no choice but to move back to the "house" she had lived in before—just a platform a foot or two off the ground with a low, sloping palm-frond roof and no walls. A plastic tarp on bamboo poles provided a porch. It was there that her husband passed away. When the hospital could do nothing for him, she brought him home to die. Her home held no obvious possessions. Whatever they owned was still in their cottage on the colonel's property, and Let Ting said she was afraid to go back. It was getting dark. Neighbors came by bringing food. One middle-aged woman was frying some fish over a wood fire. The pan rested on three stones. "We could earn 50,000 riel in that job," she volunteered. That's $12.50 a month. "Now, I don't know what I am going to do."

Even though Leang Saroeun's murder was a heinous crime, it barely stood out among the various acts of brutality and carnage that Cambodians wrought on each other every day. About once a week, on average, police reported an acid attack, often committed by a wife intent on destroying a woman suspected of sleeping with her husband. Typically, she would splash battery acid on the victim's face. The numbers of attacks were increasing so fast that a victims' group called Cambodian Acid Survivors Charity opened to treat victims who could not get help anywhere else. It worked with more than two hundred victims between March 2006 and December 2009, including scores of children. For its part in 2002 the government refused to pass a law making it illegal to possess acid for use as a weapon. Only in 2010, when government officials became concerned that the nation faced an acid-attack epidemic, did the National Assembly impanel a committee to study the issue.

Keo Srey Vy was one of the victims. Her brother-in-law doused her with sulfuric acid because she was trying to stop him from selling his young children into sexual slavery, she told the *Cambodia Daily*. But like most other acid victims, she was afraid to go outside and show her hideously disfigured face because "she is fed up with the common assumption in Cambodian culture that she must have done something wrong to deserve her devastating wounds," the paper said. That may have been why the National Assembly refused to pass that law.

At the same time, child rape was reaching the level of a pandemic. Sexual assaults against toddlers were so frequent that hardly anyone took note any longer. Human-rights groups said they investigated one or two each week, on average, and in 2009, 80 percent of the nation's rape victims were children. Then in the fall of 2010 police and human-rights groups reported 300 rapes in the year's first seven months. Two-thirds were children, some as young as four years old.

All shock seemed to have been drained from this crime, as incidents were reduced to short notes on newspaper police blotters that recounted the horror in a dull, formulaic monotone. In January 2009 the *Phnom Penh Post* reported, "Two incidents of child rape happened on Friday and Saturday" in "Banteay Meanchey province. Phaing Bor, 28, was arrested for raping a four-year-old girl on Saturday near her grandmother's house. The suspect had been asked to look after the girl by her grandmother, who trusted the man. The other case happened on Friday when a 20-month-old girl was raped after her mother had gone to market, leaving her home alone. The perpetrator escaped."

In most cases, if police arrested the rapist, they pushed him to settle the case with a cash payment to the victim's parents. Then the policemen took a cut of their own. Police reported 468 rape cases during calendar year 2009, 24 percent more than during the previous year. But the police figure was probably just a fraction of the total. Every woman who was raped knew that the police would demand a bribe before even offering to help. "Police only work if you have money, if you pay," Amnesty International quoted the father of one young victim as saying. "But we don't have that. And if you don't pay, the police just ignore you."

Adult rape victims were often ignored as well. Friends and family viewed them as tainted, spoiled. Often these women then had to leave their families and move away.

Many judges were just as eager to take money as the police. After all, many of them had paid large sums of money to get their job. A Voice of America investigative report in 2009 quoted student jurists saying that, when they graduated from the Royal Academy for Judicial Professions, they had to pay $20,000, $30,000, or more to get assignments in the nation's court system—but with the understanding that they would "earn" it back through bribe payments.

Nov Mal, a twenty-four year old in Pursat, was charged with raping an eighteen-year-old girl who lived in the same community. She said he attacked her as she was walking home from work at a store that rented CDs and DVDs. But when Nov Mal came to court, the judge freed him. Shortly after his release, he rode his motorbike out to his victim's home. "He drove a motorbike past my house and teased my sister and me," said Kem Vuthy, the victim's brother. "He said that now he is free from jail and that he paid money to the court rather than paying money to us." The victim, scared for her life, asked the local office of Adhoc, a human-rights group, for protection. "The victim is here now, in care of an NGO," living in hiding, said Ngeth Theary, head of Adhoc's Pursat office.

In Bopha, the judge on the case, offered an unconvincing story to explain why he let the man go. "In this case, the two loved each other very much, for a long time, but it was secret. Someone saw it. The girl saw that her reputation was destroyed by that. That is why she complained. The physical exam did not produce evidence she was raped. It confirmed she had sex. There were friends nearby, and when they saw her, she screamed: He raped me!"

Most Cambodian malefactors didn't have enough money to buy off judges. But foreigners usually did. Given that Cambodia remained a favored vacation spot for pedophiles from around the world, judges saw a steady stream of them standing before them in the dock. In 2003 the government began to recognize its reputation as a haven for pedophiles and announced an antipedophile campaign. Even so, in the courtroom money still managed to trump any government initiative.

Philippe Dessart, a forty-seven-year-old Belgian, was first sentenced by a Cambodian court to eighteen years in prison for sexually abusing a thirteen-year-old boy. A Belgian court had previously convicted him of child rape, in 1994, and he'd moved to Cambodia after completing his jail term. When he appealed his Cambodian conviction, the court reduced his sentenced to three years, but the judge let him out right away—after serving only six months. Human-rights groups were appalled. "It is an incentive for Dessart and other offenders to continue abusing our children," warned Samleang Seila, country director for Action Pour les Enfants, a French NGO. "It's very concerning."

Sure enough, as soon as he got out of jail, Dessart moved back in with the family of the little boy he had abused. Soon he was seen in the provincial government offices applying for a marriage license. He professed to be interested in marrying the victim's mother. Human-rights officers hypothesized that Dessart had seduced the boy's mother with his relative wealth. He bought the family a house and a motorbike.

Asked about Dessart, the provincial police human-trafficking chief told the *Cambodia Daily* he was unaware of Dessart's return from jail but couldn't do anything about him unless he was found to have molested the boy again. But he promised to "keep an eye on him."

Dessart's was not an isolated case. Some payoffs were so brazen that even fellow government officials were angry. Bribes seemed to work particularly well in Sihanoukville's municipal court. A judge there sentenced Nikita Belov, a twenty-six-year-old Russian, to three years in prison for abusing three boys aged seven to thirteen but then released him two days later. "Police worked hard to arrest him, but the court just released him," Deputy Prime Minister Sar Kheng complained during a conference on human trafficking.

The same court freed John Claude Fornier, a sixty-four-year-old Frenchman charged with sexually abusing an eight-year-old girl, even before his trial. Then the very same court in Sihanoukville sentenced Fabio Cencini, a forty-three-year-old Italian, to two years in prison for sexually abusing four girls and two boys between eight and fourteen years old—but then let him out on "bail." He disappeared.

And then there was the case of Alexander Trofimov. Another Russian pedophile, Trofimov was convicted of sexually abusing seventeen young girls. A court in Phnom Penh charged a senior Justice Ministry official with trying to forge an extradition request for Trofimov that would have allowed him to be released from prison, in exchange for a $250,000 bribe. This official got in trouble because he crossed a line. It wasn't the appearance of taking a bribe, though. In the process of forging the extradition request, he had tried to forge Hun Sen's signature. As for Trofimov, whose real name was Stanislav Molodyakov, he was sentenced to seventeen years in prison. On appeal in August 2010, the appeals court, inexplicably, cut nine years off his sentence so that he would be eligible for parole in less than three years.

Ouk Bounchhoeun used to be the minister of justice. After he left that position, he was appointed to the senate and became chairman of the Legislation and Justice Committee. Even as a CPP legislator, he found the state of the court system appalling, and so he opened a wide-ranging investigation with the hope that he could convince his government to act.

What he found were problems both in individual judges and with the system itself. "The judges and the prosecutors are facing difficulties implementing the laws," he said, because "there are a lot of technical terms they don't understand. We also don't have any law, or code of ethics, to ensure that a judge is not influenced by anyone else." Judge In Bopha in Pursat Province raised a similar concern. "There is no debate or discussion here. The law, it does not work, but we never discuss it. We should set up a national conference."

Senator Ouk Bounchhoeun wore one of those tan safari suits; a Cambodian flag sat on his desk. Small signs affixed to every piece of furniture and equipment in his office—the sofa, file cabinets, telephone, even a Cambodia map on the wall—said "Property of The Honorable Ouk Bounchhoeun," as if he feared someone might walk off with all of it at any moment. He added, "We have to seriously look at the problem of paying money to win a case. If you don't pay, you don't win; this is one of the issues I am looking at. Sometimes it's not the judge, sometimes it's a middleman who runs the paperwork and takes the money."

A week before this conversation Yorn Than, a circuit court clerk in Ratanakiri Province, acknowledged to reporters that his boss, the judge, had asked him to request five hundred dollars from relatives who wanted a young man released from prison. When the relatives complained about the bribe request, Yorn Than acknowledged asking for the bribe but warned that he would sue them "for defamation or disinformation" if they kept talking about it. Often disputes like that ended in violence.

Juanita Rice, an American jurist from Minnesota who volunteered in Cambodia, working to improve the court system, said she witnessed all of the malfeasance and criminality the court system offered. She said one court official in Kampot Province told her, "The Khmer Rouge created a nation of liars and thieves." The government's occasional proposed legal reforms, she said, "are like spraying air freshener on a trash dump."

Senator Ouk Bounchhoeun wanted to make clear that every class of citizen shared guilt. "Even wealthy people get to court, and the trial does not satisfy them. So they make a secret plan to kill someone. It's not just the poor people who commit violence. I do not agree with what some people say, it is a result of the Khmer Rouge." That, he suggested, was just an excuse. He shook his head and said, "We need to reform everything."

———

Not surprisingly, domestic violence was even more widespread than rape or sexual abuse of children. Many men viewed beating their wives to be a cherished Cambodian tradition—taking to heart the Cambodian proverb "Men are like gold; women are like cloth."

In 2003, women tried to force the issue. Government figures then showed that 25 percent of all women nationwide were subjected to serious domestic violence in any given year. Yet when a bill came before parliament that would punish men for beating up their wives, legislators erupted in anger. They accused the sponsors of trying to bring Western fads to Cambodia. "They called me a revolutionary," said the women's affairs minister, Ing Kantha Phavi. "They said this was a family matter," not something the state had a right to adjudicate. The bill died.

The ministry came back with a new version in 2005, and this time it passed. Human-rights advocates were jubilant—but not for long. Like so many other laws the rulers did not like, the government simply declined to enforce it. Violence continued and even increased, as reports newspapers printed almost every day in 2008 and 2009 made clear.

- "Khim Ny, 44, was severely beaten by her husband after she went to retrieve him from a gambling club about 200 meters from their family home in Kampong Cham Thursday. Khim Ny's husband broke her leg with a long pole after she rebuked him for gambling and not earning money for the family."
- "A Khmer-American man has confessed to pouring gasoline on his fiancée and her sister and burning them at their home in Cambodia's northwestern Battambang province, authorities here say, amid what the government describes as a worsening pattern of violence against women."
- "The headless and naked bodies of Nhaem Phoeun, 37, and her daughter Bun Savy, 8, were found floating on Prek Chhlaung River in Snuol district, Kratie province, on November 11. Police have arrested Sem Bun, 48, the husband and father of the victims for the murders, when the suspect's oldest daughter, Bun Saron, 20, alerted the authorities after her father confessed his crime to her. She said her father had been sexually abusing her for one year, and

she believes he killed her mother and sister because they knew of the rapes."

The government had been shamed into passing a law it did not agree with. Its solution, as usual, was to do nothing. As a result, four years later the Women's Affairs Ministry conducted another national survey and found that the incidence of domestic violence had actually increased. In 2009, one-third of the nation's women reported that they were subjected to physical abuse. "We have a lot of good laws; the problem is the enforcement of the laws," said Ing Kantha Phavi, using the bureaucratic understatement required of a minister serving in the government she is criticizing.

Dr. Mam Bunheng, the minister of health, addressed the worsening statistics with a furrowed brow and a worried tone. "Yes, now we see more domestic violence," he acknowledged. "We had it before but not as much. A big part of the problem today is that so many people like to drink." But then he brightened. "Also look at how we inform people about this now, educate people."

Given the bleak statistics, that didn't seem to be helping. In fact, in late 2009 the Women's Affairs Ministry conducted a nationwide survey and found that 70 percent of all respondents, male and female, said they believed physical violence against women was sometimes permissible. More surprising, 55 percent of the women surveyed said they deserved to be beaten if they questioned their husbands about spending habits or extramarital affairs. Isn't that what the *Chbab Srey*, required reading in the schools until 2007, had been teaching Cambodia's children for generations?

Pailin is a scruffy town near Cambodia's western border with Thailand. It is distinguished by its role as the former Khmer Rouge "capital." In Pailin, Chhoun Makkara represents the human-rights organization Adhoc, which pursues human-rights cases in court—often a fruitless endeavor, given the corruption endemic to the legal system.

One morning in the summer of 2009 Chhoun Makkara heard about a double murder in town, including a hanging—an extreme example of domestic violence, it appeared. He went to have a look, "because this kind of hanging is increasing," he explained. Really, not much happened in Pailin, but this looked interesting. Now he was looking at grisly photos from the murder scene. A ceiling fan rotated slowly overhead—too slow to create a breeze. A fluorescent light hung from the ceiling just above the fan, creating a slow, eerie strobe effect. The room was bare, save for a desk, a table, and a couple of chairs. "I don't think the police will drop this case," he added, as if that were unusual. "They are doing an investigation."

A few hours earlier, I had accompanied two uniformed policemen as they walked down a narrow dirt path behind a small neighborhood of one-room Cambodian homes on stilts. The path led down to a small stream where residents went to bathe. Just one mile from Pailin's city center residents had no electricity or running water. Down a short rise they came to the stream, little more than a creek three feet across, not even two inches deep, littered with small empty shampoo and liquid-soap squeeze tubes.

A low tree hung over the stream, and as soon as the police made a turn in the path they saw the first victim, forty-three-year-old Sorn Phalla, bare-chested, hanging from a rope tied to a low branch, his chin at his chest, eyes wide open, tongue sticking out. He was a muscular fellow with short-cropped black hair and faint blue tattoos all over his chest in a serpentine Asian design. Some Cambodians believed tattoos like that protect you from harm. They did not appear to have worked that day. His feet were bare and dangled a few inches from the ground. No stool or other object lay beside him, nothing he could have jumped from to hang himself. But then, he was not the only victim. Two yards away Ream Sokny, a women in her midthirties, lay dead on the ground, faceup, coils of heavy wire wrapped tight around her neck. Apparently, she'd been strangled. Her legs splayed wide open, and water dribbled around her bare feet in the stream. She wore a yellow sarong and bra but was otherwise bare-chested. Her eyes were closed, her mouth open, her face expressionless. A large green and white bath towel lay beside her in a pile.

Along the rise overlooking the scene a dozen townspeople crouched, watching silently. One policeman wandered among them taking statements while the other looked over the bodies. In short order the woman's husband made his presence known. He wore a beige shirt that looked like it had once been white and black pants rolled up to his knees. Crouching on the ground just above his wife, he muttered loud enough so that everyone could hear him. "I was away at the Thai-Cambodian border," he said to no one in particular. The border was fewer than twenty miles away. "I drive a bulldozer. I come home just once or twice a month." He gazed at the scene with a sour, pursed-lip expression. "I just received an award for good work on the road project, and I didn't even get to tell her."

An older man in a sleeveless white T-shirt wandered around the scene, his face etched with hostility. He, too, spoke to no one in particular, but his manner was angry, pugnacious. "I share a fence with her, so we are like brother and sister. And this man killed her!" he declared, pointing urgently at the dead man hanging from the tree.

A policeman pulled the dead man's shorts down and examined his genitals with a gloved hand, looking for evidence of recent sex. When he finished he left the shorts pulled down so that the dead man presented an even more inelegant image, if that were possible. The officer then found a scythe and cut the dead man down. The body was stiff as a pole and simply fell back into a crook in the tree.

The husband said, "He has tattoos, and she is scared of tattoos. He's not handsome; he does not look like a movie star. I don't think my wife had an affair with this man." Just then the pugnacious older neighbor marched over to the tree, positioned himself behind the dead man, and gave his back a strong kick, knocking the body forward so it fell to the ground with a loud and sickening thud that raised a cloud of dust and stilled the crowd.

Everyone watched intently until the dust finally settled and they could see him facedown in the dirt, his naked butt looking up to the sky. Within a few minutes ants were crawling over the body. The husband roused himself and walked over to his wife, the wire still coiled around her neck. He picked up the big green bath towel and covered her.

Up the hill, in the little neighborhood where the couple had lived, another policeman was questioning a young girl who was sitting in the doorway of the dead woman's small home—one room with wooden walls and a tin roof. A car battery powered a single fluorescent light. The couple had an actual bed, an unusual luxury in a Cambodian home—a straw mat on wooden slats. The woman had hung red, lacy curtains around it. On faded posters tacked to the walls Chinese models posed in fashions from ten or fifteen years before. A small photo album from their wedding sat precariously on one of the rafters. Inside, the victim, a pretty young woman, stood smiling in front of statues and pagodas. Her new husband was not shown; he must have been taking the pictures.

The young girl said she sometimes stayed in the house when the husband was away and told the police that the dead man knew the woman and occasionally came over for dinner. "But they talked in a normal way," suggesting that she had not seen any improper behavior.

At the Adhoc office later that day, Chhoun Makkara, looking at his photos from the scene of the crime, said police told him that "they found sperm on both people. There was no trail in the grass, no crushed plants, so in my opinion, they were killed while they were getting ready to take a bath. They brought a towel. She's only in a bra. He's in shorts. But it's hard to draw a conclusion." Obvious questions, he admitted, included: How did it happen that the husband, who seldom came home, happened to be there that day? Did he catch the two of them in the act and, in a fit of rage, kill them?

That evening, Chhoun Makkara said a friend at the police station told him that the police would likely charge the husband with the crime. A few days later, however, the police rendered a different, far-fetched judgment. The young man killed the woman and then hung himself, raising the obvious question: Did the husband pay off the police?

Just outside the Pursat town center one summer afternoon a week or so after the hanging and murder in Pailin, police were manning a traffic checkpoint on the main east-west highway. They'd placed a metal fence in the road so that it blocked the east lane of traffic. There, a policeman wearing an orange emergency vest stood under an umbrella, waving tractor-trailer trucks to the curb with an orange truncheon. Cars and small trucks were allowed to pass unhindered. Another officer stood behind another fence doing the same thing with traffic heading west, and at any given moment two or three trucks were idling beside the road in each direction.

The officers said nothing to the trucks' drivers. They didn't have to. One by one, each driver hopped down from the truck cab with a handful of bills in his hand. He trotted over to the side of the road where three other officers stood behind their patrol car. Wordlessly, each of the drivers plopped the bills onto the squad car's trunk as the officers watched, then ran back to his truck and drove away. One driver, stopped and questioned a short distance up the road, said he had paid 5,000 riel, or about $1.20.

Capt. Sim Rath was standing under an umbrella behind the squad car, collecting the cash as the drivers dropped it off. He said nothing to the drivers as they paid their bribes; they exchanged not a word or even a glance. The captain looked both nervous and defiant as I approached. I asked him, "Why are you taking their money?"

"They don't have drivers' licenses, or their trucks are too heavy," he said without pause.

"How do you know the trucks are too heavy if you don't have a scale?"

"I can tell. Some of these trucks were inspected before." He pointed to his ticket book, folded open to one page that was filled out with a notice of infraction. But then, none of the drivers were leaving with tickets in their hands. Was the ticket book for show? Was it a threat? Give me some money, or I'll give you a ticket that costs more?

"We give them a receipt," the captain insisted. Just then another driver trotted up, dropped 10,000 riel on the trunk without a word, turned around, and jogged back to his truck. The for-show ticket remained in the book.

"What did he do wrong?"

Capt. Sim Rath paused for a moment, considering, then said, "He already knows what he did wrong."

Later that day, around lunchtime, the fences and umbrellas still sat by the road, but the officers were gone—taking a break from their labors. Checkpoints like that one dotted the highways nationwide. At another in Kandal Province, ten policemen ignored all the cars and motorbikes and small trucks. They stopped only big trucks loaded with goods. Truck drivers got out, trotted over to the table, just as they had at Capt. Sim Rath's checkpoint in Pursat Province, left some money, and then got back in their trucks and drove off. But at exactly 5:00 p.m., the police gave the table and chairs they'd been using back to the businesses they had requisitioned them from. They took off their helmets and police shirts and walked across the street to their cars carrying briefcases, one of which held the money they had just purloined.*

Government officials were not unanimous in their disapproval of this practice. Chhay Sareth, the Pursat council chief, called it "a big

---

*It seemed odd that police were extremely reluctant to use new radar devices, donated by an NGO, to catch speeders or Breathalyzers to catch drunk drivers. Wouldn't this equipment provide new opportunities to demand cash payments from drivers? But even after extensive training and public announcements that warned drivers, police simply refused to use the new devices. In Channy, the president of Acleda Bank, explained, "Cars are hard to recognize. Sometimes army officers or senior government officials will get caught," and then the police would get in serious trouble. Better not to use the equipment at all.

issue for me; I hate it." Prach Chann, governor of Battambang Province, acknowledged that police checkpoints dotted his roads but called them "a small thing. Not a big deal."

Police generally targeted fully loaded tractor-trailer trucks because the drivers, carrying rice or corn or cassava, knew they would have to pay bribes to get their produce to market, so they came with cash in their pockets.

Ma Buth was a produce broker. His trucks picked up corn from farmers in western provinces and drove it across the country for sale in Vietnam. "On the way, at all the checkpoints," he explained matter-of-factly, "we will have to pay the police a total of about $50 and then at the border another $50. Each way. We make about $300 on the truckload, minus the bribes. So really it's $200. It's getting worse. Hun Sen said they shouldn't do it anymore. But nothing has changed. In fact it's getting worse. It's a big problem. They extort money from us, and so we cannot pay as high a price for the product, meaning the poor farmer is the one who suffers." In his line of work, from every direction, he said, someone was trying to cheat him. "I've been at this since 1985. Corruption in previous years was not as serious. Now it gets worse and worse. They see me doing business, so they want to make some profit from me." In 2008 the United Nations, quoting a recent survey, said, "89 percent of encounters with the traffic police resulted in a bribe."

While police and the courts took money to let criminals go free, judges also readily accepted orders from above. In fact, they usually didn't need orders. When Hun Sen or some other senior member of his government filed charges against someone, the judges knew they had to find that person guilty—if they wanted to keep their jobs. For a few judges, failure to do so had resulted in immediate dismissal. So it was for Moeung Sonn, president of the Khmer Civilization Foundation, dedicated to protecting and promoting the nation's cultural heritage. In 2009 the government started putting up lights at Angkor

Wat, the twelfth-century temple that remained the symbol of Cambodia's former glory. The Cambodian flag featured a line drawing of Angkor Wat. The idea was to begin a nighttime show for tourists.

Moeung Sonn said he was concerned that putting up the lights might damage the temple. Right away, the government sued him for disinformation and incitement. He fled to France. Meantime, Dave Perkes, a *Phnom Penh Post* writer, had a look at the walls where the lights had been mounted and found "regular, oblong holes about 10 cm long" that had been cut in the walls above "the cornices opposite the bas reliefs." Exercising the extreme caution that journalists had to display, so as not to attract their own lawsuits, Perkes concluded his short column saying, "I cannot say for certain whether additional holes had been cut" to put up the lights, "but I can see how people get the impression that serious damage had been done."

A court convicted Moeung Sonn in absentia. Judge Chhay Kong said, "We find that the accused damaged the government's reputation and caused anarchy and disorder in society." He sentenced the defendant to two years in prison. Moeung Sonn remained in France. This was just one in a spate of similar lawsuits against opposition politicians, journalists, and other assorted government antagonists. Among them, once again, Sam Rainsy found himself caught in this trap.

In the fall of 2009, Vietnam put up several posts that were intended to demarcate a portion of Cambodia's disputed border with Vietnam. This was still a volatile issue for Cambodians, as many still did not recognize Vietnam's claim to the Mekong Delta region in southern Vietnam. In response, Sam Rainsy pulled off a perfect politician's publicity stunt. With reporters in tow, he yanked six of these border posts out of the ground and made a show of lambasting the government for "enforcing a Vietnamese government order." Hun Sen immediately slapped him with a lawsuit. But first he had to strip Rainsy of his parliamentary immunity, which his parliament promptly did, for the third time in the previous few years—during a closed assembly session.

Rainsy had often promised to stop provoking Hun Sen. In 2000 he told interviewers, "I will soften my stance. I realize that my aggression seems to create confrontation, which is not productive." Ron Abney, his longtime friend and adviser, said he often told Rainsy: "You've got only one issue, pal, and that's Hun Sen. That's the way it was, and that's the way it is now."

A few weeks before his border show, Rainsy told me, "We need to go back to what we should have been doing. Telling how we will address the concerns of the everyday people. Land issues, education. How we will put people back to work. We will concentrate more on issues, not on persons. We'll talk less about Hun Sen."

That resolve didn't last long, and after the assembly acted against him, Rainsy took off, to plead for support from his friends in the bleachers. He was in France when a court sentenced him to two years in prison for "racial discrimination and damaging public property." In a televised address to his followers a few days later, Rainsy put on a pitiable expression and vowed to remain in (comfortable) exile in his Paris home "until all people jailed in land disputes are set free and their land returned."

In the meantime, he promised to do what he liked best: complain about Hun Sen to sympathetic foreigners. "Now," he said, "is the time for diplomatic and political approaches to friendly nations and international organizations." Hun Sen responded by filing new charges against him, for "using fake border documents"—the maps Rainsy had proffered to show where the "actual" border was. Meantime, two villagers who had helped Rainsy rip out the border posts had been convicted at the same time as Rainsy. Now, while Rainsy plotted in his Paris *palais*, they were serving their long prison sentences. One was reported to be seriously ill. In September 2010 a court sentenced Rainsy in absentia to another ten years on charges of "spreading false information." Hun Sen said he had no intention of intervening in Rainsy's court case. For the moment, at least, Cambodia was effectively a one-party state.

Across the board, all of these cases ended badly. Leang Saroeun's killer was never punished. A few weeks after the crime, the colonel who set him on fire moved to Vietnam. Top Chan Sereyvudth remained the undisputed chief prosecutor of Pursat Province. No one was prosecuted for hanging and strangling the victims in Pailin. Moeung Sonn and Sam Rainsy remained in exile. As Youk Chhang put it, "Everywhere you turn around, there is no justice today."

# CHAPTER THIRTEEN

When a society is sick, then even the institutions that are intended to make people well are infected. Ask Cambodians what their government does for them, and they still cite roads, bridges, and reservoirs—the public works of the Angkorian kings. But sometimes, just sometimes now, they also cite health care.

For some people Cambodia's hospitals and health clinics are a life-saving godsend in a nation that had no modern health care until just a few decades ago. Naturally, that applies only if they're among the lucky few who can afford it. Health care is supposed to be free for everyone. But then, this is Cambodia. And so for many people hospitals are the source of nothing but pain, sorrow, and untimely death.

Erin Soto, head of USAID's office in Cambodia, had a meeting one day with the deputy minister of finance. They were going to discuss problems in the nation's health clinics, "how people have to sit in a clinic for hours and hours to see a nurse—while the people who pay something up front get served right away," she recounted. "And he told us: 'It's just like a restaurant. You have to tip to get good service.' It made me realize we have a long way to go. They just thought" that paying bribes "was the way it was supposed to work."

That was the way it worked for Let Ting. Her charred husband had been shuttled from a small regional hospital to a bigger one until finally he wound up at Preah Kossamak Hospital, a large facility in downtown Phnom Penh. At the smaller so-called "referral" hospitals, doctors and nurses had given Leang Saroeun intravenous fluids and salve for the burns. That's all. "We arrived at Kossamak Hospital at midnight," Let Ting related. "They, too, gave him an IV and an injection and then walked away. Several hours later, a doctor came in. He told us the burn was very serious, and he needed to clean the wounds. But we would have to pay him $100. He told this to my grandmother. She is old, and she had just lost a leg to a land mine. Through the evening, the price increased to $150. I was crying. I told the doctor I didn't have $150. The doctor said, 'Well, I guess we don't need to clean the wounds.' He took off his gloves and walked away." That was the last they saw of him. Leang Saroeun, the victim, "was crying through this," she went on. "He was in a lot of pain, saying, 'I'm too hot, I'm too hot.' He just laid there until the next day. Nothing but an IV. By now his body was starting to swell. So we packed him up and took him home. We had no options. All they were doing was giving him IVs. And he was swelling up, very, very big." The next day he died.

Chhay Sareth, the provincial council chief, said he never heard about this case. "I think the authorities have covered it up. But if you commit a crime like this, you are like Pol Pot."

Teng Soeun, director of Kossamak Hospital, was a troll-like fellow, short and round. But his manner was concerned, soothing, and seemingly sincere. "As the director I feel sick that a man died without any treatment," he said. "It is against the ethics. I have to tell you that any patient who comes here, they have to get treatment. We have this hospital to help the poor even if they cannot pay for treatment." He said all that with a straight-eyed stare and an unwavering manner of conviction.

"I was on duty that day," said Ek Sonsatthya, a nurse. She and several others who had been involved in Leang Saroeun's care were sitting on a sofa in the director's large office. (Missing, of course, was the doctor who had asked for the bribe.) On the floor was an inexpensive oriental rug. "He got a prescription injection on 20 June and an IV," she said, consulting the dead man's case file. "His wife stayed with him. He had burns on 80 percent of his body. It was so bad that it was hard to find a vein to make an injection."

"His condition was very serious," said So Saphy, chief of the hospital's intensive care unit. "I told the patient's mother."

"According to our rules," the director interjected, "we have to treat the patient to the last breath. And if a patient dies here, we give them a free coffin. We cannot force them to leave, and we usually advise them carefully. But if he dies," he said again, "we give him a free coffin."

But what about the demand for $150?

"There have been cases in the past," the director allowed. "I agree in past times there was corruption. But now no more. We will try to clean up all this mess. We try to implement the regulations. Our hospital is one of the honest hospitals." Of course, any other hospital director would say the same, he acknowledged, chuckling.

When the discussion ended, So Saphy offered a tour of the intensive care unit, downstairs. Fourteen patents lay on battered old metal beds with straw mats they'd brought from home, laid on bare wood frames. The ICU had two respirators, three oxygen saturation machines, and no other medical equipment. In the adjoining medication pantry, So Saphy pointed to a glass cabinet that held two dozen IV bottles, neatly arranged. "This is the serum for patients who pay," she said without expression. Then she pointed to a low cabinet on the other side of the room and slid open a metal cabinet door. The cabinet was full of rags and other debris, but she reached toward the back and pulled out two IV bottles. "This is the serum for patients who can't pay." She held up one bottle. The expiration date, in bold blue letters, was five months earlier. She allowed me to look at the drugs in the medicine cabinet, assorted bottles and jars, nearly all with expiration dates long past—six months, a year, two years. Looking at one dated the previous year, So Saphy just pursed her lips and shook her head.

Asked about that later, the health minister, Dr. Mam Bunheng, a gynecologist, offered scant reassurance. "That is not allowed," he insisted. "We have a monitoring system. We check every year." But that may have been among the least of his problems.

Mith Ran, forty-nine, had a well-worn artificial leg and a doleful expression affixed to his face. He had served in the Khmer Rouge army and lost his right leg to a land mine. Decades later he lived in Pailin, still home to many Khmer Rouge veterans. Mith Ran's wife was recently deceased, another unfortunate death, and as a result four of his seven children, the youngest of them, were in an orphanage because, he said, he could not care for them alone. The others, pulled from school, were at work in a cornfield.

One evening, he sat on the front steps of his little home just like all the others: one room, small, dark, and bare. An empty bag of corn lay on the ground beneath him. Chicks pecked at the few remaining kernels as he told of his wife's death. She was pregnant; this was her eighth baby. One night the previous month, when she said she was ready, he rushed her to the hospital in Pailin at about ten o'clock. The medical staff wheeled her to the maternity ward, "and thirty minutes later a doctor looked at her and said she was not ready. I said, 'Please help my wife. This is her eighth baby.'" He told the story as if he had related it more than once before, which he had. Human-rights workers had come to see him and promised to take his case to court.

She went into labor at 3:00 a.m., he said, and "asked me to wake up the nursing staff. I knocked on the door several times, but the nurses were asleep. I pounded on the door. They would not come out. At 3:30 one of them finally did come out, a girl with slightly crossed eyes, and she brought in the doctor. I asked him please to take her to the delivery room. The doctor said, 'Do you have any money with you?' I asked how much. He said 100,000 riel," or $25. For Mith Ran the sum might as well have been $25 million, given how unapproachable the doctor's bribe request was.

"I said no. He asked where I lived. I told him."

"Do you have relatives there who can lend you the money?"

"No." Then, like the doctor at Kossamak Hospital, this one "pulled off his gloves and walked away."

Later, his wife's water broke, and "I called the medical staff. I banged on the door. They would not come out for a long time. I pleaded with the medical staff, 'Please, please, help my wife. I am poor. Please!'"

He sat on his false leg; a battered black wing-tip shoe covered the artificial foot. He looked at the ground and shifted from his story into a litany of woes. "I own no land. I am just a worker on other people's land. I did own land, but I had to sell it to get treatment for my leg. I stepped on a land mine in 1993. The bone was infected, so it was expensive. I am a former Khmer Rouge soldier in Battambang. I cannot read and write. I didn't go to school. I joined the Khmer Rouge when I was thirteen. My parents were killed, beaten to death by a plantation owner." Then he broke free of his dark reverie. "Help my wife," he said again, looking up. "I asked the nurses, 'Please, help my wife!'" A few hours later his wife and their baby died.

At the Pailin hospital maternity ward the next afternoon, two women lay with their newborn babies on wooden-slat beds covered with straw mats the patients had brought from home. Fluid from an IV bottle dripped slowly down a tube into one of the women. The clear plastic bag hung from a crooked bamboo pole tied to the side of the bed with white string.

If the ward had a nursing staff, the nurses were out of sight. But then a blue door was closed—the same door Mith Ran had pounded on over and over again. A sign on the wall above, in Khmer, declared "Duty Room." Now, once again, repeated knocks on the door brought no reaction. Not a sound. So I opened the door. A nurse, in bed, asleep under a blanket at three in the afternoon, woke up with a start, rubbed her eyes, and slowly got out of bed. Minutes later she came out. Sun Thida was her name, and she said she was the duty nurse. She was thirty years old and wore a red shirt festooned with panda cartoons. Her eyes were slightly crossed.

"I wasn't here" when Mith Ran's wife died, she averred. "That wasn't my shift. But I heard about it. That was a complicated case. But I was not on duty." Sun Thida said she had been a nurse "for five or six years. I had twelve years of school and a short course in nursing once I got here. A seminar, three days."

Dr. Sou Vichet, the hospital's new director, had a nervous tic. He simultaneously blinked and squinted when he was nervous. Now he was blinking away at a pace so rapid that he could barely see. "That night I was not here; I didn't have this job yet," he said. "But I've investigated. At that time there were two or three nurses and two or three medics on duty" in the entire hospital. "The doctors were gone. Some were at a seminar to improve their education. The director of the hospital was not here, either. I can't say if they were violating regulations."

He sat at a battered old gray metal desk in the hospital's administrative office. He'd been on the job only a few weeks, but now, he said, doctors were required to be on duty around the clock. As for sleeping during the duty shift, "I don't blame her. She probably had a late shift," but then, blinking away, he insisted, "It is not routine that medical staff sleep during their duty shift like that."

As for the bribe demand, Phab Sou Vichet said he had no knowledge of that. "Patients are not required to pay." The doctor in question had not been penalized; the hospital seemed to accept his argument that all of the problems were the woman's fault. He was still on staff, just like the doctor at Kossamak Hospital in Phnom Penh who refused to treat Leang Saroeun.

Dr. Meng Huot, the hospital's deputy director, interrupted the conversation to say, "A reporter came to us and said he would not print a story about that case if we paid him $100 to $250. I don't know his name. He wanted me to send the money someplace. I didn't pay him," perhaps because the *Phnom Penh Post* printed a story about the woman's death a day or two later. (These blackmail attempts were not uncommon; the "reporters" wrote for small papers and, in these cases, published stories under pseudonyms.)

Meng Huot spoke with an omnipresent sneering grin but took on a more serious tone when he volunteered that "in this area, the education of the medical staff is quite limited. If people are educated, they don't want to come here to Pailin. If they come, they don't want to stay. So the only people we have to take care of these poor people are not the best in their profession."

"If the doctor had given her a normal delivery, on time," said her husband, Mith Ran, rocking slightly as he lamented, "she would have survived. If she'd had a C-section, she probably would have survived. But she died."

Mith Ran probably hadn't known it, but if he had asked the doctor for a C-section, he might have gotten the physician's attention. In maternity wards around the country, C-sections were all the rage. Normally, "between 5 and 15 percent of births require a C-section," said Dr. Paul Weelen of the World Health Organization office in Cambodia. But nationwide, a far larger number of women giving birth (no one was counting) were subjected to surgery instead of being allowed to give the child a natural birth. The reason for this was simple. "The fee structure for maternity is as follows," said Dr. Sin Somuny, executive director of Medicam, which represents all the donors involved in health-care issues. "A midwife costs $15; $20 for a regular delivery— and $150 for a C-section."

In a maternity ward at Battambang Hospital, one of the nation's major health-care facilities, two women lay in bed with their new babies. Both said they had been given C-sections. Yoeun Chantho was still in pain; dark bloodstains spotted the front of her blouse. "This is my second baby and my second C-section," she said. Her oldest son, nine years old, held her IV for her, dangling from the end of a bamboo pole. It looked like he was holding a fishing rod. "The last time they said I had high blood pressure; this time they said the baby was in the wrong position."

In an adjoining room Hop Thoeum looked to be near tears. Her mother sat on a mat on the floor beside her. They had no baby. "The doctors told us the baby was about to die, so they gave her a C-section," said the mother, Run Hon, fifty-six. "But the baby died. They said he drowned. They didn't ask for money this time. In this case whether we paid or not wouldn't have helped. It was not about money; it was related to capability."

In fact, at Battambang Hospital and a growing number of health facilities nationwide, money was becoming less of an issue because, as several patients said, "the NGOs paid for it." In a small office at the hospital's entrance, several workers sat at computers emblazoned with big, bold USAID stickers. The workers were employees of health-care donor organizations. Their job here was to certify patients as truly poor, under a new government program.

Until 2009 a poor person who fell ill had been required to visit the communal government office and get a document certifying that he or she was indeed poor. The problem was, a really sick person did not have the time or capability to travel there, wait for the offices to be open (usually just two or three hours a day), and bribe the responsible officer.

Under the new program, the government was distributing identity cards to poor people, which meant that they would not have to pay for their health care. In the Battambang Hospital office, a stack of these cards sat on the desk of one worker. "We help them fill it out," he explained. "Most of these people can't read or write. Most of the interviews for these cards are done in the villages, but if they show up here we do the interview here." Outside a naked baby boy, by himself, toddled past the door.

This new program was an important change, pushed by the donor community and accepted by the government. However, across the country the administrators were employees of donor organizations. The government had agreed to implement the program only so long as it did not have to administer it. As it was, the Battambang Hospital's administrative staff, about a dozen people sitting at desks with a television on a shelf above them, spent that afternoon watching WWF wrestling.

With the new card in hand, patients were entitled to free care. That did not necessarily prevent doctors from demanding bribes, but they might have been less likely to exploit people who were certified to be poor.

Perhaps the greater problem, as the dead baby's grandmother had said, was the quality of care. How many Cambodian doctors had been accepted to medical school with a score of 25 percent on the entrance exam? How many of them had bribed their way through their medical education and training? How many had access only to expired medications and primitive or nonexistent equipment? For example, not one Cambodian hospital had a bacteriological lab, used to test for infections.

Cambodian women faced a high risk of death when they got pregnant. In 2009 the United Nations reported that 1 out of every 185 pregnant women died during childbirth. (In Vietnam the number was 1 of every 666 women. In the United States it was 1 in every 4,800.) But the UN said the larger problem was that Cambodia's miserable statistic had not improved in decades.

In response, Hun Sen called for the recruitment and training of more midwives—while proposing no new program or funding to accomplish such a goal. Michael O'Leary, head of the World Health Organization office in Cambodia, shook his head. "Midwives are one part of the solution," he said, "but that alone will not bring the rate down. It's a multifactoral problem. You need emergency obstetric care."

Even if that were available, most people lived too far from a health clinic to reach one in time. And in fact, most clinics were open just two or three hours a day. Like teachers, the government paid doctors, nurses, and paramedics so little that they could not afford to work at the clinics all day. They had to find other jobs. Doctors opened private clinics. In their hospital jobs they earned fifty to eighty dollars a month, the health minister said. Oftentimes they worked in the hospital for only a few hours a day. That was the probable reason no doctors were on staff when Mith Ran's wife died at Pailin's hospital. "What you are getting now is more and more doctors working in private clinics—when they are supposed to be at the hospital," said Sin Somuny of Medicam. "So they end up working in the hospital just to promote their names, and then they poach the patients. This is leading to a collapse of the public health system."

With or without doctors, a patient could not survive in a Cambodian hospital without the help of a family member or friend. Many services are inaccessible to anyone who is seriously ill.

Battambang Hospital provided lunch and dinner. A woman rolled a wheeled lunch wagon around the campus and waited for patients to come out to get the food. One afternoon a woman with an apron and a gray chef's cap parked her wagon outside the maternity ward. Patients or their relatives came out with plastic bowls they had brought from home; the "chef" doled rice and beans in prodigious portions out of large plastic buckets sitting in her cart. Behind her, across the street, was the six-grill "kitchen"—just concrete pits with three-post pot stands. Patients had to bring wood for fire, pots, pans, and food for any patient or family member who wanted to make their own meals. When doctors told patients they needed ice, they had to trudge over to the hospital icehouse, pay seventy-five cents, and carry the ice back to their rooms.

The emergency-room duty nurses' station, a large open room, was empty. But a green door was cracked. Three women were inside, sitting on beds, eating bananas and rice cakes. One of them spotted me looking through the crack of the door. She jumped up in a rush and pulled on her white coat. "Just a minute," she said, obviously embarrassed. The other two nurses were bumping into each other as they scrambled to put on their coats and nurses' caps, shove the bananas under the bed, and come out of the room. Two of them scurried down the hall.

I asked the third nurse how many people had been admitted that day. "Ten new inpatients," she said, distracted, embarrassed. "They are being treated for high blood pressure, encephalitis, dengue fever, and malaria." All the windows in the emergency room were open to the outside. No screen, no glass, nothing to keep malarial mosquitoes out of the ward. The nurse's name, on her name tag, was Meas Sudhan, R.N. "Another patient was bitten by a poisonous snake," she added. Then she, too, hurried out of the room—all of a sudden attentive to her patients.

Just then a woman came in the front door, barely able to walk, leaning heavily on her husband. Her breathing was heavy; sweat rolled down her forehead. Trailing behind her, three family members carried large bags of food and gear. A doctor led her to a bed—just a steel frame with wooden slats. He stood still with the woman, whose legs seemed ready to collapse beneath her, while family members dug hurriedly through their bags until they found a straw mat, woven with green and yellow flowers, and laid it across the bed frame. One of them, who looked like the sick woman's sister, pulled a pillow from another bag and laid it on the bed. Only then did the doctor help the patient onto the bed, take out his stethoscope, and begin to examine her.

At Battambang Hospital and every other health-care facility across the nation, patients arrived with illnesses, often fatal, that were almost never seen in other nations, including Vietnam and Thailand. A large part of the problem was hygiene. Ninety-eight percent of Thai had access to clean drinking water; 95 percent of them had a toilet in their homes. In Cambodia about 14 percent of the population had access to clean water. Just 22 percent had a toilet, and in rural areas the number was 16 percent.

At the end of 2008 UNICEF and Cambodian government statistics estimated that 9.7 million people were treated for diarrhea and other sanitation-related illnesses each year, most often from dirty water. That was 72 percent of the population. Each year nearly 10,000 people died. "It's routine to have diarrhea here," said Loch Pheach, vice chief in the village of Sangkum. "It happens a lot."

Chea Sophara, the minister of rural development, did not dispute the World Bank's numbers. They had barely improved in decades. So he offered one of the government's facile promises: "We want all rural people to have clean and safe water to avoid diseases. By year 2015, we believe 50 percent of rural people will have access to clean water, and by 2025, everyone in the country will have clean water." Opposition lawmakers, as usual, noted that the government was dedicating no money toward the goal; officials seemed to be waiting for donors to step up and take on this problem.

But then when the World Bank gave the government $11.9 million for seven major rural sanitation projects, in short order the bank found that the money was being squandered in a typically Cambodian festival of corruption. This included "solicitation and acceptance of bribes as a condition for allowing companies to participate in bidding, rigging of bids for construction contracts and manipulation of procurement, fraudulent bid securities, price fixing and collusion to manipulate tenders, inflated bid prices, fixed outcomes of competitive procurement procedures, and submission of fraudulent bids by unqualified bidders who misrepresented both their financial statements and prior experience," the bank said.

Furious, bank officials demanded their money back. Hun Sen hemmed, hawed, and stalled until finally he found a fall guy. Mour Kimsan, former deputy director general at the Rural Development Ministry who now was working as a consultant there, was charged with embezzling $880,000 of the bank's money. The bank canceled its sanitation project.

In Bon Skol, near the Vietnam border, village chief Mou Neam was among the more prosperous people in town. He had an outhouse beside his house, a little shed with a seat over a deep pit he had dug. When the pit filled up, he could dig a new one and move the shed. As it happened, just ten yards away he had also dug a well with a pump. There he could draw water from the same aquifer into which his septic pit drained.

Mou Neam's situation was not at all unusual. It was the norm. Viey Savet, a twelve year old from the village of Chong Kneas near Siem Reap, told the Red Cross as part of a study on sanitation problems, "I wake up and wash my face and brush my teeth using water from the lake. I go to the toilet. Our latrine goes straight into the lake. My parents both bathe in the lake. To make dinner, my parents boil water from the lake to use for cooking. I bathe three times in the lake each day with soap." So, "the passive genocide continues," as Dr. Beat Richner put it.

Richner, a Swiss physician, was an irascible fellow, contemptuous of people he considered to be fools and scoundrels. In Cambodia he believed he saw one every time he turned around. Richner operated a pediatric hospital in Siem Reap, and the difference between his facility and Battambang's public hospital could not have been more striking. Kantha Bopha Hospital was large, clean, modern—and free. Patients were not charged for their care; doctors and staff were paid a living wage and did not ask for bribes. Kantha Bopha and Battambang Hospital shared one common feature: the patients.

Standing at the entrance to one ward, where twenty children rested in real beds, Richner waved his hand across the room as he looked at a chart. "They have malaria, dengue fever, encephalitis, hepatitis, meningitis, pneumonia, diarrhea." Then he launched one of his rants. "We have thousands of typhus cases. We had forty-two cases of dengue in the hospital and ninety-five new ones this morning. Eighteen meningitis cases. If in Switzerland you had three cases of meningitis in the whole country, it would be all over the newspapers. Here if you go to a health clinic, they charge you sixty dollars. But which child has sixty dollars? We do tuberculosis research. It was not known before that TB can cause encephalitis. We are going to publish in November. Twenty-five percent of Cambodians have hepatitis B or C, and 63 percent of them are infected with tuberculosis."

Tuberculosis can lay dormant for years. In the developed world 1 or 2 percent of the population has it even in dormant form. Illness, age, or malnutrition can trigger active tuberculosis, and Richner said he could gauge the state of the nation by watching the prevalence of the active disease among children. "Now it is up," he said. A spike in TB cases indicated that malnutrition was increasing. "Eighty percent of our malnutrition cases also present TB."

In 2008 high food prices nearly doubled the rate of severe malnutrition, to 16 percent of all children, the government reported. The next year, even after food prices had declined, the figures showed no improvement. "TB is a bellwether for malnutrition," said Mam Bunheng, the health minister. "And, yes, it is rising."

Richner moved without pause to another complaint. "Corruption is a killer," he said as he hurried down a hall between wards, always a few steps ahead of his guests. "It takes thousands of lives. If you show up and you can't pay, no one will help you. Here the nurses' station is in the ward." He pointed to a large rectangular table in one ward, where nurses sat at computers and worked with charts. "They are not in the back, hiding."

Richner, a pediatrician, was a portly sixty-two year old who first found himself in Cambodia in the early 1970s, working for the Swiss Red Cross. Like most westerners, he left as the Khmer Rouge approached Phnom Penh. "At that time Cambodia had 943 doctors. Only about 50 of them survived. I do have a conscience. Leaving in 1975, leaving behind all those doctors who did not survive, I still feel a little guilty."

After the war, King Sihanouk "asked me to come back to fix Kantha Bopha Hospital in Phnom Penh. So I said, 'Oh, okay, I will do it.' I thought I would at least try but was not sure I could do anything. I was aware of the problem of corruption."

In fact, Cambodia captured him. Driven by anger, guilt, contempt, and, yes, compassion, Richner raised tens of millions of dollars and opened his first hospital in 1993. Now he operates five of them. All of them provide free care to any child who comes in. "The first year we had 5,367 patients; last year, 1.3 million." He liked to say he treated 85 percent of the nation's children, a figure that was easy to believe but difficult to prove. Every morning starting at four o'clock hundreds of mothers with children in tow poured into the Siem Reap hospital's lobby and sat cross-legged on mats, waiting for treatment. By seven they were sent to triage doctors who determined whether the children were likely inpatients, generally about 10 percent of the new patients, or could be treated and released. "We have 640 new patients so far today," Richner said with a boastful tone, just after seven o'clock. Already a large sweat stain permeated the back of his shirt. Already the cries of wailing babies came from every direction, muted in each ward by the sound of forty-two ceiling fans, whirring at full speed. "Yesterday the number was 1,200."

The hospital was as well equipped as most any in the West. It had CAT scan and MRI machines and a bacteriological lab. Expectant mothers were given ultrasound exams. The hospital had 800 staff physicians, 400 nurses, and 590 regular patient beds, 100 in the delivery ward. No other hospital in Cambodia came close—except Richner's other facilities. But all of it depended on donations, and he needed $26 million a year, more if he wanted to expand or buy new equipment. His detractors—and his abrasive manner ensured that he had many—said his model was not sustainable. Who can raise $26 million each and every year? "Hun Sen gave us $3 million," Richner said, "directly to us, not through the ministry so they could take some." He had several other more reliable donors. Richner was also a cellist, and every Saturday night he gave a concert for tourists who were in town to see Angkor Wat.

Before taking their donations, he liked to tell them of his war with Dr. O'Leary at the World Health Organization in Phnom Penh. He offered a synopsis of his weekly speech: "The creed of WHO is that treatment should correspond to the economic reality of the country," he said with fresh anger and resentment, even though he had made that remark hundreds of times. "But the economic reality of Cambodia is zero. They also expect Cambodians to pay. But they are all farmers. How can they pay? The WHO's view of 'appropriate care' for this country is a Maoist idea. Poor people deserve poor care. That is their idea of justice." Allowed to, Richner would have prattled on into the afternoon, listing the woes of the Cambodian people and the uncaring venality of the nation's health-care establishment.

Asked about Richner, O'Leary, the director of WHO, wouldn't take the bait. "Good things get done," he said without apparent emotion. "It's parallel work. Our jobs are different. Our job is to support the government and by extension the people." But people in his office, talking not for attribution, disparaged Richner's combative attitude and his refusal to coordinate his work with the donor community—a charge Richner heatedly denied.

Richner was a prodigious fund-raiser, but he walked a tightrope—pushing, struggling to raise tens of millions of dollars every year. So what would happen when he retired or died? "A successor has been chosen," he said. "He can run this." But what about raising all that money? "Well, that is a concern. We are now looking for permanent sources. But this is an obligation we will fight for. It is a war."

Beat Richner ran the largest and most expensive health-care operation in Cambodia. James and Cara Garcia had more modest plans. He was an emergency medical technician, she a registered nurse. They lived in South Carolina and knew nothing of Cambodia's tortured history and byzantine present. But in 2008 they found themselves on vacation in Cambodia, indulging Cara's new interest in Theravadist Buddhism.

Moving around the state, they saw what every visitor sees: a seemingly gentle people living in abject poverty. "Children playing with broken flip-flops—or a frog tied to a tree," Garcia said. Infants left to walk around naked because their parents could not afford diapers. Families eating fried grasshoppers for dinner.

But the Garcias also looked at the Cambodians through the eyes of health-care professionals and saw a host of debilitating medical conditions that were being left untreated. Suddenly Cara was seized with the idea of uprooting their lives, moving to Cambodia, and opening a health clinic for the poor. Her husband eventually agreed; this would solve some problems in their lives, and they would live an adventure!

Without realizing it, they had stepped into a drama that proved Ambassador Joseph Mussomeli's prophetic warning about the state. As he had always told visitors, "Be careful because Cambodia is the most dangerous place you will ever visit. You will fall in love with it, and eventually it will break your heart."

The Garcias sold almost everything they owned, netting about $40,000, and managed to raise another $16,000 in donations. With that, they set off for Phnom Penh, hoping to open a clinic and begin treating patients right away.

Altruism is a rare commodity. While Garcia was telling the truth when he said, "We were just trying to do a good thing," the couple did have other motivations. Cara had a mental disorder. She was bipolar and considered disabled. What's more, six years earlier, she was caught, twice, stealing prescription drugs from the pharmacy in a hospital where she worked. The South Carolina State Board of Nursing censured her. Needless to say, all of that made it virtually impossible to get a job. The new venture might give her a fresh start.

They met with Mam Bunheng, the health minister. He'd run the Health Ministry since 1983 and had become a master of ingratiation. Donors large and small streamed in and out of his office day after day, and he offered each of them a smiling blizzard of words about his goals and how far the nation had come since the Khmer Rouge killed all the doctors. He soothed and flattered the donors. "We develop policy together," he liked to say. "Ownership. Every donor has ownership.

The health sector is one of the most effective at using international funds." When the inevitable difficult questions popped up, Mam Bunheng was a master at deflecting them. Bribe payments to doctors? "You heard about this because they know they have the right to talk. This is a free society. That's good."

So it was with the Garcias. He gave them permission to open a health clinic in Kampong Thom Province that would be an official part of the state's health-care system, Garcia said. The Health Ministry would provide the clinic with the supplies it needed. So, using their own money, they began seeing patients, hundreds of them—more than nine hundred every month. But when they asked the local Health Ministry office for supplies, the drugs and medications they needed, the local representative said the warehouse was bare. "We put in request after request but were always told they had no medications," Garcia said. Then one evening the Garcias happened by the ministry's local warehouse when the doors were open. They saw that it was fully stocked with all the medications they had been requesting. Garcia asked why his requests were turned down but said the warehouse manager told him simply, "'None of this is for you.'"

Not long after, while Cara Garcia was out for a walk one night, she said she saw two SUVs pull up to the warehouse doors. Two men were filling the vehicles with medications and equipment. When the Garcias asked about this during a local donors meeting, they began to broach the second part of their Cambodian adventure, under Mussomeli's gloomy formula. Most likely, they were told, the men were carting off the drugs, intending to sell them and keep the money. Across the province the Health Ministry operated nineteen clinics, more or less like the Garcias', but most of them were closed, some boarded up permanently. Three or four were regularly open, though only for a few hours a week. The rest of the time, the nurses and paramedics were off working other jobs. With so many clinics shuttered, bureaucrats at the Health Ministry could pocket the salaries of ghost employees. Suddenly, in October, the Garcias' good intentions ran full force into the ingrained customs of the nation they were trying to help.

Cara Garcia, particularly, did not like it. She raged at government officials, questioned their honesty, blamed them for the deaths of patients the Garcias could not properly treat. Cambodian corruption, she kept shouting, was killing little children. "You should be ashamed of yourself!" she told them, wagging her finger.

Her husband was used to her "severe mood swings," as he put it. That was a feature of her illness. But Cambodians found her insulting in the extreme. To them she seemed to know nothing about the Asian need to save face. She also obviously had not read the *Chbab Srey*, that piece of folk literature that told women what their place in society should be. As those Swedish anthropologists had found in the 1990s, Cambodians were ill-equipped to deal with these direct affronts and often reacted with extreme violence.

A few nights later, the Garcias said, Cara was walking home from a meeting when several men jumped out of a car, dragged her into a rice paddy, beat and raped her for several hours, then left her for dead. She didn't die, but she was broken.

The Garcias complained to the police in several locations. All of them were unresponsive. When asked about the attack later, they claimed that Cara Garcia had been running down the road, stark naked. Now the couple was radioactive. No one wanted to touch them. Finally, they gave up. They began packing up their belongings and settling accounts—only to discover, Garcia said, that their office assistant had been stealing from them for months. They had nothing left, "no home, no car, no possessions or belongings except what was in our suitcases," Garcia lamented. They had no more money and had to solicit help to get home.

Back in the United States, Garcia reflected on their journey: "We gave all we had," he recalled. But Cambodia "defeated our spirit"— and broke their hearts.

# CHAPTER FOURTEEN

J oseph Mussomeli had little knowledge of Cambodia before he became U.S. ambassador in 2005, though he had hung on to his anger
over America's perceived role in the nation's destruction thirty years
earlier. "In college I helped organize a demonstration against the U.S.
invasion of Cambodia," he recalled. "It has haunted me ever since. So,
when I was presented with a list of Asian countries where I could serve
as ambassador. I didn't hesitate even five seconds. Cambodia."

This was his first ambassadorship; most recently, he had served as
deputy chief of mission in the Philippines. And a year or so after he
arrived, when he invited several senior CPP officers to his house for
dinner, "I was shocked," he said, eyes wide. Referring to the United
States, not necessarily the new ambassador, the Cambodians told him:
"You never trusted us. You are always trying to embarrass and undermine us. You cut off direct aid in 1997. For so long, you have only supported our political opponents."

All true. American relations with Cambodia were frozen in time.
Almost ten years later the ban on direct aid, ordered after the so-called
coup in 1997, remained firmly in place. Most American aid projects
had to be funneled through NGOs or other private enterprises; almost

none could be given to the government. At the same time, many in the U.S. government still loathed Hun Sen and worked to promote Sam Rainsy. Hun Sen remained a persona non grata in Washington.

A few years earlier, when Kent Wiedemann was ambassador, angry officials in Washington had pulled back from any real involvement with the state, a result of the "coup." "We don't have any major national interests there," Wiedemann had explained. "So we say, let's make human rights the principal or perhaps the only foreign-policy objective." This, of course, meant that the embassy was constantly battling Hun Sen and the CPP, the villains of human-rights advocates. That was the embassy Mussomeli inherited—even though the formative experience in his mind was the U.S. bombing and invasion of Cambodia during the Vietnam War.

By now all of the major State Department figures who had been players during those heady days of the UN occupation and the first elections in 1993 were retired or working in positions far removed from this issue. More than fifteen years had passed since Secretary of State James Baker had pushed Cambodia to the top of America's foreign-policy agenda for a few months in 1990. The UN occupation in 1992 and 1993 was now a historical footnote—too far past to be part of the active political debate, too recent to be in history books.

Since then the United Nations had placed smaller, less ambitious peacekeeping forces in Eritrea, East Timor, and Darfur, among other spots. The world had tried to face up to more recent genocidal spasms in Bosnia, Sudan, and Rwanda. Although far more people died during the Khmer Rouge era than in any of these later murderous rages, Pol Pot's crimes against humanity no longer seemed so unique.

Now, as Mussomeli served in Phnom Penh, the United States was at war in Iraq and Afghanistan. At the State Department, the assistant secretary of state for East Asian and Pacific Affairs, Christopher Hill, was so preoccupied with North Korea's nuclear-weapons program that he liked to say, "People are calling me the assistant secretary for North Korea." Hill had met Hun Sen once, when he was in Phnom Penh for the dedication of a new U.S. Embassy building. That was the time Hun Sen had arrested two human-rights activists, and, when Hill asked about them, Hun Sen promised to let them go, saying, "I am releasing them as a gift to you." Talking about Hun Sen a few years later, Hill still held his nose. "This is not a guy you are going to confuse with Thomas Jefferson," he said, straining to maintain a diplomatic veneer.

All of this meant that Mussomeli was free to formulate U.S. policy for Cambodia more or less on his own. No one else really cared. So he set out to right a wrong, as he saw it. No, he was not trying to make up for the bombing of Cambodia. Still, this was his turn to make a difference.

In 2007 he told Washington he wanted to restore direct aid to the Cambodian government. Hill got the request and approved it without a great deal of thought. "The ambassador was all in favor of it," he explained with a shrug. But then, on reflection, he added, "That doesn't mean we are just going to hand money over to some minister."

The Hun Sen haters in Congress had moved on, too. "It became very, very clear to us that he was a permanent fixture," said a senior congressional official who had been deeply involved in Cambodia issues. "When the administration comes up with a coherent policy, Congress steps back." As Twining, the former ambassador put it, "You know there's now an international consensus that we have to deal with Hun Sen. Cambodia—it's just not worth fighting over anymore."

"There's a status quo now," said Richard Solomon, the former State Department official who had helped negotiate the UN occupation. "And it's better—certainly better than it was under the Khmer Rouge." In the end, for Washington and much of the world, that seemed to be enough. They'd given up on the promise of the UN effort the United States had helped start. They'd turned away.

No one in Washington even seemed to notice when Hun Sen, in 2005, dropped public observance of October 23, the day in 1991 when all Cambodian factions including the Khmer Rouge signed the Paris Peace Accords and agreed to lay down their arms and seek a new day for their nation. Once a national holiday, this was no longer an event Hun Sen felt any need to celebrate. As Sam Rainsy put it, the world seemed to be saying, "If you continue living like you did a thousand years ago," when Jayavarman II reigned, "you are still better off than you were during the Khmer Rouge."

Hun Sen was pleased. Mussomeli's relationship with him improved and became the closest since Ken Quinn had served as ambassador. The ambassador appreciated having the ability to see Hun Sen when he needed to, like the time, he said, "when they were renovating the park" across the street from the old parliament building, where the 1997 grenade attack occurred, now a bright, clean grassy park often frequented by tourists who knew nothing of the grenade attack. "And as part of process, they were going to take out the monument to the grenade victims. I asked Hun Sen about this. He swore he didn't know anything about it. But he stopped it."

Still, Mussomeli fully recognized that Cambodia was riddled with debilitating problems. He had lunch with Hun Sen's son once, and waiters were serving the meal when Mussomeli pointed to one of them and said, "You could throw him off the roof, and no one would touch you." His host protested: "If my father found out, he would put me in jail forever!" Mussomeli retorted, "But he'd never find out because everyone would be afraid to tell him."

While Mussomeli tried to strike a balance in America's relationship with Cambodia, elsewhere in his embassy the staff was still working full-throttle to expose corruption and related government villainy. No other embassy remained so obsessed. "We are the outlier," acknowledged Erin Soto, the USAID office director.

Her office sponsored a broad range of efforts, some of which seemed quixotic. This was particularly true of the program to train Cambodian journalists in investigative reporting. Even the program director, Mike Fowler, wondered about its efficacy. "It's absolutely problematic," he said, shaking his head. "You write an investigative story here, and you'll end up being charged and put in jail."

Another program was far more ambitious but reached a similar conclusion. In May 2008 a convoy of motorcycles and rickshaws pulled up in front of the National Assembly building to deliver a petition signed by 1.1 million Cambodians from across the nation—almost 10 percent of the population. Most of the signatures were actually just thumbprints, since few Cambodian adults could write their own names. The petition urged the assembly to pass the anticorruption law that had been languishing for almost fifteen years. The U.S. Embassy paid for the petition drive. "Our assessment was that there was not the political will to pass the anticorruption law," Soto said. "When political will does not exist, it must be built." Up to then, nothing else had worked. Neither did this. The drivers of those motorcycles and rickshaws were unloading the boxes when a national assemblyman came out to greet them. He told them the assembly refused to accept the petition.

Mussomeli said he preferred a low-key approach to all of this. "I think the effective way to deal with the corruption problem is not to pontificate. It is to talk about destiny rather than morality. 'You are so far behind your neighbors, Vietnam and Thailand. You will become a vassal state if you don't take this last chance to compete. You cannot afford the luxury of corruption.' That's what I tell them. You know," he added, "when you say critical things, they are genuinely afraid the West is trying to undermine or subvert the government. In fact, we should be able to offer criticism as a concerned friend." But he quickly learned that being a "concerned friend" of the Cambodian government was difficult work.

At about the time the United States restored direct aid in 2007, the British NGO Global Witness finally published its report on illegal logging. Three years of research produced a ninety-four-page document, entitled *Cambodia's Family Trees*. It documented what most Cambodians already knew, that "a kleptocratic elite, led by Hun Sen, is stripping Cambodia's forests."

Cambodia's luxury-wood trees had been a source of wealth for Cambodians since the beginning of time. After the Khmer Rouge fell from power, their soldiers demonstrated for the first time that the trees could be harvested in bulk and sold abroad. They introduced

Cambodia to the concept of deforestation. Learning from their example, almost as soon as Hun Sen took power in 1993 he had made his deal with his co-prime minister, Ranariddh, to split the proceeds from illegal logging. The two of them wrote the secret letter to the Thai prime minister saying that, effective immediately, only the Defense Ministry had authority to export timber. Part of the motivation was to undercut the Khmer Rouge. But if that had been the order's only purpose, the two would not have kept it secret.

Secret as the order may have been, the result was quite visible. While Charles Twining was chief of mission and then ambassador during the early 1990s, he said he discovered that "the military was heavily involved in forestry issues." He urged the government to control that, he said, but as he saw it, "the state had such weak institutions then."

Once the military got a taste of the logging business, it became an addiction. As the problem grew worse and worse, the World Bank pushed the government to hire Global Witness as the nation's forest monitor. But then in 2002 Hun Sen angrily expelled the organization's investigators. Others filtered back in to continue the work, until finally they published their report.

It decried the duplicitous system under which Hun Sen had awarded his *oknya* vast tracts of forested land as "plantations," like the bogus eucalyptus farm in Pursat Province. Global Witness mapped the broad network of illegal logging, cataloged the bribe payments, and named names—dozens of government officials, army officers, as well as the prime minister's relatives and cronies who were said to be complicit. It asserted that Hun Sen's 4,000-man bodyguard unit "serves as a nationwide timber trafficking service. It transports illegally logged timber all over Cambodia and exports significant quantities to Vietnam." The haul from one illegal lumber mill alone amounted to $13 million a year.

Hun Sen was livid. As usual, he refused to discuss the findings and instead assaulted the organization that offered them. First he forbade any Cambodia newspaper to report on the Global Witness document. When the French-language paper *Cambodge Soir* ignored the threat, the government fired the editor and shut the paper down. Lem Pich-pisey, a reporter for Radio Free Asia, fled to Thailand after his life was threatened because he, too, reported on the Global Witness investigation. Hun Sen's brother Hun Neng warned: If anyone from Global Witness comes back to Cambodia, "I will hit them until their heads are broken." The report had said his wife and son were involved in the trade. For his own part, Hun Sen made a point of describing his contempt with one of his trademark metaphoric barbs: "This can probably be explained in the same way that dogs are happier to lick the bones found in the domestic waste."

But the truth was, for all the foment over the Global Witnesses report, by the time it was published, in June 2007, most of Cambodia's luxury-wood trees had already been felled. Illegal logging, deforestation, was a dying business. Hun Sen and his *oknya* had already moved on to a new line of work: seizing and selling off Cambodia's land—even if Cambodians lived on it.

On June 6, 2006, soldiers and police showed up in the middle of the night outside Un Phea's crude home in the Sambok Chap neighborhood near central Phnom Penh. They threw her family and more than 1,000 others into the street and then torched their shelters before Un Phea and the others had time even to retrieve their meager belongings. Then soldiers herded all the residents onto truck beds and ferried them fifteen miles out of town, to an area called Andong. There, soldiers dumped them in a rice paddy without so much as a bottle of water or a tarp for cover. "Even the landowner is scared," Yeng Virak, executive director of the Community Legal Education Center, said, recalling that night. "He had not been told. Suddenly there are 1,000 people on his land."

After that the soldiers left—though a few stayed behind to turn away the aid workers who came out to drop off emergency rations. As if all of that were not traumatic enough, incidents like this set off many people's preexisting mental illnesses. "Older traumas, they are going to influence current responses to things like land seizures," said

Nigel Field, the psychologist who studied PTSD among Cambodians. After all, that scene Quinn had witnessed with his fiancée, atop the Vietnamese hill on the Cambodian border in 1973, was eerily similar. Khmer Rouge soldiers had thrown residents out of their homes, then burned them to the ground and trucked the people off to a relocation camp.

"Out here, I cannot make business," Un Phea complained two years later, with considerable understatement. "They dumped us here and gave us no money, no land title. Nothing." She sat in the mud outside her shanty house—one small room with palm-frond walls and roof, on poles three feet off the ground. One of her naked children sat underneath, eating a small bowl of rice. Un Phea was peeling bamboo shoots into a plastic bowl—still seething. "Before, I sold water and some eggs in front of the royal palace and made a good living. Here it is hard to work."

In Phnom Penh the community had electricity, clean water, and, for what they were worth, schools and medical clinics. Most people had jobs. There in the rice paddy, they had none of that. They were now a forty-minute drive from downtown, past the airport and a sign that said "Bon Voyage. See you again."

"We have to buy water from the water seller," Un Phea said, nodding toward an earthen cistern beside the house. Mosquito larvae seemed to roil the water surface. An NGO had tacked a poster to her shelter's front wall. In Khmer and English it warned of dengue fever, a mosquito-borne illness that was epidemic that year. But of course, Un Phea couldn't read.

Her case was among several thousand more or less similar land seizures across Cambodia in the previous few years. The government said at least 3,000 people were appealing the seizures to a government agency set up for that purpose.

The problem was not entirely new. "Land conflicts were there even before UNTAC left," Twining said. "I pushed the government to create land records, but that didn't seem to go anywhere." Back then much of the land the government seized was covered with trees the military wanted to harvest. But as the trees began to run out—replanting was not a Cambodian practice—the government and its friends began eyeing the land itself. They seemed not to notice the people who lived on it.

Valuable property in Phnom Penh, like Un Phea's neighborhood, was the favored target. The Swedish anthropology team that studied Cambodia in the mid-1990s noted that during the Vietnamese occupation, "land was state property, and this idea still lingers. So, every time a title is recognized, it is felt that 'the State' is giving away its property," although "they are responsive to bribes."

When this trend, kicking poor people out of their homes and dumping them somewhere outside of town, began in earnest in the late 1990s, diplomats and donors pushed the government to pass a law regulating land seizures. "It was just a big, horrible problem," said Wiedemann, who was U.S. ambassador then. "During the Khmer Rouge time, all the titles were destroyed, and when the people came back from the refugee camps in Thailand, they just settled where they could. When the government decided they wanted the land, they just told them, in effect, we have the guns, now get off! So we pressed them to pass the law."

In the late 2000s Phnom Penh was booming, and when a developer spotted a choice piece of land, he simply paid off the proper official to win a newly minted land title. "What happens is they bribe the judge, and then they have the title," said Javier Merelo de Barbera Llobet, who served as an aid worker in Battambang. "Then they can prove the land is theirs."

"It's a very effective way for developers to do it," said Yeng Virak, of the Community Legal Education Center. The government has "the paper, and you pay for it." After that, the victim's only choice was to take the case to court. But the land's new "owner" had bought the deed from Hun Sen, and, and if forced to, he would defend it in Hun Sen's courts.

When that was done, the new owner had only to rid the property of its residents—almost always poor, uneducated people. Once the developer had paid for the new title, the government sometimes charged the residents with trespassing and vandalism and threw them in jail. In one typical case soldiers helped the Heng Development Company expel residents from a piece of property the company had "bought" in Kandal Province. Soldiers opened fire and wounded several residents who refused to leave. The *Phnom Penh Post* reported that the developer bought 9,900 acres and then decided he wanted some adjacent property, too. When those residents refused to sell, the developer went back to Phnom Penh and bought another title for that land as well. Soldiers opened fire again as they chased these new victims away.

The Land Law, enacted in 2001, attempted to address this dilemma by giving anyone who lived on a piece of land for at least five years ownership and the right to a legal title. Well, like so many of these laws, the government never wrote the enabling regulations and chose not to enforce or abide by it. And as property values rose—in 2007 land in downtown Phnom Penh cost about the same as land in downtown Chicago—the land seizures escalated into an epidemic.

NGOs and other donors took up the cause and tried to hold workshops to apprise villagers of the Land Law's protections. The government would not countenance that. On more than one occasion provincial authorities sent a fire brigade to disperse the workshop by spraying everyone with a fire hose. "Fire brigades is one way they do it," said Youk Chhang. "But they also disperse crowds with electric batons, kick you with their boots, beat you. It's so wild! There are cases where they beat people to death."

As the eviction problem grew to a frenzy, the nation's newspapers carried two, three, four, or more stories about land seizures every single day. Human-rights groups cataloged evictions affecting 79,155 people in 2007, and the number rose in following years. The seizures grew ever more brazen. The State Department's 2009 human-rights report recounted one episode in dry diplomatic language:

In April, representatives of the Phnom Penh Tonle Bassac Group 78 (G78) met with Phnom Penh Governor Kep Chuktema regarding a

2006 eviction notice. While authorities claimed the land was state land, the government did not provide documents classifying it as state property, and the land did not meet the 2001 land-law definition for state land.

According to the 2001 law, the land was eligible for transfer by the state into private land. Many of the families had lived on the land since the 1980s and claimed ownership under the 2001 law. G78 community members stated that the municipality offered compensation that was approximately equal to 2 percent of a November 2007 independent assessment of market value, plus one plot in a Phnom Penh eviction resettlement site per family. The community remained under threat of eviction.

Then, in July 2009, security forces forcibly evicted the residents.

Watching all of this, the World Bank decided to step into the fray. After its deforestation debacle, it now tried to fight the land-seizure problem. The bank began buying land titles for poor people all over the country. "We've paid for teams to research these land titles, and almost 1 million have been granted!" a senior World Bank official in Washington boasted in 2008.

Stephane Guimbert, senior economist in the bank's Phnom Penh office, explained how his office chose the plots of land. "This is driven by the government," he acknowledged with a dry tone. In other words, the government told the bank which pieces of property it could title for its residents. Wasn't it obvious that the government would steer the bank away from land it intended to seize? Guimbert nodded. "We have done some of the easiest areas—areas that are not controversial," he said matter-of-factly. A year later his office got into trouble once again, for ignoring perhaps the most brazen, audacious land seizure thus far.

Right in the center of Phnom Penh sat a beautiful lake of about 220 acres, called Boeng Kak. Green islands of morning glories floated on the surface. On the east side sat a gold-domed mosque. Metal and wood shanty homes for more than 4,000 families ringed much of the remaining perimeter. Over the past thirty years, they had been built out over the water on piers, and a sinuous network of wooden-plank walkways wound among the homes and businesses. Lake water glistened beneath. One resident operated a boatyard. Another worked in a studio weaving rattan artwork. Most others eked out a living on the streets.

Right from under these people's feet, the Phnom Penh city government leased the entire lake and surrounding land to a private developer. That was in 2007, and the Chinese government news service, Xinhua, issued a press release saying that officials from "the Yunnan Southeast-Asia Economy and Technology Investment Industry and the Cambodia's Shukaku Company signed agreements in the presence of Cambodian Deputy Prime Minister Sok An and Governor of China's Yunnan Province Qin Guangrong. Under the agreements, the two sides will cooperate to develop the Boeng Kak Lake area in Phnom Penh into a multi-purpose living and recreation center called the New City of the East." No one knew exactly what that meant, but everyone knew that a prominent CPP senator, Lao Meng Khim, and his wife, owned Shukaku. Lao Meng Khim was the same *oknya* who bought rights to the last remaining forest in Pursat Province, where he professed an interest in planting eucalyptus trees. Now the government had given him a ninety-nine-year lease on 330 acres—the lake and the surrounding neighborhoods, where thousands of people had lived for decades.

A year later the developer made his intentions plain. With no notice or explanation, the company ran a fat pipe from the bottom of the Tonle Sap River, through Phnom Penh neighborhoods, and into Boeng Kak. When a worker flipped a switch, heavy-duty pumps began pulling sand from the river bottom, carrying it through the city, and then dumping it into the lake. Though no one said anything publicly, suddenly the goal became plain: Fill the lake with sand, obliterate it, and suddenly the developer would have 220 acres of new prime real estate, right in the middle of the city. The price Lao Meng Khin paid for this: $79 million. Journalists could find no record of a deposit for that amount in the national treasury.

By the summer of 2009 a tongue of sand reached more than halfway across the lake. Of course, the water level was rising, and the city began telling Boeng Kak residents that they needed to leave. Early in 2010 the sand reached the sewage intake pipe and blocked it off so that raw waste began backing up under the residents' homes. "The sewage water is rising day by day, and I worry my house will be flooded," one resident told the *Cambodia Daily*. The residents complained of a terrible stench, and some were getting sick. Several residents showed reporters documents showing that they had lived in their homes since 1979—more than long enough to claim ownership under the Land Law. But that didn't matter.

The government, behaving as it usually did, forbade residents to hold a town-hall meeting to discuss their situation. As for the Land Law, the precise regulations had never been written. The developer did offer one public disclosure; he put out an environmental impact statement that said filling the lake was environmentally useful because the lake was "dead." The residents, it asserted, "were living in anarchy." So filling Boeng Kak would not have "major effects on the environment" or "major potential impacts on society."

*Cambodia Daily* reporters tried to get someone with the Shukaku company or the government to explain what was happening to this lake, a major landmark right in the middle of the city. "A visit to the municipal office of the Boeng Kak Development Committee on the northeast coast of the lake resulted in police, military police and what appeared to be undercover police racing to reporters, demanding that they immediately leave the office compound," the paper wrote in the summer of 2009.

"No entrance to the area around Boeng Kak," said an employee who declined to give his name. "Want to ask questions? Ask city hall." At city hall, "Municipal Governor Kep Chuktema could not be reached for comment," and Deputy Governor Pa Socheatvong declined to discuss the lake, referring questions to Mr. Chuktema's cabinet. Cabinet chief Nuon Sameth said he was too busy to discuss the lake, before hanging up on a reporter. Daun Penh District Governor Sok Sambath referred all questions about the lake to Shukaku, saying, "Our authorities will just continue to cooperate with the company in order to facilitate the development fast." But "Shukaku officials, who have not once spoken to the press about the lake development, could not be reached for comment." By the summer of 2010 so much sand had been pumped into the lake that water spilled out into the streets, flooding dozens of homes.

As this saga progressed, human-rights groups began asking the World Bank: Why aren't you offering legal representation to Boeng Kak lake residents? The obvious answer was that the government, not the World Bank, chose the out-of-the-way areas where the bank was allowed to represent residents—plots of land so remote that no developer would ever offer to buy them. All of that spawned a new World Bank internal investigation whose findings were a mirror of the office's forestry-program investigation a few years earlier.

Investigators recognized "a disconnect between institutional, legal and policy achievements and insecurity of land tenure for the poor, especially in urban areas, and for indigenous people. This disconnect can be attributed in part to the design of some of the project's components, in part to the way the project was implemented." In other words, bank officials set up a program and allowed it to run for years, boasted about the number of titles granted—and ignored the egregious land seizures they could have seen if they had bothered to look out their office windows.

The investigation cited "a decision, during design, in line with Cambodian law that the project will not title lands in areas where disputes are likely until agreements are reached on the status of the land. Clarifying the status of the land would have required the development and implementation of clear procedures for state land classification." That was never done.

Chastened by Washington once again, the bank asked the government to change the program so that it addressed some of these problems. It also offered to help resolve the Boeng Kak dispute. But the government refused, and in the fall of 2009 the bank canceled the program. All told, the bank had spent $24.3 million. And during the program's course the government had evicted tens of thousands of its citizens from their homes. In one instance, on a vacant lot in midtown Phnom Penh, twenty families, every one of them HIV positive, had built a little shanty village for themselves, not far from the hospital where they got their maintenance medications. No one forced them to live together in this modern-age leper colony. They said they simply found it convenient. In 2008 the Tourism Ministry decided to build a new headquarters adjacent to this lot, and the next year the minister announced that he wanted to plant a garden beside his ministry, exactly where the HIV families lived. The new ministry headquarters was only half built, but a billboard in front of the construction site showed a grand Asian palace with happy people strolling in the plaza. The HIV families' village was off-frame.

The city gave each family 10,000 riel, or $2.50, and with only a few hours' notice trucked them to an eviction site about fifteen miles from town. There, the government had put up new housing for them: a complex of large green corrugated-metal buildings divided into several dozen rooms. Each family got one bare room, roughly fifteen by twelve feet, that looked like the inside of a garden shed. The site offered no kitchen, no bathrooms, no electricity or running water, though there was a water pump outside. It pulled up murky water that tasted like chemicals. Farmers working a flooded rice paddy behind the site had probably been using fertilizer.

Four days after they had arrived at the eviction site, forty-one-year-old Suon Davy, thin as a rail, sat in a hammock and lamented her state—ill and dispossessed. "All of us are sick," she said. "We lived at the old site since 2000 but never registered it because I was always too sick. Since we have been here, no authorities have come to see us. They dumped us and ignored us. They left us out here to die."

They were hardly the only ones. Nai Chineang's home in central Phnom Penh sat in the shadow of a ten-story apartment building put up in 1960. The spot was called Dey Krahorm. It sat just down the street from the parliament building. Nai Chineang's house was built of scrap wood, corrugated metal, and blue plastic sheeting. In the early 1990s the United Nations had handed out thousands of these blue plastic tarps, to be used for cover. Among the poor they were still in service.

The house looked like other shanties around town but for one thing: A government document was tacked over the front door, dated July 2003. Hun Sen's Council of Ministers wrote that the government had granted "land concessions for the poor communities in the following locations." One of them was "Dey Krahorm, which is a former public park" of about twelve acres where "there are 1,220 houses, 1,465 families with 5,854 people. They shall be provided a land concession" of about nine acres.

That made Nai Chineang and the others lucky indeed—until the city changed its mind. A developer named 7NG decided it wanted the land, paid whomever it needed to get a deed, and then tried to buy the land out from under the legal owners, Dey Krahorm's residents. The company's Web site showed Hun Sen hanging a gold sash over the CEO's shoulder. Its caption said, "Cambodian National Award from Samdech Akka Moha Sena Padei Techo Hun Sen, Prime Minister of Royal Government of Cambodia."

Hundreds of residents took the offer, generally about $3,500 and a home of sorts almost twenty miles away. But hundreds refused, so 7NG and its allies in the government began harassing them—driving bulldozers onto the property and knocking down buildings.

Foreign human-rights groups and others took up Dey Krahorm's cause. A German filmmaker moved into a vacant home there as an act, he said, of "pure solidarity." Yash Ghai, the UN human-rights representative for Cambodia, marched with the Dey Krahorm residents, prompting Hun Sen to say, "You are regarded just as a long-term tourist" and should leave the country because "I will not meet with you even if I live 1,000 years." Soon after, Cambodia media reported, police and 7NG employees pelted the residents with rocks and bags of urine. "It's too obvious now," Kek Galibru, head of Licadho, the human-rights group, said in the summer of 2008. Licadho was providing legal representation for the residents. "They can't say the land belongs to the state, so now they try to scare them. Now it seems they changed a bit their method. Now in the last year, when their reputation is so bad, they are trying both the carrot and the stick" by offering more money.

She and other human-rights advocates began to believe they were winning. The government had finally realized the law was not on their side. Buoyed by this optimism, the remaining residents refused to take the new cash offers. "They want to kick us out, want to take our land," Nai Chineang said. "They offered me $7,000. I can't do anything with that. I want to stay here, in the city."

They were wrong. In January 2009, three years after 7NG made the first offers to buy Dey Krahorm property, company enforcers showed up to expel the remaining 152 families. The residents had barricaded the streets and were lobbing stones at the police, but eventually they were rounded up, loaded on trucks, and carted away. As bulldozers knocked the houses down, the Council of Ministers' land-grant documents were still tacked above the doors. More than a year later two dozen evicted families were still living in tents on the outskirts of town.

As the clamor about land seizures from the United Nations, human-rights groups, and foreign governments grew louder and more frequent, Hun Sen up a new government agency whose stated purpose was to ensure that evictees were treated fairly. He named it the National Land Authority and appointed Chum Bun Rong as deputy director. He was an older man, plump, confident, and self-satisfied. He'd been a second lieutenant in Lon Nol's army. "I took off my uniform and ran" when the Khmer Rouge marched into Phnom Penh, he said. "I lived a lot of years in the jungle and ate insects."

After the Vietnamese invasion he had served as spokesman for the Foreign Ministry. He started there while Hun Sen was still the foreign minister. More recently, he said, Hun Sen had assigned him to "act against negative information from outside the country. I am sort of a quick-response person, the national spokesman." A great deal of negative information coming from the outside now related to land seizures, and he said he was continuing to act as a special spokesman, even in his new job.

Chum Bun Rong said his agency had received more than 3,000 land-seizure appeals since he took office. Of those, he admitted, only about 50 had been judged in favor of the impoverished people whose land was seized. But the National Land Authority was not the final authority. Those 50 cases were sent on to the Cadastral Commission. There, the deputy director said, "some of those cases were resolved. Some were not. Sometimes they are resolved in a day. Sometimes the cases disappear." When that happens victims call him, not the Cadastral Commission, he said. "But if a land concession is not organized properly, it's the role of an NGO or a journalist to make sure the victims are heard."

Boeng Kak, Andong, Dey Krahorm, and all those other terrible stories of evictions, "you have to think this is a case of propaganda," he insisted. "There are different kinds of people who use these issues for their own political interests. We can say we are not doing perfect. But if you don't like what we are, don't vote for us. If the government does bad things, the people will rise up. Sometimes we protect the people. Sometimes we protect the interests of investors." After all, he added, eyes wide, "some millionaires are behind some of these projects!" Thank goodness Hun Sen has his national spokesman on the job to protect evictees.

Chum Bun Rong said 200 people worked in his office. They had more than 700 appeals in hand just then, waiting for disposition. He gave a tour. Perhaps two dozen workers sat in offices. Some were looking at papers. Others appeared languorous, indolent. In 2006 Japan gave the Land Authority $615,000 for a departmental computer system, to help speed up the work. Japan, unlike the United States, then gave money directly to the government. During the tour, I saw a dozen ordinary desktop computers, worth perhaps $30,000 altogether. Asked about that, Chum Bun Rong grew agitated and said, "Oh, but there's a server in the basement!" He didn't show it, but a server for a dozen personal computers would have to be gold-plated to cost $585,000.

By the summer of 2008, two years after the residents of Sambok Chap had been dumped in the rice field, physicians working for Licadho, the human-rights group, had visited Andong hundreds of times and performed almost 15,000 medical consultations, the group said. The residents' most common health problems, the doctors found, were "malnutrition, typhoid, dengue fever, hepatitis A or B, hypertension, respiratory-tract infections, gastro-intestinal illnesses including stress-related ulcers, depression and anger management problems."

With all of those afflictions, the largest outside presence at the eviction site was a church, built by a Korean philanthropist who had decided what those Buddhist refugees needed most was a Christian church. So he built one, the only masonry building there, at the entrance to the Andong camp—the Happy Church, a sign out front announced. The preacher, thirty-four-year-old Thong Sopheak, could not identify the church's denomination. He spoke vaguely of Protestantism and wore a yellow T-shirt that said in bold letters, "You! Man of God." He said he did not deliver sermons.

The church started a school, and the preacher said 160 children attended. The teacher, twenty-eight-year-old Touch Vireak, said, "Last year we sent 12 students to junior high school. Two of those say they are preparing for high school." But then he acknowledged that, perhaps, a Christian church may not have been the answer for these people. "The biggest need here is food. Food is very important. Some people don't have enough, so they borrow from neighbors. Some of them are deeply in debt." The preacher added: "They are still angry. They need help. They need electricity, they need water. They bought power from a local man who had a generator. But he charged very high prices. But the generator has been broken for two months. In my house I use candles and car batteries."

By 2009, three years after the eviction, Andong had settled into a community of sorts, shambling bamboo huts sinking into the mud along soggy, rutted dirt paths, most too narrow for a car to pass. Un Phea was gone, working in Pailin Province, harvesting corn and cassava. Sam Nhea, her twenty-three-year-old brother, was staying in her house. He was asleep on a front porch, a wooden platform he had added to her house two weeks earlier. Only shreds remained of the dengue-fever warning poster that had been tacked to the side of the house. Sam Nhea said he'd tried to tear it down. But he was an indolent sort and hadn't finished the job. He said he worked construction but had stopped work to take care of his son. "He has a cold; he is not so healthy." The boy lay naked on the wooden porch beside his father. He was five years old but looked to be about the size of a three year old. At noon, he was motionless, lapsing in and out of consciousness. When awake, his face offered only a blank stare. His father lifted the boy up by his hands. He was only about thirty inches tall. Here was malnutrition and stunting in the flesh. The boy could stand on his own as his father held his hands. But he was mute, and his big brown eyes did not evidence any awareness of his surroundings. His father let him down slowly, and once again the boy lay flat on the hard wooden porch and closed his eyes.

A tiny three-year-old girl laying in a hammock looked to be in the same shape. She was the size of an infant. "My wife usually breast-feeds her," Sam Nhea said, pointing to the tiny, motionless girl. "That and some rice and maybe a sweet cake. But she's not here now, so we just eat rice. I buy rice every day, one kilogram. This feeds four people, breakfast, lunch, and dinner. Since my wife is away, I'm too busy to take them to the hospital."

How would he take them even if he had time? "I would have to borrow a motorbike." But he acknowledged he did not even know where the health clinic was. As we left, he lay down on his new porch and fell asleep again. Passing by an hour later, he still slept as his sick children lay quietly beside him, barely conscious.

Trying to institutionalize this wretched camp, the CPP appointed a village chief, Chhin Sarith. He built a real house with a concrete foundation and sat at a table in his two-car garage, beside an old Toyota.

"Sam Nhea, he worked as a street sweeper," he said. "He was a drug addict. Amphetamines. He says he gave them up in 2008." The chief ragged on his neighbor without restraint. "He was also a trash scavenger. Sometimes he worked as a beggar."

Almost 1,400 families now lived at Andong. Directly behind the last row of homes, the rice paddy picked up again. But out by the highway, some rich person, probably an *oknya*, had built an eighteen-hole golf course, the Royal Phnom Penh Golf Club. Hun Sen played there from time to time.

Chhin Sarith talked up the benefits of this evictee camp. "Yes, people say they are still angry. It's normal in this community for people to feel that way. But they know that where they lived before was not legal. Here we have the right of ownership. I consider myself lucky because I now have a piece of land—my own personal property. Here we are far away, yes, but in the old place my children did not go to school. Here they do. There are no drugs, no crime here, unlike the old place. Living here is far better."

Un Sophal disagreed. She was Sam Nhea's mother and lived down the road. All of her five children lived in Andong. She was forty-five and missing half of her bottom teeth, all on the right side, as if someone had slugged her. "I have no choice but to live here. I have no place else to live." Without being asked, she told of the day, still fresh in her mind, when they were evicted from their homes. "The police, 300 or 400 of them, were there. They said if we refuse to leave they would bulldoze down our homes. They put us on trucks and took us out here and dumped us. There's no business out here except picking bamboo and other wild things from the forest or shellfish out of the lake, three or four kilometers from here."

A friend was making dinner as Un Sophal talked. She had mixed mashed rice with water until she had a thin gruel, a batter. She poured it into a frying pan resting on a three-arm concrete fire pit stuffed with burning twigs. As the batter hardened into a yellowish crepelike form, she filled it with bamboo sprouts that Un Sophal had cut up with a little knife. Then she folded over one side of the rice crepe.

"I am still angry, but I can't do anything to them," Un Sophal said, her voice hard-edged, more than three years after she and the rest of her family had been violently evicted. "I just keep it in mind. The CPP kicked us out of there, mistreated us a lot." She was waving the knife over her head. "No electricity, no power, no water. Nothing!"

Thousands upon thousands of people, evicted from their homes, lived in makeshift camps like Un Sophal. Meanwhile, the government's enablers were meeting regularly in Phnom Penh, helping ensure that Hun Sen could continue abusing his people at will.

# CHAPTER FIFTEEN

In March 2008 the assorted NGOs, donors, and foreign govern-ments that had been giving money to Cambodia since 1992 met in Phnom Penh once again to make their pledges for the coming year. As usual, the U.S. ambassador addressed the group, which included Hun Sen and almost every cabinet member.

Ambassador Mussomeli had thought about what to say, and in the end, addressing Hun Sen and the rest of his government, he told them, "In all candor, we, your development partners, are perplexed by the apparent lack of priority given to the anticorruption legislation. Anticorruption is the base of your development strategy and central to everything you hope to accomplish—yet, after ten years, the law re-mains in draft." Since Charlie Twining's time in office, most of Mus-someli's predecessors had said more or less the same thing.

In fact, by the time Mussomeli took his turn, the anticorruption law had become a uniquely Cambodian chimera lost in a shell game. Thir-teen years had passed since Hun Sen, trying to mute growing donor concern about corruption, had first promised to approve the law—thirteen years since Ambassador Twining had warned, "We are not threatening to cut our support at this time, but it is true that there is a lot of competition for our aid dollars." For the following few years nothing much happened but more promises—until no one was paying attention any longer as the nation fell into chaos culminating in 1996 and 1997, with the grenade attack, the "coup," and the ugly aftermath. Soon after, however, pressure to pass the bill resumed. Donors, NGOs, and interest groups began publishing reports that were reflections of their growing frustration. In 2000, for example, the International Crisis Group published a widely read report entitled *Cambodia: The Elusive Peace Dividend.* "Cambodia remains a strongman state," it asserted, "replete with lawlessness, human rights abuses, grinding poverty, corruption, bloated security forces, and an economy thriving on prostitution, narcotics trafficking, land grabbing and illegal logging." The government, it insisted, must enact the law.

That same year, the Council of Ministers finally approved the anticorruption bill and passed it on to the National Assembly for final passage. But then, another year passed, and the next word was that the Council of Ministers Secretariat was once again "examining the law," the same one it had already approved twelve months before.

Donors were growing frustrated and angry. Ian Porter, director of the World Bank office in Phnom Penh, warned at a donor meeting that if Cambodia did not make progress fighting corruption, including passage of the law, "support will not be at the same level." He was the first prominent donor to warn Hun Sen, once he became the nation's sole leader, that the donors would hold back money if the government did not pass the bill. Hun Sen then promised to have an anticorruption law "ready for debate by June 2003."

For 2001 and 2002 the donors gave Cambodia $615 million. Then in 2003, as promised, Hun Sen put the bill before the National Assembly for a vote. That was when the assembly, out of the blue, decided that seven-eighths of its members had to be present for the vote. For some unexplained reason, just enough CPP members failed to show up so that the vote could not be held. Nonetheless, that transparently disingenuous effort was enough to satisfy the donors. They gave Cambodia $635 million that year.

The yearlong postelection stalemate began the next month, but soon after it ended the World Bank published its own broadside, *Cambodia at the Crossroads*, in November 2004, just before the donor meeting. The 143-page publication spoke of "weak governance and the failure to control corruption and enforce the rule of law, underscoring the country's limited institutional capacity and the lack of trust among the elite—and strong resistance to reforms from powerful invested interests." But for the first time, the bank also laid blame on itself and other donors. "Cambodia's international development partners are strongly committed to Cambodian development and are anxious to be a part of the solution. But they may also be part of the problem. The failure to speak out for Cambodia's poor with one voice or to link financial and technical support to performance and outcomes has sent mixed signals to the country's leadership, which has shown itself adept at doing just enough to win donor support." Porter, the director, threatened again: "If there is little progress, then we would certainly be concerned that the overall pledges for Cambodia could well come down."

That year Hun Sen vowed, "The government will encourage the ratification of an anti-corruption law as soon as possible." Late in 2004 he explained that a draft of the law "has been already prepared and needs some further review and the final approval of the National Assembly." At the donors' meeting he shook his fist as he said that corruption represented a "life or death" struggle for the nation. Charles Ray, the American ambassador at that time, then accused the government of misusing aid money "for personal gain" and demanded "verifiable and successful investigations and prosecutions of corruption cases. According to some accounts, not a single case of corruption or embezzlement has ever been prosecuted before a court in Phnom Penh." Undeterred, donors gave $504 million that year.

In the summer of 2005 the draft bill was still languishing at the assembly, but the government promised to pass it that year. "To free society from corruption, I believe that we need good laws and good governance both in public management and private business," Hun Sen averred. "The draft law has emerged, and we are opening the debate on the law." But once again nothing happened, and by 2006 some international observers were growing so angry that they took up a new strategy.

A coalition of human-rights groups, including Human Rights Watch and the Asian Human Rights Commission, tried to stiffen the spines of the other donors who always seemed to look the other way and hand over their money regardless of performance. "Since the last donor meeting," the group said, "the government has made no tangible progress in meeting its commitments. The courts are still used to conduct sham trials, impunity prevails in government abuses." And then it issued the annual call: "Donors should make it clear that continued assistance will depend on the government keeping its promises," including "passing asset disclosure and an anti-corruption law that meets international standards."

Basil Fernando, executive director of the Asian Human Rights Commission, cautioned, "Donors should not be lulled into thinking the situation has improved. This is a decade-old pattern: assurances by the government right before the meetings, followed by return to the old ways afterward." The next day donors pledged to give Cambodia $601 million.

Later in 2006, the law still had not been passed, and Hun Sen offered a new stratagem. Cambodia, he told the donors, had to pass a new penal code before it could enact an anticorruption law. "I would like to inform" the donors, he said, "don't misunderstand that the government lacks will."

In 2007, inexplicably, the draft law was no longer at the National Assembly awaiting a vote. Now, Hun Sen, said, "it is in the final stage of discussion with detailed consideration among the government ministries and institutions concerned before it is forwarded to the National Assembly and the Senate for approval." Later that year the bill seemed to have regressed even further. Hun Sen told a conference on economic development that he was "determined to prepare an anti-corruption draft law."

Next came word that the draft bill was back at the Council of Ministers, which had first approved it seven years earlier. That year, the human-rights groups' annual press release was even more strident; key passages were in boldface: "Donors should hold the Cambodian government accountable!"

Hun Sen stood before the donors once again in 2007 and declared, "The fight against corruption in Cambodia must remain a very high priority for the government, and in that context, the passage of an anti-corruption law would be very important." At about that time, the prime minister began building himself a massive mansion on the most important corner in central Phnom Penh. It had four stories plus a basement and looked to offer 10,000 to 15,000 square feet of living space. A heliport sat atop the roof. He still kept his country estate with the eighteen-hole golf course—all of this, in theory, purchased with his government salary. The donors gave him $689 million, 15 percent more than the previous year.

In 2008, the year Mussomeli spoke, Khieu Kanharith, the government spokesman, said the National Assembly would pass the bill within a month. But then the next month Deputy Prime Minister Sok An revealed that the Council of Ministers had reviewed only "40 of the 700 articles of the new Penal Code," two years after that project had begun. After the new penal code is finally complete, Sok An added, "the government will continue to inspect the anti-corruption law."

The annual donors' conference came at the end of the year, and opposition lawmakers including Sam Rainsy pleaded with the donors not to give money until the government enacted the long-awaited law and took "concrete measures to stop grave violations of Cambodia's laws and serious violations of human rights," as Rainsy put it. "It's a ritual, an annual ritual between the government and the international community," lamented Ou Virak, president of the Cambodian Center for Human Rights. "They said exactly the same things last year, the language is the same, the outcome is always the same—we finish the ritual with a stamp of approval, and then it's back to business as usual."

292 | CAMBODIA'S CURSE

One more time Hun Sen opened the meeting promising he would finally pass the bill. He tried to sweeten up the group, declaring out of the blue, "We are better off to keep the forests as a national reserve and not try to get money from logging." An easy promise to make, for by then nearly all of the valuable trees had already been cut down. Recent UN and International Monetary Fund (IMF) studies had found that between 1.7 and 3.4 percent of Cambodia still consisted of what they called "primary forest." The Cambodian Forestry Ministry put the number at 59 percent.

Even so, the donors appeared pleased. They showered Hun Sen with gifts unimaginable. They gave Cambodia almost $1 billion, more than any time since the early days of the modern state, nearly double the amount the government legitimately took in from taxes, fees, and other revenues. The next year promised to be a good one for builders and flat panel–television dealers.

A few months before that meeting, Carol Rodley was sworn in as the next U.S. ambassador to Cambodia. She had been deputy chief of mission in Phnom Penh, the number-two position, when Ken Quinn was ambassador ten years before. And a few months after the $1 billion meeting, she agreed to speak at a rally and concert several NGOs were staging to emphasize the need to fight corruption.

More than 50,000 people showed up, filling Phnom Penh's Olympic Stadium. Rodley was just one of several speakers, and even she admitted that most of the audience likely came for the performers. Young people filled the seats. On that date anyone born the year Hun Sen first promised to enact an anticorruption law would be old enough to attend high school.

In her speech, just like her predecessors, Rodley urged the Cambodian government "to deliver on its promise to enact the anti-corruption law." She quoted the USAID study from a few years earlier, the one that said corruption gobbled up as much as $500 million—enough, she said, "to build 20,000 six-room school buildings" or "to pay every civil servant in Cambodia an additional $260 per month." And with that she was more specific than any previous American ambassador had been.

She was the first to describe exactly what Hun Sen could be doing for his people with the money he and his aides were stealing.

The government was enraged. The Foreign Ministry issued a warning to her and other ambassadors that "the diplomatic corps must maintain their neutrality and refrain from interfering in the internal affairs of Cambodia." Rodley's remarks, it added, were "based on a biased assessment" that the government "absolutely refutes." The Council of Ministers expressed its "sadness." Om Yientieng, head of the government's putative anticorruption unit, called the speech "irresponsible. We don't accept her statement, and we do not understand it."

In spite of the furor, the embassy refused to react. For weeks, when reporters called, all they would get was: No comment. Later, Rodley told me, "I have to admit I was a little surprised. A lot of those were things I had said many times before. They were not new. There have been several similar estimates." Then she vented. "What I learned from this is that these people have a long way to go to get the thickness of skin that you need to live the life of a public official."

A few days before that conversation, the embassy held a Fourth of July celebration. Representing the government was the minister of defense. As usual, scores of diplomats, civil-society leaders, and Cambodian government officials were there. Just before the party began embassy staff wheeled in a six-foot-tall Statute of Liberty ice sculpture. It served as a metaphor for the Western effort to bring democracy to that place. The evening heat was typically torrid. The statue's torch melted away by six thirty, and Lady Liberty's left arm fell off just after seven o'clock.

———

At the end of 2009 the National Assembly finally adopted the new penal code, and Cheam Yeap, a senior CPP lawmaker, said, "I would predict that the anti-corruption law will be approved during the first three months of 2010." Then in mid-December the Council of Ministers approved the draft bill one more time and said it was being sent to the National Assembly for approval for the third, or possibly even the fourth, time. Hun Sen issued a statement, saying, "The former Royal Cambodian Armed Forces Supreme Command headquarters in Phnom Penh will be the home for the new national anti-corruption body." But no one outside of government was being allowed to have a look at the draft bill.

In January 2010 Hun Sen said, "The anti-corruption law will be adopted in the near future." In March the parliament said it was beginning to debate the bill all over again. By then even the NGOs had grown weary and resigned. For several years the government had refused to show anyone its draft bill, causing concern that the reforms it promised would be hollow. The office of Douglas Broderick, the UN chief in Cambodia, put out a statement, saying that "to its knowledge, no draft bill has been shared with interested stakeholders, including civil society, since 2006." Even if the government ever did manage to enact a law, wouldn't it go the way of the Land Law, the Domestic Violence Law, and every other law the nation's leaders had enacted under pressure, since King Norodom promised the French he would end slavery in the 1870s?

The anticorruption bill "doesn't really matter anymore," Sara Colm, the longtime head of the Human Rights Watch office in Phnom Penh, said with a resigned, war-weary tone. Hun Sen seemed to be offering the same point when he told a group of businessmen, "The anti-corruption law will not be a magic pill that will eliminate corruption."

He was certainly right. On March 11, 2010, fifteen years after Hun Sen first promised to enact anticorruption legislation, the National Assembly finally passed the bill, by a unanimous vote of the ruling party's members. Everyone else had walked out because it was clear the new law was a cynical ploy, "nothing but an attempt to impress foreign donors," the Human Rights Party asserted. Around the city Cambodians and foreigners shook their heads and sighed—disappointed, deflated.

The law was doomed by design. The very heart of any effective anticorruption law, anywhere in the world, must be the public declaration of assets. For years and years donors and diplomats in Cambodia had made that point so many times that it grew to be a mantra. Only when an official's holdings are held up to public scrutiny can anyone see whether his financial dealings are aboveboard. The new Cambodian law stipulated that asset declarations would remain secret. The only people who could see the corrupt officials' accounts were other corrupt officials—if the declarations were made at all. And since the entire process was to be kept secret, who would ever know?

Far from being independent, the new anticorruption body would report to the Council of Ministers, made up of the very officials the new unit would likely need to investigate. Sok An, the deputy prime minister, who lived in that 60,000-square-foot house theoretically purchased with his government salary, was the council's chairman. The anticorruption body reported to him.

To make matters worse, the law forbade gifts, or "commissions" (i.e., bribes), to government officials in exchange for favors, such as forest or land titles. But that provision had an exception. These gifts were permissible when they were "in accordance with custom and tradition." Well, paying bribes for government positions, or for economic opportunities, had been "custom and tradition" for 1,000 years. Finally, the law gave the government authority to file defamation or disinformation suits against anyone who filed a complaint that "leads to useless inquiry." Imagine what would happen to anyone who filed a complaint against any influential government official.

Om Yientieng, a Hun Sen crony, was the longtime head of the government's existing anticorruption unit, and the prime minister appointed him head of the new body. A look at his existing operation offered a picture of the way the new anticorruption body would likely operate. The most visible symbol of his office was a small sign hanging from the side of a building on a busy street in downtown Phnom Penh. "Office for the Complaints on Corruption," it said in English and Khmer.

To reach the building entrance, complainants have to squeeze through a parking garage crammed with motorbikes and a few cars. The building's proprietor sits in a corner of the garage, watching television. A policeman questions anyone trying to enter the building and then says the complaints office is on the fourth floor. The elevator is broken, but to the left is a dark, dingy stairwell with industrial matting worn through at the steps' edges, laying bare gaping holes that look decades old. On the fourth floor gold-colored plastic sconces in the stairwell lobby have no bulbs. Instead, fluorescent tubes flicker and hum, casting scant light. A photocopied piece of paper on one door says "Office for Receiving Complaints," suspiciously in English. Who was the office's true audience?

Inside is a small room, maybe ten by twelve feet, with three desks, two of them empty, and no place for the complainant to sit. Navanny Son, the complaint receiving officer, pulls out an unoccupied desk chair. "We ask the person to fill out a form," he explains, holding one out. But then many adults can't read or write. He nods and adds, "We take the information if the person cannot write."

What exactly is his job? "Here, we only wait to receive complaints," he answers. I ask how many have arrived today. Navanny Son and his secretary look at each other and giggle. Okay, how many so far this year? Navanny Son nods to his secretary. She looks up the number on her computer and then says, "I dare not answer the question."

"Some months," Navanny Son acknowledges, "we don't get any complaints."

For the few complaints that do come in, "we have our expert groups look at them," says Neath Mony, another worker—one of ten employed in the complaints office. "If it is about land, we send it to the National Land Authority. If it's about courts, we send it to the court. We send it to whichever institution is involved." In other words, the office sends each complaint to the very office the complainant is accusing—with the complainant's name attached. "We ask that institution to let the complainant know what happened," Neath Mony says.

You forward the note; that's all? "We do have an investigations unit. I don't know what they do. The investigators do investigate some irregularities. Their work is secret"—just like the anticorruption agency chartered under the new law promised to be.

---

In 2009 more than 2,000 donor and NGO organizations were based in Cambodia—more per capita than most anyplace in the world. And the money they disbursed per person far exceeded the average for poor countries receiving foreign aid. Some donors were huge government agencies, like the U.S. Agency for International Development or the Department for International Development in Britain. Others were large international organizations, like the United Nations, World Bank, or International Monetary Fund. Still others were small, local groups, like the Alliance Association for Rural Restoration. It appeared to have fewer than a dozen employees.

Overall, so many donors and NGOs were pursuing projects in Cambodia that they were tripping over each other. Several reports on their work noted that many didn't coordinate with each other and ended up spending time and money on duplicative projects. The government often had no idea what they were up to. "Some of them, particularly the smaller ones, I don't know what they are doing," said Im Sethy, the education minister. No matter. The foreigners stationed in Cambodia savored the lifestyle. "People move here just because it is a nice place to live," said Sara Colm of Human Rights Watch. "There's Internet, restaurants."

For many aid workers this was a delightful change, given where they had been based before. Jean-Pierre de Margerie, head of the World Food Program office in Phnom Penh, had just moved from a posting in North Korea. Richard Bridle, head of the UNICEF office, and Douglas Broderick, head of the UN's mission in Cambodia, had been stationed there, too. In Pyongyang they led controlled, constricted lives. "The government was always playing mind games," de Margerie recalled. Phnom Penh, in comparison, was quite pleasant.

But for the WFP and other UN agencies much of Cambodia was still listed as a hardship post, just like North Korea or Burma, with commensurate salary supplements. In those other countries, though, they couldn't walk along the riverfront and stop in any of half-a-dozen espresso bars and pick up one of the two better than average English-language newspapers.

Teruo Jinnai, head of the UNESCO office in Phnom Penh, had worked previously in Tanzania—and Rwanda "just after the genocide," he said. By comparison, he said, Cambodia was like a ball of clay that he could shape any way he wanted. "Here I have found my own passion. Here, I can work and cause the result I am after. In France, or America, you don't see results. But here I can set my own target. If I want Cambodia to be like this or that, I can see the result. So that gives you more power, more energy, more passion."

Critics of the donors and NGOs often noted that they favored expensive Basque, northern Italian, and Japanese restaurants that charged more for a meal than some Cambodians earned in a year. That may have been unfair; you don't have to live like the people you are helping to be compassionate and effective. Nevertheless, it was clear that these people had a lifestyle they wanted to protect.

Though their work was challenging, it was often rewarding. Many were highly paid, and Cambodia charged no income taxes. They could live in sumptuous homes and hire as many servants as they wanted.

If they cut off aid to the government, as the human-rights groups were demanding, many donors would lose their jobs, or at least their postings. In a Brookings Institution report entitled *Aid Effectiveness in Cambodia*, two Cambodian economists argued that donors were eager to begin programs that required their continuing participation and assistance because they "wish to maintain their presence in Cambodia." The donors' favorite project: good governance, an objective certain to require many years of work. So far it had produced few if any useful results. At one point in 2008, the Brookings study found that donors were pursuing 1,300 different projects nationwide, and 710 of them were ongoing, meaning they required a continued donor presence to keep them running.

So what happened each year when the donors' meeting came around again? Hun Sen stood before them and one more time said, *this year*, we are going to reform education, health care, land usage. Every year human-rights groups and opposition candidates cried out: Hold back your donations until they end land seizures, illegal logging and corruption, until teachers stop selling test scores and doctors stop demanding bribes!

But most every donor in the audience had spent the past few months negotiating contract renewals with their home states or organizations, agreements allowing them to continue their work for the coming year. Here at the meeting they were to announce what they were now planning to do and how much they intended to spend. Human Rights Watch and the others were asking them to rip up their new contracts and go home, jobless.

Naturally, none of the donors said that bleak possibility was the reason they would not hold back aid. Instead, they argued, "If you hold back money, the people most affected would be the poor," explained In Samrithy, the NGO liaison coordinator for the Cooperation Committee of Cambodia, a donor umbrella group. He acknowledged that corruption was so rife that government officials helped themselves to money and goods that donors had dedicated to the poor. Even when they "distribute rice to the poor who they have evicted from their homes—they take some for themselves," said Kek Galibru, director of Licadho, the human-rights group. "They can't help it. It's a habit." Still, In Samrithy said, "the poor won't get the services they need," if aid is cut off. As for the corruption, he explained it away. "Some money goes this way or that way. But it's useful if some of it reaches the poor. Not all of it does, but some does. That's better than nothing." That was a popular rationalization among donors.

A few months after parliament passed the 2010 anticorruption law, a routine government census turned up about 2,000 ghost workers—phantom employees whose salaries went into their supervisors' pockets. The government declined to prosecute, saying, "We must first warn those individuals who are getting money from ghost names," as Cheam Yeap, a senior member of parliament, put it.

The next month, Hun Sen addressed the annual donors' conference once again and promised one more time that soon "we will have the capacity to fight against this dangerous disease" because "corruption will damage our institutions." The donors awarded him $1.1 billion—the largest pledge in a generation.

Some Cambodians and others remained astounded by the donors' behavior—even people who worked for them. "I don't understand their policy," said Chhith Sam Ath, executive director of another donor umbrella group. "The government has learned that the donors are not serious." He leaned forward in his chair and spoke softly, as if he were confiding a secret. "They do not stand behind what they say. Sometimes I don't think some of the donors are really here to fight corruption."

Year after year the foreign donors continued meeting with the smiling health minister who flattered, and coddled, them. They reached agreements to begin new projects and then joined their friends or lovers at the new Greek place for dinner. After the donors handed over the money to build a new health clinic, the deputy minister took out enough to pay his son's school tuition bill. The assistant minister took enough to buy new tires for his car. His deputy simply stuffed some cash in his pocket. After all, government commerce was carried out entirely in cash. When the clinic was finally built, so little money was left that the contractor had to use cheap and flimsy building materials, raising the real risk that the structure would collapse in the next big storm—just like that new school building in Kampong Thom.

Broderick, the lead UN officer, was a big, beefy New Yorker, a UN bureaucrat who seemed primarily interested in projecting a positive image of the UN's work. He sat in a large leather chair, surrounded by several cabinet officers. "The donors and the international community are getting smarter," he asserted. "We are chipping away at the edges. We are drilling down on the corruption issue where it affects the people."

In contrast, Richard Bridle, director of the UNICEF office, one of Broderick's agencies, complained that donors remain complacent, "unable to change. We are too comfortable with our control mechanisms." The donors "are embedding and enabling the mentality of dependency," said Theary Seng, who was director of a local advocacy group, the Center for Social Development. The Cambodian government, after all, had been dependent on foreign patrons since the Angkor empire fell in the fifteenth or sixteenth century—the Thai, the Vietnamese, then the French, the United States, the United Nations, and finally the world's NGOs and donors.

But some donors pointed to Theary Seng and the other critics and said: Look, this government is not so bad. "There's a free press," Peter Jipp, a senior specialist with the World Bank, offered with a cheery grin. "You don't find that in other states—Laos, Vietnam. There's a developing civil-society network. So, in the parlance of the donor community, these are the champions!"

Kek Galibru saw all of that as a bitter irony. "At least the government can use us," she said. "Our presence helps them a little bit. They need money from the international community, so they can say: Look at Licadho. They are free!"

Mu Sochua, a senior Sam Rainsy Party parliamentarian, liked to take her case to Washington, just as her boss, Sam Rainsy, was wont to do. "In Cambodia, the pillars of democracy are all there," she told an audience at the National Democratic Institute. "But you have to look at the quality, the functions. It's really just a facade."

So it also seemed for newspaper editors. Michael Hayes, founder and executive editor of the *Phnom Penh Post*, was a cynical, hard-bitten journalist from Massachusetts, but he acknowledged that the government needed the semblance of a free press to keep the donors happy. Still, Hun Sen sued the paper for defamation in 1994 and threatened to sue several times after that.

Khmer-language papers were generally affiliated with the government or political parties and were fairly predictable. But they, too, were targets of the government's wrath. In the summer of 2008 two men speeding by on a black motorbike with dark-tinted faceplates shot and killed Khim Sambor along with his twenty-one-year-old son as they walked down the street in downtown Phnom Penh. Khim Sambor was a reporter for the *Khmer Conscience*, an opposition newspaper, and not surprisingly the paper had been writing critically about the government. That year, the government sued twenty-five journalists for defamation or related pseudo-offenses. Defamation lawsuits Hun Sen filed against several opposition newspapers in the summer of 2009 forced some of them to close.

By and large, though, the government did not worry so much about the two English-language newspapers. Hardly anyone in the country could read English, only donors, diplomats, and some government officials. Still, even those papers could be only so free.

For most of its life, until 2008, the *Post* published once a week. "When we were weekly, I would read everything," Hayes said. "Sometimes I would cut out stuff or change the tone" to keep from angering government officials. He pointed to that day's paper. Inside was an interview, and the interviewee had said something critical of the government. "I sent a message to my staff: 'We have to be more careful. We could get nailed for this!'"

Sure enough, in 2009 the government sued the *Cambodia Daily* for defamation, saying it had quoted an opposition politician who criticized the Cambodian military. The paper had made no accusation. It had simply quoted someone else. Isn't that what newspapers are supposed to do? Still, Judge Sin Visal told the court, "The article published in their paper caused confusion among the Cambodian people and

damaged the dignity of the military officers." The government did not
review or censor stories before publication. But lawsuits and intimidation forced editors to censor themselves.

The donors knew all of that. The papers reported it. They also
knew that their image was poor, their effectiveness questionable.
They realized that their continued support of Hun Sen and his government served as a prop holding him up. They knew that many of
the senior government officials who told them how concerned they
were about corruption were sitting on fat wallets. "There are some
reformers in the Finance Ministry," a senior World Bank official observed. "But I think even they are corrupt." So, some donors were taking small, tentative steps to address the problem. "Good governance"
was the catchphrase for this.

However, even those projects faced justifiable skepticism. "Since
NGOs cannot seem to have any influence on government, they say
it's better to get good governance projects going," said Peter Manikas,
who managed the National Democratic Institute's Asia programs.
"Why they think that would possibly work is beyond me."

One World Bank governance project served as the poster child
for this kind of absurdity. In 2009 the bank allotted $20 million for
a program called Demand for Good Governance, intended to help
"grassroots groups, independent media, trade unions, etc." demand
"transparency and accountability" from the Cambodian government,
the bank said. "It will enhance the capacity of non-state actors to
constructively engage with the government in support of better development outcomes and improved governance."

So what was the bank going to do with that $20 million? Hand
it over to the government. Stephane Guimbert, the economist in the
bank's Phnom Penh office, spoke about this plan with a straight face
that betrayed not even a hint of recognition that the whole idea was
ludicrous. "A small component of this money goes to nongovernment
actors," or NGOs, he noted, and then explained that the bank had
asked the government for permission to do even that. "But we think

the government itself could do a number of things to improve transparency. If there is no information coming out of government, what good does any of this do? The public is not going to accomplish anything." He sat in the bank's comfortable, air-conditioned conference room, at a conference table where bank officers often worked on white boards to lay out their development plans. "All sorts of scenarios have been piloted in Cambodia," he acknowledged with a smile. This was one of the rooms where bank officials plotted their forestry and land-registration programs—while failing to look up, out the window, to see army officers felling the forests and developers burning residents' homes.

"This is like a jungle to them," said Ok Serei Sopheak, a former government official who was serving as a consultant to the World Bank. "It's not very easy to understand the mind-set of this place."

Foreign medical NGOs didn't look out the window often enough, either. Ask any one of them what had been accomplished in the past few years, and he would most likely say: We defeated HIV/AIDS! Prodded and funded by foreign governments and private groups, Cambodia reduced the prevalence of HIV/AIDS in the general population from more than 3 percent to just under 1 percent—a major public-health victory. But that laudable accomplishment masked a darker truth.

Medical experts working in Cambodia allowed the nation's health policies to be determined by the priority or caprice of officials in Geneva, Washington, or Berlin—not Phnom Penh or Battambang. That gave the country a skewed health policy that made little effort to address the patients' most pressing needs.

"Everybody talks about AIDS," complained Dr. Sin Somuny, executive director of Medicam. "It affects 0.09 percent of the population. Well, diabetes now affects 10 percent of the population. But no one talks about that. Funding for diabetes is twenty-five to thirty times less."

O'Leary, director of the World Health Organization office, explained that international donors "want to give money to the big thing of the moment. Right now," in 2009, "it's influenza," better known as swine, or bird, flu.

Beat Richner, that hospital director from Switzerland, was scornful. "They care about bird flu because a bird may fly to California," he said. "But a mosquito flies only 120 meters." Hence, the dearth of funding for malaria or dengue fever, two mosquito-borne illnesses. "Two years ago 22,000 children in this country had dengue fever. But did the WHO care? No. They cared about bird flu."

When he spoke only nine people in Cambodia had contracted swine flu, but Richner's hospital was full of children afflicted with malaria, dengue fever, encephalitis. Not one Cambodian hospital had a bacterial lab, but donors did put one in a French medical-research clinic in Phnom Penh—to conduct swine-flu tests. "Infectious diseases, infectious diseases," Sin Somuny said, shaking his head. "If you care about the lives of the people, it should not just be infectious diseases."

"You know, beggars can't be choosers," countered Dr. Paul Weelen, another WHO official. "Donors set the agenda for what is done in these countries. Where there's no money, not much is happening."

---

When Charlie Twining was ambassador, just after the UN occupation and the first national elections, "our countries put a lot of money into the UN operation," he said, "and we pushed hard to have the UN and other agencies open offices there. We very much wanted to see the apparent success continue. We were very much drawn into that way of thinking."

Now, said Broderick, the UN chief, "we are pretty much at a stalemate, and there is a lot of frustration." He was speaking about the debate over corruption, but that was a comfortable metaphor for the donors' larger presence in society. "We continue to engage the government" but seldom gain much from that. "We need to move away from the narrow-minded focus on the law and find individual entry points" direct to the

Cambodian people. Meantime, the government had learned to play the donors like a fiddle. "It's not uncommon for senior opposition leaders to be charged and convicted without evidence, and to be subsequently pardoned" to "soften up international donors before crucial pledging conferences," the United Nations Human Rights Council noted in 2008.

Government officials also used the donors' complacency as justification for their own behavior. When a human-rights group issued a statement criticizing the government for failing to pass the anticorruption law, Information Minister Khieu Kanharith shot back, "If the government was not good, then donors would not have provided aid to Cambodia. They have not provided us with millions of dollars for useless spending."

And so the donor community talked and then talked some more. While continuing to give Hun Sen the money that kept him in power, more and more every year, they eagerly awaited the opening of exciting new restaurants or cultural attractions. "You know, there was a small theater at the Royal University, a subcampus, in 2002 and 2003," said Jinnai, head of the UNESCO office. "But then the government sold the site to a developer in 2004, and they tore the theater down. Another theater burned down. They sold that land to a developer, too." Though for most people working in Cambodia, this parable would bring to mind images of land seizures and corruption, not so for Jinnai. Instead, he went on with a wistful tone, saying, "Culturally, 2002 and 2003 was a good time here. I'm still hungry for this sort of culture now."

The United Nations and the developed world spent more than two years and $3 billion to redeem Cambodia in 1992 and 1993, bring it back from the abyss, and offer it a doorway into the modern age. Then the world turned away, and the nation fell back into habits that had pertained since the Angkor era. For a while, particularly after the "coup" in 1997, the United States and some other nations grew angry and tried to punish Hun Sen. In time, though, the world simply gave up. Their efforts had failed. To them, Cambodia had become just one more sad little state, like Senegal or Laos—beyond redemption, of little note. All the while, donors and NGOs made a home in Cambodia. They lived well and did good work. Each one could take pride in some small accomplishment, a problem assuaged, a life improved. But they also grew to be enablers.

By 2010 donors had given at least $18 billion. The government relied on them to provide social services, then took credit for most everything they did and boasted about these "accomplishments" at election time. Government officials also maintained their comfortable lifestyles by ladling money out of the donor accounts. In fact, "the government has succeeded in persuading donors to pay salary supplements to its employees with remarkable regularity, despite regulations in virtually every donor organization against doing so," the USAID corruption study noted.

Just before the $1 billion donor meeting in December 2008, Heng Samrin, the CPP's honorary president, blithely promised once again that the government "will ensure sustainable development, poverty reduction, the promotion of the rule of law and equity in social justice, as well as the elimination of land-grabbing, deforestation, illegal fisheries resources and the prevention of national income loss and the strengthening of public order." Standing at a podium, he was the picture of smiling beneficence.

Yet by 2010, 80 percent of Cambodia's people remained desperately poor and barely educated. Cholera broke out nationwide soon after the dengue-fever epidemic abated, while malaria, tuberculosis, and dysentery remained commonplace. Almost 1 Cambodian of every 10 had diabetes, while World Health Organization figures showed that every year nearly 10,000 people, most of them children, died of diarrhea-related illnesses, all of them easily preventable. Five women died during childbirth every day.

The government had passed a law in 2009 legalizing land seizures in certain circumstances and also began selling off government-ministry buildings in prime downtown locations, relocating workers to the suburbs. *Oknya* Lao Meng Khin bought one building belonging to the Ministry of Cults and Religion. (His companies were also behind the eucalyptus plantation in Pursat Province and the destruction of Boeng Kak lake.) Another developer with close connections to Hun Sen was given permission to buy the colonial-era government headquarters compound in downtown Siem Reap. The provincial government moved to new buildings more than ten miles from the city center.

Meanwhile, Hun Sen, trying to show he was sensitive to overspending during the world economic crisis, promised that "we won't spend money buying cars for government officials." A few weeks later the government said it had signed a fifteen-year contract with a limousine service to provide one hundred Mercedes Benz 280S sedans, with drivers, for those same government officials. In the meantime, outside the capital 95 percent of the nation's roads remained unpaved.

The Cambodian Human Rights and Development Association reported that in 2009, 235 "human rights defenders" had been charged with crimes for doing their work—more than ever before. Life expectancy remained stuck, at sixty-one. So had the average per-capita income, at somewhere between $500 and $600. But 42 percent of the children still suffered from stunting. Fewer than 20 percent of Cambodian families who lived outside of the cities had access to a toilet or clean water. At least one-third of the people lived on less than $1 a day.

What, exactly, had $18 billion in aid accomplished? "The pain, the suffering continue, in spite of Cambodia being the highest per capita recipient of foreign aid, for more than five years," Bert Hoak and Ray Zepp wrote on a Cambodia news blog in 2008. Hoak had owned a bookstore and guesthouse in Phnom Penh for many years; Zepp wrote a travel guide about Cambodia. They, like so many foreigners who held affection for the state and its people, were growing ever more distressed. "The deforestation increases, in spite of foreign aid," they wrote. "The human rights abuses, the killing of journalists and editors, dissidents and others continues, and will continue, in spite of foreign aid. Our continued aid will only serve to prolong the misery, to prop up a despotic regime, to prolong the ecological devastation, even to the point of no return."

In 2007 the *Cambodia Daily* reported, "There had been brief discussion of postponing the next" donor meeting "until an anti-corruption law is enacted, said a Western diplomat on condition of anonymity. That radical proposal, however, didn't last very long before it was shot down."

What would happen if the donor community did in fact stand up to Hun Sen? What if they stood together as one and announced that they would withhold all but humanitarian aid until Hun Sen lived up to his promises to address the donors' concerns about education, health, food security, corruption, sanitation, land seizures, and the rest?

In the meantime, the World Food Program would continue delivering school meals. Other organizations would help poor patients receive ID cards, enabling them to receive free medical care. Every manner of direct humanitarian aid to the poor could continue. But all of the other initiatives, the "governance" programs and others from which government officials fed, would be put on hold. Sure, Hun Sen and Sok An could continue seizing land and selling it to *oknya*—even sucking sand from the river bottoms and selling it to Singapore.

But most government employees would find they had to live on their actual salaries, fifty or seventy-five dollars a month. More important, the developed world would be delivering a strong statement—stronger, even, than the one the UN occupation offered, since Cambodians quickly realized then that the UN was a toothless, clawless tiger. Now, after decades of complicity and neglect, the developed nations would at last declare: We are here for the Cambodian people. It is your job to serve them.

The government's invulnerability, its invincibility, might be thrown into doubt. When the CPP could no longer reliably provide for its members, perhaps the model would begin to break down. Maybe, just maybe, after 1,000 years, Cambodia's rulers might finally be forced to give the people their due.

# CHAPTER SIXTEEN

I eng Sary was a key intellectual architect of the Khmer Rouge approach to governance. In the 1950s he attended school in Paris with Saloth Sar—Pol Pot—and there they planned their genocidal revolution. While the Khmer Rouge held power, Ieng Sary served as foreign minister.

After the government's fall, after the disclosure that 2 million people had been killed, after years of bloody insurgency, Ieng Sary took up Hun Sen's offer of amnesty in 1996 and, in time, simply moved back to Phnom Penh, where he settled into a mansion, by Cambodian standards, in a housing development for ruling-party officers—just down the street from the Senate Golf Range. There he lived comfortably among his former victims, protected by legions of bodyguards.

For foreigners working in Cambodia, donors or diplomats, this seemed little different from allowing Joseph Goebbels or Rudolf Hess to move back into their Berlin homes after World War II to live out the rest of their days in peace and comfort. Yet Cambodians found it utterly unremarkable that a Khmer Rouge leader lived openly among them. Ask anyone how that could be, and all you'd get back was a puzzled look.

If nothing else, Ieng Sary fed the state's omnipresent culture of impunity. If he, with the blood of 2 million people on his hands, faced no penalty, no censure, no retribution, how hard was it to accept the killing of a journalist here, a trade-union official there, a crane operator riding his motorbike down the street—even a servant thrown off the roof? As Theary Seng, the advocacy-group director, put it, the Khmer Rouge crimes remained "the baseline. This is thirty years later, but we are still comparing ourselves to the Khmer Rouge. Today, the government can say it took 10 lives, or even 100 lives—but what's that compared to 2 million? That's still the Cambodian standard," and most foreign governments felt the same way.

Maybe most Cambodians were quiescent about living among the former Khmer Rouge killers. But foreign diplomats were appalled. As Thomas Hammarberg, the UN human-rights officer in Phnom Penh in the late 1990s, delicately put it, "This led to a contradictory situation. First, it became obvious that it would no longer be possible to avoid a real discussion about justice." At the same time, he noted that in the days leading up to the "coup" in 1997, both Hun Sen and Ranariddh were actually courting the Khmer Rouge, hoping to recruit their fighters for the battle to come.

Still, Hammarberg and others at the United Nations were convinced that these mass murderers, the Khmer Rouge leaders cavorting around town, must be put on trial. In April 1997, the United Nations Commission on Human Rights passed a resolution requesting Hammarberg "to examine any request by Cambodia for assistance in responding to past serious violations of Cambodian and international laws as a means of bringing about national reconciliation, strengthening democracy and addressing the issue of individual accountability."

The United Nations wanted at last to put the Khmer Rouge leaders on trial. Actually, the Vietnamese had already tried to do the same thing. In 1979 they staged a show trial and condemned them to death, in absentia. (Later, King Sihanouk pardoned them.) But the UN, in another bureaucratic understatement, called that trial "flawed." One could only wonder why the United Nations wanted to jump into that pool again after the "flawed" occupation and election just a few years earlier. But for human-rights officers, the reemergence of the Khmer Rouge leaders in everyday Phnom Penh society was such an affront that they could not help themselves.

In the days before the "coup," Hammarberg had asked the co-prime ministers, Ranariddh and Hun Sen, if they would like to ask the United Nations for help in staging a trial. They both agreed, though one can only imagine what was running through their minds. At that moment both were focused on the certain battle ahead. And when thinking about a trial, Hun Sen could not help but consider that he and many members of his government were former Khmer Rouge officers. Nonetheless, they both signed a letter asking for help, because, they said, "Cambodia does not have the resources or expertise to conduct this very important procedure." They were too busy to argue about this now; there'd be time to undo it later.

The street battles of July 1997 put all discussion on hold. And when Hun Sen emerged as the victor, almost every nation on earth angrily blamed the coup on him. For a while Cambodia's seat in the United Nations sat vacant once again until someone could decide whether it would be given to Ranariddh, as he argued, or Hun Sen. Neither the Security Council nor the UN General Assembly wanted anything to do with Hun Sen. The trial idea lay dormant.

Just then Kent Wiedemann arrived in Phnom Penh as the new U.S. ambassador with a mandate from Washington, he said, to push the government to hold a trial. "It stemmed from the belief," he said, "that there should be a firm structure in place for the rule of law. Anyone who commits these crimes against humanity should be put on trial." Still, "this was just after the coup d'état, the kind of atmosphere when nobody was willing to rely on Cambodia for justice."

In Washington, all the while, the departments of State, Defense, and Justice were furiously negotiating with Thailand and other countries so that the United States might seize Pol Pot and spirit him into

Thailand so he could be flown away into custody and put on trial. The air force was said to be prepped for the operation, and the islet nation of Palau said it was prepared to take him. To a world dulled to genocide, given the spate of more recent cases, State Department officials hoped to make the point that the Khmer Rouge had killed more than twice as many people as had died in Rwanda and almost twenty times more than were killed in Bosnia. The *New York Times* reported that President Clinton issued a written order to organize the logistics for capturing and holding Pol Pot until he could stand trial.

But in April 1998 Pol Pot died, still at home in the jungle. Officials in Washington were disappointed, deflated. Soon, however, they turned their attentions to Ta Mok, the Khmer Rouge military commander, and other former senior officials. For the United Nations, though, Pol Pot's death "was a reminder that time was running out," Hammarberg said in his account of the debate, written for the Documentation Center of Cambodia. "Other Khmer Rouge leaders were aging."

In 1998 two more Khmer Rouge leaders, Khieu Samphan, who had been the head of state, and Nuon Chea, who had been known as "Brother No. 2," accepted the amnesty offer and received a warm welcome when they showed up at Hun Sen's country estate. The prime minister told them, "The time has come to dig a hole and bury the past." This remark came back to haunt him. Was that the attitude of a man who wanted to put the Khmer Rouge leaders on trial?

A few days later, Khieu Samphan and Nuon Chea went on a road trip, as local and world media reported. Here's how the Associated Press described their journey:

> Two Khmer Rouge leaders went on vacation today, buoyed by promises of amnesty, while a UN officer said the world body still hoped to try those responsible for Cambodia's genocide. After basking in VIP treatment in Phnom Penh for the past two days, Khieu Samphan and Nuon Chea began a tour of the country that they helped turn into a vast slave-labor camp when the Khmer Rouge held power from 1975–79.

The two drove with their families in luxury vehicles to the seaside resort town of Sihanoukville, the first leg of a tour that will take them to the ancient Angkor temple complex and their home provinces.

Hun Sen insisted that he still wanted to put on a trial for the Khmer Rouge. But then, complicating the matter, he added new crimes to the list of events he wanted prosecutors to investigate, including the American bombing of Cambodia and Chinese support for the Khmer Rouge. So began a tortured minuet between Hun Sen, who did not consider a trial to be in his best interest, and the United Nations, whose leaders felt trapped by the process they had initiated. Now, of course, they also held no real enthusiasm for dealing with Hun Sen.

Over the following few years Hun Sen and his aides threw up one objection after another. They worried about national stability. They complained about infringement upon their sovereignty. They insisted that any trial take place in state courts, even though Hun Sen knew full well that his court system was thoroughly corrupt. Reforming the courts had been on his own campaign agenda during the most recent election. "If foreigners have the right to lack confidence in Cambodian courts," Hun Sen said, "we have the right to lack confidence in an international court. Why? Because those who mandate an international court used to support the Khmer Rouge."

Still, the UN repeatedly objected and refused. In Washington administrations changed, and the government lost interest in capturing the aging leaders. "It became such a difficult, convoluted, lengthy, very, very difficult process," said Wiedemann, largely because "as far as the UN was concerned, and others, there was no Cambodian qualified to participate in the tribunal in any meaningful way. The secretary-general wanted to appoint judges with eminent standing in the international community."

Finally, Kofi Annan, the secretary-general, threw up his hands and said he'd had enough. Hun Sen must "change his position and attitude," he declared, and "send a clear message that he is interested in a credible court, a credible tribunal which meets international standards." Until that day came, the United Nations was backing out of the discussions. When several UN ambassadors complained about his decision, Annan directed them to Hun Sen. In Phnom Penh the prime minister retorted, "I now suspect that political tricks are being played by the United Nations to protect the Khmer Rouge."

Ten months later the United Nations General Assembly, the entire world body, stepped into the debate and rescinded Kofi Annan's previous order when it passed a resolution directing "the Secretary-General to resume negotiations, without delay, to conclude an agreement with the Government of Cambodia, based on previous negotiations, on the establishment of the Extraordinary Chambers to try those suspected of being responsible for the atrocities committed by the Khmer Rouge." Too many nations, including the United States, were unhappy with Annan's decision.

Soon enough, Cambodia and the UN agreed to establish a hybrid court with both Cambodian and international judges and prosecutors. They called it the Extraordinary Chamber in the Courts of Cambodia, to differentiate it from Cambodia's much-maligned court system. David Scheffer, the U.S. ambassador at large for war-crimes issues, visited Cambodia and came up with the idea that made the negotiations succeed. Under Scheffer's plan, a majority of the trial judges could be Cambodian. But no decision could be reached unless at least one international judge agreed to it, too. Scheffer called that a "supermajority," and that formula broke the logjam. "I'm afraid there was no magical historical reflection or precedent that brought it to mind," Scheffer said later. "I simply tried to figure out how to manage a Cambodian majority on the bench and determined that requiring the vote of at least one international judge could establish the minimum threshold of international oversight." One analogy, he added, "deeply influenced my thinking—the requirement for unanimous jury verdicts in common-law criminal trials. Why shouldn't a ruling in a criminal trial require more than a bare majority of judges' votes, when our American criminal trials require all twelve jurors to render 'guilty' verdicts before a defendant in fact is found guilty?" Thanks to Scheffer's efforts, in 2003, after six years of acrimonious discussion, Cambodia and the United Nations finally agreed on a formula for trying the murderous leaders of the Khmer Rouge regime.

Anticipation was keen, expectations grandiose. "For Cambodia, this will fill a blank page," said Khieu Kanharith, the information minister. "It shows you cannot kill on orders from your bosses." That sounded odd from him, given the long list of government-ordered assassinations. But sometimes, just sometimes, government officials seemed to step partway out of their roles and express genuine hopes for a cleaner, gentler state, one that actually cared for its people. Even so, they stepped only partway out because they knew that in such a state, they would be a lot poorer. Even advocating that outcome could cost a job—and conceivably even a life.

Wiedemann, the ambassador, viewed the trial as a way "to salve the wounds, close the chapter, to recognize the suffering in Cambodia and show that the international community will not allow it to happen again." The State Department, he added, "believed quite strongly that it would inculcate a tradition of justice in Cambodia. The legal system had profound shortcomings, and if the tribunal was run on international standards, that would serve as an object lesson and bring the Cambodians along." For its part, the United Nations said the trial would demonstrate once and for all that in Cambodia, "there can be no impunity for violations of human rights."

Authorities finally arrested Ieng Sary on November 12, 2007, and took him to a holding cell in a converted military facility on the outskirts of town. It was being renovated, outfitted as a high-profile courthouse. Joining him there were his wife, Ieng Thirith, the Khmer Rouge minister of social affairs; Kaing Guek Eav, who was commander of the Tuol Sleng jail, where 15,000 Cambodians died; and two other senior leaders, Nuon Chea and Khieu Samphan.

Three years after the 2003 agreement to stage the trial, David Tolbert, a UN lawyer working at the International Criminal Tribunal for the former Yugoslavia, got a call. Could he please go to Cambodia and try to straighten out the war-crimes courtroom there? Nothing was moving. The court was stuck. Tolbert was a tall, garrulous North Carolinian with long, straight yellow-blond hair. He had an easy smile but a world-weary manner. His job took him into the heart of the world's worst genocidal moments. And now he was to bring that experience to Cambodia. There, the problems were altogether different.

The court had been organizing itself for several years now, but when Tolbert arrived, "it had no administrative leadership, particularly with respect to court management, including translation and interpretation and the witness-protection program. The international side had essentially given over judicial management to the Cambodian side." But "there was really very little judicial management in place. The Cambodian staff in charge had virtually no knowledge or experience, as most had no judicial background. And yet there were a large number of them," hundreds in fact. "There was no way the court could stage a trial at that point."

Tolbert spent a few weeks drawing up a series of recommendations to get the process moving. Then he returned to Yugoslavia. Almost a year later he got a call from a court employee in Phnom Penh. You suggested a new staff position, the employee said. Could you please send a job description? Tolbert realized: The place was still moribund.

In 2008 UN Secretary-General Ban Ki-moon appointed Tolbert as a special expert, an assistant secretary-general, to try one more time. He quickly found that five years after the agreement to set up the court, "very little progress had been made. I proposed reducing the budget by 35 percent. The staff was bloated. They had fifteen gardeners, which looked like a job-creation program to me." So he pursued four specific goals: "Financial stability. Giving donors confidence in the budget. Providing the administrative staff a new direction. And addressing corruption."

Yes, once again corruption had reared its head. Cambodian staff members were being forced to give up 30 percent of their salaries to their bosses. The delays and corruption allegations were demoralizing for the few Cambodians who knew about the court. They began giving up on the lofty hopes they had placed on this trial. But one poll in 2008 found that 85 percent of the population didn't even know the trials were under way. That was not so surprising. Given that Cambodia was managing court administration, no one even thought about informing the public. Cambodian public institutions were notoriously closed and secretive, better to hide the graft and indolence.

Over the years that Hun Sen battled the United Nations over the trial, by all accounts his overriding concern was control. He wanted to make sure that the UN did not set up an autonomous body inside his country that he could not manipulate to protect himself and his fellow former Khmer Rouge friends. But as he and the rest of the world soon discovered, the Khmer Rouge trial presented a new and different liability for Cambodia's leaders. It exposed Cambodia's way of doing business—incompetent, rapacious, corrupt—to everyone in the world. Half of the court was staffed by foreigners, UN employees and others, mostly from Western nations. People like Tolbert. Cambodian business as usual, generally practiced behind locked doors, was now exposed for the world to see—like a dollhouse with no back wall. The scene inside wasn't pretty.

Heather Ryan arrived in Phnom Penh in 2005 to serve as a court monitor for the Open Society Institute, George Soros's human-rights NGO. She, too, was a lawyer, and independently of Tolbert, she came to conclusions similar to his.

The Cambodian operation just wasn't competent. The nation didn't have a real court system, just a collection of courtrooms staffed by lawyers and judges who had bribed their way through school, bought their positions in court, and ruled by bribe, fiat—or orders from above. They just didn't seem to understand or appreciate the law. As an example, in Ratanakiri Province, police impounded a pickup truck that had been used in a robbery and double murder. It was to be held as evidence. But then provincial court judge Thor Saran decided he liked the truck, picked up the keys, and drove it home. He kept it for more than a year. After a human-rights group complained, saying, "normally, evidence is kept in its original form to be shown in court," the Justice Ministry investigated and then cleared the judge.

When Cambodian jurists were paired with Western lawyers and judges, the disparities were glaring. For example, Ryan said, "interviewing witnesses—they're just not good at it." Legal interviews, like police or journalists' interviews, have to be informal and unthreatening so that the subject relaxes and feels comfortable talking. Well, the Cambodians, Ryan said, "call the village chief and tell them to contact the witness and set things up. Way too formal. And then they show up in a white car, four or five people," and pile out, a troop of official-looking people, there to do an interview.

Then in 2007 Ryan uncovered the kickback scheme. "We spoke to lots of staff members; they had come to us anonymously." They told her that the Cambodian staff director, Sean Visoth, was the ringleader ordering and directing the 30 percent kickback system—netting $30,000 to $40,000 a month, local media reported. He, in turn, had to turn most of the proceeds over to the people in government who had appointed him to this rich position.

Cambodia reacted as it always does. Officials attacked Ryan. Sok An, the deputy prime minister, declared that she could never again set foot in the courthouse. She had observed that foreigners working at the court did not really understand Cambodia. As it turned out, she didn't entirely understand Cambodians, either. With surprise and exasperation, she complained, "All I did was call for an investigation. But instead, it became simply a debate over our allegations"—and about her. She was learning the immutable rule of Cambodian behavior. If accused, a Cambodian generally will not respond to the accusations. Instead, he will attack the accuser.

The court's Cambodian judges, who more than likely had to kick back part of their own salaries, took umbrage at Ryan's allegations and issued a statement saying Ryan needed to "correct by appropriate

means this unsubstantiated allegation" because it "created public confusion and seriously undermined the reputation and integrity of all
national judges appointed to the tribunal."

Those judges didn't have much of a reputation to begin with. For example, Human Rights Watch said Kong Srim, the chief judge, "developed a reputation for handling cases in a political manner rather than
according to the law and the facts. He prosecuted suspects in absentia,
played a key role in the release of Hun Sen's nephew, Nhim Sophea,
against whom there was compelling evidence of murder, and was crucial in engineering the imposition of the deputy prime minister's own
candidate, Ky Tech, to be president of the Cambodian Bar Association."

Needless to say, hardly anyone doubted that the corruption charges
were true. In fact, Ryan said some of her donor friends told her, "This
is Cambodia. What do you expect? Back off." A short time later the
court dismissed Sean Visoth's deputy. A "red herring," Ryan said.

Nonetheless, the new charges roiled the court. Donations to support the trial dropped off. Defendants' attorneys began filing motions
saying their clients could not get a fair trial in a corrupt court. And
those Cambodians who were paying attention grew even more disil-
lusioned. The *Phnom Penh Post* noted that "feelings of hopelessness
and a sense of mistrust came to the fore" at a 2008 forum staged by
Theary Seng's NGO. "A significant number of participants expressed
growing disillusionment because of delays and a lack of information
about what the court personnel are doing."

To quell the growing anger, Sean Visoth appointed corruption
monitors: Chief Judge Kong Srim and Helen Jarvis, a middle-aged
Australian woman, a former librarian, who was a longtime Cambodian
government hanger-on then serving as a public affairs officer at the
court. Neither of them would threaten Visoth's reign over patronage
and graft. Right away court watchers labeled them the foxes guarding
the henhouse.

While the court's administrative side slowly disintegrated in acrimonious finger-pointing, the legal side actually filed charges and brought

the first defendant to court: Kaing Guek Eav, the commander of the Tuol Sleng torture chamber. He was known as Duch, pronounced "Doik." Police took him into custody in 1999. He claimed to have been an evangelical Christian since 1979 and had told interviewers he welcomed the chance at repentance. On July 31, 2007, he got his wish.

The court charged him with crimes against humanity. Researchers had found his written directives ordering the executions of scores of victims, generally people viewed as enemies of the revolution. Through torture, guards forced them to confess to fantastic crimes. Once they had confessed, they were executed, whacked on the back of the head with a club, and then thrown into a mass grave. At Tuol Sleng 15,000 people were believed to have died that way. But years would pass before Duch's trial would begin.

Meantime, in 2008 the United Nations validated Heather Ryan's corruption allegations, saying it had received significant evidence of its own. The UN withheld funding for the trial until the allegations were settled. UN investigators had found what one official called "prima facie" evidence that Sean Visoth, the Cambodian-staff director, was also the corruption ringleader. Tolbert became the first in a parade of UN officials sent to Phnom Penh to negotiate a way out of this typically Cambodian impasse.

Tolbert's job was to convince Deputy Prime Minister Sok An that Sean Visoth had to be removed from his job. Sok An could be a nasty fellow, drunk with money, power, and self-importance. He was the one who lived in the 60,000-square-foot chalet. He was also fat, an embodiment of the Cambodian paradigm that only senior government officials, like the kings of yore, got more than enough to eat. Some UN officials had a nickname for Sok An. Privately they called him Jabba the Hutt, the hideously obese figure in the *Star Wars* movies.

At first, Sok An refused to see Tolbert. In time, he got an appointment, and when Tolbert finally walked into the deputy prime minister's office Sok An was cold. "It was a very difficult meeting," Tolbert said. "He of all people lectured me on due process." Tolbert pushed him to fire the man responsible for the graft problem. Sok An resisted, "but I pushed hard." Finally, Sok An told him he would take care of the problem "at the appropriate time." Tolbert went home, and a few months later Sean Visoth left his job on sick leave. He never returned, but that did not clear up the problem.

A parade of UN and U.S. officials stopped by to see Hun Sen or Sok An, trying to work out a new corruption-reporting system. For the visitors, it remained vitally important that graft victims be able to report to a neutral third party—not a government operative. For the government, however, it remained essential that they maintain full control over this, too. Who knew what some third party would say or do? Meanwhile, the court was running out of money. Some months, the staff got no pay.

The government stood tough. In fact, when the United Nations raised its corruption allegations, officials responded as they always did, as they had when Heather Ryan first brought the issue to public attention in 2007, by attacking the accuser. A spokesman for the Council of Ministers announced that the government was now "monitoring all international staff" at the court because "the international side has corruption, too." Naturally, he backpedaled when he realized he had offered a tacit admission of government graft and suddenly insisted that corruption on the Cambodian side hadn't been proved.

Attention to the infighting receded as Duch testified in court in the spring and summer of 2009. He electrified the audience. In his opening statement, he said he was sorry for the atrocities he had committed. "I would like to apologize to all surviving victims and their families who were mercilessly killed" at his prison, the former commandant said. "I would like to express my regret and heartfelt sorrow." He sat behind a luxury-wood dock with armed guards to his left and right, a withered old man with white hair. He was sixty-six, already five or six years past the typical life span for a Cambodian male, facing a panel of judges wearing crimson robes with black and white sashes. Behind him Cambodians and foreigners in the audience watched from behind a large, panoramic picture window. In the front row sat a few monks in saffron robes who would have been executed had they found their way into Tuol Sleng when Duch was in command.

Duch spoke for almost twenty minutes. "My current plea is that I would like you to please leave an open window for me to seek forgiveness." He faced the possibility of a life sentence; Cambodia had no death penalty. In the following days, his few surviving victims gave terrible testimony, describing torture and seemingly indiscriminate death. Some told of electric shock or being hung upside down, trying to hold their heads out of a bucket of water. Some said guards ripped out finger- and toenails. "Every night I looked out at the moon," one of the victims, Bou Meng, sixty-nine, recalled while testifying. "I heard people crying and sighing around the building. I heard people calling out, 'Mother help me, mother help me!'" During the night, guards trucked the condemned out to a field on the edge of town for execution. Every night, Bou Meng said, he waited for a guard to come get him. "But by midnight or 1 a.m. I realized that I would live another day."

Cambodia televised the trial, and some people watched it on their car-battery televisions. In many cases, they reacted to the testimony as Bou Meng did—furious that these mass murderers were living comfortably in a cell with air-conditioning and three meals a day, delivered. "I am extremely envious of Duch and the treatment he receives. I don't understand why the court treats him so well, much better than me."

One television viewer, Saloth Nhep, eighty-four, had a different reaction. He lived in Prek Sbov village, just outside Kampong Thom, and one afternoon he had just come from a bath and was sitting in a black hammock under his modest house, shirtless and damp. His face was heavily furrowed, his hair white and thin. He was calm, philosophical, and polite as he considered the trial. "I don't know how to say it," he said. "I am not educated. But the court is not really Cambodian. It is partly international. The way Duch speaks it sounds like a confession. I remember Duch saying that if he did not do those things, someone would kill him." Saloth Nhep had never met Duch or any of the other defendants, even though they had been close friends and compatriots of his older brother, Saloth Sar—Pol Pot. "Brother Number One" had died eleven years earlier, and at that time Saloth Nhep had grieved. "When I heard the news I was very sad, and I felt my heart slow down," he said then.

Even with a creased face and white hair, Saloth Nhep held a striking resemblance to Pol Pot. Whatever anger he still retained toward his brother related primarily to Saloth Sar's neglect of his family—not his role in the deaths of 2 million Cambodians. Before joining the Cambodian Communist Party, Saloth Sar studied in France, and after he came back from France, "he came to see us only twice," Saloth Nhep complained. "He did not care about family. He has never even seen the face of my oldest child." That was especially painful. As children, the brothers had been best friends, inseparable.

For much of the time the Khmer Rouge held power, "I did not know the name Pol Pot, did not know he was my brother," Saloth Nhep recalled. Even as the president's brother, he was swept into the vortex of the Khmer Rouge horror. Unlike his older brother, he was an illiterate rice farmer—just the kind of Cambodian the Khmer Rouge respected. "They treated me like everyone else; they didn't know he was my brother. I didn't know Pol Pot. The work was very hard, and there was no freedom." But then in 1977 he saw a picture of Pol Pot on a poster. He stared, shocked. "What I was thinking was that he should not be leading the country this way and letting people starve to death." After that he said he did not tell anyone that Pol Pot was his brother. Asked why, he just shrugged. He continued working with little if anything to eat until the Vietnamese invasion in 1979. Neither during the war nor after did he ever see his brother again.

Still, Saloth Nhep was content now. At rest, his expression was serene. Villagers respected him. They knew his history and appreciated that he was a pleasant, respectful neighbor. "The present government is better than the previous regime," he averred. "There is freedom of travel, and we have security." Like most Cambodians, that's all he seemed to expect—except, he said, to see his brother's former comrades, on trial in

Phnom Penh, convicted and sent to prison. But he did not live to see that. On February 4, 2010, Saloth Nhep passed away.

Around the country tens of thousands were unable to watch the trial. They didn't have a television, or an antenna able to pick up the station. Asked about that, generally they shrugged. They didn't really care. Still, Youk Chhang, head of the Documentation Center of Cambodia, took it on as his mission to bring the trial to the people. One morning in the town of Kampong Speu, west of Phnom Penh, residents started arriving before eight o'clock, middle-aged men and women, poor rice farmers mostly—damaged survivors of the Khmer Rouge regime. Youk Chhang and his staff had brought a video projector and set it up in a monk's pagoda near the center of town. They showed a DVD featuring highlights of Duch's trial testimony. "I want to contribute to engaging the victims in the court process," Youk Chhang explained. "Some Cambodians have moved on, but there are others who still suffer, and these are the ones we are targeting." And that's just who he got. For an hour about seventy-five people watched transfixed as Duch described his crimes and told how he supervised as his soldiers executed victims by whacking them on the back of the head. In the video Duch looked directly at the judges with a calm and confident gaze, seeming to be the commandant still, as he confessed to his terrible crimes, apologized, and asked for forgiveness. "I was given a directive to use a plastic bag to suffocate prisoners," he acknowledged.

When the video excerpts ended, the room sat silent—stunned, it seemed. One of Youk Chhang's aides asked audience members to talk about what they had seen. The DVD was paused on a scene in which Duch seemed to be staring directly at the crowd with a stern, almost threatening, gaze. The first woman who raised her hand took the microphone and promptly broke into tears. "Forgiveness is not acceptable," she declared, wiping her eyes. "They killed my father and two older brothers." Next a middle-aged man told of how six of his relatives died, and as he spoke his large brown eyes grew red and filled with tears. Still another man was choking up so that his words were hard to understand. "I was a child, and I was starving," he stammered. "They gave us no food, and sometimes I would fall down and pass out and then wake up again." And so it went.

The problem, of course, was that almost half the adult population of Cambodia, those over thirty-five or forty years of age, showed symptoms of post-traumatic stress disorder. And for them, psychiatrists said, watching a video like the one those people saw was like poking a stick in a hornet's nest. It triggered all of the symptoms: pain, rage—even violence.

Daryn Reicherter, the psychiatrist at Stanford University, served as a consultant to Youk Chhang's Documentation Center a few months earlier and came back angry. "Those people at the documentation center have no background or knowledge of anxiety or the risks associated with trauma. But it turns out they are dealing with this stuff every day. There needs to be some medical follow-up with these people" after the show has ended, "but they aren't getting it."

By the summer of 2009 the Documentation Center had trucked more than 10,000 villagers to Phnom Penh to see the trial—or brought DVD excerpts to show in their own villages. Reicherter described taking part in one of these "outreach" trips.

They go to a village and round people up, anyone who wants to come, 100 or so, and then they put all of them into the backs of trucks and drive them an hour to Phnom Penh. They go into this air-conditioned courtroom, put on headphones and listen to Duch describing torture and murder. And then they put the people back in those trucks and take them home. Some of these people are likely to have emotional breakdowns. I asked Youk's people, "Is there any follow-up with these people?" One of them said, "We have some information on our Web site."

Reicherter grimaced and shook his head. "I told him, 'You're kidding!' He wasn't."

Youk Chhang said he understood the doctor's concerns but pointed out that he is a researcher, not a treatment specialist. The government, he insisted, should provide any needed psychiatric services. Of course, he knew the government could not, would not, do that in any case. Cambodia had only about twenty-six psychiatrists in the entire nation. Most of them worked in hospitals, handing out pills "because that pays more," said Muny Sothara, a psychiatrist with the Transcultural Psychosocial Organization. He was one of only three or four clinical psychiatrists in the country. He grew agitated when he discussed Youk Chhang and his outreach program:

> Exposure like this can trigger serious reactions. These people need to be prepared before exposing them to such terrible things. We need to give them a briefing on what they are going to see. These scenes can provoke a reaction. Their staff does not have the capacity to deal with this. It can provoke fear, anger, a drive for revenge. Intensified post-traumatic stress disorder can lead to hyperarousal, panic attacks, and, if they have a predisposed condition, a heart attack. If they don't know how to deal with feelings of revenge, they can do harm to others through aggressive behavior. There can be domestic violence—or if you are in a position of leadership, bad judgments, making aggressive decisions at work. When you are angry, you cannot think clearly.

Sophearith Choung worked for Youk Chhang for several years but quit, he said, in part because he could not bring himself to participate in the outreach project any longer. "How many people died, and we didn't know anything about it? I have a big concern about that project. I feel guilty. The problem is, with mental health there's a delay in dying. I saw in some cases they were very emotional as they left. I want to understand how physical problems and mental health are related. This was an activity I could not accept."

At the Kampong Speu event, Yim Choy, a forty-four-year-old farmer, shouted at the crowd, saying that he had been conscripted to a child-labor team. "I cannot forgive Duch!" he declared, his voice hard, his tone bitter. "How can I when I saw him throw little boys against a tree?" Afterward, he said that, even now, he cannot talk about those times without growing angry. Yet he had a hard time keeping the thoughts out of his mind. He even dreamed of the horrors almost every night—a hallmark of PTSD. "I see myself with my hands tied behind me." All of that made him angrier still. He clenched his fists; veins pulsed in his neck.

Youk Chhang was a bright man, college educated in the United States. But in this case he strove to show that he did not understand the consequences of his actions. It was also plain that he felt marginalized. The Documentation Center had been the sole source for information about the Khmer Rouge. But the tribunal usurped that role, even though much of its evidence had come from the center's files. And now psychiatrists from the Transcultural Psychosocial Organization, often known as the TPO, were sniping at him. "Fifteen years ago, who wanted to talk about the Khmer Rouge tribunal?" he said with a curled lip. "Not the TPO. They stayed away from this" until it got popular. "And now they are just doing it for fund-raising. That's all. But we are here to assist victims—not to victimize victims. We are sensitive to this problem to the best of our abilities. We have had a long association with them. They trust us. And Cambodians are good followers. They will follow people who lead them, particularly people they trust."

There lay the crux of the problem. It was not unique to Youk Chhang's victims. Youk Chhang was bright, educated, well-off. His victims, raised in a culture that respected class hierarchy, followed him—right over the cliff. He may truly not have understood how much damage he was doing.

After his presentation in the Kampong Speu pagoda, sobbing former victims staggered home. Meantime, Youk Chhang led his volunteers—fresh-faced young women from the United States, mostly, who looked up to him as a teacher and mentor—on a short tour of the surroundings. They stopped at a clearing where townspeople had built a two-story glass shrine and filled it with skulls of Khmer Rouge victims. Youk Chhang reflected on the event in the pagoda, and then he cheerily invited all of them to lunch at a nearby restaurant, "where they make the best roast chicken in a special Khmer way." Then they all climbed into a van and drove off.

But then Youk Chhang's victims were not alone. Across society, older people, particularly, decried the trial. "PTSD, everyone has it," said Khieu Kanharith, the information minister. "That's why Cambodians don't want to bring this up again. The wounds are deeper than anyone could imagine." Kek Galibru lamented, her voice heavy with the pain, "It is still a trauma, and the trial has reopened the wound." She was director of Licadho, the human-rights group. "Now they say they are going to clean the wound. They didn't clean it. It's hemorrhaging!"

In the courthouse, meanwhile, the corruption allegations were stymieing any hope of progress. The Cambodian employees had gone unpaid for so long that even Kong Srim, the Cambodian chief judge, suddenly decided he wanted the investigation concluded. "I see this as our most important challenge," he said in March 2009, "as it hardly seems reasonable to continue working without remuneration."

Another UN official, Peter Taksoe Jensen, assistant secretary-general for legal affairs, met with Hun Sen and Sok An repeatedly, trying to resolve the disagreement between the UN's insistence on autonomy for a corruption monitor and Cambodia's determination to remain in control. At about that time a defense attorney produced a government memo of uncertain provenance that plainly showed Hun Sen's direct control of the trial thus far. He and Sok An had handpicked the Cambodian judges and all of the court's Cambodian legal staff, even though the government's Supreme Council of the Magistracy was supposed to have done that. When asked, government officials evaded questions about the memo. All the while the international judges were saying they wanted to bring in more defendants, additional senior Khmer Rouge leaders still at large—such as Meas Muth, former Khmer Rouge southwestern division commander.

Meas Muth was seventy years old now, but still active—and wealthy. He wasn't hiding. He lived in southwestern Battambang Province, part of the area he controlled as Khmer Rouge commander. His house was lavish by Cambodians' standards—a three-story wood-frame structure powered by generators, with a shiny blue-tile roof decorated with ornate Asian filigrees. Two cars, both large SUVs, sat out front under custom-fit tan covers. Two satellite dishes on his roof fed programming to flat-panel televisions inside. In numerous interviews Meas Muth insisted that prosecuting him would be a mistake because that might destabilize the nation. "To add five, six or 10 more, or more than that, that's not for justice, but to stir up Cambodia, causing instability," he told the Voice of America.

One afternoon in the summer of 2009 he was not home, but his son was there: Meas Savuth, thirty-four. He adored his father and pointed to a wooden shrine of sorts he had built for his dad on the occasion of his seventieth birthday. It looked vaguely like a gallows. "I had been separated from my father since I was six years old," said Meas Savuth, a handsome, rugged-looking young man wearing flowered shorts and no shirt, eating lychee nuts, and throwing the shells on the ground. He was born in 1974 and during the Khmer Rouge years lived with his mother and father, the military commander.

He was five years old when Vietnam invaded. While most Cambodians rejoiced, his parents fled. "Everyone ran off in all directions," he recalled. "My mother went one way, my father disappeared. They left me with my aunt. She was killed by the Vietnamese. I had foster parents. I lost track of my father." Along the way he never went to school. He remained illiterate. "But then in 2002 I heard he was here. I came here in 2002 and saw my older brother. But he did not trust me. Did not believe it was me. He said the rumor was that I had been killed by the Vietnamese. He wouldn't believe me, so I went away." Later, "I went to a fortune teller who told me to look for my father. She told me, 'You cannot see your father until your daughter is a teenager.' So when my daughter turned thirteen, I came back." That was in 2007. "This time they accepted me."

Down the road, Sit You Sous, a sixty-one-year-old blacksmith, grew excited when asked about Meas Muth, his neighbor. He had been twenty-eight years old when the Khmer Rouge took power, and he had been certain then that he would die. He'd been thrown into a rice field to work, he said, though he had never spent a day as a farmer. "Other people from my village surrounded me in the field, hid me, and chanted that I could make knives, axes, and machetes," he recalled, sitting shirtless in his front yard. His grandchildren, giggling, crawled in and out of a small wooden box lying in the dirt. "A Khmer Rouge soldier heard that and pulled me out. I was very frightened. I thought they would kill me. But they brought me some tools and asked me to make something. I did, and that is what they had me do for the rest of the war." Even now, he had a blacksmith shop around the back of his house with a foot-powered bellows.

Across the road one of his daughters was doing laundry in a little stream. She wet clothes then laid each one on a board resting in a tub of soapy water and scrubbed it with a brush. Sit You Sous said he didn't know what to do about Meas Muth now. "I don't know how to feel angry because this is the system here. But that regime was too brutal. I will let the government take care of it. I depend on the government. That's its function." He sprang up from his chair all of a sudden, saying he wanted to get something out of the house.

He brought back some papers on U.S. State Department letterhead. "I applied to go to America because I want my children to see the developed world. I dream that they can go to a better school in the modern world, then come back to help this country." The letter showed that he had applied for a residency permit in early 2006. The department sent back that letter simply acknowledging receipt and informing Sit You Sous that the application would expire if further documentation was not supplied by June 1, 2007—two years earlier. "I have been holding on to this," he explained, waving the papers, "waiting for someone to come by who could read it to me."

As soon as word about prosecuting additional suspects began leaking out of the court, Hun Sen went on the offensive. He had already said anyone criticizing the trial's Cambodian judges "are not human; they are animals," who "even want to seduce their own parents." As for the additional defendants, he insisted, "This will not happen on my watch. The UN and the countries that supported Pol Pot to occupy Cambodia's seat at the UN from 1979 to 1991 should be tried first. They should be sentenced more heavily than Pol Pot."

Then later that year he took up a new, illogical argument. "If you want a tribunal, but you don't want to consider peace and reconciliation and war breaks out again, killing 200,000 or 300,000 people, who will be responsible?" he asked. "Finally, I have got peace in this country, so I will not let someone destroy it. The people and the nation will not be destroyed by someone trying to lead the country into instability."

During the early debate over the trial ten years earlier, Wiedemann said, several senior government officials, including Sihanouk, had openly worried that calling for a trial would spook Khmer Rouge officers and their men still living in Pailin, prompting them to leave the jungle and "make trouble again." But Hun Sen, Wiedemann added, never voiced that concern back then. Now, the prime minister never explained exactly how or why the unrest he predicted would come about, given that the Khmer Rouge movement was dead. Most Cambodians had ignored the Duch trial; there'd been no known incident of unrest. Another time he lashed out against the idea of more prosecutions. "I would rather see the court fail than let the country fall into war."

Even so, in the court's offices sat more than a dozen legal investigators, foreigners on the UN payroll who were researching new suspects and couldn't care less what Hun Sen had to say about it. And in the fall of 2009 the court did announce that it intended to charge additional suspects. Though the judges did not name them, speculation centered on Meas Muth and a few others.

On July 26, 2010, the court convicted Duch of crimes against humanity and sentenced him to thirty-five years in prison—by almost every reaction an exceedingly light sentence for a man who oversaw the torture and deaths of 15,000 people. But he will not serve even thirty-five years. After subtracting his time already spent in jail, more for cooperation and good behavior, and more still for a period of illegal detention in a military jail, the court left him with nineteen years to serve. When the judge sentenced Duch, he was sixty-seven years old, meaning he could conceivably walk out of prison a free man one day.

This was the first time in recorded Cambodian history that a former senior government official was actually sentenced to prison for a human-rights violation. And as best as anyone can tell, this was also the only trial ever conducted in Cambodia under true international standards of justice. Still, many surviving victims were distraught. "This is a slap in the face," said Bou Meng, who had testified against Duch. Shouting at the crowd in the muddy yard outside the courtroom, Chum Mey, another survivor, complained, "We are victims two times, once in the Khmer Rouge time and now once again. His prison is comfortable with air conditioning, food three times a day, fans and everything!" So limited was Chum Mey's existence, like those of most Cambodians, that a life in prison seemed preferable.

Most people involved with the court wondered if that would be the last trial. After all, Duch had been the youngest of the defendants. His trial took three years—and he was cooperative; he readily admitted his guilt. All of the others were in full denial. In fact, Ieng Thirith threatened that anyone who accused her of murder "will be cursed to the seventh circle of hell." Ieng Sary was eighty-four, and since he was put in jail he'd been hospitalized several times for heart problems and blood in the urine. He could barely walk. Khieu Samphan and his wife were both in their seventies and in frail health. Nuon Chea was in his eighties and no better off. Which of them would still be alive in three years?

But there was more. Everyone involved with holding the trial was by now battered and weary. Every step along the way had involved brutal fights with Hun Sen and Sok An, constant threats, and manipulation. Most reporting on the trial focused on corruption, political manipulation, and money shortages. No one spoke any longer of their dreams that the trial would strike a blow to impunity and injustice. In fact, the trial had offered new demonstrations of impunity and injustice. Already donors had given more than $100 million to the court, knowing that some was lost to corruption. Now the court was asking for another $93 million for just the next two years—not enough time, more than likely, to complete another trial.

But then in the fall of 2010 the court surprised everyone by issuing indictments for the four remaining defendants at the same time, charging them with crimes against humanity, genocide, murder, and religious persecution. Mindful of their ages and health, the court planned to try them together. All of them were members of the government that ordered the killing. But unlike Duch, these people probably did not actually kill anyone themselves.

The United Nations and other assorted international organizations that followed the trial were pleased. But, as usual, Cambodians were barely aware. Various surveys and anecdotal evidence—I asked every Cambodian I met about the trial—showed that most people simply weren't paying attention. They didn't have a television, or they couldn't get the station that aired the trial, some said. Others shrugged and professed to have little interest. They were too busy. The trial was on during the day, when they were at work in the rice paddies. If they had time to watch TV, they wanted to be entertained.

The trials might finally bring some Khmer Rouge leaders to justice. But so many other hopes had also been attached to it. The trials would wake up the Cambodian people. They would demand an end to impunity and use the Khmer Rouge trials as an example for reforming the state's dysfunctional court system. None of that came to pass.

The government and United Nations did finally agree on the selection of a corruption monitor. They chose Uth Chhorn, Cambodia's auditor general, a seemingly independent official. But then no one in Cambodia's government was truly independent. In the end, after more than a year of argument and debate, the UN seemed simply to have given up.

Uth Chhorn had been running the National Audit Authority whose job was to review the finances of government agencies. Of course, honest reports on that subject were certain to be toxic, so the authority was years behind in issuing its findings. When Uth Chhorn did issue a report, the government forbade him to publish it, though the law required that the authority's work be made public. If Uth Chhorn had fought back against any of this, there was no public record of it. Now he was to be the court's corruption monitor, someone victims could trust to take their reports and complaints in confidence. But he was given no investigative authority or mandate, and a few weeks after his appointment, Uth Chhorn betrayed his true intent. He told reporters it was not his job to resolve corruption charges. Instead, he said he would simply pass complaints to senior UN officers—and to Sok An, the deputy prime minister, as well as other Cambodian officials, the very people the complaints were likely to be about. Just like the Office for Reports on Corruption in downtown Phnom Penh.

Only four people came to see him in the first six months. And in 2010 donors to the trial wondered why he deserved a $140,394 salary, given that all he did was make a few phone calls and hold an occasional meeting. Uth Chhorn's salary was cut to $32,000, recognizing his role as a cipher in the courtroom—nowhere near the robust and independent corruption investigator the UN had wanted.

Hun Sen had beaten the United Nations once again.

# CHAPTER SEVENTEEN

S erge Thion, a French sociologist, said it best: "Explaining Cambodia is typically a foreigner's business," he wrote. "For about one century, foreigners have been providing explanations."

In downtown Phnom Penh, a few doors away from the World Bank's offices, not far from the U.S. Embassy, Monument Books offered shelf after shelf of books about the Khmer Rouge era and other periods of Cambodian history, all written in English or French, all by Western historians, journalists, or other chroniclers. Books written by Cambodians were rare, and in almost every case those authors were expats educated in the West who had written memoirs, typically about their experiences under the Khmer Rouge.

Part of the explanation was education. For all of time, until the French occupation of Cambodia, the nation had virtually no books, just short scribbles on palm leaves. Until the 1960s few Cambodians could read or write. Even in the twenty-first century, illiteracy was widespread. And of the few people who were capable of writing a book about Cambodian society, most probably considered it too dangerous. When Tieng Narith, a political-science professor at Preah Sihanouk Raja Buddhist University in Phnom Penh, wrote a book about modern-day Cambodian society in 2007—unpublished, only for use in his classroom—he was immediately arrested. A judge convicted him of "printing false documents" and sent him to prison for two and a half years. But this isn't the only explanation, either.

For decades, foreign authors have tried to puzzle their way to an understanding of the paradox that is the Cambodian personality. It may seem a broad generality to refer to it this way, but every state has certain common personality characteristics, even if not every citizen displays them.

While trying to understand Cambodia, foreign writers sometimes fall into glib stereotypes and generalizations. In the nineteenth and early twentieth centuries, French writers routinely characterized the people as "obedient and lazy." These people liked to note that Cambodians would plant just enough rice to feed their families and then go home. If fertilizer or a hybrid rice seed allowed them to double the size of their crop, they would grow only half as much. Philip Short, the British author, made the same point, concluding that "the perception of indolence has become part of the country's self image, an explanation for its failure to keep up with its neighbors."

Michael Coe, author of a book about Cambodia's Angkor period, recounted a legend that he offered as a parable for the Cambodian people. In 1594 the Thai army attacked the town of Lovek, he wrote. The city was "surrounded by a fence of bamboo hedges. The invaders fired a cannon containing silver coins at the fortifications. The Khmer cut the bamboo to the ground to get the money" and "left themselves defenseless." Soon after, the city fell.

David Chandler, the dean of Cambodian historians, offered his own assessment of other writers, while offering his own analysis of the Cambodian personality: "The inherent stability of Cambodia, often the subject of absurd romanticism among colonial writers, has rested throughout nearly all of Cambodian history on the acceptance of the status quo as defined by those in power. Because the people in the countryside have never been asked to play a part in any government, they saw few short-term rewards in resisting those in power."

Michael Vickery, another academic and author, served as a school-teacher in Cambodia in the early 1960s, under a U.S. government aid program. He learned Khmer and made study of the nation his passion. In one of his books he told of his visit to a remote Cambodian village in 1962, where he saw "wild looking boys" carrying "dead lizards strung on sticks like freshly caught fish" they were taking home for dinner. Their village, in a remote corner of Banteay Meanchey Province, was home to people Vickery found "strangely hostile." These villagers made it clear "they did not like city people." But Vickery also noted that they had a "valuable cottage industry. The villagers made beautiful silk." He offered to buy some, but the villagers steadfastly refused, saying it was only for their own use. Vickery's money, no matter how much he offered, was of no value because "there was nothing in the market they wanted." Just like the farmers the historians had described. Of what use was that extra rice? Vickery concluded that "for reason of climate, inaccessibility and incompatibility," these villagers, like so many others around the country, "had evolved a nearly autonomous, autarkic lifestyle, wanting only to be left alone."

And so it remains. In 2006 and 2007 Jeffery Sonis, a physician at the University of North Carolina at Chapel Hill, conducted a survey on the prevalence of PTSD among Cambodians and sent teams of surveyors across the nation to ask questions. Though he originally intended to ask the subjects to sign forms, he had to abandon that plan. Cambodians, he found, were too suspicious of outsiders. "In Khmer Rouge times, they ask you to sign a form, and then they kill you," Sonis said he learned. "Now, unscrupulous businessmen ask you to sign a form, and then they take away your land." The people trusted no one. They just wanted to be left alone.

Cambodians themselves are the first to tell you that they hold no real national identity. They seldom feel "Cambodian." That has been true through the ages. But the Khmer Rouge era hardened this trait. "The survival instinct has taken over," said Ing Kantha Phavi, the minister of women's affairs. "Surviving doesn't mean giving help to others. If you help others, you may be betrayed. A lot of people did a lot of bad things to survive. So people are more individualistic. They think only of themselves. They think first of survival. They don't think of society at all."

Beat Richner, the hospital director, saw the results of this firsthand. His maternity-ward doctors refused to talk to their patients. "After the Khmer Rouge, no one is talking to anyone. They don't want to be in interrogations." Even now, "older docs still keep to themselves. They do not talk to others"—including their patients. Yet this underlying personality trait existed long before the Khmer Rouge ruled. Sihanouk used to call it "individualism" and once described that as "a national failing."*

Still today, "in this society there is no one else you can count on," said Chandler, the historian. "They don't think a society really exists." That tendency proved useful for most of Cambodia's history, as the nation lived through successive wars with its neighbors. Most Cambodians focused only on family and village life. These were their only havens as foreign troops ranged over the nation and government leaders schemed and connived for their own accounts. Egoism was of undeniable value during the Khmer Rouge era. To survive Cambodians had to behave as Kok Chuum, the Dang Run village chief, did. "I ate wild potatoes I found in the woods," he said. "I did it secretly. I told no one." Presumably, back then, others near him were starving to death, as workers did all over the nation.

---

*Once in modern times, Cambodians did unite as one in fervent agreement on an issue. In July 2008 UNESCO listed Preah Vihear, a small, disputed nine hundred–year-old temple on the Thai-Cambodian border, as a World Heritage Site. Predictably, that led to an angry argument between Bangkok and Phnom Penh. The two states had argued over ownership of that temple for decades, and in short order both sides sent troops to the border. Though this did not exactly spawn a shooting war, a few soldiers died in short firefights. More interesting, the Cambodian people seemed to rally around their leader in support of this military standoff with their longtime foe, the Siamese. "For the first time in living memory, the entire Cambodian population was unanimously and fiercely united on a single issue," wrote Michael Hayes, editor of the *Phnom Penh Post*.

But in the twenty-first century individualism, this shared personality trait, ensured that Cambodians would remain hungry and illiterate. By and large they could not, would not, stand up and advocate for themselves.

Imagine that Bulgarians or Indians, Malay, Bolivians, Poles, or citizens of most any nation ruled by a government styling itself as a democracy instead sold off the nation's harvest each year, leaving its people without enough to eat. Evicted thousands of people from their homes, burned down their houses, then dumped the residents into empty fields and sold their property to a developer. Amassed vast personal fortunes while 40 percent of the children were so malnourished that they were growing up stunted. Allowed schoolteachers to demand bribes from six year olds and doctors to extort money from patients, letting them die if they did not pay. Presided over a state in which 80 percent of the people lived under conditions little changed from 1,000 years earlier so that everyday lives remained simply battles for survival. Would any of these other populations stand for this? Even in Iran, a brutal theocracy, the people arose in furious opposition to the government in 2009 for far less.

But Cambodia is home to a world-class paradox. In 2010, 60 percent of the nation's population was born after 1979, when the Khmer Rouge fell from power. "You'd think," said Kent Wiedemann, the former American ambassador, "that if these people look around at their neighbors and see that they are relatively more prosperous, they would not want to spend their lives grubbing around in the mud, in the rice paddies. They would demand something more from their government."

As it happens, though, the International Republican Institute conducted national surveys of Cambodians every few years to gauge their view of current issues. Their pollsters spoke to people nationwide, urban and rural, young and old, well-off and poor. The IRI was the U.S.-government funded agency that employed Ron Abney, who was injured in the 1997 grenade attack. The agency's leaders had long disliked, even loathed, Hun Sen. Yet year after year the group found that 75 or 80 percent of the Cambodian people said they were satisfied with their lives. They expected nothing more. The country, these people said, was going in the right direction.

The *Cambodia Daily* reported on one of those surveys in February 2009. It showed that 82 percent of the respondents said the country was on the right track. Some other headlines in the same paper read, "U.N. Agencies Alarmed by Jump in Child Malnutrition," "Prosecutor Accused of Bias in Land-Dispute Case," "Panelists Criticize Government's Lack of Budget Transparency," "Banteay Meanchey Man Charged in Rape of Two 6-Year-Olds," and "Prime Minister's Son Promoted to Rank of 1-Star General."

The poll respondents said they were happy because the government provided infrastructure: roads, bridges, wells, schools. Kimber Shearer, a director of the International Republican Institute's Asia Division, tried to explain the seemingly contradictory finding, saying the "people specifically give credit to Hun Sen for building all of this—no matter who really built the schools." In fact, foreign donors, or Hun Sen's *oknya*, built most of the infrastructure that Cambodians appreciate. The poll findings were not new. In 2003 the Asia Foundation conducted a similar survey and came up with similar results: Only 9 percent of the population said "the country is headed in the wrong direction."

Hun Sen's government touted these surveys as validation, a fact that certainly rankled the IRI's leaders. But the principle behind the people's point of view kept Hun Sen in power. If 80 percent of the people lived hardscrabble, subsistence lives in the countryside—quite literally hungry, barefoot, and illiterate—what did they care about the newspapers that reported about criminality, corruption, or malfeasance? The papers didn't circulate where they lived. Even if they did, they couldn't read them. Most people did have television, but the government controlled all of the stations. Regular news-program fare showed Hun Sen standing in a village, pointing to an *oknya*, and asking him to build a new road or bridge, "presented as requested." "Control of the electronic media is a serious problem," Ambassador Mus-someli asserted. "Until they open up TV and radio, no, you cannot have a free and fair election."

Local human-rights groups put all sorts of reports on their Web pages that detailed government abuses. Licadho's site featured reports like these: "Police and Military Burn and Bulldoze Houses During Land Eviction in Cambodia's Northwest" and "Cambodian Teacher Convicted of Defamation in Land Dispute with School Principal." But who saw these reports? Journalists and other NGOs, perhaps. In 2009 the Cambodian Chamber of Commerce reported that Internet penetration nationwide stood at .0014 percent. About 20,000 of the 13.5 million Cambodians had an Internet subscription. (Still, in 2010, the government started discussing Web censorship, saying, "If any Web site attacks the government, or any Web site displays inappropriate images such as pornography, or it's against the principle of the government, we can block all of them.")

Javier Merelo de Barbera Llobet lived in western Cambodia for more than two years, helping villagers as a worker for Jesuit services. He spoke to dozens of them during the 2008 election campaign, and he said he observed a constant theme: "People were very afraid of the CPP losing. They were very afraid of change." After all, for centuries change in Cambodia has generally led to misery or death.

Chan Sophal, chairman of the Siem Reap provincial council, said his government "is encouraging the people to change their way of living. Train them in business farming, chickens or pigs. Give them microfinancing." But wasn't he dealing with an intensely conservative population that resisted change? "In your question, you are proving my reality. The biggest challenge we have is facing the state of mind of our people. They don't want to change. This will require lots of time; this will need education." In the meantime, "our goal, if we can achieve it, is improved infrastructure—better roads, bridges, and irrigation for remote rural people."

The governor pointed to a similar problem. "A big part of this challenge now," he said "is fishing." The government was trying to enforce a ban on fishing during the spawning season; fish stocks were severely depleted. The problem was, for all of time Cambodians have eaten rice and fish and very little else. The annual flood of the Tonle Sap River washed millions of fish into the Tonle Sap lake. Water from the lake flooded rice paddies even miles inland, carrying fish spawn.

At the evictee site for HIV/AIDS patients outside Phnom Penh, the residents dragged through the afternoon, still depressed about losing their homes in the city a few days earlier. They were dispirited and hungry. But then at dusk, one of them walked down to the rice paddy behind their tiny refugee camp, dropped a small net into the water, and came back with a few dozen tiny fish, each at best two inches long. The mood in the camp suddenly changed. Children giggled; smiling parents eagerly gathered sticks and started little fires in their earthen cauldrons. Dinner was here! Who was going tell these people they couldn't fish?

Nonetheless, Hun Sen ordered a fishing moratorium in 2009. If you eat fish roe, the prime minister told his people in a television address, it's like eating thousands of fish. But convincing Cambodians to stop catching fish was as unlikely as persuading them to stop growing rice—or to accept microloans and start agribusinesses, as council chief Chan Sophal was proposing.

Chnok Trou was a fish hauler on the shores of the Tonle Sap lake, in Pursat Province. Her job was to carry the fishermen's catch from the boats to the wholesaler at the end of the dock. She lived in a bamboo hut that might have been eight feet long by eight feet wide and six feet high. As the Tonle Sap flooded each year she and other fish haulers lugged their homes away from the water's edge and up a slope in stages, five times as the water rose, and then back down in stages as the water receded. She lived at the end of a long line of these little huts, dozens of them, most with TV antennae strapped to the end of bamboo poles, high in the air, swaying in the breeze.

Chnok Trou was idle just now. The fishing ban "has been here every year for generations," she explained. "But this year they are very strict about it, more than any other year." She said she had saved money from last season and hoped it might help her get through this ban. In past years "there was still some fishing" during this, the spawning season. She shook her head. "We may run out of money this year. If we do, we will borrow until next year to buy food."

Just then a motorboat pulled up to shore in front of her. Four men wearing straw hats began unloading half-a-dozen large blocks of ice, each one six feet long. They piled the blocks onto a truck bed and drove off. What was the ice for? Chnok Trou looked embarrassed. She paused a moment and then whispered: "To keep the fish fresh."

Sit You Sous, the sixty-one-year-old blacksmith who lived near Pailin, said he voted for the CPP year after year "because of the support for poor families, the development and the construction." He pointed to a small wooden bridge over the stream that ran beside his house. "Also because they liberated the country on January 7, 1979, so I vote for them out of gratitude—and for keeping us safe. They are the ruling party, and I trust them."

About that time, the Gallup polling organization made public a major survey it had conducted throughout the world over several years, asking tens of thousands of people to score their own well-being. Were they "thriving," "struggling," or "suffering"? Cambodians' own view of themselves was darker than that of any other Asian nation. Just 3 percent of Cambodians said they were thriving, 75 percent said they were struggling, 22 percent were suffering. But then most of them simply believed that was their lot. Asked if he was satisfied with his life, Sit You Sous nodded. "Yes, I am. Like the old people used to say, life is hard, but I survive."

Mu Sochua, an opposition member of parliament, said her party had striven to use the "change" mantra that opposition parties offered worldwide. With so many destitute, miserable people, how could they not want change? "But we can't use change anymore," she acknowledged with a frown, "because the people don't want change."

Thirty-six-year-old Ten Keng lived in deep-rural Battambang Province, near Pailin. She grew corn and made just enough money to feed her family. Ten Keng volunteered that she was illiterate. But, in a conversation, her manner was chilly, unwelcoming. She was dismissive of government. "They don't do anything for us." Her only real interaction came once, when she contracted malaria and had to go to the hospital. "I had to pay 60,000 or 70,000 riel to the hospital," fifteen or twenty dollars, she said. "But then when the doctor came to see me, he said I should pay him another 50,000—as an incentive. This was at Battambang hospital. I got good care after that." What did she see ahead for herself and her nation? She pursed her lips and shrugged, as if to say, "I don't know. That's not my business."

# EPILOGUE

I n 2002 the Cambodian government sold the rights to explore for oil off its coast to Chevron Oil Company. Of course, the government said nothing publicly about this and never disclosed how much money it received or where it went. Chevron was mum, too. After having worked in Burma for many years, the company's policy, it seemed, was to avoid mixing politics with business wherever possible.

Within a year Chevron found oil, though the size and market-ability of the deposits remained unclear. Then in 2005 Chevron put out a statement, saying, "We are very encouraged to find oil in each of the first four wells of this drilling program." Two years later the International Monetary Fund ventured an estimate. Within a decade, it said, Cambodia could begin taking in $1.7 billion in oil revenues each year. That's when the panic began.

Cambodia chartered a new national regulatory agency, and Hun Sen gave the oil portfolio to Sok An, the deputy prime minister. The new company operated in total secrecy; one human-rights group charged that state oil-company employees were forbidden even to use the telephone. Hun Sen talked about using the profits to reduce poverty and promote development. No one believed him.

The IMF urged Cambodia to pass financial-management laws before pumping even the first gallon of oil. John Nelmes, the fund's resident representative, said, "One of the keys is that they have to put in place strong macro-economic management. That means budgetary policy that is sound and that directs money toward productive uses."

His advice was the first in a chorus from donors and diplomats who warned that setting up a state-owned oil company from which corrupt officials could skim profits was the perfect formula for afflicting Cambodia with still another serious malady: the oil curse. The World Bank pressured Cambodia to sign the Extractive Industries Transparency Initiative, an international agreement that would require public disclosure of oil and gas revenues. "This is a big thing for Zoellick," said a senior World Bank official. Robert Zoellick was the bank's president. But in 2008 Hun Sen refused and called external criticism of his oil policies "crazy." Then, in the fall of 2010, opposition politicians grew so frustrated about all of this that they wrote a plaintiff letter to twenty-two U.S. senators, saying, "Cambodia is ripe for disastrous extraction of our oil reserves" because the government was granting "99 year concessions for enormous swaths of land" over presumed oil reserves "in exchange for private pay-offs to a small number of associates at the top of the ruling party." As usual, that brought no useful result.

But what would happen if oil wealth began sloshing over Hun Sen's government with no oversight or control? Donors and NGOs feared he would not have to put up with them any longer. As Kek Galibru had put it, now "the government can use us. Our presence helps them a little bit. They need that money from the international community." With oil wealth the government might not need donor money any longer. Would Hun Sen shut down Licadho, take over the newspapers, tell USAID and the World Bank to mind their own business? "This has been in our minds for some time," said Guimbert, the World Bank officer in Phnom Penh. "The little that has come out now suggests that the pockets of oil are more scattered and may be less commercially viable. That could be a blessing in disguise. But I don't want to discount the black scenario. It could still happen. That's why we have to try to develop systems" that bring transparency to government spending. "And, yes, there is a sense of urgency here."

Then in 2010 the reason for the urgency became clear. The U.S. Securities and Exchange Commission opened an investigation into whether one oil company paid a $2.5 million bribe to government officials in 2007 for the right to look for oil. At that time, one government minister, Lim Kean Hor, called the payment "tea money," a euphemism for an under-the-table bribe. When Hun Sen learned of the SEC investigation three years later, he said the money had gone into a "social fund" for schools and hospitals. "It's not under-the-table money." But he refused to say exactly how the money had been spent. Traveling the country, talking to governors, looking at schools and hospitals, no one told me of any significant new projects. And, of course, the new anticorruption agency chose not to take up this case.

As if that were not trouble enough, late in the decade China became Cambodia's single largest donor. When donors pledged almost $1 billion in December 2008, $257 million of that came from China. Beijing actually spent billions more to build dams and roads and other infrastructure. And, of course, China's aid came with no strings—except that Hun Sen had to endorse Beijing's "one-China" policy on Taiwan. He did, and after that the Chinese couldn't have cared less whether he enforced an anticorruption law or ended land seizures. "Loans or grants from China have released Cambodia from certain kinds of political pressure from international countries," Hun Sen once remarked. As Hun Sen dedicated a new bridge China had built for him in 2009, he lauded his new friend—once the Khmer Rouge's patron state, as he had caustically complained in previous times. "A total of $6.7 billion of Chinese capital has been used in Cambodia," he boasted. Chinese aid, he added, "helps strengthen Cambodian political independence."

So where is Cambodia heading? "I have become so dispirited," lamented Yeng Virak, executive director of the Community Legal Education Center. He sighed heavily and shook his head. "The foreigners, the donors, they say Cambodia is so much better off than in the past. But I feel sad and worried. We are falling off a cliff!"

One resident of the Boeng Kak lake community in Phnom Penh watched the fetid water rise under his floor as the developer continued pumping sand. On the side of his house, he painted a declaration: "Stop evictions!" The government sued him for defamation.

"It's just like the kingdom again, but now it's the twenty-first century," Keo Phirum said with as much wonder as anger. He was a provincial counselor for the Sam Rainsy Party.

When the government finally enacted an anticorruption law of sorts in 2010, ruling-party legislators rushed the bill through parliament, giving opposition lawmakers and civil-society leaders almost no time to study it. Douglas Broderick, head of the UN offices in Phnom Penh, noted publicly that the government had not shared a draft of the bill with anyone since 2006. Right away, Foreign Minister Hor Namhong sent him a threatening letter, complaining of "flagrant and unacceptable interference in the internal affairs of Cambodia." The foreign minister warned that "repetition of such a behavior would compel the Royal Government of Cambodia to resort to a 'persona non grata' decision." The government would expel Broderick—heir to the UN authorities who tried two decades earlier to give Cambodians a fresh start in the world. After that, Broderick insisted that he had to keep a "low profile" in the state his organization had spent $3 billion to create.

"Cambodia is not a perfect democracy yet," insisted Hem Hong, Cambodia's ambassador to the United States. "We need to improve ourselves." But all of the available evidence showed that the state was moving quickly in the opposite direction.

"I don't know if it is right," Ok Serei Sopheak, a former government official, said matter-of-factly. "But a lot of people think we are moving toward Myanmar's model."

———

Cambodians have been abused by so many leaders over so many years that they expect nothing from their government. In fact, they remain convinced that any change at all will be painful, if not fatal. As Vickery put it, they want only to be left alone.

Around the world billions of people live under evil, autocratic governments. In Darfur and southern Sudan thousands of people live in small grass huts, even more primitive than Cambodian homes. They wear the old clothes that Americans donate to Goodwill. I saw a young man who lived in Rumbek, in southern Sudan, wearing a tattered uniform shirt from a Chrysler dealership in Arkansas that had the worker's name on a patch sewed over the breast—Clem. Still, Sudanese were more prosperous, on average, than Cambodians. The Sudanese government slaughtered hundreds of thousands of people, but in both places rebel groups fought back—eventually bringing the conflicts to a military standstill. Cambodians are incapable of that.

In Burma a self-interested military junta offered its people little if anything but continued oppression, and when a cyclone ravaged the country in 2008, the government refused to let many international relief agencies deliver shipments of food and medicine, afraid the aid workers would subvert their rule. But in normal times, Burmese are far more productive. They grow almost twice as much rice per acre and generally are more prosperous. Occasionally, they stage massive pro-democracy demonstrations, even knowing that the government will strike back. Cambodians are incapable of that.

In North Korea the regime kept its citizens locked down tight and ignorant of what was happening in the rest of the world. Occasionally, the nation suffered a famine. All the people knew about anything was what government radio told them. But then most everyone in the nation had electricity to play those radios, though there were frequent outages. North Korea's average per-capita income was three times higher than Cambodia's, and the government at least offered meager food rations. Not so in Cambodia.

Haiti remained the poorest nation in the Western Hemisphere and one of the poorest in the world. As in Cambodia, most residents did not have electricity, toilets, or clean water. But by almost every measure Haitians were better off. For example, UNICEF reported that 29 percent of Haitian children under age five suffered from moderate or severe stunting, largely a result of malnutrition. In Cambodia the number was 42 percent. In 2007 10 percent of Haiti's people had access to the Internet. In Cambodia the number was close to zero.

Of course, Cambodia is hardly the only corrupt country. When Joseph Mussomeli was the U.S. ambassador, he said he would "always tell the Cambodians that we put about six hundred American government officials in jail each year for corruption. It reminds me that we also have a corrupt society and that we are doing the right thing about it. We're putting them in jail. There's no shame in admitting corruption; the shame is in denying it and not doing something about it."

In fact, the Cambodian government almost never imposed any real penalty, even when an official was caught red-handed. In 2007 Ly Vouchleng was president of the National Court of Appeals when she was exposed for taking a $30,000 bribe in exchange for releasing two human-trafficking suspects from jail. She lost her job. Soon after, however, she was appointed legal counsel to the Council of Ministers. In 2009 the government removed Ke Kim Yan from his position as commander in chief of the military because he'd been caught in several shady land deals. Less than two months later Hun Sen appointed him deputy prime minister. And in the spring of 2010 a Phnom Penh court convicted an assistant to Interior Minister Sar Kheng of fraud and sentenced him to two years in prison for taking a $25,000 bribe in exchange for a job at the ministry. Upon convicting him, the court let him go, saying time served, a few months, was enough.

———

Many nations have suffered dark histories that left sad legacies. Many of those same nations are ruled by leaders who mistreat the people now. But no nation has suffered so much in the recent past.

No other people lived through an era when their own leaders killed one-quarter of the population—only to find that when the offending government fell, uncaring, avaricious leaders replaced it. No other nation's population is so riven with PTSD and other traumatic mental illnesses that are being passed to a second generation and potentially to a third—darkening the nation's personality.

All of that offers the Cambodian people a toxic mix of abuse unmatched anywhere in the world. But given their history, given the subservient state Cambodians have accepted without complaint for more than a millennium, they don't seem to care.

Once, just once, they dared to hope. The world's major nations gave them the chance to choose their leader for the first time in history. Almost every Cambodian embraced it; 90 percent of them voted. But then their leaders betrayed them, and the world deserted them.

Now, once again, most expect nothing more than they have. They carry no ambitions. They hold no dreams. All they want is to be left alone.

———

Nine Cambodians out of ten may not hope, or care. But change is coming. Even for a nation lost in the past, the modern world encroaches, far more slowly than in most any other place, but inexorably still.

In the late 1960s Ken Quinn, the State Department officer working in Vietnam who later became ambassador to Cambodia, watched as villagers in South Vietnam replaced their thatched roofs with metal—an anthropologist's measure of social improvement. Soon he began to hear radios and see televisions in these homes, and not long after that he watched families send their children to middle schools. Quinn credited the roads the United States was building in South Vietnam back then. They opened the villages to commerce. While he was ambassador to Cambodia during the late 1990s, Quinn pushed Washington to build more roads. But growing violence, culminating in First Prime Minister Ranariddh's "coup," put an end to those plans.

Ten years later, however, the Chinese stepped in and began building important roads and bridges, particularly in neglected rural areas. In some of those places now served by roads, a few farmers are buying tractors of sorts. Really, they are motor scooters with a till attached. But that's a big step above tying a rock to a plow pulled by an ox.

But then prosperity came to those Vietnamese in the 1960s because they also adopted the modern rice-cultivation techniques that the Americans offered. That increased their yields—and their wealth. Cambodians, on the other hand, resist change. Dr. Yang Saing Koma, president of the Center for the Study and Development of Agriculture, in Battambang, knows that as well as anyone. "The most important thing is just to change your thinking," he said. "The problem is you have to have a better way to explain the new techniques to the farmer. In a very simple way." When his group does that, "we ask them to do a pilot project, test it first" on a small plot of ground. "And once that happens, some of them are receptive. But now the government is in it; they're pushing this, too."

It's hard to know how quickly farmers may adopt modern agricultural techniques. But the metal roofs, motor scooters, and now even a smattering of cell phones in rural areas suggest incremental change.

The nation grows ever more prosperous, too. For all his faults, Hun Sen has given Cambodians one very important thing: more than a decade of stability and calm that bring some predictability to their lives for the first time in centuries. Stability is important not just for Cambodians. It encourages more tourists to visit the Khmer Rouge sites in Phnom Penh and the monuments left behind from the Khmer empire at Angkor. Tourism, one of the three legs of Cambodia's economy, continues to grow. Leopard Capital, an investment-fund manager in Southeast Asia, said tourist arrivals increased by 26 percent between 2008 and 2009. In the first half of 2010, 1.2 million people visited Cambodia, another large increase.

Foreign investment is still slow to come and is unlikely to grow significantly, as long as businessmen see that so many hands will be reaching into their pockets as soon as they arrive. For now, few Western companies dare to try. But Cambodia's commerce with its neighbors is growing fast. In the first quarter of 2010, trade with Vietnam grew by 127 percent compared to the same period a year earlier.

Yet all of this skirts Cambodia's largest problem: Hun Sen and his organization, the Cambodian People's Party. A variety of Cambodians and Cambodia experts, asked about the state's future, seemed to agree that fundamental change cannot come until Hun Sen leaves the scene. He was born in 1952, so he could potentially remain in power into the 2020s or '30s. "In 2013, I will be only 61 years old and still firm," he proclaimed at a university graduation ceremony. "Even now I have already become the longest ruling prime minister in Asia and made a historical record." He suffered a bout of swine flu in 2010 but still seemed healthy and robust after that and evidenced no interest in stepping down from office.

Don Jameson, who served as a political officer in the U.S. Embassy during the 1970s, married a Cambodian woman and remains intimately involved with the state. He visits often and follows events day by day. "As long as Hun Sen remains in power, which could be another twenty years or so," he said, "it is hard to envision any basic changes in direction." Still, he and others also pointed to a growing number of urban Cambodian college graduates; 40,000 people start college in Cambodia each year, and a growing but uncounted number study abroad. Many of these people are quite skeptical of the government and seem poised to push for change when the time is right.

David Chandler, the historian, has been following events and writing books about Cambodia for decades. And "when I was in Cambodia last month, I faced several large audiences of university students," he told me in the summer of 2010. "Queues of questioners" lined up, "and some even sent follow-up e-mails. They asked some probing questions." That had never happened before. In past times, he said, students were passive, uncritical.

"A French official with UNESCO, whom I met officially, told me that the quality of local personnel coming into the UN system in Cambodia is higher every year," Chandler went on to say. UN and NGO officials told me the same thing. All of this led Chandler to conclude that educated, urban Cambodians, at least, "are not simply sitting back and letting things wash over them" any longer. "This doesn't mean that they are politically foolhardy. It means that they are more skeptical and responsive than Cambodians have generally been."

Thousands of educated young Cambodians are no longer willing to accept the current state of affairs, unlike generations of students before them. But what can they do? For now, not much. They cannot speak up or organize without risking their lives; none of them wants to see two helmeted men on a motorbike with no license plate approaching from behind.

They have little choice but to bide their time, wait for Hun Sen to step down—or for some unforeseen external event to intervene and rattle the status quo. But when that day comes, these Cambodians will have a distinct advantage over similar groups in other countries that faced moments like this. The UN occupation, for all its faults and failings, did leave Cambodia with an enduring gift—a true democratic system of government. Cambodians are accustomed to voting, and the government is properly divided into executive, parliamentary, and judicial branches that have the ability to check one another. The current regime distorted it, turned it into a one-party, job-protection racket. But, in the right hands, all of that could be undone. "A series of events, actions, and circumstances" as yet unseen "could converge to precipitate a tipping point," said Gaffar Peang-Meth, a Cambodian with a doctorate earned abroad, at the University of Michigan—one of the very few Cambodians with these qualifications in all of time. He's a professor of political science who recently retired from the University of Guam. Not only are some students and recent graduates dissatisfied, he said, but "I also know some people in the current regime, in the military as well as in the bureaucracy, who are unhappy." Maybe, just maybe, he offered, "if the right spots are pushed at the right time, a seemingly unchangeable situation can be altered. Call me a dreamer if you will, but thoughts give rise to dreams, and dreams to actions."

All of that amounts to little more than a warm breath of hope. But for Cambodians, that's more than anyone has offered in a very long time.

# ACKNOWLEDGMENTS

I have many people to thank. James Hoge, who was editor of *Foreign Affairs* magazine, trusted me to write that first article about Cambodia, in the spring of 2009. Researching that piece, I saw the book. The Pulitzer Center for Crisis Reporting gave me a grant for travel expenses. So did the Fund for Investigative Journalism. Later, after I had written the magazine article, Peter Osnos, who was the editor of my first book in 1989, trusted me to write this one. Lindsay Jones served as an outstanding editor. Thank you all.

In Cambodia, Phann Ana, an outstanding reporter for the *Cambodia Daily*, worked as my research assistant and translator for two summers. Van Roeun and Phorn Bopha also were able colleagues for shorter periods.

In the United States, Don Jameson, who follows Cambodia hour by hour, kept me abreast of the latest developments. And Luke Henesy worked tirelessly as my research assistant here at Stanford.

Most of all I thank my family. Researching and writing this book, while also writing a weekly op-ed column and holding down my job at Stanford, required an incredible commitment of time. My wife, Sabra, and my daughters, Veronica and Charlotte—to whom this book is dedicated—put up with me, even encouraged me, all the while.

# NOTES

## A Note on Sources

Over two years, I interviewed more than two hundred people, Cambodians and others with experience in the country. I read twelve books and parts of several others as well as probably a thousand newspaper and magazine articles—not to mention scores of government and private-organization documents and reports. The *Cambodia Daily* and the *Phnom Penh Post* were important and reliable sources. My database contains 7,387 distinct digital records.

Far more important than any of that, of course, are the months I spent traveling the country in 2008 and 2009. Looking back after more than three decades in journalism, those experiences were among the most fascinating, even amazing, I have ever had.

In most cases I attribute remarks, statements, and sources as I cite them, just as you would in a newspaper or a magazine. But this is not a newspaper or a magazine. So in many cases, including specific attribution with source and date got in the way of telling the story. I offer some further explanation here.

Books cited are listed in full in the bibliography. When someone is quoted without explanation, in nearly every case it means I spoke to him or her. In some other cases, a public official is quoted without attribution when his or her remarks were widely reported and not disputed. Following are some other statements and remarks that are not fully attributed.

9 **UN agencies say:** On its Web site UNICEF puts Cambodia's literacy rate at about 70 percent, but in my own observation almost everyone I met outside the cities was illiterate.

18 **The best surviving account:** Zhou Daguan's descriptions of Angkor-era Cambodia were taken from *A Record of Cambodia: The Land and Its People*, translated by Peter Harris.

19 **In AD 245:** Information about the AD 245 fact-finding mission to Cambodia came from Michael D. Coe, *Angkor and the Khmer Civilization*, 57.

23 **Writing in 1834:** The observations of Emperor Minh Mang of Vietnam, in 1834, came from David Chandler, *A History of Cambodia*, 152.

27 **The author wrote:** Young Saloth Sar's remarks about the king came from David M. Ayres, *Anatomy of a Crisis: Education, Development, and the State in Cambodia, 1953–1998*, 42.

49 **A few weeks earlier:** Noam Chomsky offered his views about the Khmer Rouge in the *Nation*, June 6, 1977.

50 **In February 1978:** Lewis Simons offered his views about the Khmer Rouge in the *Washington Post*, February 19, 1978.

56 **Zbigniew Brzezinski:** Elizabeth Becker described Zbigniew Brzezinski's decision to encourage the Chinese to support the Khmer Rouge in her book *When the War Was Over: Cambodia and the Khmer Rouge Revolution*, 435.

56 **After the UN vote:** Samantha Powers wrote about Robert Rosenstock's interaction with Ieng Sary in her book *A Problem from Hell: America and the Age of Genocide*, 150, 152.

60 **Henry Kamm:** Henry Kamm wrote about his visit to the Khmer Rouge jungle lodge in his book *Cambodia: Report from a Stricken Land*, 179–180.

70 **In October 1991:** The *New York Times* published its editorial on the danger that the Khmer Rouge might return to power on October 24, 1991.

72 **"The process is unfolding":** The *Washington Post* editorial was published on September 12, 1990.

73 **Discussing this:** Hun Sen's conversation with David Roberts appeared in his book *Political Transition in Cambodia, 1991–99: Power, Elitism, and Democracy*, 40.

93 **"Over the last 10 years"**: The *Toronto Star* printed the quoted story on June 23, 1994.

93 **A bit later:** The AP distributed its interview with Sam Rainsy on August 31, 1994.

94 **He told a reporter:** The *Christian Science Monitor* published its story quoting the information minister on October 26, 1994.

116 **As Seth Mydans:** The *New York Times* published its story about the 1997 grenade attack on March 31, 1997.

118 **"I have no intention":** *Mother Jones* published its article on the grenade attack online in April 2005. Later the authors, Rich Garella and Eric Pape, posted the article, tapes, and other research at http://www.cambodiagrenade.info/main/.

131 **The United Nations "left the four parties":** The *Washington Post* quoted Benny Widyono on the failings of the UN occupation on July 20, 1997.

133 **Seth Mydans of the *New York Times*:** The *New York Times* published Seth Mydans's story about the village with victims' "ghosts" on May 27, 1996.

135 **Typically, the victim would recall:** The journal *Cultural Medical Psychiatry* published Devon Hinton's research on Cambodians with PTSD on March 31, 2009.

137 **In San Jose, too:** The *Journal of the American Medical Association* published the study "Mental Health of Cambodian Refugees Two Decades After Resettlement in the United States" on August 3, 2005.

138 **In about 2004 Cambodian officials:** Government statistics on men who beat their wives came from interviews with government officials.

160 **An editorial in the *Washington Post*:** The *Washington Post* published an opinion piece with the headline "Saddam Hun Sen" on July 20, 1997.

160 **The *New Republic* called him:** The *New Republic* titled an article about Hun Sen "Hun the Attila" on August 4, 1997.

160 **The first one:** The *Boston Globe* published Senator Mitch Mc-Connell's first op-ed on Cambodia on August 1, 2001.

182 **Sixty percent of these payments:** Steven Heder published his account of the agreement between Hun Sen and Ranariddh to split "commissions" in the journal *Southeast Asian Affairs* in 2005.

Heder attributes his finding to "FUNCINPEC and diplomat interviews, March–November 2004."

183 **"Grand corruption involving illegal grants":** The USAID published its report *Cambodian Corruption Assessment* on August 19, 2004.

208 **An NGO study:** A group of NGOs, part of a coalition called "Clean" that is dedicated to fighting corruption, published a study in November 2006 that described the "facilitation fees" school principals had to pay. The study was titled *Local Public Services: Performance and Unofficial Fees*, 7.

208 **In late 2009 the *Phnom Penh Post*:** The *Phnom Penh Post* published its story on schoolteachers doubling their bribes on October 27, 2009.

224 **But when one reporter asked:** The *Cambodia Daily* published its article about the Pursat prosecutor Top Chan Sereyvudth the week of February 14, 2009. The *Phnom Penh Post* published its own article on June 30, 2009.

233 **Violence continued and even increased:** The *Phnom Penh Post* published the police-blotter shorts on various dates in 2008 and 2009.

255 **At the end of 2008:** Statistics on sanitation conditions came from various UNICEF and Cambodian government reports.

288 **In 2000, for example:** The International Crisis Group published its report *Cambodia: The Elusive Peace Dividend* on August 11, 2000.

289 **The yearlong postelection stalemate:** The World Bank published its report *Cambodia at the Crossroads* in November 2004.

298 **In a Brookings Institution report:** The Brookings Institution published its report *Aid Effectiveness in Cambodia* in December 2008.

306 **"It's not uncommon":** The United Nations Human Rights Council published a report that included an observation on pardons before pledge conferences on February 29, 2008, 12.

307 **while World Health Organization figures showed:** Data on child deaths from diarrhea-related illnesses, and maternal deaths, came from interviews with World Health Organization officers and hospital officials.

308 **"The pain, the suffering":** Bert Hoak and Ray Zepp's observations about foreign aid were distributed on the Camnews Listserv on May 22, 2008, and then posted at http://www.mekong.net/cambodia/aid_ess.htm.

314 **The *New York Times* reported that President Clinton:** The *New York Times* published its story about American plans to seize Pol Pot and put him on trial on April 9, 1998.

314 **For the United Nations, though:** The Documentation Center of Cambodia published Thomas Hammarberg's account of negotiations on the Khmer Rouge trial in its magazine, *Searching for the Truth*, on June 18, 2001.

314 **Here's how the Associated Press described:** The Associated Press distributed its story on the Khmer Rouge leaders' vacation on December 31, 1998.

321 **Human Rights Watch said Kong Srim:** Human Rights Watch put out its news release on the Khmer Rouge trial and Kong Srim, the chief judge, on December 5, 2006.

321 **The *Phnom Penh Post* noted that:** The *Phnom Penh Post* published its story about despair over the direction of the Khmer Rouge trial on November 21, 2008.

342 **The *Cambodia Daily* reported on one of those surveys:** The *Cambodia Daily* reported the results of an International Republican Institute survey the week of February 14, 2009.

342 **In 2003 the Asia Foundation conducted:** The Asia Foundation published its public-opinion survey of Cambodians on May 16, 2003, and posted it on its Web site.

345 **Just 3 percent of Cambodians said:** Gallup published its worldwide survey on attitudes toward well-being in 2009 and said "results are based on telephone and face-to-face interviews with more than 137,000 adults, aged 15 and older, conducted between 2005 and 2009 in 139 countries."

# BIBLIOGRAPHY

Ayres, David M. *Anatomy of a Crisis: Education, Development, and State in Cambodia, 1953–1998.* Honolulu: University of Hawaii Press, 2000.

Becker, Elizabeth. *When the War Was Over: Cambodia and the Khmer Rouge Revolution.* New York. PublicAffairs, 1986.

Bit, Seanglim. *The Warrior Heritage: A Psychological Perspective on Cambodian Trauma.* 1991.

Chandler, David. *A History of Cambodia.* 4th ed. Boulder: Westview Press, 2008.

Coe, Michael D. *Angkor and the Khmer Civilization.* London: Thames and Hudson, 2003.

Kamm, Henry. *Cambodia: Report from a Stricken Land.* New York: Arcade Publishing, 1998.

Ovesen, Jan, Ing-Britt Trankell, and Joakim Ojendal. *When Every Household Is an Island: Social Organization and Power Structures in Rural Cambodia.* Uppsala Research Reports in Cultural Anthropology, No. 15. Stockholm: Sida, 1996.

Powers, Samantha. *A Problem from Hell: America and the Age of Genocide.* New York: Basic Books, 2002.

Roberts, David W. *Political Transition in Cambodia, 1991–99: Power, Elitism, and Democracy.* London: Curzon Press, 2001.

Short, Philip. *Pol Pot: Anatomy of a Nightmare*. New York: Henry Holt, 2004.

Solomon, Richard H. *Exiting Indochina: U.S. Leadership of the Cambodia Settlement and Normalization with Vietnam*. Washington, DC: United States Institute of Peace Press, 2000.

Tully, John. *A Short History of Cambodia: From Empire to Survival*. New South Wales, Australia: Allen and Unwin, 2005.

Vickery, Michael. *Cambodia, 1975–1982*. Boston: South End Press, 1984.

Zhou, Daguan. *A Record of Cambodia: The Land and Its People*. Translated by Peter Harris. 1296. Reprint, Chiang Mai, Thailand: Silkworm Books, 2007.

# INDEX

# ABOUT THE AUTHOR
# AND PHOTOGRAPHER

**Joel Brinkley** is a professor of journalism at Stanford University, a position he took in 2006 after a twenty-three-year career with the *New York Times*. There he served as a reporter, editor, and foreign correspondent. He won a Pulitzer Prize for his coverage of the fall of the Khmer Rouge regime in Cambodia in 1979.

At Stanford, Brinkley writes an op-ed column on foreign policy that appears in dozens of newspapers and Web sites in the United States and around the world each week, syndicated by Tribune Media Services.

He is a native of Washington, D.C., and a graduate of the University of North Carolina at Chapel Hill. He began his journalism career at the Associated Press and over the following years worked for the *Richmond (Va.) News Leader* and the *Louisville Courier-Journal* before joining the *Times* in 1983.

At the *New York Times*, Brinkley served as Washington correspondent, White House correspondent, and chief of the Times Bureau in Jerusalem, Israel. He spent more than ten years in editing positions, including political editor in New York. In Washington he served as foreign editor, projects editor, and investigations editor following the September 11 attacks. He also served as political writer in Baghdad during the fall of 2003 and as foreign affairs writer in Washington.

Over the past thirty years Brinkley has reported from forty-six states and more than fifty foreign countries. He has won more than a dozen national reporting and writing awards. He was a director of the Fund for Investigative Journalism from 2001 to 2006. He is the author of five books and lives in Palo Alto, California, with his wife, Sabra, and two children, Charlotte and Veronica.

**Jay Mather** has been a working photojournalist since 1972. He accompanied Brinkley to Cambodia in 1979 and shared the Pulitzer Prize.

His interest in documentary photography began while he was a Peace Corps volunteer in Malaysia. That led to jobs at newspapers in Denver, Louisville, and Sacramento.

During his career he has covered a wide range of subjects and people from the rich and famous to the poor and nameless. Mather received the Robert F. Kennedy Photojournalism Award and was a Pulitzer finalist in 1991 for his project on the centennial of Yosemite National Park. He was the photographer for the *Sacramento Bee*'s 1992 project "The Sierra in Peril" that won the Pulitzer Prize for Public Service.

Mather also worked extensively with the Sacramento Ballet as their production photographer and documented the company's first international tour to China in 2007. He now lives with his wife, Diane, in Sisters, Oregon, where he volunteers his photographic work for the Sisters Folk Festival, among other organizations and events.